Is There a Middle East?

Is There a Middle East?

THE EVOLUTION OF A GEOPOLITICAL CONCEPT

Edited by Michael E. Bonine, Abbas Amanat,

and Michael Ezekiel Gasper

Stanford University Press
Stanford, California

Stanford University Press
Stanford, California

Printed in the United States of America on acid-free, archival-quality paper

Library of Congress Cataloging-in-Publication Data

Is there a Middle East? : the evolution of a geopolitical concept / edited by Michael E. Bonine, Abbas Amanat, and Michael Ezekiel Gasper.
    pages   cm
  Includes bibliographical references and index.
  ISBN 978-0-8047-7526-7 (cloth : alk. paper)—ISBN 978-0-8047-7527-4 (pbk. : alk. paper)
  1. Middle East—Historical geography.   2. Middle East—Historiography.
3. Geopolitics—Middle East.   I. Bonine, Michael E., 1942– editor of compilation.
II. Amanat, Abbas, editor of compilation.   III. Gasper, Michael Ezekiel, 1963–
editor of compilation.
    DS44.9.I8   2012
    911'.56—dc23   2011026603

Typeset by Westchester Book Group in 10/14 Minion

CONTENTS

LIST OF FIGURES

LIST OF TABLES

CONTRIBUTORS

ROGER ADELSON is recently retired as Professor of History at Arizona State University, Tempe, where he taught beginning in 1974. After receiving his Ph.D. at Washington University, St. Louis, he was Alistair Horne Senior Research Fellow at Oxford and taught at Harvard University. Dr. Adelson's research has focused on British and U.S. policies toward the Middle East since the mid-nineteenth century. He edited *The Historian* from 1990 to 1996 and has published more than one hundred articles, essays, and reviews in history journals. He is the author of *Mark Sykes: Portrait of an Amateur* (1975), *London and the Invention of the Middle East: Money, Power and War, 1902–1922* (1995), and *Churchill and the British Impact in the Middle East* (2009). He is presently writing *Truman to Bush: The Impact of the Middle East on the U.S. Presidency.*

ABBAS AMANAT is Professor of History and the Director of the Iranian Studies Initiative at Yale MacMillan Center for International and Area Studies at Yale University. He received his B.A. from Tehran University in 1971 and his Ph.D. from Oxford University in 1981. He is the author of numerous works, including *Pivot of the Universe: Nasir al-Din Shah and the Iranian Monarch, 1831–1896* (1997) and *Resurrection and Renewal: The Making of the Babi Movement in Iran, 1844–1850* (1989), and editor of other books. Amanat was a Carnegie Scholar of Islamic Studies in 2005–7 and the recipient of the Mellon-Sawyer Seminar Grant for Comparative Study of Millennialism in 1998–2001. He is a consulting editor and long-time contributor to the *Encyclopedia Iranica* and in 1991–98 he was the editor-in-chief of *Iranian Studies.* He is currently writing *In Search of Modern Iran: Authority, Nationhood and Culture (1501–2001)* as well as a biography of the Babi leader and poet Fatima Baraghani Qurrat al-'Ayn (Tahirah) and a documentary history of Qajar Iran (in Persian).

MICHAEL E. BONINE is Professor of Geography and Professor and Head of the Department of Near Eastern Studies at the University of Arizona, where he has been since 1975. He received his Ph.D. in geography in 1975 from the University of Texas at Austin, completing a dissertation on city-hinterland relationships based upon two years of field work in Yazd and central Iran. He was executive director of the Middle East Studies Association (MESA) from 1982 to 1989. He is the author of numerous articles as well as the author/editor or coeditor of several books, including *Yazd and Its Hinterland* (1980), *Modern Iran: Dialectics of Continuity and Change* (1981), *Qanat, Kariz and Khattara* (1989), *Middle Eastern Cities and Islamic Urbanism* (1994), and *Population, Poverty, and Politics in Middle East Cities* (1997). He is working on a manuscript on the Imperial Bank of Persia and its banknotes, as well as a coauthor of a manuscript called *The Sacred Egg and the Elegant Plume: The Ostrich in Africa and the Middle East.*

DIANA K. DAVIS, a veterinarian and a geographer, is currently Associate Professor of History at the University of California at Davis. She received her doctorate of veterinary medicine in 1994 from Tufts University School of Veterinary Medicine and her Ph.D. in geography in 2001 from the University of California at Berkeley. She has conducted research with Afghan and Moroccan nomads, and she has worked extensively in the British and French archives. Her first book, *Resurrecting the Granary of Rome: Environmental History and French Colonial Expansion in North Africa* (2007), was the winner of the George Perkins Marsh Prize, the Meridian Book Award, and the James Blaut Award. Davis has also published articles on various Middle Eastern topics in geography and other scholarly journals. She recently has been named a Guggenheim and Ryskamp (ACLS) Fellow for her new research book project on imperialism and environmental history in the Middle East.

MICHAEL EZEKIEL GASPER is Assistant Professor in the History Department at Occidental College in Los Angeles, California, where he teaches classes on the cultural, social, political, and economic history of the modern Middle East. He received his M.A and Ph.D. in history and Middle Eastern studies from New York University and has previously taught at Yale, NYU, York College of the City University of New York, and Albright College. In 2008–9 he was named a Carnegie Scholar for his research project, "Rethinking Secularism and Sectarianism in the Lebanese Civil War (1975–1990)." His first book, *The Power of Representation: Publics, Peasants and Islam in Egypt* (2008), explores nationalism and religious identity in intellectuals' writing about peasants and how their constructions drew the social boundaries of modern Egypt.

JAMES L. GELVIN is Professor of History at the University of California, Los Angeles. He received an M.A. in international affairs from the School of International and Public Affairs at Columbia University and a Ph.D. in history and Middle East studies from Harvard University. He is the author of three books: *Nationalism and Mass Politics in Syria at the Close of Empire* (1998), *The Modern Middle East: A History* (2004, 2007), and *The Israel-Palestine Conflict: One Hundred Years of War* (2005, 2007). He is also author of numerous articles on the social and cultural history of the Middle East (particularly the region of Greater Syria during the early twentieth century), nationalism, the Middle East state system, and Islamic movements. He is currently working on a manuscript titled *From Modernization to Globalization: The United States, the Middle East, and the World Economy in the Twentieth Century.*

WALEED HAZBUN is Assistant Professor of Political Studies and Public Administration at the American University of Beirut since fall 2010. Until summer 2010 he was Assistant Professor of Political Science at The Johns Hopkins University in Baltimore, Maryland, where he taught international relations and Middle East politics. He received a Ph.D. in political science from MIT. He is the author of *Beaches, Ruins, Resorts: The Politics of Tourism in the Arab World* (2008) and has published articles on the politics of travel, geopolitics, and decolonization. He is currently working on extending his work on the cultural political economy of tourism by investigating issues of historical memory, identity, and travel in new forms of tourism development based around history, religion, and the environment across the Middle East. Another project explores the influence of notions of modernity and the politics of modernization on U.S. foreign policy in the Middle East and cultural and intellectual relations between the United States and the Middle East.

ARASH KHAZENI earned a Ph.D. in modern Middle Eastern history from Yale University in 2006 and is Assistant Professor of Middle Eastern and North African History at Pomona College in Los Angeles, California. In 2009–10, he was a Robert W. Mellon Research Fellow at the Huntington Library. His research is focused on the Islamic world since 1500, with an emphasis on the social, cultural, and environmental history of Iran, Afghanistan, and central Eurasia. He is the author of *Tribes and Empire on the Margins of Nineteenth-Century Iran* (2010), which received the 2010 Houshang Pourshariati Iranian Studies Book Award from the Middle Eastern Studies Association. He is currently working on an environmental history of the borderlands of Iran, Afghanistan, and central Eurasian steppes, c. 1500–1850.

RAMZI ROUIGHI is Assistant Professor of History at the University of Southern California. He received an M.A. in historical studies at the New School for Social Research in New York in 1999 and his Ph.D. in history in 2005 from Columbia University. His dissertation, "Mediterranean Crossings, North African Bearings:

A Taste of Andalus in Bejaia, 1250–1400," examined the migration of Andalusians into Ifrīqiyā in the thirteenth and fourteenth centuries. Expanding on that research, he is now completing a book manuscript titled *The Making of a Mediterranean Emirate* that investigates the processes that led to the making of Ifrīqiyā as a region. Rouighi's main research interests focus on the medieval Mediterranean and the Sahara, the production of medieval history, and conceptions of power and the past in medieval and modern times.

GAGAN D. S. SOOD has been the Vasco da Gama Research Fellow at the European University Institute in Florence, Italy, since 2009. Educated at the University of Cambridge, Sciences Po, and Yale University, he received his Ph.D. in 2008, with a dissertation titled *Pluralism, Hegemony and Custom in Cosmopolitan Islamic Eurasia, ca. 1720–90,* from the Department of History at Yale University. His larger research agenda centers on the history of the Middle East and South Asia in the early modern world and of the region's differentiated transitions into modern times. He has carried out archival work in Oman, Yemen, Syria, India, France, and the United Kingdom, and at present he is engaged on a project that explores the structures of everyday life in this region and their transformations after the demise of the great empires of the Ottomans, Safavids, and Mughals. His articles have appeared in the *Journal of the Economic and Social History of the Orient* and *Modern Asian Studies,* and he is working on a book manuscript, provisionally titled *An Ecumene Unravelled.*

DANIEL MARTIN VARISCO is Professor and Chair of Anthropology at Hofstra University in Hempstead, New York, where he has taught since 1991. He received his Ph.D. in anthropology from the University of Pennsylvania in 1982, based on eighteen months ethnographic fieldwork on irrigation and water resource use in a highland Yemeni village. During the 1980s he consulted on international development in Yemen and Egypt and received four postdoctoral grants for research on the history of Arab agriculture and folk astronomy. His most recent books are *Reading Orientalism: Said and the Unsaid* (2007) and *Islam Obscured: The Rhetoric of Anthropological Representation* (2005). He has published more than forty articles in professional journals and edited *Yemen Update* from 1990 to 2002. He serves as coeditor of *Contemporary Islam,* editor of the online journal *Cyber-Orient,* and webshaykh of the academic blog *Tabsir.* He is currently working on a comprehensive history of Yemeni agriculture in the Islamic era titled *Arabia Viridis.*

HUSEYIN YILMAZ is Assistant Professor in the Department of History, University of South Florida, Tampa. He received his Ph.D. in 2005 from Harvard University in history and Middle Eastern studies. From 2005 to 2008 he was a postdoctoral fellow at the Introduction to the Humanities Program at Stanford University, and in 2008–9 he taught in the Department of History, Stanford University, as acting assistant professor. His research interests include geographical imaginations, social stereotyping, translation, cultural formation, and political thought in the early modern era. He has published articles and book chapters on Ottoman constitutionalism, imperial ideology, and historiography. He is currently working on a book examining imageries of leadership in the sixteenth-century Ottoman Empire.

PREFACE

ON DECEMBER 17, 2010, a 26-year-old street vendor of fruits and vegetables, Mohamed Bouazizi of Sidi Bouzid, Tunisia, humiliated when the police confiscated his produce, doused himself with gasoline and set himself on fire. He died of his burns on January 4, 2011, and thus began the Arab Spring, with protests that spread to the rest of Tunisia and then throughout the region—from Libya and Egypt to Syria and the Arabian Peninsula. Nearby Iran had its highly contested election of summer 2009, and its Green Movement has continued to stage demonstrations since that time. The populations of this region, particularly the young, with their social media, fed up with corruption, inherited leadership, economic injustices, and human rights abuses, have erupted in massive riots and protests against their own governments. With a predominantly Muslim population, this region also has been accused of fostering and harboring "Islamic terrorists," from the earlier Muslim Brotherhood of Egypt to the terrorist network of the now-killed Osama bin Laden.

But where are we talking about? Is this indeed a coherent geographical and cultural region? What is the significance for scholarship and government policies for treating and understanding the Middle East as a "region"? Is North Africa part of the Middle East? These subjects are the focus of this volume, which tackles the question, "Is there a Middle East?" If we consider the events of the Arab Spring, as well as the typical front-page news of the last decade, from the invasion of Iraq and the attempts to eliminate al-Qaeda and the Taliban from Afghanistan and Pakistan to the world's dependency on oil, we begin to understand that we are indeed talking about a most significant geopolitical region. Whereas the term "Middle East" is certainly common usage among scholars and the media, exactly (or perhaps inexactly) where is this? How did this term and usage come about? Is it a valid way to conceptualize and understand this region? And what are the impact and consequences of this abstract category and its use?

This volume addresses these questions. It shows how the Eastern Question of the nineteenth century provides much of the framework for the conceptualizing of the Near East and Middle East of the twentieth century, with the latter term predominating after World War II. These essays will show that the Middle East is a complicated and changing region, with often conflicting definitions, usages, and impacts. Some of the chapters will bring out other identities and allegiances for parts of the region, particularly for periods before any of this area was called the Middle East. Today this region, including the "Greater Middle East," has evolved as a geopolitical concept that influences how governments approach the region in terms of their foreign policy, foreign aid, and military assistance (or intervention). The U.S. general public also views the Middle East as a region of Islamists, war and conflict, oil, and massive foreign and military aid. It certainly behooves us not only to ask, "Is there a Middle East?" but also to provide an answer to that question, and to why that answer is significant for understanding today's complicated world. That is the task of this volume.

The kernel of an idea for this book came from an earlier workshop in May 2006 at the Center for International and Area Studies (now the MacMillan Center) at Yale University. We acknowledge and appreciate support from Yale University's Edward J. and Dorothy Clarke Kempf Memorial Fund and thank the organizers and supporters of that event, including August Ranis, then Director of YCIAS, Nancy Ruther, Associate Director, Barbara Papacoda, administrator of the Council on Middle East Studies, and the staff of MacMillan. We acknowledge and thank the editors and staff of Stanford University Press, whose competence and encouragement have enabled this book to come to fruition. We thank two anonymous reviewers for their thoughtful comments and recommendations. For helping to make the book a reality, special recognition goes to Mirela Saykovska, a research assistant at the University of Arizona, whose technological and organizing skills were instrumental in bringing the manuscript to completion. We also thank the University of Arizona for the support of a subvention for publishing illustrations and maps as well as paying for permissions and for the redrawing of several maps by Stanford University Press.

As educators and coeditors, we greatly benefitted from the contributions to this volume, and we believe that specialists, students, and the general reader will find it useful for teaching, study, and further research.

Michael E. Bonine
Abbas Amanat
Michael Ezekiel Gasper
May 17, 2011

Is There a Middle East?

INTRODUCTION: IS THERE A MIDDLE EAST?
Problematizing a Virtual Space

Abbas Amanat

WHEN THE FIRST television network started broadcasting in Tehran in 1958, its adopted motto was "The first private television in the Middle East." For many Iranian viewers the novelty of the new medium brought with it the idea that their country was a part of a larger region called the Middle East. Iranians aside, this of course was not the first encounter with the term. One can find references in geographical textbooks of the 1950s to the oil fields of the Middle East, or to the wartime Anglo-American Middle East Supply Center established in 1941 to aid the Allies' war effort in the region. The 1956 Suez War was often labeled in the headlines as a Middle East crisis, while the luxuriously produced journal *Aramco World*, first published in 1949, displayed glimpses of the region's natural beauty and material culture. The accidental way the Middle East nomenclature entered our geographical horizon enabled many specialists in the West, beginning especially from the late 1950s, to increasingly identify themselves with the nascent field of Middle East studies, then barely distinguishable from Oriental studies or Islamic studies.

Decades of scholarship and teaching about this region and its history, society, culture, and politics does not seem to have resolved the Middle East as a puzzling entity. Under its rubric we teach courses, organize conferences, publish books, define our field, and wage academic brinkmanship. In the harsher world of geopolitical realities, real conflicts have been fought in the Middle East, from World War II and the Arab-Israeli conflict to the Persian Gulf wars and Afghanistan. Such conflict seems indelibly tied to the notion of the Middle East as a playing field for the Cold War, which involved, often inadvertently, many of the countries of the region. The often unfavorable view of the

1

Organization of Petroleum Exporting Countries (OPEC) in the Western media and of course anxieties in recent years over the real or assumed threat of religious militancy further perpetuated the ambiguity. Today the ongoing popular movements of protest in the Arab world (and prior to that the Green Movement in Iran in the spring of 2009) cast on the region an entirely new light stressing a greater degree of social homogeneity and a shared quest across the region for democracy, openness, and political accountability.

Yet a century of increasing usage of the Middle East as an organizing principle, and its ever-growing boundaries, stretching today (at least for some observers) from Pakistan and Afghanistan to Morocco, have not clarified many conceptual issues related to this elusive term. The long overdue task of problematizing it from geographical, historical, cultural, and sociopolitical perspectives hence is the focus of this volume. It can be argued that the countries of Western Asia and North Africa that are put together on the map as the Middle East neither constitute a continental landmass nor sufficiently bind together by any unifying characteristics. Marshall Hodgson's well-known "Nile to Oxus" stretch, which he considered as the Islamic heartlands, represents a plausible geocultural entity that was carved in the midst of the Eurasian landmass together with a part of Africa. Yet Hodgson was the first to admit that this "venture of Islam" was above all about sharpening of diverse cultural identities, emerging ethnolinguistic communities, sectarian divisions, and modern national identities.

Although today the Nile to Oxus world roughly matches the boundaries of the Middle East (that is if one excludes Central Asia and North Africa), there is much that can be said about the circumstances leading to the rise and prevalence of the term *Middle East*. We may ask, for instance, why the old legal notion of *dar al-Islam* (the abode of Islam) was never translated into sustained geopolitical boundaries on today's regional and world maps—what Hodgson called the "Islamicate." Is it because Islam could no longer operate as a unifying principle perhaps as early as the sixteenth century when the Ottoman, Safavid, Mughal, and Uzbek territorial empires each appeared independent from the other as "guarded domains" (*mamalik-i mahrusa*) in the historical and geographical works in Persian and Turkish? The European cartographers too honored these imperial divisions. For a long time, moreover, along with the imperial notion of the "guarded domains," a range of indigenous terms such as *mulk* (kingdom), *mamlakat* (realm, country; at times *mamlakat-i Islam* or more recently *mamalik-i Islami*), *ard* or *sarzamin* (land),

and *iqlim* (climate) served their purposes without an apparent need to conceptualize a broader notion of regional territory before the twentieth century and reconfiguration by Western imperial imagining.

As has often been noted, the "east" (*mashriq*) and the "west" (*maghrib*) of the Islamic world up to the twentieth century remained intrinsic: the latter exclusively a reference to North Africa, and the former a vague reference to Iran and eastern neighboring lands, the so-called Persianate world of Marshall Hodgson as opposed to the Arabic cultural and linguistic world of Arabia, Mesopotamia (Bayn al-Nahrayn, Iraq), Syria (Shamat), Egypt, and North Africa. The West, in reference to Europe (or more specifically to western Europe) continued to be identified as the land of Franks (Arabic: *al-Afranj;* Persian: *Farang;* Turkish: *Ferenj*) following nomenclature that came about after the early Islamic empire's contacts with the Carolingian empire of the Franks. Before the age of Muslim discovery in the nineteenth century, there were also the Russians (*Urus*), the Slavs (*Saqalib*), and other a host of non-Westerners known to Muslims. They included Christian Abyssinians, the Muslims of Western China (*khata*) and China proper (*khutan* and *chin*) stretching beyond as far east as Japan, and of course the *Hindustan* ("province" of India), which was envisioned, as were many other lands surrounding the Islamic empires, as a province attached to the outside of the Islamic core. This indigenous geopolitical culture, confident of its own place in the world, seldom felt the need for differentiating between the Islamic empire (or Muslim empires of early modern times) and Christendom or the heathen world of the "Other."

As late as the mid-twentieth century the new defining concepts that originated in Europe and the United States did not entirely supplant these older indigenous notions, nor were these modern terms adopted uncritically by the peoples of the region. Western geopolitical nomenclature that had divided the ancient East into the Near East and the Far East, by the early twentieth century also discovered a Middle East in between almost as an afterthought. In the nineteenth and early twentieth centuries these concepts of "near" and "far" were forged by Europeans in contradistinction to the concrete perception of the West as the Self. The people of the former Muslim empires who no longer were subjects of the "guarded domains"—specifically the Ottoman Empire—thus became citizens of infant nation-states. Under the auspices of European mandatory powers some of the former provinces of the Ottoman Empire after the First World War were carved out or lumped together to create Iraq, Syria, Lebanon, and Jordan. These countries together with Iran, Egypt, and Arabia in turn were placed in a newly constructed category of the Middle East. Abiding by the East-West cultural dichotomy vis-à-vis the all-powerful West (Arabic: *al-gharb*; Persian: *gharb*), they were as diverse culturally and linguistically as in their historical experiences and exposure to modernity. Even Iran, with frontiers that remained relatively intact since the thirteenth century (and often identified by Europeans as continuation of the Persian Empire of ancient times), was brought into the Middle East construct along with Egypt, another ancient land of independent identity, the new Republic of Turkey, the last remnant of the old Ottoman Empire, and a host of new states in the Eastern Mediterranean and Persian Gulf.

Absence of an intrinsic regional notion and identity in the postcolonial era added greater weight to the Middle East nomenclature as an extrinsic construct. Even with its curious history it eventually gained global acceptance. Rooted in the ancient Greek cosmographic division of the world into the *Orient* (where the sun rises) versus the *Occident* (where the sun sets), it was embedded in a prehistoric notion of a yet undivided Eurasian landmass. Whereas connotations of the Orient in the twentieth century have become mostly cultural—as in the discourse of Orientalism and its critics—the East took on a more geopolitical undertone (even as it served as a neutral nomenclature for an academic field). Yet if it were not the old Orient, it still betrays a deeply Eurocentric arrangement. "East of where?" we may ask, and the answer is obvious. The universal usage of the term *Middle East*, not only in Europe and in the Americas but in East Asia, South Asia, Southeast Asia, and Australia, further proves preponderance of an essentially colonial construct.

Whereas today the term *Near East* is largely relegated to archeology and studies of ancient civilizations of the eastern Mediterranean, and the term *Far East* has almost disappeared as a geographical denominator (except perhaps in travel guides and travel literature), the term *Middle East* is alive and well. The remarkable endurance of the term to the present day, in the headlines and in the political sphere, may best be attributed to tensions in its cosmogony: geopolitics and imperial power rivalries, oil exploration and thirst for energy, territorial and ethnic disputes arising from Western vested interest (such as in Israel/Palestine and Iraq), inefficient and authoritarian regimes in the region, and more recently resurgence of religious extremism. Even if one avoids resorting to the rhetoric of attributing all the ills of the Middle East to the colonial past, the fact remains that in one way or another, in imagination and in reality, these ills directly or indirectly concern the mixed legacy of the West in this region for over a century.

Does it matter how the term *Middle East* came about and that it is a Western construct? To most scholars the question seems secondary. It can be argued that to a historian who writes about modern Egypt, or an anthropologist who works on Iran, or a geographer who studies the ecology, demographics, or urbanization of the region, the Middle East is merely a framework, very much like colleagues working on countries of Latin America, Africa, and Eastern Europe. Pragmatic concerns aside, it is undeniable that academics as well as journalists, politicians, and economists are operating within a broader regional framework that has created its own narrative and its own dynamics over at least half a century; some are more viable than others. This collection is an effort to explore both the shaping of the Middle East narrative and the operating dynamics that have given it continued viability.

Yet we still can envision scenarios whereby the Middle East as an entity can be broken down—deconstructed—to more realistic and historically viable units. The Egyptian delta and eastern Mediterranean lands, for instance, have enjoyed a close interaction for millennia. Egypt also maintained ancient connections with the Sudan and interiors of Africa, whereas the rest of North Africa maintained an active trans-Saharan trade with the lands to the south of the great desert, as well as with the Iberian Peninsula. The Iranian plateau shared historic ties with Central Asia, the Caucasus, and eastern Anatolia as well as with the Mesopotamian hinterlands and through the Persian Gulf with India, the rest of South Asia, and East Africa. The Arabian Peninsula too shared much across the Persian Gulf, the Red Sea, and the Indian Ocean, including with East Africa, India, and beyond. Western Anatolia was part of the eastern Mediterranean world that included mainland Greece and the Balkans and the Black Sea littoral, as well as Egypt and the Levant.

Of course virtually any region on the world map, it may be argued, is divisible into smaller units, and any region or subregion cannot be seen in isolation and without ties with neighboring lands. The Middle East no doubt is not an exception, yet its case is somewhat distinct because many of the cultural, economic, and ethnic bonds with its immediate lands were weakened or severed in modern times after the demise of the old Muslim empires and through the experience of colonialism and even more so by the postcolonial rise of nation-states. These older connections were at one time the basis upon which the region thrived economically and culturally. Of course these ties also brought military clashes, nomadic invasions, slavery, and exploitation of hinterlands.

The Middle East today, much like Europe of the early twentieth century or East Asia, is a land of contested memories and historical animosities. The nationalist narratives of Shi'i Iran (and even southern Iraq), for instance, are fundamentally at odds with the Sunni narrative of Arab nationalism and Pan-Arabism, and both run counter to the Ottoman imperial legacy as appropriated by nationalist secular Turkey. And almost all are in contrast with the Unitarian or Wahhabi narrative of today's Saudi Arabia and the Salafi movements of dissent across the region.

Perceptions of modern history in these countries of the region reflect diverse directions and individual logics. Most Arabic-speaking countries experienced British and French colonial presence in one way or another during the nineteenth and twentieth centuries, whereas Turkey and Iran were never colonized per se, even though their histories were greatly impacted by European military, diplomatic, and economic interventions. Anger and resentment toward colonizing Europe thus was, and still is, a powerful unifier that has fuelled nationalism and nationalist revolutions in Iran, Egypt, and Algeria, as well as in other countries of the Middle East. In the postcolonial era, however, such animosity quickly projected itself to Israel and the Zionist movement, which has been seen almost unanimously in the Arab world as a Western-sponsored intruder and a legacy of the colonial period. Stories and images of occupied Palestine and the stateless Palestinians generated sympathy and symbiosis, especially after 1967, when they reached beyond the Arab world and gradually became symbols that increasingly appealed to all Muslims.

Yet beyond anger towards Israel and the United States, an experience now shared by nearly all countries of the region, the realities of today's Middle East encourage greater and more positive interregional dialogue. Some countries no doubt benefited from natural resources to build stronger economies and more prosperous societies even though there are remarkably few interregional and cross-regional markets and meaningful organizations of regional cooperation. The ideological, territorial, and sectarian tensions, much of them the legacy of nation-building since the First World War and the nationalist ideologies that came with it, diminished the chances for regional interconnectedness along the lines that in the past connected the lands and the communities in this part of the world through caravan and pilgrimage routes and maritime trade. Yet recent democratic "revolutions" in Tunisia and Egypt had a remarkable impact on the rest of the region, inspiring a "chain reaction" that may suggest shared sociopolitical dynamics and in due course greater economic or cultural integration.

The modern Middle East thus has become a virtual space with political tension and resentment but also prospects for social and cultural homogeneity—a region still waiting to be reconstructed in ways more viable and more beneficial to its own population. Appeals to a common Islamic heritage, advocated by individuals, movements, and regimes in the region, can only go so far before facing sectarian, nationalist, and ethnic barriers. Extremist currents of Islam, even though adhered to by relatively few, nevertheless weaken the appeal of Islam as a civilizational and a cultural unifier. Becoming "Middle Eastern" as an identity still thus remains a challenge to its inhabitants, who opt to give their allegiances to democratic, nationalist, sectarian, and ideological causes.

This collection of ten essays focuses on many of the above issues and their historical and conceptual manifestations. The chapters are grouped into three different sections. First is "The Middle East: Defined, Obliged, and Denied," which contains four chapters that focus on the historical evolution and use of the terms *Near East* and *Middle East*, or the lack of such use. The second part, "Historical Perspectives of Identities and Narratives in the Region Called the Middle East" provides historical perspectives that are significant in understanding that the Middle East is indeed a more recent conceptualization imposed from the outside and that there were other ways and divisions in which (parts of) the region were understood in the past. The last section, "Challenging Exceptionalism: The Contemporary Middle East in Global Perspective," focuses on the Middle East in the contemporary period, where globalization and geopolitics combine with oil and political extremism to create a region that has become one of the most critical, significant, and relevant ones not only for the United States but also for the entire world. A brief concluding chapter provides a further overview of the content and message that the ten chapters provide the reader.

THE MIDDLE EAST: DEFINED, OBLIGED, AND DENIED

Part I

1 THE EASTERN QUESTION AND THE OTTOMAN EMPIRE
The Genesis of the Near and Middle East in the
Nineteenth Century

Huseyin Yilmaz

NEAR EAST OR MIDDLE EAST maps were first drawn at the height of intense interest in what Karl Marx labeled "the Eternal Eastern Question."[1] It was the content of this question that defined the geography of this region that came to be known as the modern Middle East. Later attempts to give a consistent geographical or cultural definition to the term all followed major international developments or were made in anticipation of major geostrategic shifts, ultimately creating multiple "Middle Easts" that were based on different sets of criteria.[2] Two such attempts in recent memory were the redrawing of the Middle East following the end of the Cold War and the Greater Middle East Partnership discussed in the G-8 summit in 2004.[3]

Despite staying at the center of international politics for more than a century, the region still has no standard textbook definition.[4] In the popular imagination as well as academic studies, the Middle East is often conceived of as the locus of an international question rather than a geographically or culturally definable region. Except for the questions it posed, there is hardly any common element that defines the various "Middle Easts" constructed in the media, academic scholarship, and political agencies. As the nature and scope of the Middle Eastern Question change, so do the region's boundaries. There has been no secular organizing principle to make the Middle East a meaningful region other than a historical memory built by the very term itself.

At the beginning of the nineteenth century, the term "the Eastern Question" was generically applied to almost all conflicts taking place in Eastern Europe, including those in Poland, Macedonia, and the Caucasus. Toward the late nineteenth century, however, within the context of a broader confrontation between

Europe and the Orient, the scope of the Eastern Question was extended to all of Eurasia, producing such formulations as "the Afghan branch of the Eastern Question."[5] Even Americans conceived of their western entanglements as "our Eastern Question" in reference to American-Japanese conflict.[6] Reflecting this holistic view in 1878, Victor Duruy presented the three core problems of the Eastern Question as Constantinople, *l'Asie Centrale*, and *l'Océan Pacifique*.[7] In some Christian apocalyptic literature, however, "the Eastern Question" referred specifically to the holy land where the demise of the Ottoman Empire would signal the coming of the Armageddon.[8] For them it was a matter of divine providence foretold in scripture and that was unfolding to fulfill prophecies.[9]

Views on the scope and historical depth of the Eastern Question ranged from a mere Great Power rivalry to an existential conflict between two incompatible worldviews with no beginning point in time. John Marriott, who wrote the now classical account on the subject, stated in 1940 that "from time immemorial, Europe has been confronted with an 'Eastern Question.'"[10] For him, conflicts between the Roman Empire and Hellenistic monarchies and between Christianity and Islam reflected this confrontation. Although the semantic range of the term "the Eastern Question" was extended to include the whole scope of relations between the West and the Orient, unless specified it commonly referred to the Euro-Ottoman context. Albert Sorel, who wrote a widely read textbook on the Eastern Question in 1898, argued that "since the first entry of the Turk into Europe, there has been an Eastern Question." It was this perception of the Eastern Question that gave rise to the notion of the Near Eastern Question by the late nineteenth century, from which current conceptions of the Middle East originated.[11]

The term "the Eastern Question" entered into wider circulation with the 1815 Congress of Vienna. Ironically, among the many eastern questions of the nineteenth century, the Eastern Question that formed the focal theme of European thought and diplomacy for much of this and the early part of the twentieth century initially emerged not as Europe's Turkish problem but as the Ottoman Empire's Egyptian problem. European interest on the Eastern Question seems to have been prompted by the internal crisis of the Ottoman Empire in 1831–40 when Muhammad Ali, the governor of Egypt, captured Syria and much of western Anatolia, a crisis overcome by the intervention of Britain and Austria. The French press, which was more acquainted with the region because of Napoleon's invasion of Egypt a few decades earlier, was the main source of information for the broader Europe.[12] In fact, during the 1830s the British press commonly referred to the crisis as "the Oriental Question," a literal translation of the standard French term *la Question d'Orient*.[13] The reason the Egyptian crisis brought about such an uproar in European public opinion was the possibility of an imminent collapse of the Ottoman Empire that might lead to a total reshuffling of power among major contenders in Europe. Already in 1836, Leopold von Ranke prophetically noted that *die Orientalische Frage* was of universal significance.[14]

THE QUESTION OF THE OTTOMAN EMPIRE
IN EUROPEAN IMAGINATION

Contemporary conceptions of the Middle East are intimately connected with the way modern Europe was constructed and the Ottoman Empire was perceived since the early modern period.[15] More specifically, the depiction of the Ottoman Empire in modern cartography and geography was part of the same process by which modern images of the Middle East were constructed. However, defining Europe and placing the Ottoman Empire in any meaningful geographical category were no easy tasks. Lacking any meaningful physical or cultural commonality, the landscape under the Ottoman rule had no unifying element other than being a political geography shaped by an administrative grid and elite culture. The extensiveness of the Ottoman territories, running from the Caucasus to North Africa, presented no shared historical memory other than the one constructed by the Ottoman Empire itself, a memory fiercely contested by newly emerging national formations in the course of the eighteenth and nineteenth centuries. Indeed, earlier political conglomerations such as the Roman and the Byzantine empires similarly left few lasting unifying features within these lands.

Cartographic and geographical representations of the Ottoman Empire produced in Europe since the sixteenth century hardly accorded it a geopolitical unity. It was typically depicted as a fragmented structure stretching over three continents and considered to be primarily belonging to Asia or the Orient. It was portrayed as a contested space for different faiths, languages, ethnicities, and historical memories. European cartographers, in continuum from the Ptolemaic representations of scientific geography, presented the space from Eastern Europe to Persia in accordance with their own needs, with little attention given to representative markers of the Ottoman Empire. Western European travelers, who were usually less equipped to perceive the unifying elements of Ottoman society, often found themselves baffled by the myriad

ethnicities and languages they came across between Belgrade and Constantinople, thus having difficulty attributing any sense of unity to the land they
were crossing.

As Palmira Brummett recently showed, despite a surge in European interest in the study of the East and the Ottoman Empire, most authors were still
much better versed in the antiquated perceptions of the area than in contemporary realities.[16] They had very little knowledge of, or regard for, Ottoman
administrative divisions, regions, or city names. Instead, they primarily re-
sorted to Greco-Roman and biblical terminology in their representations.
Early modern European information gathering and representation provided
the Eastern Question debate of the nineteenth century with a picture of the
Ottoman Empire that was geographically fragmented, socially divided, linguistically disunited, and culturally incoherent. Such views formed the staple
of the Eastern Question debate in which the Ottoman Empire was considered
to be a non-European entity confined to Asia.

REGIONS IN PREMODERN MUSLIM GEOGRAPHY

The Eurocentric regionalization of the East not only supplanted the reality
of the Ottoman Empire while it was still largely intact, but also it superseded
indigenous geographical regimes. Medieval Muslim geographers conceived
the world in broad spatial constructions in reference to a center that was
Baghdad, Cairo, Jerusalem, or some other Muslim locality of significance.[17]
One such theme was "the middle of the earth," which came from a variety of
traditions Muslims came into contact with and was integrated into the self-
image of the Abbasid Caliphate. The ninth-century historian al-Dinawari, for
example, discussed the middle of the earth in the context of Noah's distribution of land among his sons where he granted the center piece (*wasat al-ard*)
to Shem, an area which was watered by five rivers: the Euphrates, Tigris,
Seyhan, Ceyhan, and Qaysun.[18] For the tenth-century geographer al-Mes'udi,
however, Shem's possession of the middle of the earth (*wasat al-ard*) consisted
of the area from the sacred land (Mecca and Medina) to Hadramawt, Oman,
and 'Alij.[19] This was for al-Mes'udi the middle of the land. In his formulation,
which included the oceans, he pointed to the equator as the middle of the
earth (*wasat al-dunya*).[20] Yet for the middle of the world he pointed to al-
Iraq.[21] In his analysis of climes, the twelfth-century scholar Ibn al-Jawzi also
noted that the center of all climes (*awsat al-aqalim*) was the fourth clime,
Babil, of which al-Iraq constituted its center.[22] Further, the center of al-Iraq

was Baghdad, "the finest part of the Earth" (*safwat al-ard*) where the finest of human races infused and beauties of all corners of the world convened.[23] For Muslim geographers working during the high Abbasid Caliphate, the center of the world was Baghdad, from which perceptions of the East and the West were organized.

Muslim geography produced a rich nomenclature of refined geospatial conceptions across the West-East spectrum. The Arabic terms *sharq* and *mashriq* were derived from the same etymological root and could be used interchangeably in reference to the East. However, *mashriq* is more than a directional concept; it is grammatically a place noun, meaning the abode of the sunrise, reminiscent of *levant* in French and *oriens* in Latin. *Mashriq*, in the geospatial sense, could refer to the whole eastern part of the world or a specific region in the East with reference to a perceived center. These terms were further specified through qualifiers of distance. *Aqsa al-sharq* or *al-sharq al-aqsa* (the Far East) could refer to a distant East, most commonly to the area centered on China. A fifteenth-century geographer, Ibn al-Wardi, for example, used the term "from the Far East to the Far West" (*min aqsa al-mashriq ila aqsa al-maghrib*) in reference to the two end points of the known earth encircled by the ocean (*min al-muhit ila al-muhit*).[24] In this horizontal space, he considered Sudan between the East and the West (*bayn al-mashriq wa al-maghrib*).[25]

Muslim geography did not develop standard lines of division between the East and the West or within these broad zones. Geographers often developed their directional perceptions in reference to the lands of Islam, their own locations, or Mecca, the universal point of direction for prayers. Ibn Khurradadhbih, who wrote one of the earliest Muslim accounts on geography in the ninth century, pointed to the subjectivity of perceptions in regard to the East and the West: "Egypt is for us part of the West but it is the East with respect to al-Andalus. Similarly, Khurasan is for us the East but it is the West with respect to China."[26] He nevertheless not only used spatial directions but also came up with more complex designations. His conception, the "middle of the East" (*wasat al-mashriq*), for example, referred to a region that roughly corresponds to a part of today's Central Asia.[27] The fourteenth-century historian al-Dhahabi, however, used *al-Sharq al-Awsat*, the standard term for the Middle East in modern Arabic, in reference to a specific locality somewhere between Baghdad and Damascus.[28]

Muslim conceptions regarding the West, the *gharb* and the *maghrib*, were similar to those regarding the East, but with more certainty in terms of its regional references. The west of the Nile was commonly divided into three regions that resembled the modern Eurocentric division of the East. In Ibn al-Wardi's account, the three divisions were *al-Gharb al-Aksa* (the Far West), *al-Gharb al-Awsat* (the Middle West), and *al-Gharb al-Adna* (the Near West).[29] These were almost the mirror images of the nineteenth-century reconstruction of the Orient as the Far East, the Middle East, and the Near East. In some views, the area was divided broadly as *al-Maghrib al-Sharqi* (literally, the Eastern West) and *al-Maghrib al-Gharbi* (the Western West).[30] Although this division was generally formulated for North Africa, for some, it also included al-Andalus or Muslim Spain as well. Ibn Khaldun, from Muslim Spain by birth, employed the term "the Middle West" (*al-Maghrib al-Awsat*) extensively in reference to al-Andalus throughout his universal history, *al-Ibar*.[31]

THE END OF THE EXOTIC ORIENT

In the nineteenth century, whether driven by strategic and colonial interests or scholarly curiosity, exploration and information gathering about the rest of the world enabled European observers to reconstruct the single Orient in a partitioned form. The historical geography between the Balkans and the Indus Valley enjoyed a special status in the European imagination within this broader Orient. According to meta-narratives of history crafted since the Renaissance, the origins of modern Europe lay in the eastern Mediterranean, making this area its civilizational homeland. Christians had a more intimate and passionate connection to the same land, not only as the repository of their past but also in apocalyptic thought as its destined future as well. For linguists and ethnologists, the origins of Europe could be traced all the way to India, making Persian and Sanskrit close cousins of principal European languages and the Caucasians their blood relatives. More important, this part of the Orient fell within the historical reach of Europe from the Romans to the empire of Alexander the Great. For European observers this space was not an alien place. Unlike new frontiers such as China and Africa where Europeans sought new discoveries, visitors to the area between the Danube to the Indus Valley were thought to be exploring their own origins. Thus the European study of the East, the Eastern Question, and the construction of the Middle East were intimately linked and had more to do with the making of Europe than its Orient.

Friedrich Hegel's conception of "Hither and Farther Asia" (*Vorder und Hinterasien*) was based more on racial and civilizational affinity than spatial proximity to Europe. He considered India and China as Farther Asia, belonging to the Mongol race and therefore strictly Asiatic, in "prodigious contrast" to European character. Hither Asia, however, which included Iran, was Caucasian and related to the West with inherent European dispositions, virtues, and human passions. Beyond Persia was the land of peoples with the "most repellent characteristics."[32] But some of Hegel's contemporaries were less nuanced and were greatly disturbed by their observation that this repellent Asiatic or Oriental character existed in the very midst of continental Europe. More specifically, the eastern part of physical Europe was populated by or under the occupation of Asia or the Orient represented by the Turks, the Jews, and the Slavs. As vividly recounted in Karl Franzos's travel account of 1876, *Aus Halb-Asien*, when viewed by an enlightened eye, southeastern Europe was semi-Asian.[33]

Prince von Metternich may have been sarcastic when he remarked in 1820 that "Asien beginnt auf der Landstraße" in Vienna.[34] But when Alexander Kinglake noted in 1834 that the East began at Belgrade, he was only one of many other west European travelers who were struck by a different world.[35] His sentiment was shared by perhaps the most well-known historian of his time, von Ranke, for whom "noch immer beginnt in Belgrad der Orient."[36] Likewise, for Hippolyte Desprez, "l'Orient commence aux frontières occidentales de la Hongrie."[37] Observing the same difference in Malta, Pierre Victor Ad Ferret noted that the island displayed a dual character involving both European and Asian civilizations.[38] An 1848 article in *Der Orient* described Hungary as being "between the East and the West, between European cultivation and Asiatic coarseness."[39] Eduard Alletz, who wrote one of the earliest accounts of the Eastern Question, considered the inhabitants of this frontier as intermediaries between Turkey and Austria, the Orient and the Occident, and Islam and Christianity.[40]

The Orient in the Europe-versus-the-East contrast was a wider space than that of the Orient in the West-versus-the-East distinction. The Far East and its cognates in reference to the easternmost corner of Asia was an area that both Muslim and European geographical accounts recognized. The vast regions between Western Europe and China, however, were defined in various ways by a number of terms ranging from the "Middle Orient" to the "Central East." The Malay Peninsula, for example, was sometimes considered the Middle East, whereas the Philippines was classified as part of the Near East.[41] Because of the British involvement in India and China, "the Near East" was used in English with more geographical consciousness where it was often juxtaposed against "the Far East."[42] As the perception of China and its environs came to be accepted as the Far East, the land mass in between was referred to by a number of different regional terms, such as "Front Asia," "Hither Asia," "Western Asia," "Near Asia," "Central Asia," and the like. The Eastern Question debate provided meanings to these terms as it was extended to include Europe's relationship with all of Asia.

CONCEPTUAL ORIGINS OF THE NEAR EAST

The term "Near East" enjoyed a long and colorful history in European languages and thought. The eighteenth-century Italian uses of the term "the Near East" (*il vicino Oriente*) lacked geographical specification, and in most cases it was used in literature imbued with metaphorical connotations.[43] For example, Stanislao Canovai's use of the phrase "the Near East and the Far West" (*al vicino Oriente ed al remoto Occidente*) in 1817 still referred to directional space with very little sense of geography.[44] Carlo Tenca in 1847 used *il vicino Oriente* in the context of Cossacks and Lithuanians in a vague sense of identity and geographic location.[45] In 1857, *La Civiltà cattolica* employed the term *l'Oriente vicino* in reference to a neighboring culture with respect to Italy.[46] Despite these uses, the term did not produce a clear geographical image and so remained in Italian without making its way into the mainstream of European thought.

Its German equivalents, however, were used with more civilizational consciousness and geographical underpinnings. By *der Vordere Orient*, Johann Kanne in 1808 and Johann Wagner in 1815 specified the eastern Mediterranean as a cultural space. An 1834 article in *Bilder-Magazin für allgemeine Weltkunde* used the same term specifically in reference to an area that included Greece, Asia Minor, Egypt, Syria, and Palestine. The 1833 edition of *Jahrbücher der Literatur* extended the geographical space of the term all the way to India. In 1849 Georg Rosen mentioned Bursa and Constantinople as major cities of *der Vordere Orient*. From the 1820s onward, *der Nahe Orient* or *der Nahe Osten*, often used interchangeably with *der Vordere Orient*, came to be more commonly used. In 1827 Carl von Rumohr provided no geographical certainty when he used the term *der Nahe Orient* when he talked about its cultural influence on Greece and Christianity. Georg Donop in 1834 and Constant Dirckinck-Holmfeld in 1838 used the term in the context of Mesopotamia and Eastern Europe, respectively. In 1875, Hermann Vámbéry portrayed the extent of the "Mohammedan nation" *vom nahen Osten bis ins Innere Chinas.*[47]

British commentators, who had been more engaged in other parts of the world from India to China and Africa, showed an increased interest in the Ottoman Empire during the 1853–56 Crimean War when Britain participated in the alliance against Russia. Not surprisingly, then, early uses of the term "Near East" were mostly devoid of the historical and cultural content found in the German tradition. British discourse on the Near East centered on political and commercial interests of the British Empire, and with relatively few exceptions, such as Frederick Townshend's *A Cruise in Greek Waters*, the term was often employed in English in juxtaposition to the Far East.[48] Thomas Meadow and an anonymous article in *Fraser's Magazine* in 1856 both referred to the Near East as the Ottoman Empire in comparison with China—the sick man of the Near East versus the sick man of the Far East.[49] Lucy Mitchell in 1883 conceived of "the Near Orient" as a civilizational space with clear inspiration from the German conception of the term.[50] The preference given to "Orient" in the construct is telling as it accommodated more cultural and civilizational content than its more secular equivalent "East," which was more suitable in referring to geographic spaces reflecting strategic and commercial interests. From 1895 onward, when the British press started its extensive coverage of the Ottoman Empire prompted by uprisings in the Balkans, even provincial papers employed the term "the Near East" with regard to the general geographical context of specific political conflicts.[51]

The European construction of "the Near East" seems to have largely originated from German scholarship on the Orient that was bereft of political or strategic references. By the mid-nineteenth century, *der Vordere Orient* or its cognates established themselves in the German imagination as a cultural space with some degree of geographical clarity, albeit without neatly drawn borders. Whether it was *nahe* or *vorder* and combined with *Orient*, *Ost* or *Morgenland*, almost all constructs of "the Near East" in German pointed to a less definite geographical space while certainly implying a marked civilizational contrast. The German imagination of the Near East was shaped by scholarly study of the Orient in the eighteenth and nineteenth centuries; particularly important were the works of the highly respected Ottoman specialists Dimitrie Cantemir and Joseph von Hammer-Purgstall. Since Paul Rycaut's monumental work published in 1667, *The Present State of the Ottoman Empire*, British commentators were generally more interested in the political economy of the Orient than in its culture, at least until the latter half of the nineteenth century.[52]

In various accounts, throughout the nineteenth century and beyond, "the Near East" indicated a cultural space distinct from that of Europe that might encompass the whole geographical area between Western Europe and India (or some part of it). Often, it simply referred to the former or current Ottoman lands. As such, it sometimes included Eastern Europe and Persia but most frequently it was represented as comprising the Balkans and Asia Minor. Whereas the term "Orient" remained part of the construct in French and Italian, it was less common in English and German. Although it was sometimes used interchangeably, "the Near Orient" often implied the Asian and African parts of the Ottoman Empire whereas "the Near East" referred to Eastern Europe and the Balkans.[53] This distinction was made clearer when the term was used together with continental designations such as "the Near East of Europe" or "the Near East of Asia."[54] Further, although "the Near East" and "the Near Orient" were used as synonyms, their semantics were not identical. More precise scholars seem to have used "the Near East" in reference to the civilizational space from where modern Europe originated and still historically connected, whereas "the Near Orient" referred to a non-European cultural space that may include an Islamic presence.

A close cognate of "the Near East" was "the Nearer East," which was used interchangeably with the former. It was mostly used in British writing and was used even more commonly than "the Near East" in the second half of the nineteenth century.[55] In early uses of the term its geographical space closely corresponded to the Ottoman Empire, in most cases the area stretching from the Balkans to Mesopotamia. Authors who preferred this term over "the Near East" also displayed more geographical consciousness as they often attempted to give a visible definition of the terrain it represented. Richard Burton, a serious student of Islamic culture, and his wife Isabel Burton comfortably used the term in their works without feeling it necessary to define its geographical space (but which appears to be the area between the Nile and the Euphrates).[56] In 1873, W. J. Lamport used the term in his discussion of the religious sects of the Levant.[57] In the British press it was used almost synonymously with "the Near East" within the broader political context of the Eastern Question. In the aftermath of the Russo-Turkish War of 1877–78, the British papers the *Pall Mall Gazette* and the *Newcastle Courant* used the term in reference to an area from the Balkans to Central Asia, an area where Britain had an uneasy relationship with Russia.[58] As in the case of "the Near East," the term became a media staple from 1895 onward, commonly referring to Ottoman space in discussions of political conflicts.[59]

But what really distinguished "the Nearer East" from "the Near East" was its distinctly Christian character. More specifically, it was the preferred term to signify the biblical space of the Old and New Testaments centered on the Holy Land. By extension, depending on the subject in question, it could refer to the broader Christian space between Western Europe and Persia. But it also alluded to a temporal proximity as opposed to the old Near East of pre-Christian antiquity. As in the case of Hegel's "Hither Asia," the adjective "nearer" in this construct implied historical and religious affinity more than geographical and spatial proximity.

In writing on the history of Christianity, some authors were still thinking of the Nearer East from a comparative perspective within the parameters of the contemporary British Empire. Among them, Sir James Tennent in his *Christianity in Ceylon* pointed to the area between Persia and Greece as the Nearer East as one of the travel routes in the dispersion of the Aryan family.[60] In 1860, a review article on the New Essayists in the *Ecclesiastic* portrayed Jesus as "the Gospel of the Nearer East" and considered Buddhism "the Gospel of India."[61] Henry Wilson, who shared the same vision of Buddhism, although in a slightly different formulation, stated that "the Gospel of Jesus was proclaimed in the Nearer East."[62]

The biblical scholar Francis Upham provided a more tangible geographic definition of the Nearer East geography in 1875, based on his reading of the scripture and etymological analysis.[63] For him, the "Biblical East" had two meanings: in the singular it referred to Mesopotamia whereas in the less definite plural it denoted Persia. When considered as such, the East mentioned in the Bible in the context of Ezekiel, Isaiah, and Solomon must be understood as "the Nearer East." In addition, in the Hebrew scriptures, "the Far East" meant Persia, and so Cyrus was "the man from the Far East" and the "wise men" were Persians.[64] Taken from Upham, this image of the Nearer East was further romanticized and even introduced in Sunday school curricula. The *London Quarterly Review* in 1872 used "the Nearer East" as the geographical space for medieval relations of Christianity and Mohammedanism. For the *Journal of the Anthropological Institute* in 1876 the Nearer East spanned from Egypt to Assyria where the Genesis myth spread. In the same year, Van Lennep provided a detailed study of biblical geography that centered on the Nearer East.[65]

By the 1880s, "the Nearer East" as the lands of the Bible was firmly established in British thought.[66] Around the turn of the twentieth century, Christian authors placed a neatly defined biblical geography within the Orient of the European imagination. Francis Griffith defined it as an area that included "Babylonia, Assyria, Phonecia, Syria, Asia Minor, and Egypt." In Hubert Bancroft's depiction, it included "Palestine, Syria, and Egypt." Thus when Justin McCarthy wrote about the conflict between "Greece and Turkey" as "the question in the Nearer East," he was using a distinctly Christian view of the Eastern Question.[67]

Writing at a time when a number of different regionalizing conceptions were already in circulation with overlapping references, the British archaeologist and scholar David George Hogarth attempted to develop a coherent definition of the Nearer East by taking into account physical features, current politics, economic interaction, human distribution, civilizational traits, and historical memory. He thus came up with a region that corresponded to a land mass from the Adriatic Sea and Black Sea to the Indian Ocean and Caspian Sea. Land was demarcated by straight lines overriding existing political boundaries and natural physical features (see Figure 2.1). Although he conceived of the area primarily as the hinterland of three ancient civilizations, the Aegean, the Nile, and the Mesopotamian, surprisingly, he included the whole Arabian Peninsula, which occupied the largest as well as the central-most section of this region, producing a Nearer East not imagined by most other authors. He marked the boundary between the Nearer and the Farther East in Sind, which was considered by many of his contemporaries as part of the Middle East. For the northwestern boundary of this conceived region, Hogarth could not think of any obvious marker other than a civilizational divide:

> For want of an effective natural division, the north-western limit of the East depends largely on political conditions. Where centres of the superior civilization of the West lie so near at hand as to exercise an intrusive influence in any case, occupation by a Power, which does not derive its origin from the East, quickly decides in favour of the West. . . . [W]e must set the north-western limit of our "Nearer East" at the Balkan water-parting; but somewhat arbitrarily and without begging the question that there East and West are divided in any very obvious manner, or will long continue to be divided even as obviously as now.[68]

Yet what made Hogarth's conception of the Nearer East compellingly appealing for his contemporaries was his reasoning within the parameters of the Eastern Question.[69] The area was conceivable as a region where Western civilization originated, including the Christian code of ethics. For him, the ancient Nearer East included both East and West but now turned into a "Debatable Land" thanks to the spread of Western civilization over this region. This change turned "the Nearer East" into an "Intermediate Region, serving for the communication of the outer West, that itself has created, with an outer East which also owes it much."[70]

This comprehensive reconstruction of "the Nearer East" as the area that fell roughly within the domains of the Ottoman Empire was then readily adopted by mainstream scholarship and media and projected to contemporary geographic understanding of the area.[71] Thus, apart from the distinctly Christian writings, authors with less essentialist and more nuanced views of the East also seem to have found "the Nearer East" a useful term. Among them were scholars of antiquity who could not easily place the origins of modern civilization in either the then-perceived Occident or the Orient. Benjamin Wheeler, a scholar of Greek and comparative philology and former president of the University of California, was comfortable in using both "the Nearer East" and "the Near East" when referring to ancient civilizations between Mesopotamia and the Nile, including the Aegean. However, when viewing the same area in relation to Indo-Chinese civilizations he preferred the term "the Nearer World." For him, "in this fabric of the Nearer World joined of the West and the East, the East supplied the informing spirit, the ordered life, the civilization; the West, the moving will and the arm of power."[72]

THE EMERGENCE OF THE MODERN MIDDLE EAST

If the terms "Near East" and "Nearer East" created geographical uncertainty, then the term "Middle East" only added to this complexity. It has been a convention among modern scholars to credit Valentine Chirol, Alfred Mahan, and in some cases General Sir Thomas Gordon for coining the term "Middle East" around the turn of the twentieth century.[73] The term itself and its various cognates, however, not only were in circulation during the nineteenth century but existed in both European and Islamic sources in premodern times as well. In describing Alexander's reception of the legation of Spaniards and Gauls in Babylon, the fifth-century Spanish historian Orosius, in his *Historiae Adversum Paganos*, located that realm in the middle of the East (*medio Oriente*).[74] Examining this account of Orosius in 1863, Reinaud translated *medio oriente* as the heart of the East (*le coeur de l'Orient*) where Babylon was located.[75] In a more cultural sense with no geographical certainty, a 1641 letter written in French used *medio oriente* in reference to a place where Hebrew and Oriental books could be found.[76] The term survived in Italian (*il Medio Oriente*) and Spanish (*el Oriente Medio*) and became the standard equivalent of what came to be known eventually as the "Middle East" in English.[77]

In the nineteenth century, "the Middle East" and its equivalents in European languages often signified two different regions: either Persia and India together or the area encompassing from Persia westward through the Balkans. In 1819 Goethe used the term *Mittler Orient*, a term still in use in contemporary German, in reference to Persia and her neighbors.[78] Due to Goethe's profound influence on German and the broader European intelligentsia, his conception of "the Middle East" came into wide usage and also had an enduring impact on thinking about Persia and India as part of this region.[79] In 1875, a French positivist, Pierre Laffitte, defined what he termed *l'Orient occidental et l'Orient moyen*, based on ancient conceptions, as an area comprising Arabia, Asia Minor, Syria, Armenia, and Persia. James M. Ludlow, a pastor and prolific author, in 1896 defined "the Middle Orient" as an area centered on Asia Minor but excluding Persia, similar to the definitions of "the Nearer East" preferred by biblical scholars. An 1897 piece in the *Catholic World* referred to the Middle East alongside Egypt in the context of biblical lands. The travel writers Marius Bernard in 1885 and Hiram Stanley in 1897 included India when they used the terms "the Middle Orient" and *le Moyen Orient*, respectively. In 1901, the British historian Charles Beazley defined the Middle Orient as an area beyond the Nearer East, which included the Levant, Syria, the Euphrates, and the Caucasus. In 1906 the historian William Morey included Babylon, Assyria, and Persia in his conception of the Middle Orient.[80]

In British usages, the term "Middle East" and its near cognates were increasingly used to refer to India and its immediate vicinity. An influential work that spread this perception was Lord Curzon's 1894 book, *Problems of the Far East*.[81] In the words of its reviewer, "to the author there is a Near East—Russia and Persia; a Central East—India and the adjoining lands; and the regions beyond India, or the Far East."[82] This conception of the Central East, also referred to as the Middle East, became the standard British perception. Indeed, from 1895 onward, British newspapers and magazines commonly employed the term "Middle East" in reference to India and its neighbors.[83] General Sir Thomas Gordon's 1900 article, "The Problem of the Middle East," discussed Afghanistan and Persia within the context of Anglo-Russian rivalry.[84] In 1902, the navy officer and professor Captain Alfred T. Mahan gave the term "Middle East" a strategic and geopolitical cast by defining it in relation to maritime routes essential for military control of the area.[85] Although he was an American naval officer, Mahan's region was an exclusively British definition of the area constructed in response to the objectives and capabilities of sea power. In his 1903 book *The Middle Eastern Question*, Valentine Chirol tied the India Question to the Eastern Question.[86] Addressing the British audience, Arminius Vambéry's *Western Civilization in Eastern Lands*, a study on the British-Russian contest in Central Asia, was published in 1906 with "the Middle East" in its subtitle.[87]

Although "the Nearer East," "the Near East," and "the Middle East" were firmly established in European imagination during the second half of the nineteenth century, for the layperson this diversity of concepts may have looked chaotic. So, as a matter of clarity, many authors opted to use both terms together in combination as "the Near and Middle East." What they intended to imply was the conventional East or the Orient of European imagination or simply the sum of the contents of both terms. The use of these composite terms conveyed a sense of authority and learnedness. Yet others used the composite term to simply avoid their equivocality. Boundaries between Europe and the Far East were easier to conceive than the boundaries between the Near East and the Middle East.

Yet the more usual use of this combined construct was in fact quite learned and intended for the sake of its semantic range, particularly in British conceptions. As Britain's military and colonial involvements spanned from Egypt to India, this construct was found to be more convenient for writing on international affairs. More important, the Eastern Question was now thought to represent the whole set of relations between Europe and the East. Further, the late nineteenth century also witnessed the rise of non-Western ideologies articulated in a universal language and shared sentiments aimed at particular contexts, most notably the pan-Islamic movement. In the face of such developments, "the Near and the Middle East" was conceived to have referred to the broader spatial content of the Eastern Question from the Balkans to India. When used as such, the construct was largely devoid of its historical content and mostly used in reference to current affairs. Ironically, its geographical content was more definite than all other regionalizing concepts discussed above.

By the early twentieth century, there were quite a variety of terms and usages for this region. For instance, Victor Dickins in 1903 divided the Orient into two broad parts, the Near and Middle East versus the Far East, to point out the civilizational contrast between the two. Charles Eliot in 1907 referred to an area from Constantinople to Delhi in juxtaposition with China. In 1904 Ludwig Wilser used *der Nahe und Mittlere Ost* to criticize German ambitions to expand in an area where Britain already had a firm hold. Henry Steed in 1915 used the term in reference to the German projects to settle the Eastern Question, having in mind Eastern Europe. In 1909, Henry Dyer's use of the term excluded India. In 1916 Charles Seymour employed the term "the Near and Central East" in reference to an area from the Ottoman Empire to China, including Central Asia. The Missionary Survey of the World in 1917 established "the Near and the Middle East" among the major divisions of the world for missionary activity. In 1918 Thomas Holdich, who also used "the Near East" and "the Middle East" separately, preferred the combined form when referring to the geographical area between the West and the Farther East.[88]

Although this composite form was gaining favor, it was not a product of a new geographic vision. Rather it merely added the spatial content of the two terms involved. In any case, its life was cut short to a great extent by Toynbee's simplification of this conceptual complexity. Toynbee confined the geographical spaces of both terms to the same area and defined them from a strictly civilizational point of view. In sharp contrast with his wartime views and reflective of his subsequent trip to Asia Minor, he distinguished the two terms on the grounds of historical experience rather than contemporary geography. For him the term "Near East" denoted "the civilization which grew up from among the ruins of Ancient Hellenic or Greco-Roman civilization," whereas the Middle East referred to "the civilization which has grown up from among the ruins of the ancient civilizations of Egypt and Mesopotamia."[89] His Near East map therefore excluded Iran but included Libya and Macedonia.[90] He further argued that the West and the Ottomans belonged to different civilizational genealogies with distinct origins and diverse historical trajectories. Unlike its kin in the West, Near Eastern civilization (except in the case of Russia) broke down in the eleventh century due to the premature development of its state structure. However, Middle Eastern civilization broke down in the sixteenth century despite the political and military genius of the early Ottoman Empire. For Toynbee, the terms "Near East" and "Middle East" referred to the same geography but two distinct civilizations and historical trajectories.

What turned these terms into staples of media lexicon was their association with the Eastern Question. In early uses of "the Middle East" and its cognates, the term's reference was more spatial than ideological. During the nineteenth century, within the context of the Eastern Question, it gained its ideological content and came to refer to a particular cultural and human geography with which Europe had a troubled relation. From 1895 onward, "the Eastern Question" was more specifically referred to as "the Near Eastern Question," "the Near East Question," "the Problem of the Near East," and the like.[91] The entire historical content of "the Eastern Question" was already embedded in this more specific terminology. Albert Hart, writing in 1923, argued that "the Near Eastern Question" was already twenty-five hundred years old, having first been conceived with the clash between the Athenians and the King of Persia.[92] At the same time, "the Nearer Eastern Question" was used synonymously with "the Near Eastern Question" but often with a distinctly Christian perspective.[93] In British perceptions, "the Orient" was not only demystified by its increasing replacement by "the East" but also partitioned along strategic colonial projects and disenchanted from indigenous geopolitics. Local entanglements were situated within the context of a more abstract and broader confrontation between the West and the East and retranscribed as a new series of "questions." Thus the China Question became the Far Eastern Question, the India Question and Persian Question became the Middle Eastern Question, and the Turkish (Ottoman) Question became the Near Eastern Question.[94] The first maps of this region were drawn only after the Eastern Question was dismantled into the Near Eastern Question and the Middle Eastern Question.

In broad terms, the Eastern Question was about establishing a new world order. In other words, it was European intellectuals' self-proclaimed mission to accord order to the rest of the world. Yet, more specifically, it was about envisioning Europe vis-à-vis the Ottoman Empire, for it represented an alien civilization still surviving on the same continent these Europeans saw as the dispenser of modern civilization, uncompromised by inferior races and cultures. The Eastern Question in this way became integral to the process of purifying Europe from cultural contamination by enlightening or driving out its Asiatic elements. It was a shared pursuit, if not a project, to create and reinvigorate a common historical memory, reclaiming lost lands, and repossessing its classical and Christian heritage, a project that entailed establishing first what Europe was not, a negative definition that created oriental stereotypes to identify, compare, and rid. Obsessive discussion of the Turks was, in this context, an inherent part of existing discourses on civilization, commercialism, racism, and feminism that were forging the European self-image.[95]

In political terms, much of the Eastern Question debate since the Congress of Vienna focused on the post-Ottoman configuration of the contested space from the Danube to the Euphrates. As symbolized by the sick man metaphor, the Ottoman Empire was a relic of past failures, a nonentity without a future whose survival could only be sustained by Great Power rivalry.[96] In this respect, the Eastern Question was part of the anti-Ottoman appeal for a united Europe. For as soon as the Eastern Question was answered, the Ottoman Empire would have ceased to exist. The Ottoman Empire's existence was thus inseparably tied to the Eastern Question. A growing number of European authors then saw no incompatibility in covering the Ottoman Empire not as a separate unit but as chapters of the Eastern Question. A significant outcome of the Eastern Question concerning the construction of the modern Middle East was its regionalizing effect. As it was neatly depicted by the *Historische Karten zur Orientalischen Frage*, published in *Brockhaus' Konversations-Lexikon* (Figure 1.1), the very geographical scope of the Eastern Question created its own regional paradigm.[97] Thus "the Middle East" and its cognates were conveniently associated with the geographical locus of the Eastern Question. As the marked transition from "the Eastern Question" to "the Middle Eastern Question" and its cognates reveals, the Eastern Question remained embedded in the Middle East as its principal signifier.

THE LOCAL NEAR EAST, MIDDLE EAST, AND ORIENT

Although imposed from outside, identification with "the Near East" and "the Middle East" was readily received by the locals under the authority of European image making. In the case of the Ottomans, the terms were meaningless but nevertheless adopted as part of the prevailing language in the international press and diplomacy. Once proudly defining themselves as the Rumis, the Ottoman elite first conceded to perceive themselves as easterners in the nineteenth century and then started to imagine themselves as part of "the Near East" by the turn of the twentieth century with almost no inquiry into the meaning and implication of this term.[98] This adoption of the term owes a great deal to the presence of the American Committee for Relief in the Near East (*Amerikan Şark-ı Karib Muavenet Cemiyeti*) that was founded in 1915 to assist Christians living in the Ottoman Empire.[99] Yet, even the Ottomans found the term convenient for pragmatic purposes. Having seen the emergence of powerful and expansionist nation-states that were once part of the empire, the Ottoman elite considered themselves not "the problem" but a player just like others in the broader problem that came to be commonly dubbed the Near Eastern Question.

But other locals, the ones seeking independence and new identities, quickly embraced these terms mainly for their secularizing effect, in a quest to turn themselves into legitimate players on the Eastern Question. In the final decades of the Ottoman Empire and after, frequently shifting borders left ethnic and religious communities divided and relocated in newly formed political entities. As in the case of the Association for the Strengthening of Near Eastern Circassian Rights (*Şark-ı Karib Çerkesleri Temin-i Hukuk Cemiyeti*), these communities used "the Near East" in a diasporic sense.[100] Turkish press during the War of Independence found the term "Near East" useful in discussing the area that once was under Ottoman rule.[101] For successor states of the Ottoman Empire, self-identification with the Near East also meant proximity to Europe, an act of dissociation from the more exotic "Orient," and a proof of disowning their Ottoman past.

The "Orient" and its equivalents in local languages are now mostly used in the (exotic) tourism industry as a relic of the past. However, in the nineteenth century, it was widely adopted as a supra identity among the peoples of Asia and North Africa before it was partitioned into subregions. From Morocco to Japan, intellectuals and statesmen in the main felt themselves part of the greater Oriental community and, in symbiosis with their peculiar cultural and political identities, could comfortably speak for the whole Orient. Their exposure to colonialism and European claims of civilizational hierarchy created a defensive solidarity and cooperation. European exclusivism and involvement in North Africa and Asia not only created an imaginary Orient with definable qualities but also actually led to an Oriental consciousness among the locals, ultimately creating a more tangible Orient with greater interaction among its leaders. So the Orient became at least in part a reality. The 1905 war between Russia and Japan, for example, was hailed throughout Asia as a victory of the Orient against the West.[102] In the face of this strengthening anti-Westernist wave toward the late nineteenth century, envisioning the Orient through regions that suit European views and colonial designs was strategically conducive to break the threat of Oriental consciousness. The same Orient created by European imagination was thus partitioned into separate units. In the age of flourishing pan-movements, differentiating the newly conceived regions of Asia from each other certainly did not fare very well for such threatening ideologies ranging from Pan-Islamism to Pan-Asianism.

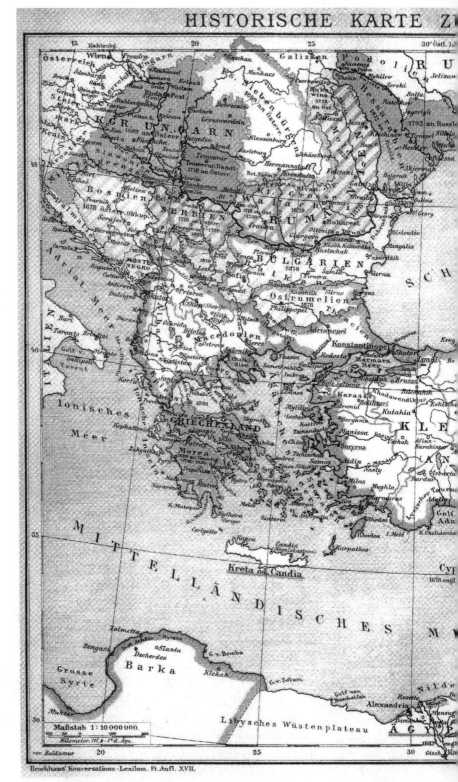

Figure 1.1. Historical Map of the Eastern Question. *Brockhaus' Konversations-Lexikon*, 1894–1896, 818a (original in color).

CONCLUSION

Despite the rise of modern geography and cartography in the contemporary era, the term "Middle East" and its variations were not created by geographers or cartographers. Rather, they provided them an enduring challenge to map out the region and define it as a coherent geography. Yet it would be meaningless, if not impossible, to trace the origins of these terms to a single historical factor or process. Throughout the nineteenth century and beyond, a number of terms were proposed by different players for different purposes, in many cases independently from each other. Many Christian authors, for example, based their views on the scriptures and considered the Near East as the area centered on the Holy Land. For many Orientalists and historians of antiquity, these terms represented the ancient origins of European civilization, which could be differentiated from the rest of the Orient and yet could not yet be considered part of contemporary European civilization. For British diplomats, "the Middle East" was conceived to facilitate the logistics of its imperial establishment. When British interests centered on India, the area was meaningful as the Middle East. When the imperial interests centered on the Ottoman Empire during World War I, the Levant became the center point of the new Middle East.

In the wake of World War I, the European discourse on the Eastern Question revolved around the widespread belief that it was now finally settled (Figure 1.2). As passionately reported by Toynbee in 1917, the Allied Powers had declared the purpose of the war as "the liberation of the peoples who now lie beneath the murderous tyranny of the Turks" and "the expulsion from Europe of the Ottoman Empire, which has proved itself so radically alien to Western Civilization."[103] Since then, it was often invoked and thought to be still unsettled but rarely used to define Europe's relationship to its East. Instead, the terms "the Near East" and "the Middle East" almost synonymously replaced "the Eastern Question," but now without the "Question" attached. The semantic cache of these terms was already charged by the historical content of the Eastern Question.

As their quick and wide reception in both media and academia show, "the Middle East" and other similar constructions proved very convenient in envisioning Europe's relationship with its East. The civilizing mission entailed prescribing order to the non-European world, a pursuit carried out in tandem with colonialism. Creating such a region enabled European powers to super-

Figure 1.2. The Revival of the Eastern Question. *Le Petit Journal Supplément Illustré 935*, October 18, 1908 (original in color).

sede local realities and render their versatile problems into a few manageable categories while freeing themselves from being drawn into existing local entanglements. European observers could then comfortably render differences and perspectives into a few essential points of conflict, undermine existing social structures and cultural formations, and disenchant geography from its inhabitants and history. In this Eurocentric view of the world, seen from the metropolis, what the periphery lacked may be seen as a shortcoming and what was different may be considered as an anomaly. By regionalizing a given geographical space and rendering its essential qualities into a few universal characteristics, it simplified dealings with the perceived region in question. "The Middle East" as such still primarily signifies Europe's historical experience. "The Middle East" provides no local imagery prior to its engagement with Europe. It is no surprise, then, that modern scholars are very reluctant to teach courses on the medieval Islamic period under the rubric of the Middle East whereas teaching the modern period of the same area is now commonly referred to as the Modern Middle East.

This one-sided and holistic approach not only saved Europeans from seriously studying what they have been regionalizing but also in fact justified or even normalized it. The number of Europeans, from all walks of life, writing on the Eastern Question and the Near East was remarkable. But more astounding was the authoritative and prescriptive language adopted by these authors in drastic contrast to their competence on the subject about which they were writing. Even the most sophisticated intellectuals, some even without seeing and some with a single glance, could read the essential qualities of Oriental societies. Even the ones who spent serious time and effort in observing non-European societies were outside viewers with little understanding and penetration of the culture. The few who displayed a genuine interest in studying societies east of Europe produced the kind of representations with which the represented might not disagree, but these views were greatly dwarfed by the flood of more popular and stereotypical writings in the media.

The common attitude of European scholarship of the time was to look for patterns and universals instead of nuances and peculiarities. As a result, writing about Near Eastern character required much less competence than writing, say, on Persian poetry. Two British observers writing in 1866 on the Eastern Question noted that Bulgaria was then less known in Britain than was Timbuktu.[104] Urquhart's observation that "the European goes into the East convinced that he is a professor of political economy, that he is in possession of the science of government, and that in every respect he is a free man of an understanding mind" could easily be substantiated by simply perusing what these Europeans wrote on the East.[105] Ottoman authors too, in refuting the common European views on the East, were often struck by how little their opponents knew about any particulars.[106] It was perhaps this simplicity of European knowledge about the East that dissuaded local intellectuals from seriously engaging with the Eastern Question debate until it became a matter of life and death. Even then, most respondents were rank-and-file intellectuals with no significant scholarly background.

The Occident-versus-the-Orient contrast had initially created a dualistic but hierarchical vision of the world. Reconceptualizing the Orient as the Near/Middle East and Far East vis-à-vis Europe reaffirmed the central position of Europe in this imagery and further peripheralized the East, Europe being the metropolis. Despite this implied degradation, institutions and businesses from universities to newspapers continue to internalize the Middle East and, at the expense of a drastic drop in the uses of "East" as impersonal names since World War I, they use the term in their names as part of their contemporary appeal. Nevertheless, the Middle East as imagined never created a shared identity among its inhabitants as Middle Easterners, and there is still no regionwide organization with any considerable representative status. The Middle East today still remains a region with few claimants from within.

2 BRITISH AND U.S. USE AND MISUSE OF THE TERM "MIDDLE EAST"

Roger Adelson

THE TITLE OF THIS CHAPTER puts "Middle East" in quotation marks because the term has been defined in a number of different ways over the past hundred years. Nevertheless, this term, with its imprecise definition and history, continues in use and importance. This essay examines the history of this neologism of fairly recent vintage, and more generally, this discussion seeks to shed light on the ways that political and bureaucratic contexts have determined how the Middle East has been defined since the beginning of the twentieth century. The term "Middle East" particularly gained currency during and after World War II, although more recently this term connotes many negative images associated with oil, Islam, and terrorism. We can trace much of the current American understanding of the Middle East back to the oil and terrorism crises of the 1970s, which were amplified of course by the events of September 2001, when al-Qaida terrorists attacked New York City and Washington, D.C. As terrorism crossed the Atlantic to Madrid, London, and other European cities, the U.S., British, and other governments declared a global war against terrorism and intervened militarily in Afghanistan and Iraq, and subsequently the Middle East has been seen as an even more troubled but most important region.

In the preceding chapter, Huseyin Yilmaz showed how the term "Middle East" evolved into the twentieth century. But why did "the Middle East" gain more currency during and after World War II, when the term was widely adopted by both government officials and the media? And then during the Cold War, North Africa came to be understood as part of the Middle East, whereas in the 1990s government officials and commentators spoke of the Central

Asian "stans" as part of the Middle East.[1] The geographical extension of the term has gained global currency and has added layers of confusion over what is and where is the Middle East. Indeed, very few in the media who write for general audiences ever attempt to delineate the region with any precision. Even specialists disagree about the scope of the term and about what commonality exists across such a geographically, ethnically, and historically diverse region. Even those who point to Islam as a common denominator in the region admit that Muslims practice their religion very differently from one place to another (beside the fact that most Muslims live outside this region—however it is defined).

DIVIDING UP THE EAST

By way of speaking to these issues, I propose to provide some brief historical background. First, we have to start with what was called the "Eastern Question" by European imperial powers in the late eighteenth century, which also has been dealt with in the previous chapter. The so-called Eastern Question was a phrase coined by the Europeans who began to ask what the Great Powers would do in the event of the collapse of the Ottoman Empire. Napoleon Bonaparte's expedition to Egypt and the Levant (which is an even older French term that refers to the countries of the eastern Mediterranean) first alerted Britain to the dangers France could pose to supply routes to British India. However, over the course of the nineteenth century, the rise of Russia and its imperial ambitions refocused British concerns on the czars as a greater potential rival to British overseas dominance. Because the subcontinent of India was the foundation of its Afro-Asian empire, Britain saw czarist Russia as a threat not only to the Indian subcontinent but also to its other interests in Asia as well. With this strategic picture in mind, during the Crimean War in the 1850s, the British allied with the French and the Turks to defeat Russia. Partly as a result of the Crimean War, British and French investments grew in the Ottoman and Persian Empires. Then in the 1890s, after Japan's defeat of China, the British concluded an alliance with Japan against Russia. These ties became stronger in the wake of Japan's victory in the Russo-Japanese War in 1905.[2]

Familiar to diplomatic historians, these events and the strategic planning underlying them led the British to begin to refer to the regions north of India as "Central Asia" and to divide the rest of Asia between the "Far East" and "Near East" (see Chapter 1). At the same time advances in the technologies of

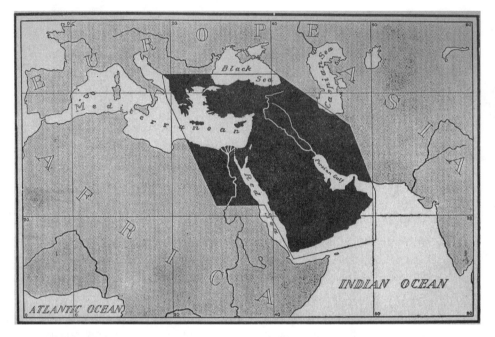

Figure 2.1. The Nearer East. Hogarth, *Nearer East,* 1902.

transportation, communication, and warfare since the middle of the nineteenth century made English-speaking peoples more conscious of Asia. Indeed, new technology partly explains some of the distinctions English speakers made between India, the Near East, and the Far East.[3]

In 1902, a book titled *The Nearer East* appeared in Britain and was soon republished in the United States with the title, *The Near East*. The author, David George Hogarth, was a noted Oxford archaeologist and geographer who launched T. E. Lawrence on his legendary career with the Arabs during World War I. Hogarth's detailed book defined the Nearer East as the Balkans, West Asia, Southwest Asia, and Northeast Africa (Figure 2.1).[4]

Also in 1902, an article appeared in the *National Review,* an influential monthly journal published in London.[5] The author, Alfred T. Mahan, was a U.S. naval officer and lecturer well known in London since the 1890s for his two books on the impact that British sea power had on history.[6] In light of the Russian advances into Central Asia and northern Persia, as well as the new Siberian railroad, Mahan believed the British must secure the Persian Gulf to defend India and its sea routes. Backing British control of the Suez Canal and

Egypt, Mahan saw moving into southern Persia as the logical next step for Britain to control the Persian Gulf, which had become a British lake. Mahan coined (what he thought) was a new term for this region: "The middle East, if I may adopt a term which I have not seen, will someday need its Malta, as well as its Gibraltar; it does not follow that either will be in the Gulf."[7] Referring to the deployment of naval power, Mahan observed: "The British Navy should have the facility to concentrate in force if occasion arise, about Aden, India, and the Gulf." Mahan did not reject the term "Central Asia," although Britain's so-called Great Game there with Russia did not trouble those, like Mahan, who were primarily concerned with naval strategies. Nor did Mahan reject the term "Near East."[8] To the latter he simply added "Middle East," which he centered in the Persian Gulf, owing to his preoccupation with securing British maritime links to India. When Mahan wrote his article, oil had not yet been discovered in southwest Iran (which occurred in 1908).

In addition, Mahan saw the German proposal to build a railway to Baghdad as a way to further strengthen British resistance to Russian expansion. The Germans were viewed less favorably by Valentine Chirol, a prominent British journalist in London. His outspoken criticism of Germany led that country's officials to ban Chirol from the country in the early 1890s. This did not deter Chirol, who became the head of the foreign department of the *Times* in the late 1890s.[9] Warning of the new Japanese threat as well as the old Russian threat, particularly for the oil wealth centered on Baku, Chirol published a number of articles that he turned into a book in 1896 titled *The Far Eastern Question*.[10] Stimulated by Mahan's article, Chirol wrote nineteen more articles for the *Times* that he then turned into another book in 1903 titled *The Middle East Question*.[11] To Chirol, the Middle East covered not just the Persian Gulf area but also all the overland approaches to India, including Afghanistan and Tibet, or as he explained, "those regions of Asia which extend to the borders of India or command the approaches to India, and which are consequently bound up with the problems of Indian political as well as military defense."[12]

Another prominent figure who concerned himself with India's defense was Halford Mackinder. An Oxford don engaged in the new field of geopolitics, Mackinder argued that the inner core of Eurasia remained the most pivotal region of the world since the Mongols had burst forth to plunder the empires of China, Russia, and Islam. Those British who followed the Great Game agreed with Mackinder's view that the Central Asian hinterland, where the Russian

Empire had gained territory at the expense of the Persian and Turkish Empires, posed the greatest Asian threat to the British Empire. In an article he published in London's *Geographical Journal*, Mackinder felt constrained to remind Mahan that most of Asia was beyond the reach of sea power.[13]

This geopolitical debate over the Middle East stirred little interest in Edwardian London, even among those who made, conducted, and influenced British policy in Downing Street, Whitehall, Westminster, Fleet Street, and the City. Whitehall officials took note of Russia's defeat by Japan in 1905 and the growth of the German navy, but few paid attention to the Persian Revolution of 1905, the Turkish Revolution of 1908, and the economic downturn and nationalistic protests in Egypt that began in 1907. The Foreign Office gave more time to the two Franco-German crises over Morocco in 1905 and 1911, the Italian-Turkish War, and two Balkan wars before 1914, which were more important to the Great Powers of Europe than to Persia, Turkey, and Egypt.

Most of London's governing establishment remained confident about the British navy's ability to overwhelm the German navy and about Britain's ability to keep a balance of power in Europe while it defended India effectively. The latter was vital because the British could send the Indian army, then one of the world's largest standing forces (and maintained at India's expense), wherever London's leaders thought necessary.[14]

The Suez Canal was another source of British concern, particularly in the city of London, the financial center of world capitalism. The Suez Canal Company was based in Paris, but almost half the company's stock was owned by the British government. The canal, completed in 1869 and used mostly by British ships, had to be kept open and its fees kept as low as possible. Benjamin Disraeli's purchase of the Suez Canal stock for the British government in 1875 set a precedent in 1914 for Winston Churchill to arrange for the British government to buy the majority of the stock in the Anglo-Persian Oil Company, a highly profitable company that became the Anglo-Iranian Oil Company in 1935 and then British Petroleum Company in 1954. As First Lord of the Admiralty, Churchill advocated government ownership of the oil company because the navy, then shifting away from coal, imported most of its oil from the United States and Mexico. To Churchill, the British navy mattered more than profits mattered.[15]

Although the British attached strategic and financial importance to the Middle East, the term itself was not employed by the Committee of Imperial Defense. Formed in 1904 to coordinate Whitehall departments and intelligence, that committee became the model for the many interdepartmental committees set up during and after the World War I. The Admiralty, War Office, Foreign Office, India Office, and Colonial Office, along with the Board of Trade and Treasury, each had its own concerns about the seas and lands lying between Europe and India. But the British government reckoned its policies in terms of empires and individual countries rather than with regions.[16] The same was true of the British Chamber of Commerce and various financiers and industrialists who backed British investments and trade routes to India. Even though they sometimes referred to the region as the "Near East" (and not the "Middle East"), they too referred to specific countries rather than the region as a whole. Likewise, religious and political activists who favored the Armenians, Bulgarians, Greeks, and Jews against the Turks continued to think in terms of political entities rather than in terms of regional formations.

There were a few exceptions to this way of thinking, such as Edward G. Browne, the Cambridge professor who taught Persian, Turkish, and Arabic. He was outspoken in his opposition to the Anglo-Russian Convention of 1907, which partitioned influence in Persia between Britain and Russia. London ignored the professor.[17]

FROM THE NEAR EAST TO THE MIDDLE EAST AT WAR

Despite the naval, military, and financial investments the British made in the war against the Turks from 1914 to 1918 and afterward, the term "Middle East" gained little currency by the British both inside and outside the government. The British were heavily involved in the region during World War I as they closed the Turkish Straits between the Black Sea and the Mediterranean; declared war against the Ottoman Empire; occupied the head of the Persian Gulf; annexed Egypt and Cyprus; and fought in several fronts to take Baghdad, Mosul, Jerusalem, Damascus, and Beirut from the Ottomans. They then occupied Istanbul, and so they established a presence on the Asian shore of the Dardanelles, along the coasts of the Arabian Peninsula, and with the collapse of the Russian Empire, in all of northern Persia and its capital, Tehran. To the British, the tens of thousands of British injured or buried in cemeteries between Gallipoli, Suez, and the Gulf seemed to justify their occupation of so much of that region. An interdepartmental committee tied to the Foreign Office was called the Middle East Committee, but it met only a few times in 1917 before it was absorbed into the Eastern Committee, which in 1918 coordinated various campaigns waged by Whitehall and its officers in the Trans-Caucasus and Trans-Caspian regions after the czar's abdication during the Russian Revolution.[18]

The press and politicians only reacted to this vast British occupation when wartime censorship came to an end, and as postwar Britain's economic situation worsened, unemployment rose, civil war erupted in Ireland, and the Allies abandoned their expeditions against the Bolsheviks. Few British took much notice of their country's deep involvement in the region until about1920, when controversy developed over the British occupation of Iraq (Great Britain was awarded the mandates of Iraq and Palestine at the San Remo Conference in April 1920). At issue was the fact that sending more troops there to put down a rebellion would add to the already heavy war burden for British taxpayers. With an estimated cost of over 400 million pounds annually, Fleet Street's most powerful Conservative newspapers opposed the high costs the British faced in Iraq.[19]

Winston Churchill, the politician most identified with the massive British losses at the Dardanelles Campaign on the Gallipoli peninsula, owed his political comeback to Prime Minister David Lloyd George. The latter dumped Palestine and Iraq into Churchill's lap early in 1921, when Churchill took over the Colonial Office. He set up the Middle East Department and convened a conference in Cairo to meet with leading British military and civilian personnel posted throughout the region. His main task was to cut costs by reducing British troops in Iraq and Palestine.

Churchill's strategy was to revert to a practice the British had adopted toward India's princes, especially after the mutiny of the 1850s. As long as the princes took their cues in external affairs from the British, the princes were left to rule internally as they wished. The British goal was to upset as few locals as possible by keeping British advisers behind the scenes and behind the thrones of cooperative leaders. The wealthiest of these leaders were expected to pay their own way whereas the poor were subsidized and armed with as little cost as possible to the British treasury. The British Raj had learned that it was much cheaper and easier for the British to pay a collaborative prince and his family than it was to meet the demands of the masses.

At the March 1921 Cairo Conference, Churchill planned an Iraqi state that cobbled together the Kurds in the north, the Shia in the south, and the Sunnis in the center. Because the Ottoman Turks had relied for centuries on the Arab Sunni minority in and around Baghdad, the British chose a Sunni leader from the Hashemite family of the Hejaz in western Arabia who had collaborated with the British against the Ottomans in the recent Arab Revolt. Having been thrown out of Syria by the French, Faisal was installed by the British as king of Iraq (and his brother, Abdullah, was soon made king of Transjordan, newly created from the Palestine Mandate). The British used air power, which, from their two bases outside Baghdad, bombed uncooperative tribes and other troublemakers. Parliament and the British press praised Churchill for cutting costs in Iraq, including his move to absorb his Middle East Department into the Colonial Office when he left in 1922.[20]

Outside of government circles, British interest groups and individual experts continued to use the term "Near East" more often than they used the term "Middle East," despite a Royal Geographical Society resolution in 1920 that prescribed that the "Near East" should denote only the Balkans, whereas the lands from the Bosporus to the Indian frontiers should be named "Middle East." The publications of the Royal Central Asian Society and the more commercially focused *Near East and India* made little use of the term "Middle East" through the 1930s.[21]

The United States was not completely alienated from the post–World War I contexts throughout the region, and although it had declared war against Germany in 1917, it did not do so against the Ottoman Turks. This disappointed the British no less than the U.S. refusal to ratify the Versailles Treaty in June 1919 did. In addition, although the Americans rejected the British invitation to take up mandates for Armenia and Palestine, they were eager to compete with British oil claims in Iraq and the Arabian Peninsula. Like the British, few Americans used the term "Middle East," although "Near East" was used by some scholars and groups. American Protestant missions continued in Syria as did charitable work on behalf of the Armenians through the Protestant's Near East College Association, Near East Relief, and Near East Foundation. Furthermore, academic programs in Near Eastern studies, with a strong focus on the ancient world, such as the one at the University of Chicago, were inaugurated around this time.[22]

The term "Middle East" came into its own just before World War II, a war that was truly more global than the 1914–18 war, or the Great War as it was first named. In that earlier war, the greatest and most decisive campaigns took place in Europe, and the British campaigns against the Turks were considered sideshows by Western strategists who opposed them. The Middle East mattered so much more in World War II mainly because of the oil required for mechanized warfare at sea, on the ground, and especially in the air. These war machines multiplied the demand for oil not only for Britain and the Allies but also for their enemies. Adolph Hitler's need to import oil helps explain the Nazi drive into southeastern Europe and Russia. Likewise the demand for oil explains Japan's bombing of Pearl Harbor: the Japanese planned to destroy the U.S. Pacific Fleet before they moved to seize the oil-producing regions in Southeast Asia.[23]

Historians now recognize that extensive war preparations took place in Britain before 1939 and that the British prewar calculations affected their mandate in Palestine, where large numbers of their forces on the ground and airplanes were required to put down the Arab revolt of 1936–39. By the mid-1930s, even nonmilitary departments in Whitehall were making elaborate plans for war in Europe, such as determining how to provide the British Isles with sufficient food, which it mostly imported. Meanwhile, the Foreign Office initiated a wide variety of diplomatic activities in light of Mussolini's ambitions for a great Italian empire in northeastern Africa; his seizure of Abyssinia combined with Italy's military occupation of Libya since 1911 demonstrated these ambitions. Looking for potential allies to oppose Mussolini and Hitler, the Foreign Office renegotiated more liberal treaties with Turkey and Egypt.

The British military made extensive preparations for war in the Middle East. The Royal Air Force reorganized the Middle East Air Command, which originally was comprised of the squadrons from Egypt, Sudan, and Kenya before the Abyssinian War of the mid-1930s. In 1938, the Middle East Air Command's authority was extended over the previously independent Royal Air Force (RAF) squadrons in Palestine, Transjordan, Iraq, Aden, and Malta. In 1939, the British army followed in the footsteps of the RAF. The British army consolidated all the separate military commands of Egypt, Sudan, and Palestine-Transjordan, and added Cyprus, British Somalia, Aden, the Persian Gulf, Cyprus, Iraq, and Iran to this conglomeration. General Archibald Wavell, charged with this consolidation of British air and military power, was designated the commander in chief, Middle East. Based in Cairo, he was responsible for vast parts of northeastern Africa and southwestern Asia. He had spent most of his career in the regions of his new command, and he was writing a biography of General Edmund Allenby, the successful commander of the British campaigns in Palestine and Syria during World War I who served as high commissioner of Egypt afterward.[24]

By June 1940, a month after Churchill had succeeded Chamberlain as prime minister, Britain stood virtually alone in Western Europe confronting the Nazis, who had taken the Low Countries and occupied northern France. The south of France was left to Vichy collaborators with Hitler, and the fall of France meant that the French colonies in Northwest Africa were tied to the Vichy regime, and thus could threaten British access to the western Mediterranean. Nazi successes on the continent convinced Mussolini that he should ally Italy with Hitler, which had the effect of cutting off British access to the central Mediterranean, with British Malta caught in the crossfire between Britain and the Axis. The closing of the western and central Mediterranean to British shipping meant that the British had to transport supplies around the vast African continent, which then raised concerns about Britain's ability to hold Egypt and the eastern Mediterranean. Early in 1941 colonial troops from the British Empire managed to defeat the Italian soldiers breaking into western Egypt, although the British and the Italians continued to battle in parts of the Horn of Africa in that year. Mussolini's forces needed to be stiffened, so Hitler sent one of his best, General Erwin Rommel, "the desert fox," to take charge of the Axis drive into western Egypt.

The next shock to the British came in the Balkans during the spring of 1941, when the Nazis occupied all of southeastern Europe and even the island of Crete, where German paratroopers defeated the British troops and the superior Luftwaffe pounded the British navy . Many Britons feared that the Nazis might dominate the eastern Mediterranean with help from the Vichy regime running Syria and press on into Iraq and Iran and their oilfields. In April, when junior Iraqi army officers staged a coup against the pro-British monarchy in Baghdad, the British sent forces from Basra and Palestine, defeated the insurgency, and put a friendly general back in charge. The British navy then bombarded Lebanon and the British military defeated the Vichy in Syria, putting de Gaulle's Free French in charge. When Rommel gained more ground in Egypt on the British, Cairo buzzed with rumors: "Rommel is coming! Rommel is coming!" Churchill replaced Wavell with General Claude John Eyre Auchinleck from India, whom he expected to take the offensive against Rommel.

An even greater concern to the British came in June 1941, when Hitler launched his massive invasion against the Soviet Union. The security of the Suez Canal and the Persian Gulf seemed in such jeopardy that Churchill's new commander publicly stated that he expected Russia to fall as quickly as the rest of Europe. But if Russia fell, what should be done about Russia's oil wells? Should the British blow up Baku as they had blown up French ships in port? The Nazi advance in Russia reverberated throughout the Middle East and encouraged Britain's enemies. Britain replaced Iran's shah, friendly to the Axis, with his son, Muhammad Reza Shah, in the summer of 1941. When shortages of food that winter led to riots in Cairo and Egypt's king wanted to name an anti-British prime minister, Churchill in early 1942 ordered British tanks to surround Abdin Palace and instructed the British ambassador to inform the king he would lose his throne unless he cooperated more fully with the British. The king complied. The British rounded up more political and religious activists in Egypt, just as they had imprisoned Mahatma Gandhi and leaders of the Indian National Congress.

Churchill was relieved at the end of 1941 by the United States' entry into the war, which was precipitated by Japan's bombing of Pearl Harbor and Hitler's subsequent declaration of war against the United States. Each of Churchill's successive campaigns had to be executed in step with United States, including his operations in the Mediterranean region and North Africa. With various operations extending from Northwest Africa, across North Africa through the Horn of Africa, and east to Iran, General Harold Alexander, the new commander in chief in Cairo, was barely able keep track of all his commanders in the field. Churchill now sent to Cairo a minister of state for the Middle East as well as the director for the new Middle East Supply Center, which coordinated all British political and economic wartime policies throughout the vast area.[25]

So, as the war progressed throughout the early 1940s, the term "Middle East" began to be used more frequently, and Churchill's wartime centralization of British military, political, and economic operations in Cairo gave greater coherence to a region referred to as the Middle East. The Americans sometimes disagreed with the British over operations in North Africa, the eastern Mediterranean, the Persian Gulf, and Iran, but Churchill's views prevailed throughout the region, part of which was often referred to as the "Middle East" and part of which was referred to as "North Africa." In 1942, Churchill tried to divide the Middle Eastern Command between Cairo and Baghdad, identifying the former as the "Near East" and the latter as the "Middle East." When he pressed for such a division, the British War Cabinet and General Staff insisted that the Middle East Command remain intact. Caught by the wartime centralization he had initiated, Churchill in his memoirs of World War II regretted the British lumping together the Near East's Turkey and Levant with the Middle East's Iraq and Persia.[26]

World War II propaganda machines on both sides of the Atlantic controlled most print and broadcast media, which quickly latched onto the term "Middle East" in their coverage of the war. The term met journalistic needs to cover North Africa and the eastern Mediterranean in ways that made sense to the public at home. British newspapers too adopted the term "Middle East," as did the British Broadcasting Company.

The war in North Africa and the eastern Mediterranean posed special problems for U.S. journalists. Stories of the determination of Churchill and the British home front were told frequently, but Allied accounts of Near and Middle Eastern campaigns ignored the wartime hardships faced by the British military and the peoples of these regions. The war on these fronts was simplified on maps to keep up Allied morale at home. The term "Middle East" was used more and more often, even though the public did not always know exactly where it meant. Defeating Hitler and Japan were still the main war goals, and the Americans had many more family and friends fighting in the Pacific or in Europe than in the largely unknown territories extending from Morocco to Iran, where British service personnel far outnumbered American personnel.[27]

By the end of World War II, for both the British and Americans, the term "Middle East" had eclipsed the "Near East" in popular usage. Only some older individuals and institutions inside and outside official London and Washington continued to use "Near East" or to distinguish between the Mediterranean-based Near East and the Persian Gulf-based Middle East, although the term "Near East" continued to be used by scholars and some university departments with interests in the ancient (pre-Islamic) world.[28] A new think tank founded in 1946 in Washington, D.C., the Middle East Institute, began to publish the *Middle East Journal*, the first U.S. journal focused on this region.

THE MIDDLE EAST AND THE COLD WAR

After World War II there was no peace conference as there had been after the Great War in Paris in 1919. By 1945, the European continent was already divided into armed U.S. and Soviet camps. The United States held sway throughout most of the world, owing to its monopoly of atomic bombs, overwhelming superiority in the air and at sea, and gigantic economy serving American consumers who had been spared the horrors that Europeans and Asians had endured. The United States also dominated the newly inaugurated United Nations, although the Soviets were able to put up some resistance with the use of their veto in the Security Council. Despite its global supremacy, the United States worried about the Soviet military occupation of Eastern Europe and Central Asia, and after 1949 the new Communist regime in China that mobilized millions of peasants against the U.S.-backed Chinese Nationalists also caused alarm.

The Cold War spilled over from Europe into the Middle East. Following World War II, Soviet forces stayed in northern Iran until 1946, several months longer than the British had agreed to in 1941, but this was a minor episode. A much larger confrontation occurred when Harry Truman granted Turkey and Greece $400 million in U.S. aid to offset Soviet influence. This had to do more with the containment of Soviet Communism than it did with events in the Middle East. The Cold War escalated with Moscow's isolation of Berlin and Washington's airlift to Berlin in 1948. The new North Atlantic Treaty Organization (NATO) was set up to counterbalance the Warsaw Pact. In 1949, the Soviets detonated their first atomic bomb and Communists defeated the Nationalists in China. This turned the Cold War in Europe into a global contest between the so-called free world and the Communist world. When North Koreans invaded the south, the United States, Britain, and the U.N. Allies, including Turkey, retaliated in a war that was waged in the name of the United Nations but run by Washington.

Truman's ideological war against Stalin upstaged Franklin Roosevelt's ideological opposition to European imperialism and colonialism that had been articulated in the Atlantic Charter early in World War II. Despite U.S.-Soviet antagonism in the Security Council, the U.N. General Assembly provided a forum for newly independent nation-states in Asia, Africa, and the Middle East. The Eisenhower Doctrine in 1958, like the Truman Doctrine a decade earlier, sought to defeat Communism. The words became cruder, and the weapons commanded by Washington and Moscow became more lethal and expensive. There were no battles in Europe's Cold War, but hot wars erupted in Asia, Africa, and the Middle East, with Asians fighting Asians, Africans fighting Africans, and the peoples of the Middle East fighting each other. Most of the weapons used in these wars were manufactured in and supplied by the United States, although more and more began to come from the Soviet Union and its East European satellites. With the establishment of the Central Treaty Organization, the Anglo-American conflict with the Soviet Union was sold to the British and U.S. public as a struggle of the free world against world Communism.[29]

One way for Washington to counter the spread of Communism in what a French sociologist in the early 1950s referred to as the "Third World" was to fund area studies at some U.S. and British universities, including several Middle Eastern centers. Area specialists at various institutions met together in 1966, establishing the Middle East Studies Association of North America (MESA), the last world cultural region to be so organized in the United States (see also the discussion in Bonine, Chapter 3). Even as the first issue of its flagship publication, *International Journal of Middle East Studies*, appeared in 1970, few U.S. programs offered much training in Middle Eastern languages or hired Middle East specialists.

While area specialists debated the boundaries and meanings of the Middle East, generalists in the media and politics continued to use this rather vague term uncritically. The Cold War ideological struggle, pitting Good against Evil, was reflected in much of the writing about the region. Thus, a view of the Middle East gained currency that tended to simplify the region's diversity and complexity, often avoiding the use of foreign words and ignoring an array of Arab states that had been added to all the other new states from Asia and Africa now at the United Nations.

Only a small number of correspondents for wire services and the most established newspapers went to the Middle East and North Africa. These journalists often found their reports shortened to make room for more pictures as newspapers competed with glossy magazines and television for attention. The public wanted pictures more than they wanted words about the Middle East and elsewhere, and the commercially driven media responded. The gap between specialist and generalist uses of the term "Middle East" during the Cold War became wider.

The withdrawal of all British forces east of Suez in the late 1960s meant that the United States had to fill the power vacuum in the Persian Gulf and Suez at the same time that the country found itself bogged down in Southeast Asia. Wanting to avoid any military encounters akin to the stalemate in Vietnam, Washington began to rely more heavily on Israeli military power in the region. The United States also encouraged and underwrote the Egyptian-Israeli peace treaty, granting both countries substantial subsidies from the United States. Iran, too, served as a bulwark against perceived Soviet interests in the region, and the United States sold large quantities of arms to the oil-rich shah of Iran and then to Arab leaders of the Gulf Cooperation Council. This strategy was beneficial for the United States through the Gulf War of 1991 (much of the cost of which was borne by Kuwait, Saudi Arabia, Qatar, and the United Arab Emirates).

Whereas most scholars argue that the Cold War ended with the collapse of the Soviet Union in the late 1980s, some historians propose that a bipolar world had already been turning into a multipolar world during the 1970s. In that decade, the Vietnam War ended, the Sino-Soviet divide deepened, the United States engaged the People's Republic of China and reached detente with the Soviet Union, and the United States started to trade with Asia more than with Europe. This is the global context in the 1970s for what some scholars refer to as the oil wars.

THE OIL WARS AND THE MIDDLE EAST

The abdication of the shah of Iran, the leading hawk among the oil-rich nations, in 1979 and the establishment of the Islamic Republic of Iran in 1979 upset U.S. strategy in the Persian Gulf. Relations were further strained when Tehran abducted Americans from the U.S. Embassy and held them hostage, thus outraging the U.S. public, who were already harboring pent-up frustrations over Vietnam, the fuel shortages, and higher prices at the gas pump. The inception of the oil wars did not mean that the Cold War completely disappeared. In fact they overlapped when the Soviets invaded Afghanistan, for it was feared that they might threaten the Persian Gulf and its petroleum production and reserves. These new contexts also fanned the flames of other social, economic, cultural, political, and religious fires in the region.

In addition, since the 1970s, the oil-rich states have become increasingly important international players. The Gulf states came to have a pronounced effect on the world disproportionate to the diminutive size of their population. The "Middle East" became more and more strongly identified with petroleum and the oil wealth of the Gulf. Scholars have written extensively about the founding of the Organization of Petroleum Exporting Countries (OPEC) in the late 1960s, as well as its Arab spin-off, the Organization of Arab Petroleum Exporting Countries (OAPEC), and the Arab oil boycott that started in the Arab-Israeli War of 1973. What merits more historical emphasis is the fourfold increase in oil prices that occurred at that time and another threefold increase in oil prices after the crisis the United States faced in Iran. The sevenfold increase in oil prices during the 1970s resulted in the largest and fastest transfer of wealth that had ever been recorded in history. The oil-producing countries now had vast amounts of money to spend. Oil revenues obviously went much farther in the sparsely populated Arabian Peninsula than they did in the more populated countries of Iraq and Iran, which helps explain why the shah was an enthusiastic backer of increased oil prices. The newly oil-rich expended their wealth both wisely and foolishly on the sacred and the profane. They spent huge sums on religious publications as well as on the construction of mosques, schools, and clinics (and ski slopes!) at home and around the world. Of course, there was still plenty left to throw away on casino tables in Las Vegas, London, and Cairo or to spend on the purchase of expensive weaponry.[30]

The oil-rich Gulf became an economic magnet for legitimate and illegitimate business. Entrepreneurs, salesmen, and hucksters from across the globe rushed to provide oil-rich customers with whatever they wanted, including arms. Similarly, many skilled and unskilled workers from the Middle East and beyond eagerly catered to the needs of the oil-rich regimes. By the time the price of oil declined in the early 1980s, the oil-rich Gulf had become economically as well as strategically vital to the United States for reasons only indirectly connected to oil. The manufacturers and suppliers of arms profited from the long Iraq-Iran War of the 1980s and the Gulf War in the early 1990s, just as U.S. arms dealers and others have profited from the Arab-Israeli conflicts since the 1960s.[31]

By the 1990s, the U.S. government and the media often added Afghanistan and Pakistan as well as the five "stans" (Kazakhstan, Kyrgyzstan, Tajikistan, Turkmenistan, and Uzbekistan) of the former Soviet Union into an even larger (Greater) Middle East, which is depicted on the larger areas represented on the covers of *Middle East Abstracts*. The volumes have also grown in number and size. In the late 1970s, all *Middle East Abstracts* were published in a single large annual volume; by the early 1990s, there were two volumes annually, not counting the years with special volumes on oil, women, minorities, and refugees; by the 2000s, there were four annual volumes, not counting all those on terrorism. The growth in interest in the region and the expansion of its conceptual dimensions also have been reflected in the range of material covered in newspaper editorials since the 1970s and in the newspapers collected by Facts on File.

The establishment of Israel on May 15, 1948, and the Arab-Israeli conflicts that have persisted since that time have also been reported and discussed in the context of the Middle East. The importation of arms into the Middle East heated up the Suez Crisis of 1956, which arose from Nasser's nationalization of the Suez Canal and led Britain, France, and Israel to occupy parts of the Sinai Peninsula and Egypt until Washington ordered them to withdraw. The Cold War intensified during the Arab-Israeli wars of 1967 and 1973. In 1973, President Richard Nixon put all U.S. armed forces on the highest strategic alert since the Cuban Missile Crisis, which has received too little historical investigation.[32]

Since the early 1970s, every U.S. president since Richard Nixon has recognized the Middle East to be strategically the most contested region of the world. Jimmy Carter's administration was so overwhelmed by the Iranian hostage crisis that his wife ended her White House memoirs by summarizing her husband's electoral defeat in 1980 in one four-letter word: "Iran." The Reagan administration, playing up the Cold War and playing down the oil wars, trained fighters from Pakistan to counter the Soviet invasion of Afghanistan and kept up a double game during the eight-year-long Iraq-Iran War in the 1980s. George H. W. Bush's administration concentrated over half a million troops in the Gulf War early in 1991 in the wake of Saddam Hussein's invasion of Kuwait. Most U.S. and Allied troops were withdrawn in 1991, but the remaining presence of so much U.S. power at sea, on land, and in the air provoked negative reactions in the Gulf, particularly among those Saudis who take the protection of Mecca and Medina seriously. Unlike the Americans, the British tried to keep their power in the Gulf as invisible as possible.[33]

The gap between the specialists and the generalists, already wide in the Cold War, has widened further during the period of the oil wars. Little of what specialists have learned about different parts of the Middle East has had much influence on the generalists, who view the region as a battleground over oil, against Muslim militants and Islamo-fascists. The changing technology in the media since World War II has also played a part. News coverage changed from government-inspired radio reports and movie newsreels in the late 1940s to fifteen- or thirty-minute network broadcasts on television during the 1950s. The independence of the U.S. media peaked during the conflicts over Civil Rights and Vietnam. In the 1970s, the sixty-minute television specials of hard news turned into the softer news magazine, with talk radio and twenty-four-hour broadcasting becoming forces of their own. Another great change occurred in the early 1990s, when most Americans followed the Gulf War through cable television. Since the 1990s, the emergence of the Internet has allowed images of Middle Eastern oil and conflict to be projected globally. Unedited blogs on the Web provide even cruder stereotypes of Arabs, Iranians, and other Muslims of the Middle East than Hollywood did in the 1970s.

There is growing skepticism about claims that 9/11 changed the world, that there is a global war against terrorism, and that fighting terrorists abroad keeps them out of the United States and Britain. Such statements, so often repeated by President George W. Bush and British Prime Minister Tony Blair, has ignored the resentments and rage that have developed over the British government's conversion of the Gulf into a British lake before the 1970s and the United States' domination not only of the waterways but also of the airways and the broadcast waves of the Gulf since the 1970s. Not surprisingly, this shared history has led some locals to be unsure about the differences between the British and the Americans. They speak the same language after all. It is perhaps equivalent to the fact that very few Americans make distinctions between Arabs of the various states. In that sense, the "sins" of the British "fathers" have been passed on to the American "sons." Rage against the Englishman over so many decades has stirred much pride, and it cannot be dismissed.

As discussed above, the British did not use the term "Middle East" much until World War II, when they coordinated their war plans over a vast Afro-Asian landmass in order to fight the Axis powers. During World War II, Washington received most of its intelligence on the Middle East from London. With help from the United States, the British held on to most of the Middle East during World War II, but by the end of the war the British were "bankrupt," to use Churchill's word. In early 1947, the British announced they would pull all their forces from Greece in a few weeks, withdraw from India in a few months, and turn the Palestine Mandate over to the United Nations. Early in the Cold War, the British offered some advice and intelligence about the Middle East to the Americans, which helped put the shah back on the throne in the 1953. The British continued to influence Egypt until the mid-1950s, and they dominated Iraq until the late 1950s. All this happened before the British withdrew from all their bases east of Suez at the end of the 1960s. U.S. intelligence has not matched the human intelligence of the British about the Middle East, although there has been no shortage of funding and gimmickry. In the Middle East the British were quite able to set up and change regimes at their own whim during World War I and World War II. The Americans have not had the same success as the British. What worked for the British earlier in the twentieth century has not worked for the Americans in recent decades. Some scholars attribute this to the United States' lack of the imperial will, tradition, and personnel that the British Empire could draw upon earlier in the twentieth century. Others fault the Americans for knowing even less about the Middle East than the British, often filling the ignorant void with ideology.

As the United States filled the power vacuum left by the final withdrawal of the British from the southern, predominantly Arab parts of the Middle East, U.S. policy makers tried to avoid another Vietnam by relying on the cooperation of Iran, Israel, and Egypt, all of whom depended on arms and/or subsidies from the United States. Saudi Arabia also bankrolled some of the more controversial and costly U.S. policies. The Americans, like the British, supported friendly regimes mostly by training Middle Eastern military forces and supplying them with weapons. With the increased oil wealth in the Gulf region, the United States first sold expensive weapon systems to the shah of Iran and then to the Kingdom of Saudi Arabia and the other members of the Gulf Cooperation Council.

U.S. ties to Saudi Arabia and the oil-rich states of the Gulf, along with U.S. leverage over Israel and Egypt, seemed to succeed through the Gulf War of 1991. However, the United States found no satisfactory solution for Saddam Hussein's Iraq that was acceptable to the Israelis and Saudis, much less to the Iraqis. One reason for the lack of U.S. effectiveness in the Middle East since the 1990s may stem from the fact that states of the region have grown more independent and less malleable than the Arab provinces of the Ottoman Empire early in the twentieth century. Whereas the British once dominated the external relations of countries of the Middle East, the oil-rich states of the Middle East now have their own resources and agendas throughout the entire world apart from the United States. Their strategic and economic autonomy has been profoundly affected not only by their enormous wealth but also by the revolutionary changes in communications in the last decades of the twentieth century.

Television brought the horrible events of 9/11 and the Iraq War into the homes and lives of Americans and the rest of the world. Whereas most of the world's viewers can tune out reports about wars in the Middle East, the people in the region do not. As a consequence of the new media access, it is quite reasonable that people in the region are suspicious of U.S. statements about the Middle East. To borrow one of the phrases of President Richard Nixon, peoples in the Middle East have been paying less attention to what the U.S. government says than to what the U.S. government does.

CONCLUSION

Despite the contrasts between the Middle East during the first decades of the twentieth century, when British influence was greatest, and in the last half of the century, when the U.S. power has grown, there are continuities and similarities in British and U.S. uses of the term "Middle East." The role of government policy makers in labeling the Middle East and intervening in the region has been no less important in Washington than it has been in London. In selling government policies to the public in Britain and the United States, the media has remained pivotal. The role of generalists, who neither know nor care much about the vast and varied parts of the Middle East, is no less great in the United States today than it has been for Great Britain. How often do U.S. and British specialists, much less politicians or commentators, admit that the Middle East is beyond the competence of any one person? Both the British and Americans should realize that there are great risks to conflating such vast areas, so diverse in geography, ethnography, and history, into one "Middle East."

Specialists on the Middle East are usually aware that they only have limited knowledge about specific peoples, parts, and periods of the Middle East. The scholars and writers with the most knowledge about the region have had to learn the language(s), conduct primary and field research there, and focus their careers on only one part of a vast and complex region. Arab specialists, for example, may be able to read modern literary Arabic in newspapers, but only a few know local Arabic dialects well enough to understand what is taking place among a small number of the more than 200 million Arabic speakers in Africa and Asia. Scholars tend to think in local rather than regional terms and focus on their discipline; policy makers, however, are easy prey to those who claim to know the entire region. Specialists and academics should be critical of the facile generalizations about the Middle East that continue to be made in politics and the media.

The pundits and politicians who theorize about geopolitics and terrorism have been all too willing to generalize about the Middle East as well as Islam. How much longer will such views be projected upon the Middle East and how much longer will they be accepted by governments and the general public? Given the long history of the British and U.S. use and misuse of the term "Middle East" during the twentieth century by policy makers, generalists, and specialists, the prospects for the twenty-first century do not seem encouraging.

3 OF MAPS AND REGIONS
Where Is the Geographer's Middle East?

Michael E. Bonine

OVER THREE DECADES AGO, in 1976, I wrote an article titled "Where Is the Geography of the Middle East?" which was published in *The Professional Geographer*.[1] In that piece, I examined how the study and teaching of the Middle East were rather sparse in American departments of geography, particularly in comparison with the study and teaching of other world regions. That situation, unfortunately, has not necessarily changed in the field of geography in the United States, despite the obvious growing importance of the Middle East for the U.S. government as well as the average American. In this chapter, I focus on what constitutes "the Middle East" for geographers and, hence, ask the question: Where is the geographer's Middle East? The answer requires an assessment of how regions have been conceptualized by geographers and how the Middle East fits into those frameworks. The field of regional geography has been a major focus of American geography since the beginning of the twentieth century, although the decline and even demise of this focus—as a specific field of study in geography—has been the case for several decades now. I examine the use of the term "Middle East" (and other terms used for this region as a whole and in part), particularly its use in world regional geography textbooks, as well as textbooks that focus specifically on the geography of the Middle East. I also provide some insights into the use of this term in maps and atlases—those essential tools of the geographer (although geographers certainly are not the sole proprietors, or producers, of such works).

REGIONS AND REGIONAL GEOGRAPHY

Is the Middle East a region? Even though there are various definitions and different shapes and sizes of the Middle East, what assumptions and what criteria are used to define this region? But first, what is a region? One of the more recent (and popular) world regional geographies, *World Regions in Global Context* by Sallie Marston, Paul Knox, and Diana Liverman, notes that "regional geography is about understanding the variety and distinctiveness of places and regions, without losing sight of the interdependence among them. Geographers learn about the world by finding out where things are and why they are there and by analyzing the spatial patterns and distributions that underpin regional differentiation and regional change."[2] They go on to say:

> **Regional geography**, which combines elements of both physical and human geography, is concerned with the way that unique combinations of environmental and human factors produce territories with distinctive landscapes and human factors produce territories with distinctive landscapes and cultural attributes. . . . What is distinctive about the study of regional geography is not so much the phenomena that are studied as *the way they are approached*. The contribution of regional geography is to reveal how natural, social, economic, political, and cultural phenomena come together to produce distinctive geographic settings.[3]

Regions can vary in sizes and scales, but generally they range from an area within a country that has a particular landscape and/or human characteristics, which may be identified by location and/or name (e.g., northern Iraq, Iraqi Kurdistan; southwestern Iran, Khuzistan), to larger areas, which are usually today conceived of as various groups of nation-states (e.g., Maghreb, North Africa, Southwest Asia, Arabian Peninsula). The largest regions are what geographers (and others) refer to as world cultural regions, and it is the use of these conceptual units that is relevant to our discussion of our region: the Middle East. For instance, in Marston, Knox, and Liverman's textbook, mentioned above, there are ten separate world regional chapters. In the order they occur in the book, they are: (1) Europe; (2) the Russian Federation, Central Asia, and the Transcaucasus; (3) Middle East and North Africa; (4) Sub-Saharan Africa; (5) North America; (6) Latin America and the Caribbean; (7) East Asia;

(8) Southeast Asia; (9) South Asia; and (10) Australia, New Zealand, and the South Pacific (Figure 3.1).[4]

What is apparent from this division of the world—these world cultural regions—is that they are mainly defined by continents or parts of continents. Our region is named as part of a continent (North Africa), but also it is one of the few non-continental names: the Middle East. Yet, as I show when I examine a number of other textbooks on regions (and our region), the designation "Southwest Asia" is also a very common name—and, so, a continent sometimes becomes predominant in naming (part of) our region. These larger cultural regions almost always comprise a number of specific political nation-states and are defined by the borders of those states. However, national boundaries usually incorporate a variety of diverse peoples and landscapes, and "seldom is an independent political territory coterminous with the territory of a self-consciously united people."[5] Nevertheless, the building blocks of our region (and the continents it spans) are nation-states, and there is an assumption that cultural identities within them are similar and coincide with political entities. "[M]ost of our encyclopedias, textbooks, atlases, and almanacs portray states as holistic entities, unified and distinct."[6]

But what is a continent? Martin Lewis and Karen Wigen's thought-provoking *The Myth of Continents* tackles the assumptions and misconceptions that have led to the construction of the world into seven continents (as well as other world divisions, such as East and West, North and South, or Third World and First World, and even nation-states). They emphasize how continents—and nation-states—have "become reified as natural and fundamental building blocks of global geography, rather than being recognized as the constructed, contingent, and often imposed political-geographical units that they are."[7] They note that world regions and continents are the products of overgeneralizations, and in fact some regions are defined according to criteria that differ from case to case. Yet, despite such problems, Lewis and Wigen "insist that world regions—more or less boundable areas united by broad social and cultural features—do exist and that their recognition and delineation are essential for geographical understanding."[8] Indeed, there must be some way to talk about the world—its diversity, patterns, and organization. So, the question is whether or not world cultural regions—and in our case, the Middle East (if it is a world cultural region)—are valid terms to use in the attempt to understand, study, and analyze a group of peoples, a group of

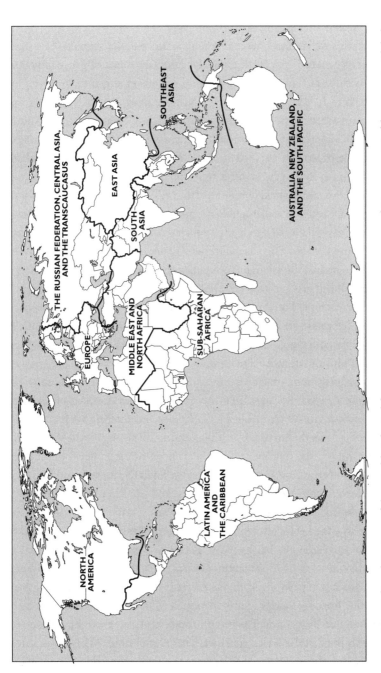

Figure 3.1. Cultural Regions of the World. Adapted from Figure 1.1 in Marston, Knox, and Liverman, *World Regions in Global Context*, 2002. By kind permission of the publisher.

countries, or a region. So in addition to the question, Is there a Middle East? there is a related and as difficult question: Where is the Middle East?

First, let us delve into how and when "world regions" came about—into the divisions generally put forth today, for example, in world geography textbooks. Basically, our present world cultural regions emerged from the period of World War II, when the lack of American international expertise and knowledge resulted in efforts to rectify that deficiency. In June 1942, the Smithsonian Institution established an ethnogeographic board, which was dominated by anthropologists but also included linguists and cultural geographers, to provide research and be a think tank for the war effort. The board met twice a year and mainly fielded requests from various governmental, military, and private agencies; one of their main products was a 187-page waterproof book titled *Survival on Land and Sea*,[9] which soldiers and sailors in the Pacific carried during the war. The board created a roster of more than five thousand individuals who had knowledge of the culture and languages of more than ten thousand cultural groups, and it divided the roster's world into the regions of Africa, Asia, Europe, Latin America, North America, and Oceania.[10] Hence, "the world regional concept that shaped postwar area studies was essentially formulated by anthropologists, and the world regional map they posited was subject to almost no debate."[11]

The establishment of major area study associations—specifically the Association of Asian Studies, Latin American Studies Association, African Studies Association, Slavic Studies Association, and the Middle East Studies Association of North America—in the decades following World War II also helped to solidify the treatment of knowledge within specific world cultural regions. Various funding agencies, such as the Social Science Research Council, American Council for Learned Societies, and Ford Foundation, began to provide research funds for work and study in specific world cultural regions. Finally, the establishment of Title VI area studies centers, funded by the federal government, led to many programs and teaching positions at major universities within departments that focused on specific language and area studies. These world divisions were the Far East, Southeast Asia, South Asia, Europe, Africa, Latin America, Soviet Union (later replaced with the Soviet Union and Eastern Europe), and the Near East (later replaced with the Middle East). As Lewis and Wigen note, "This reorganization of the global map into world areas was readily adopted by geographers, anthropologists, and other scholars. In the 1950s, a few world geography textbooks were organized around the architecture of continents, but by the end of the decade the transition to a world area framework (usually called world regions by geographers) was essentially complete."[12]

Geographers' minor role in the study of the Middle East is shown by their rather minimal participation in the emergence of the area studies programs after World War II. In November 1947, a major national conference on the study of world areas took place in New York City.[13] Slightly more than one hundred individuals participated; most were rather prominent academics but also there were representatives from government agencies, foundations, and a few other organizations. Although there were at least twenty anthropologists, five political scientists, eight historians, and more than twenty individuals from language and area study programs (e.g., Russian Institute, Institute of Latin American Studies), among them, there were only two academic geographers: Richard Hartshorne from the University of Wisconsin (one of the major figures of twentieth-century American geography) and Preston James from Syracuse University (a major Latin American geographer who wrote one of the principal regional geographies of Latin America). The conference focused on six world regions: Latin America, Soviet Union, Southeast Asia and India, Near East, Europe, and the Far East, and organized panels reported on the status of their area studies and offered recommendations. Hartshorne was with the Europe group, and of course James was with Latin America. The Near East Panel comprised ten individuals:

Walter L. Wright Jr. (Panel Chairman), Department of Oriental Languages and Literatures, Princeton University
Carleton S. Coon, Department of Anthropology, Harvard University
Mortimer Graves, American Council of Learned Societies
Philip K. Hitti, Department of Oriental Languages and Literatures, Princeton University
Frank S. Hopkins, Foreign Service Institute, U.S. Department of State
Halford L. Hoskins, School of Advance International Studies
John A. Morrison, National War College
Ephraim A. Speiser, Graduate School, Division of Humanities, University of Pennsylvania
Lewis V. Thomas, Department of Oriental Languages and Literatures, Princeton University
T. Cuyler Young, Department of Oriental Languages and Literatures, Princeton University

The panel on the Near East and the one on Southeast Asia "called attention to the neglect of these two important areas of the world by American scholarship and education, and urged recruitment and training of specialized personnel."[14] It is quite interesting that in the three pages of the Near East panel report, the issue of the use of the term "Near East" versus "Middle East" is not even mentioned.[15] The presence of archaeologists, such as T. Cuyler Young, who preferred—and still prefer the term "Near East" for this region, may certainly have been a factor for referring to the region as the Near East rather than as the Middle East. They did recognize, however, that "the interpenetrations involved in the Near Eastern area, both ancient and modern, in terms of geography, politics, and culture, mean that the area has so many facets that at present no rigid delimitation of its boundaries should be attempted."[16] Although this referred mainly to disciplinary boundaries, it might as well have referred to spatial boundaries as well.

It is also apparent how tentative their recommendations were; for instance, they focused on developing a general undergraduate course on the Near Eastern area and agreed that "the essential unity of Near Eastern history must never be overlooked, and that interrelations within the Near East and the role of the Near East in world culture must be the basic points of departure for such a survey course."[17] They also (puzzlingly) recommended that there be no language requirements for the undergraduate student of the Near East, although "complete and modern instruction in Arabic, Turkish, and Persian should be offered at the undergraduate level just as French and German are now."[18] The panels of the other areas concentrated on how to conduct research in their regions or how to teach and develop material in their graduate programs, a reflection of how further developed their area studies were (and why the Middle East Studies Association of North America was not formed until 1966—the last of the major area studies associations to do so).

GEOGRAPHIES OF THE MIDDLE EAST

Separate books on the geography of the Middle East were not published until after World War II, following geographers' new interest in major world cultural regions. Initially, however, this region was included in some of the early textbooks on Asia. For instance, in 1944, George Cressey, a major figure in American geography at Syracuse University, first published his *Asia's Lands and Peoples*.[19] In order, Cressey divided Asia into China, Japan, Soviet Union, Southwestern Asia, India, and Southeastern Asia. The chapter titled "The

Southwestern Realm" begins by addressing the terms "Near East" and "Middle East":

> The term "Near East" is an indefinite geographical expression which is frequently used but seldom defined. To some it loosely refers to all the lands between Libya and India: to others it is limited to the countries within Asia bordering the Mediterranean; and some would even include India. The words "Middle East" and "Levant" are sometimes introduced for Palestine, Iraq, and near-by areas, but the Middle East is also used variously for North Africa or even India. Like the Far East, the phrase Near East stands for no clearly defined place on the map and it is well to use it sparingly. This [Cressey's] chapter is an introduction to the eight major countries of Southwestern Asia, between India and the Mediterranean: Turkey, Syria, Palestine, Trans-Jordan, Arabia, Iraq, Iran, and Afghanistan [Figure 3.2].[20]

After about four pages of text on the Southwestern Realm, short chapters occur on the countries (or mandates) mentioned above. Although the book has about six hundred pages, only forty pages deal with this region, which includes numerous maps, photos, and graphs; hence, it contains rather limited text, much of which focuses on physical geographic descriptions. In contrast, China and the Soviet Union each have more than a hundred pages, and Japan has seventy pages (Cressey was a specialist on East Asia). With only a (rather inadequate) glimpse at the Southwestern Realm states, parts of this region are not even mentioned (e.g., the French mandate of Lebanon and British Trucial States or Oman). It is also revealing that in the acknowledgments of the book, Cressey thanks dozens of experts for their help with specific regions but mentions nobody for the Southwestern Realm—an indication of the absence of American geographers familiar with this region.[21]

The Pattern of Asia, edited by Norton Ginsburg of the University of Chicago and published in 1958, is another well-known textbook on Asia.[22] In it, the region of our concern is referred to as "Southwest Asia" (Figure 3.3), and it covers in general the same states that Cressey's work covers, except that Afghanistan has been moved to South Asia. Related to the Middle East, the text states:

> Southwest Asia forms the largest part of the Middle East region, which extends from Iran, on the east, westward to Cyrenaica, and from Turkey, on the

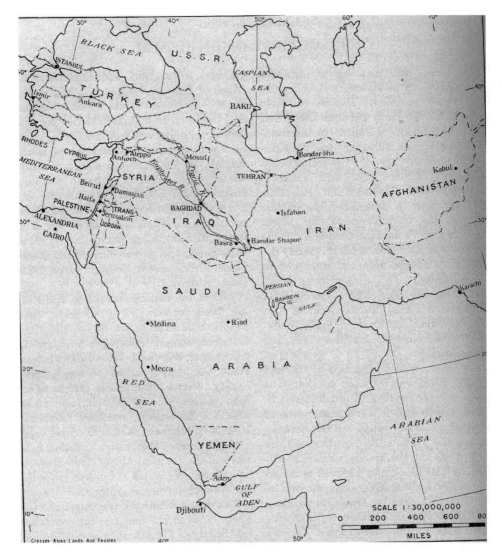

Figure 3.2. Southwestern Asia as defined by Cressey, *Asia's Lands and Peoples*, 1944. By kind permission of the publisher.

north, southward to central Anglo-Egyptian Sudan. Because of the scope of the text [i.e., Asia], Egypt, Cyrenaica, and the Sudan are not considered in detail, but one should remember that these areas, especially Egypt, are parts of an integrated unit, and that their relationship to Southwest Asia is not only obvious but also very close. . . . For the sake of convenience the term "Middle

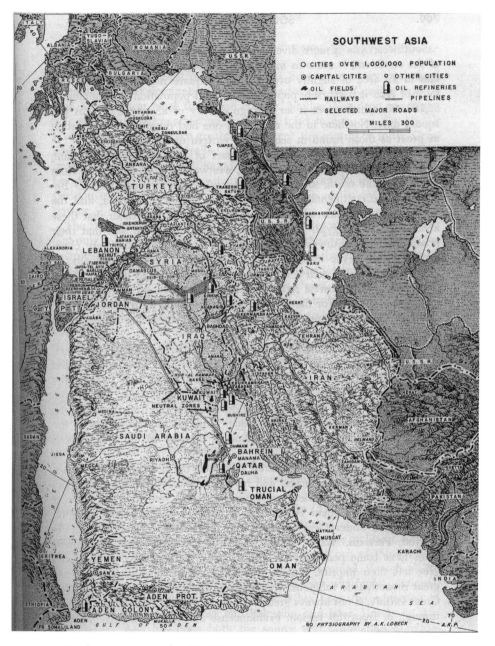

Figure 3.3. Southwest Asia as defined by Ginsburg, *The Pattern of Asia*, 1958.

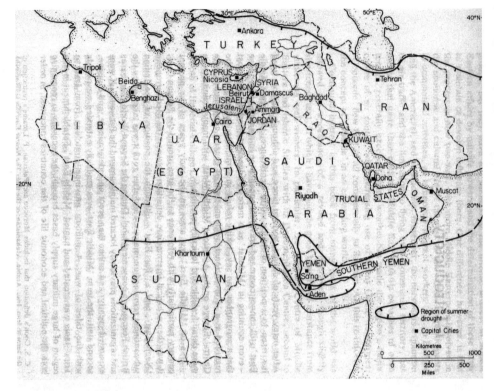

Figure 3.4. The Middle East as defined by Fisher, *The Middle East,* 1978. By kind permission of the publisher.

East" will be used here in general discussion except where the subject deals solely with Asiatic matters.[23]

The discussions of the "Middle East" countries in this book are much more extensive than those in Cressey's text; in fact, this section in Ginsburg's book constitutes almost 150 pages (out of a total of 900 pages).

Following World War II, the first textbooks that focused only on the Middle East (or Southwest Asia) were published. The classic 1950 work by W. B. Fisher, *The Middle East: A Physical, Social and Regional Geography*, went through seven editions, with the last one published in 1978.[24] Fisher, a British geographer at the University of Durham, defines his Middle East as Southwest Asia (without Afghanistan) plus Egypt and Libya. He adds Sudan in the sixth

(1971) and seventh (1978) editions (Figure 3.4). In the last (1978) edition, he has the following comment about the use of the term "Middle East":

> After many years of debate, acrid at times, and although the area itself has risen to a position of major world significance, the term "Middle East" still cannot command universal acceptance in a single strict sense—even counting in "Mideast" as a mere abridgement. Perhaps the most that a geographer can say, taking refuge in semantics, is that it can be regarded as a "conventional" regional term of general convenience, like Central Europe or the American Middle West, with many definitions in more detail feasible and logically possible.[25]

Fisher discusses how the term "Middle East" has been used by both governments and the general public of Great Britain and the United States and hence is a generally accepted term (even if the area delimited is not agreed upon). Fisher, however, goes a step further, stating that "despite the considerable geographical illogicality of 'Middle East,' there is one compensation: in its wider meaning this term can be held to denote a single geographical region definable by a few dominating elements that confer strong physical and social unity."[26]

Fisher, in fact, justifies his Middle East in a rather extreme environmental deterministic framework:

> Within a territory delimitable as extending from Libya to Iran, and Turkey to the Sudan . . . it is possible to postulate on geographical grounds the existence of a *natural region* to which the name Middle East can be applied. . . . The outstanding defining element is climatic: the Middle East has a highly unusual and characteristic regime which both *sets it apart* from its neighbours and also, *since climate is a principal determinant in ways of life*, the special climate *induces highly distinctive and particular human responses and activities*. . . . [T]he common elements of natural environment and social organization are sufficiently recognizable and strong to justify treatment of the Middle East as one single unit.[27]

He does recognize that there are some smaller areas "on the margins" that do not fit this climatically determined Middle East—such as southern Sudan, which "in its physical and human geography is in certain respects closer to Central African conditions" or where "extreme southern Arabia is brushed by monsoonal currents that give summer rain."[28] The illogic of Fisher's definition for his Middle East is illustrated in his justification for adding Sudan to his Middle East in the text's sixth edition in 1971: "Here, Islamic culture, close resemblance in some but not all environmental features to the characteristic Middle East pattern, and ideological linkages to the rest of the Middle East, could be held to justify inclusion of this extra element in the general scheme."[29] Such logic (or illogic) then begs the question, why does he not include the rest of North Africa or Afghanistan, or, for that matter, parts of Pakistan or Central Asia, in the Middle East region?

W. B. Fisher's textbook does have rather extensive physical geographic descriptions of the region, both in his general introductory chapters and within the individual regional chapters. Fisher also contributed the physical descriptions of the Middle East for the major annual reference work by Europa, *The Middle East and North Africa*.[30] Although Fisher died in 1984, the Europa publication still uses his physical descriptions of the countries included in its Middle East.

In 1966 W. C. Brice, another British geographer, published *South-West Asia*, which was part of the series titled "A Systematic Regional Geography" that was written for first-year university courses or advanced-level training college in Great Britain.[31] Other volumes in the series included, for instance, *The British Isles; Europe; A World Survey—the Human Aspect; Australia, New Zealand and the South-West Pacific; Monsoon Asia; Anglo-America*; and *The Soviet Union*. Brice's work, which omits all countries of North Africa (including Egypt), does include Afghanistan to the east, and it heavily emphasizes the physical geography, particularly the climate, landforms, and biology. "South-West Asia" is used by Brice instead of "the Near and Middle East" because the latter terms are too confusing and "have been employed by different authorities with very different implications." According to Brice, "By the Near East is understood the semi-circle of countries round the eastern basin of the Mediterranean, Libya, Egypt, Israel, Lebanon, Syria, Turkey and Greece; while the Middle East is taken to include the states of the Arabian peninsula, together with Jordan, Iraq, Iran, Afghanistan and the province of Baluchistan in Pakistan."[32] Brice also stresses the centrality of Southwest Asia in the Old World, as it is located between Africa, Europe, and the rest of Asia (Figure 3.5a).

A more widely used textbook first published in 1976, also written by British geographers, is *The Middle East: A Geographical Study* by Peter Beaumont,

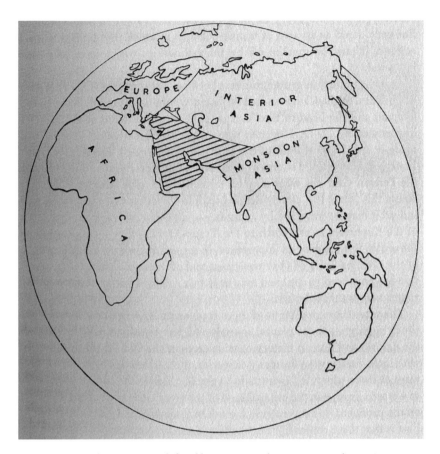

Figure 3.5a. Southwest Asia as defined by Brice, *South-West Asia*. Vol. 8, *A Systematic Regional Geography*, 1966. By kind permission of the publisher.

Gerald H. Blake, and J. Malcolm Wagstaff.[33] Beaumont and Blake were at the University of Durham and Wagstaff was at the University of Southampton when this work was first published. Their Middle East runs from Iran to Libya, but it excludes Afghanistan and Sudan (Figure 3.6). Unlike Fisher and his "natural region," however, these authors note that a wider context (such as North Africa, which then includes the Maghreb states) is often used to define the region. They assert that "the regional and subregional definitions employed in this book are . . . essentially pragmatic. The macro-region itself is defined in terms of modern states, since today these may be regarded as constituting

Figure 3.5b. The Middle East as tricontinental hub, the heart of the World-Island. Held, *Middle East Patterns,* 2011. By kind permission of the publisher.

distinctive socio-economic systems, despite a number of shared characteristics."[34] And they further state:

> Apart from political frontiers, there are no clear boundaries around the region [as] defined. . . . The sea, which penetrates deeply into the region, is as much a medium for movement as a barrier, and it is easily crossed at the Red Sea, between Africa and Arabia, and the Turkish Straits, between Europe and Asia. The upland which forms much of eastern Iran may retard movement, but well-defined corridors lead through it into Central Asia and northern India. On the south, deserts interpose not so much an impassable barrier between the Middle East, on the one hand, and the Maghreb and the Sudan, on the other, as a difficult and exhausting zone of transition.[35]

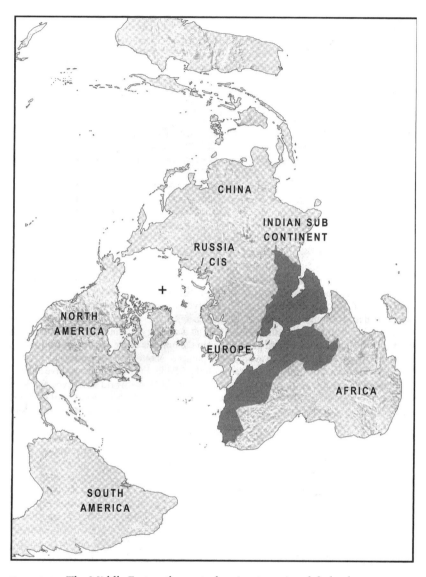

Figure 3.5c. The Middle East as the central region to major global cultures. Anderson and Anderson, *An Atlas of Middle Eastern Affairs*, 2010. By kind permission of the publisher.

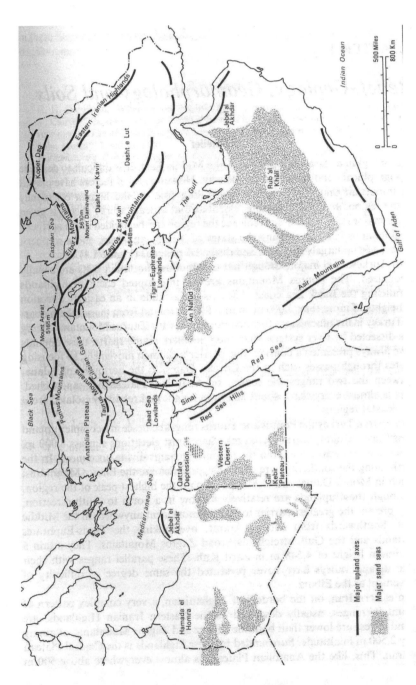

Figure 3.6. The Middle East as defined by Beaumont, Blake, and Wagstaff, *Middle East*, 1976. By kind permission of the publisher.

In their introduction, these authors emphasize the geopolitical significance of the Middle East, that junction between Europe, Asia, and Africa. Although their book has introductory chapters on the physical and human geography of the region, they group the individual country chapters thematically, focusing mainly on a specific topic within each country—such as agriculture in Iran, population growth and agriculture in Egypt, industrialization in Turkey, and the impact of oil in Libya.

The most widely used textbook today in American undergraduate Middle East regional geography classes is probably Colbert C. Held's *Middle East Patterns: Places, Peoples, and Politics*, first published in 1989, followed by later editions published in 1994, 2000, 2005, and 2011.[36] Thematic chapters on physical and cultural geography are followed by chapters on regional geography that focus on specific countries or a combination of states, such as Lebanon and Cyprus or Israel and the Occupied Territories. Unlike many of the previous textbooks, which treat the Arabian Peninsula (or Arabia) in one chapter, Held has three separate chapters for this area: "Saudi Arabia: Development in the Desert," "The Gulf and Its Oil States," and "Oman and the Yemens: The Southern Fringe." As indicated in the preface, when Held published his geography in 1989 he noted that "this is the first geography of the Middle East by a U.S. geographer since 1960. This lapse of almost 30 years between such studies is astonishing in view of the vital role of the Middle East in U.S. affairs and the equally vital role of the geographical perspective."[37] Held, who holds a doctorate degree in geography from the University of Nebraska, worked for the U.S. Department of State for sixteen years and was stationed in Beirut, Tehran, and many other parts of the Middle East during his career and then became a diplomat-in-residence at Baylor University. The fifth edition (2011) of *Middle East Patterns* is coauthored with John Thomas Cummings, who served almost thirty years in government or international organizations in the Middle East.[38]

Where is Held's Middle East? He includes the Arab states of Southwest Asia, as well as Turkey and Iran (but not Afghanistan), but only Egypt on the African continent, and hence he excludes Sudan and North Africa (Figure 3.7). This delimitation of the region represents the "core Middle East" as defined by G. Etzel Pearcy (Figure 3.8), for instance, in his 1964 Department of State publication, *The Middle East—An Indefinable Region*.[39] (Pearcy was the geographer of the Department of State," a long-defunct position.) In 1989, Held stated that "the seventeen countries that are the focus of this book are considered as

Figure 3.7. The Middle East as defined by Held and Cummings, *Middle East Patterns,* 2011. By kind permission of the publisher.

the Middle East on the latest maps published by the National Geographic Society, Department of State, Central Intelligence Agency, John Bartholomew (leading British map agency), and other international agencies."[40] Similar to Brice, he emphasizes that the Middle East is at the "Tricontinental Junction" of three continents—Europe, Asia, and Africa (Figure 3.5b)—which means that "the Middle East possesses unique geopolitical significance."[41] Regarding possible other terms, such as "Southwest Asia" and Cressey's "Swasia," Held states that "the toponym 'Middle East' is used in this book, both because it is well accepted in international usage and also because 'middle' connotes the region's central location, its function as a tricontinental hub, and its role as a strategic bridge."[42]

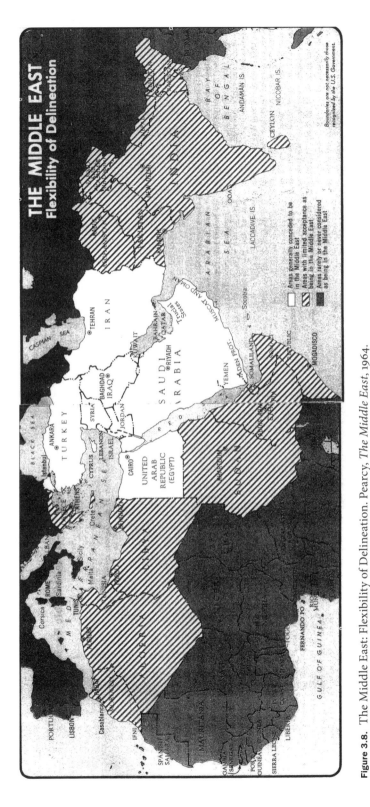

Figure 3.8. The Middle East: Flexibility of Delineation. Pearcy, *The Middle East*, 1964.

These textbooks, although varying in detail and definition of the Middle East, are rather conventional in their presentation. They define the importance of the region; have extensive descriptions of the physical geography on a regional scale; include some historical background (albeit often rather minimal); discuss the human geography in terms of languages, religion, lifestyles, and so forth (again, often rather minimally); and then have individual country chapters that go into detail on some of these subjects as well as focus on elements specific to that country.

A rather different approach is the 1985 textbook by Alasdair Drysdale and Gerald Blake, *The Middle East and North Africa: A Political Geography.*[43] Writing over two decades ago when there were no books dealing exclusively with the political geography of this region, Drysdale and Blake define this area as the Middle East and North Africa (Figure 3.9) and refer to it as one of the "Global Geopolitical Regions." They note that Fisher basically ignores political geography, whereas Beaumont, Blake, and Wagstaff include only one chapter on the political map of the region in their text. As Drysdale and Blake lament: "Possibly no other major world region has attracted so little attention from political geographers. This lacuna seems all the more surprising in view of the region's global importance and the numerous instances in which political conflicts within it have geographic origins or dimensions."[44] Unfortunately, little has changed to rectify that lacuna.

By using the phrase "Middle East and North Africa," Drysdale and Blake solve many of the problems in trying to decide what constitutes the Middle East—and it is surprising that more geographers have not followed this designation (as some scholars in other disciplines have done in their works, for instance). Southwest Asia (without Afghanistan) is their Middle East; however, they also recognize some of the difficulties in trying to delimit this region, even when North Africa is included:

The Middle East and North Africa, as we have defined them, are neither physically nor culturally bounded regions, although their physical environmental and cultural patterns endow them with a distinctive regional identity. There is no standard definition of the Middle East. . . . However the region may be defined, it is not a closed political system. Culturally, the Middle East in certain areas extends far beyond the outer limits of some of the states of the region, whereas in other areas—as in southern Sudan—different cultural regions impinge on it. The geopolitical influence of the Middle East and North

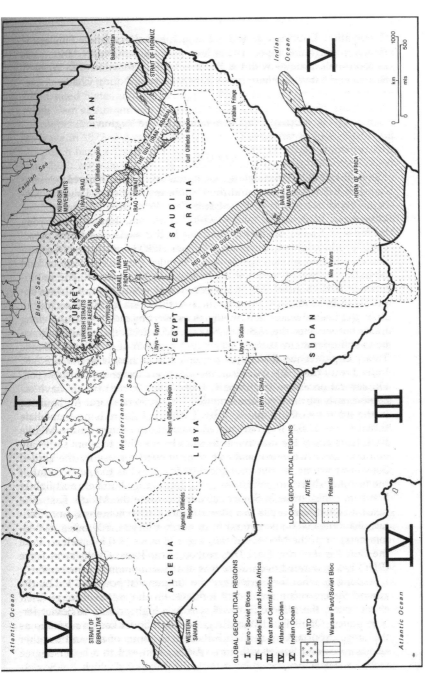

Figure 3.9. Geopolitical regions and subregions of the Middle East and North Africa (II) as defined by Drysdale and Blake, *The Middle East and North Africa*, 1985. By kind permission of the publisher.

Africa extends into Afghanistan, Pakistan, and the Indian Ocean as well as into the Sahara and the Horn of Africa. No grouping of states can claim to belong to so many geopolitical realms. The coastal states of North Africa are African, Mediterranean, Islamic, and Arab—all influenced politically and economically by nearness to Europe. Most of the states of the Middle East are in Asia, but they have strong ties with the Euro-Mediterranean world or the Afro-Indian Ocean world or both. All but Cyprus, Israel, and Lebanon are Islamic; only Cyprus, Iran, Israel, and Turkey are not Arab.[45]

Drysdale and Blake's work is certainly one of the more theoretical and thematic approaches of a geography textbook on this region, with chapters on partitioning of territory, boundary issues, offshore and ocean partitioning issues, and national and regional integration, for instance, in addition to a focus on the Arab-Israeli conflict and the control of petroleum. Although probably the best theoretical textbook on the Middle East by geographers, due to its very focus and content, it also became woefully outdated rather quickly. Unfortunately, there have been no new editions since its original publication in 1985.[46]

THE MIDDLE EAST AS A WORLD CULTURAL REGION

Having examined some major textbooks specifically on the geography of the Middle East, we now turn to how the Middle East is treated in world regional geography textbooks. Such books as *World Regions in Global Context* by Marston, Knox, and Liverman, mentioned above, are used by tens of thousands of students across the United States in introductory classes.[47] This is the way the majority of geography students—and other undergraduates — are introduced to the Middle East. Marston, Knox, and Liverman refer to the region as the Middle East and North Africa and define it as ranging from Morocco and Western Sahara to Iran, including Sudan but excluding Afghanistan (Figure 3.10). They describe the climate of the region, without ascribing environmental deterministic influences on the people, and their discussions are of high quality and present relevant material about the peoples and social issues of the Middle East. Numerous other recent world regional textbooks are available, particularly because of the rather large market for university classes. These are addressed only briefly, in order to show how they define their Middle East (and why) and the implications of those divisions and spatial patterns.

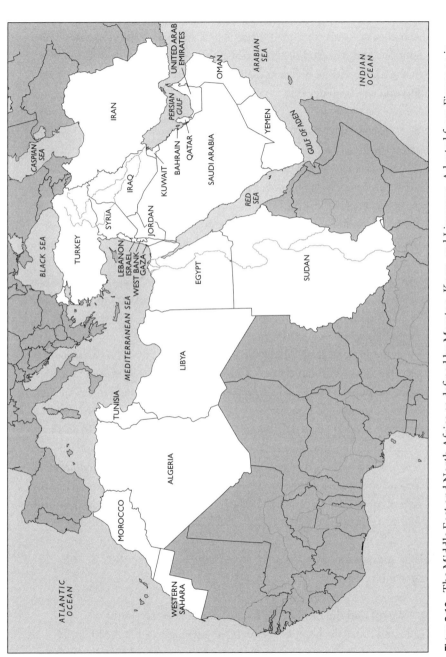

Figure 3.10. The Middle East and North Africa as defined by Marston, Knox, and Liverman. Adapted from Figure 5.1 in Marston, Knox, and Liverman, *World Regions in Global Context*, 2002. By kind permission of the publisher.

One of the most popular world regional textbooks has long been Harm J. de Blij and Peter O. Muller's *Geography: Realms, Regions, and Concepts*, first published in 1971 and continued through its fourteenth edition in 2010.[48] The authors designate the Middle East as the North Africa / Southwest Asia Realm (Figure 3.11). Regarding the term "Middle East," they mention its Eurocentric origins and acknowledge that

> the term has taken hold, and it can be seen and heard in everyday usage by schol-
> ars, journalists, and members of the United Nations. In view of the complexity of
> this realm, its transitional margins, and its far-flung areal components, the name
> Middle East need be faulted only for being imprecise—it does not make a single-
> factor region of North Africa / Southwest Asia, as do the terms Dry World, Arab
> World, and World of Islam. In this chapter we do use this name [Middle East]—
> but only for one of its regions, not for the realm as a whole.[49]

The use of the term "realm" for North Africa / Southwest Asia, in fact, enables the authors to expand considerably beyond a narrow definition for the region, and so their realm becomes quite flexible and changeable:

> Of all the geographic realms . . . the North Africa / Southwest Asian realm has
> seen the most territorial change. It has expanded, contracted, and expanded
> again in Europe and Asia, as well as Africa; its margins remain in flux.
> Islam . . . is only one dimension of it, but today it is Islam that energizes its
> borders—in West and northeastern Africa, in the Caucasus area, in northern
> Turkestan, in northwestern Pakistan. Unlike the Russian, North American,
> South Asian, or East Asian realms, this geographic realm has no dominant,
> anchoring state. . . . [H]ere is a *realm* with many core areas, linked by the te-
> nets of an ancient civilization that was infused by the prophet Muhammad
> fourteen centuries ago.[50]

De Blij and Muller then designate seven regional components of "this far-flung realm":

1. **Egypt and the Lower Nile Basin:** "This region in many ways
   constitutes the heart of the realm as a whole. . . . It is the historic
   focus of this part of the world and a major political cultural force."
   In addition to Egypt, it includes the northern part of Sudan.

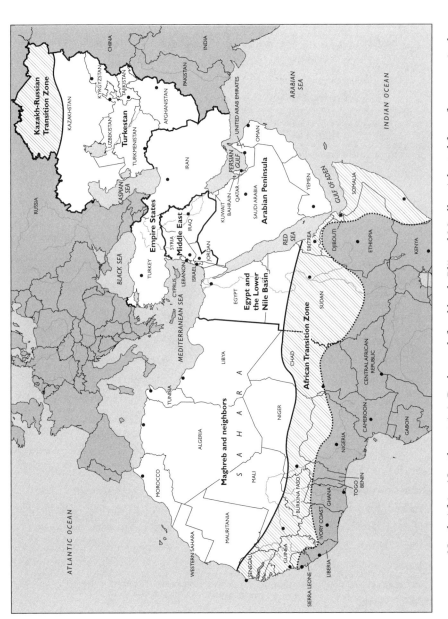

Figure 3.11. North Africa / Southwest Asia Realm as defined by de Blij and Mueller. Adapted from figure 7-10 in de Blij and Mueller, *Geography*, 2007. Reprinted with permission from John Wiley & Sons, Inc.

2. **The Maghreb and Its Neighbors:** The neighbors are Libya, Chad, Niger, Mali, and Mauritania—and the latter four are part of a transition zone into sub-Saharan Africa.

3. **The African Transition Zone:** From southern Mauritania on the west to Somalia on the east, the realm dominated by Islamic culture "interdigitates" with that of sub-Saharan Africa. There is no sharp dividing line here: "People of African ethnic stock have adopted the Muslim faith and Arabic language and traditions. As a result, this is less a region than a broad zone of transition."

4. **The Middle East:** This region includes Iraq, Syria, Lebanon, Jordan, and Israel. "It is the crescent-like zone of countries that extends from the eastern Mediterranean coast to the head of the Persian Gulf." The Palestinian territories are not mentioned as part of the definition, although they do constitute a considerable part of the discussion in the Israel section.

5. **The Arabian Peninsula:** "Here lies the source and focus of Islam, the holy city of Mecca; here, too lie many of the world's greatest oil deposits."

6. **The Empire States:** "Two of the realm's giants [are] states with imperial histories and majestic cultures . . . : Turkey and Iran."

7. **Turkestan:** This includes the Central Asian states following the collapse of the Soviet Union, with Islam a factor. "Boundaries of this region, as in the African Transition Zone, do not always coincide with national borders . . . , but regional cultural influences also radiate into China and Pakistan. Afghanistan is also part of this region."[51]

The inclusion of Turkestan (Central Asia) and the transition zones into other cultural and environmental areas, such as south of the Sahara, provides a basis, indeed, for rethinking this region—this realm—which I return to in the conclusion. However, the term "Southwest Asia" can be as nebulous as is the term "Middle East." The U.S. government, for example, recently confused the term, as evidenced by its use in Dennis Ross's title as the Special Advisor to the Secretary of State for the Gulf and Southwest Asia and its other uses as a strategic term.[52]

One of the most extensive treatments of the Middle East in a world regional geography textbook is found in Paul Ward English's *World Regional Geography: A Question of Place*, first published in 1977 and then published

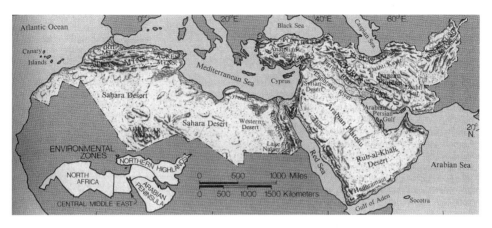

Figure 3.12. The Middle East and North Africa as defined by English and Miller, *World Regional Geography*, 1989. Courtesy of the author.

jointly with James A. Miller in later editions (1984, 1989, and 1993).[53] It is unusual for geographers who specialize in the Middle East and North Africa to be authors of a world regional geography textbook.[54] English (and English and Miller) use the term "Middle East and North Africa" to describe their region, which extends from Morocco (and Spanish Sahara in the first edition) in the west to Afghanistan in the east (Figure 3.12).

Compared with what might be included in various other definitions, this is one of the most extensive (but it excludes Sudan). The African chapter, titled "Tropical Africa" in the first edition, is rather problematic for the countries of the Sahel (Mauritania, Mali, etc.) as well as for the Horn of Africa or the southern African countries. (However, they use only the term "Africa" in the third edition). The chapter on the Middle East and North Africa has a heavy emphasis on history and culture—and on Islam—but the reason it is referred to as the Middle East (and North Africa) is never addressed. They identify four subregions: North Africa, Arabian Peninsula, the Northern Highlands (Turkey, Iran, and Afghanistan), and an area they label the Central Middle East, which comprises the Arab states and Israel "flanked on the west and east by two great river valleys, the Nile of Egypt and the Tigris-Euphrates of Iraq."[55] A focus on aspects of what English has termed the "ecological trilogy"[56] leads to discussions of nomads, villagers, and urbanites. In the first edition, English provides considerable discussion of his own work, he includes some of his studies in Iran; however, much of this is omitted in the later editions.

Some regional geographies use "Southwest Asia and North Africa" to refer to our region. In 1992, George F. Hepner and Jesse O. McKee published *World Regional Geography: A Global Approach*, which has a chapter on Southwest Asia-North Africa (written by Basheer K. Nijim).[57] The chapter includes the states of North Africa (including Western Sahara, but not Sudan) and Southwest Asia, including Afghanistan. Nijim uses the acronym SWANA to refer collectively to the two terms "Southwest Asia" and "North Africa." He never addresses the use of the term "Middle East," although it is used several times toward the end of his chapter when he discusses international trade and several international organizations. John Cole's 1996 *Geography of the World's Major Regions* has a chapter on North Africa and Southwest Asia (North Africa includes Western Sahara but not Sudan, and Southwest Asia includes Afghanistan).[58] Interestingly, Cole neither uses the term "Middle East" (or "Near East") nor addresses why the term is absent throughout the entire chapter.

Finally, in Lydia Mihelic Pulsipher's *World Regional Geography* (2000), there is a chapter on North Africa and Southwest Asia.[59] North Africa includes Western Sahara and Sudan, but Southwest Asia does not include Afghanistan. The author states that

> the term Middle East is not used in this chapter because of the Eurocentric bias it carries: the term is symptomatic of the tendency to lump the whole of Asia together, differentiating it only by its distance from Europe (near, middle, far). Furthermore, the term does not normally include the western sections of North Africa or eastern portions Southwest Asia—Iran, for example. On the other hand, the reader should know that some people who live in the region do use the term themselves.[60]

ATLASES AND MAPS OF THE MIDDLE EAST

A student looking for the Middle East might first consult a world atlas or look at one of the numerous world maps. However, after examining dozens of maps and atlases, he or she either would not find the Middle East at all or would encounter a rather wide disparity in identifying where this region is located. On a global scale the term "Middle East," or for that matter, the names of some of the other world cultural regions (e.g., "South Asia," "Latin America") often do not appear on maps or in atlases. By convention, atlases are organized by continents and countries (i.e., nation-states). Although the Middle

East remains unidentifiable on many world maps, one may find an atlas with one or two sentences that mention the fact that part of a continent has specific regional names, such as "North Africa" or "Southwest Asia" —or the "Middle East." However, large atlases published since World War II often now do have a map that is identified as the Middle East.

I could not find any use of the terms "Near East" and "Middle East" in early twentieth-century atlases. There, was, however, some rather interesting information provided about the continents where our region of the Middle East resides. For instance, the 1908 Rand, McNally *Indexed Atlas of the World*, presented the following perspective:

> The oldest of historical lands, [Asia] is yet relatively one of the least devel-oped. . . . Asia has itself been wonderfully lacking in the inner impulses of vitality and natural spurs to advancement that characterize the truly progres-sive historical countries. . . . Its ancient empires, unable to keep pace with the springing step of onward progress, either have been relegated to oblivion or have fallen backward out of the march like stragglers, their civilizations crys-tallizing, as it were, into fixed forms, offering almost insuperable obstacles to further change and progress. The very name of Asia has become symbolic of conservatism, despotism, tyranny, and official corruption, and the epithet Asiatic, when applied to the institutions, the governmental methods, or the tendencies of Western lands, is one of recognized opprobrium.[61]

The atlas contained the following about Africa: "Africa still remains a con-tinent of political chaos. Since before the Christian era it has been the seat of no important empire. Its peoples are characterized by a remarkable lack of political cohesion, living largely under nomadic conditions or divided into many petty tribes, waging incessant wars among themselves."[62] Of course, part of the reason for this condition has to be the climate: "[W]hile the north-erly continents [i.e., Europe and North America, but obviously not Asia] were endowed by nature with the conditions of accessibility and climate most fa-vorable to development and were thus the predestined scene of the greatest historical evolution, civilization in the southerly continents [i.e., Africa and South America] has been retarded by their relative isolation and enervating climatic conditions."[63]

More recent atlases (published in last half of the twentieth century), con-tain maps of the Middle East, although often with rather confusing—and differing—locations. For instance, a recent edition of Rand McNally's *Goode's World Atlas* (2005) depicts a map of the Middle East that includes from part of Libya, Chad, and northern Sudan on the west to Iran on the east.[64] Turkey, Afghanistan, and Pakistan are not part of this Middle East. There is another map titled "Asia Southwestern" ("Southwest Asia" in the Rand McNally *Quick Reference World Atlas*), and (to thoroughly confuse the reader) it includes the Arab states of Southwest Asia plus Iran, Afghanistan, Pakistan, and India—and spans east to even include Myanmar (Burma) and Tibet and southern China![65] But Turkey is still not part of Rand McNally's Southwest Asia. In the earlier Rand McNally *The New International Atlas*, there is a map of the Middle East that includes the states of Iran, Iraq, Syria, Lebanon, Jordan, and Israel—but it includes neither Turkey nor Egypt (and only parts of Saudi Arabia and Afghanistan fill out the page).[66]

So where is the Middle East in that most prominent of atlases, the *National Geographic Atlas of the World*?[67] In the Asia section of maps, there is one map titled "Middle East," which focuses on Turkey, Iraq, Syria, Lebanon, Jordan, Israel and the Palestinian territories, and Cyprus. Yet, the map includes only the western half of Iran, the northern parts of Saudi Arabia (and Kuwait, Bahrain, and Qatar), and a part of Egypt to fill out the rectangular region. In the 1990 edition, part of the Caucasus SSRs are included (reflecting part of the Soviet Union), but in the 2005 edition more of the Caucasus area is shown, and hence all the new nation-states are part of this map. What really constitutes the Middle East on this map is somewhat confusing. There is a separate map titled "Eastern Mediterranean" (Levant, Sinai and Nile Valley of Egypt, Israel and Palestinian territories, Lebanon, Cyprus, and the western portions of Jordan and Syria), whereas another map is titled "Southwestern Asia," which includes the Arab states of Southwest Asia plus all of Afghanistan and Pakistan. Interestingly, only a portion of southern Turkey is included. Another map is "Southern Asia," which is mainly India, and even part of Pakistan is not included. Unlike the 1990 edition, the 2005 edition also has a new map of Central Asia that depicts the five "stans" that emerged as separate states from the breakup of the Soviet Union.

The subregional or subcontinental maps of Africa in the *National Geographic Atlas of the World* are even more confusing in their references to world cultural regions. One map, titled "Northwestern Africa," includes all of North Africa and West Africa, east to parts of Egypt and Sudan—and on the southern borders, Cameroon and the Central African Republic—and even an edge of Zaire (now the Democratic Republic of the Congo). The map titled

"Northeastern Africa," however, includes parts of Libya and Chad, Egypt and Sudan to the Horn of Africa, and on south to Tanzania and Zaire (again, including everything that fits onto a rectangular page).

Continuing this survey, *The World Atlas* by John Bartholomew has a map titled "The Middle East," which shows Southwest Asia to western Afghanistan and Pakistan—and it does include Turkey (and parts of Egypt and Sudan fill out the page).[68] Other maps include "France and Northern Algeria," "Levant Coast," and "North-West Africa," the latter including most of the entire northern half of Africa! The 1966 *Encyclopaedia Britannica World Atlas* has no map of the Middle East, although there are separate maps for Eurasia (Europe and Western Asia, but the Arabian Peninsula is cut off), the eastern Mediterranean (including Greece and Turkey in addition to the Levant), Israel and Egypt, Iran and Afghanistan, and Northwest Africa (the Maghreb basically).[69] *The Times Atlas of the World* has a rather confusing map titled "The Middle East: Asia, South," which includes from Turkey and Egypt on the west to Mongolia and parts of Vietnam and Thailand on the east.[70] North Africa is never named as a region, and there are separate maps for (1) Morocco, Algeria, and Tunisia; (2) Egypt and Libya; and (3) Africa, West (which only goes eastward to the western part of Niger). I could cite many more examples from other atlases, however they would only emphasize the confusion and lack of agreement on how to depict the region of the Middle East (and North Africa) in world atlases and on maps.

Furthermore, the dearth of atlases produced specifically on the Middle East, despite the significance of this region on the world stage, is noteworthy. The *National Geographic Atlas of the Middle East* covers Southwest Asia (without Afghanistan) and includes only Egypt within Africa (Figure 3.13a).[71] However, the introductory sentence to the first edition sets the (melodramatic) stage: "Fixing the Middle East with ink on paper is like reviewing a play in the middle of the second act. So volatile is the region, so unpredictable its continuing drama, that we can only set the stage and name the players. The ending—what will ultimately happen to political borders, resources, governments, and peoples—is yet to be written."[72] In the first edition, "The Focus" is Southwest Asia plus Egypt (Figure 3.13a), which is called the "traditional Middle East" in the second edition. Then in the second edition the "Featured area of this atlas" adds Afghanistan and Pakistan on the east and Sudan on the west (Figure 3.13b).[73] In both editions North Africa, including Libya, has been added as part of a "broader definition of the Middle East . . . used in a cultural sense" (first edition), which is simply referred to as the "cultural Middle East" in the second edition (Figure 3.13c).

Figure 3.13a. Middle East: The Focus. National Geographic Society,
National Geographic Atlas of the Middle East, 2003.
By kind permission of the publisher.

The CIA's Middle East (at least in the 1970s), shown in its 1973 *Atlas: Issues
in the Middle East*, is from Libya to Iran (Figure 3.14).[74] The atlas contains
various topical maps (religion, agriculture, environment, etc.) as well as larger
scale maps that focus on such issues as the emergence of Israel, Palestinian
refugees, Jerusalem, and Cyprus. The preface contains the following statement about the region:

> The Middle East is torn by tension and bitterness. Hostility among ethnic,
> religious, and traditional groups constantly threatens, and at times erupts
> into, open warfare; rivalries among outside powers with political, economic,
> and strategic interests in the area pose the possibility of wider conflict. The
> issues in the Middle East that set peoples and nations against one another are
> numerous, complex, and diverse. Some are recent; the origins of others may
> be traced thousands of years into the past.[75]

Figure 3.13b. Middle East: Featured Area. National Geographic Society, *National Geographic Atlas of the Middle East,* 2008 (original in color). By kind permission of the publisher.

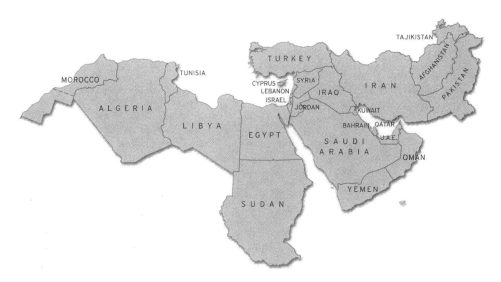

Figure 3.13c. Middle East: The Broader Definition. National Geographic Society, *National Geographic Atlas of the Middle East,* 2003. By kind permission of the publisher.

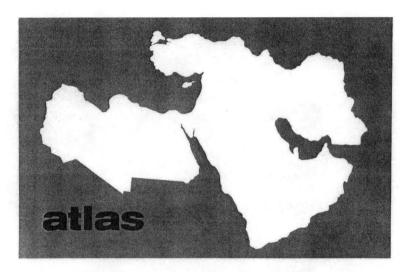

Figure 3.14. The Middle East as defined by Central Intelligence Agency, *Atlas,* 1973.

Needless to say, if this statement represents (or represented) the U.S. intelligence community's perception and understanding of the Middle East, then it is no wonder that the region has presented a puzzle and perplexity for the U.S. government.

One of the more informative atlases is *The Cambridge Atlas of the Middle East and North Africa,* which covers North Africa (without Western Sahara but with Sudan) and Southwest Asia (without Afghanistan) (Figure 3.15).[76] Although dated (1987), the series of regional maps and text, as well as specialized larger-scale maps, provide considerable useful information. The authors

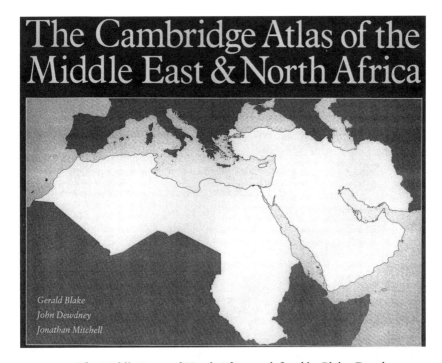

Figure 3.15. The Middle East and North Africa as defined by Blake, Dewdney, and Mitchell, *The Cambridge Atlas of the Middle East and North Africa,* 1987. By kind permission of the publisher.

emphasize that "there is no standard definition of either Middle East or North Africa," and although there is a brief history of the use of the term "Middle East," there is no attempt to justify the reason that the atlas chose the (twenty-two) countries it includes in the region.[77]

A more recent atlas is *An Atlas of Middle Eastern Affairs* by Ewan W. Anderson and Liam D. Anderson, published in 2010. The authors state that

> for this *Atlas* the Middle East will be used as a term to include North Africa and to extend from Mauritania in the west to Afghanistan in the east and from Turkey in the north to Sudan in the south. . . . This delimitation includes all the states generally accepted as Middle Eastern together with those of the Maghrib and its westward extension into Western Sahara and Mauritania. In the East it includes Afghanistan, at the present time closely linked in the public mind with Iran, Iraq, conflict and terrorism.[78]

Similar to Brice and Held (and Cummings), they indicate the central location of their Middle East, which "abuts on to all the major global cultures other than these of North Africa and South America" (see Figure 3.16 and Figure 3.5c).[79]

Published maps of the Middle East are rather interesting, for they do not necessarily follow the spatial delimitations that the various textbooks or even atlases mentioned above might use. The current maps of the Middle East available at Barnes and Noble or Borders bookstores, for instance, focus on Southwest Asia, and usually include Afghanistan and Pakistan (especially since 9/11). Usually most of Egypt except for a small southwest corner is also shown, as is all of Turkey except for a small part of European Turkey, for, similar to atlases, these maps depict what can be included in a rectangle placed upon a world map. This is also the case for the maps of the Middle East by Map Link (1:4,500,00; 1998), Cartographica (1:4,000,000; 2003), and Hammond International (titled *Near and Middle East*, 2006). National Geographic Society also has a recent map titled *Iraq and the Heart of the Middle East* (1:1,983,000; 2003), which, in addition to Iraq, includes Israel, the Palestinian territories, Jordan, Lebanon, and Syria.

CONCLUSION: IS THERE A GEOGRAPHER'S MIDDLE EAST?

So, is there a geographer's Middle East? And where might that be? We have seen the great variety of countries that different geographers (and cartographers) regard as the Middle East. There certainly is no agreement on the definition and boundaries for this region. And often the Middle East (or the Middle East and North Africa) is never defined, but instead it seemingly arbitrarily comprises a group of states in this "region." We have also seen that maps and atlases are even more confusing and inconsistent, varying widely in their depiction of the Middle East—or Southwest Asia, or Near East, or North Africa, or Northwestern Africa. There certainly is a major disparity between what academics and students learn about the Middle East as a world cultural region, on the one hand, and what the public and media perceives as the region and what atlases and maps depict as the Middle East (or Southwest Asia—and any other name) on the other hand. There also appears to be a strong geopolitical (and commercial) element to what constitutes the Middle East for many of the mapmakers and atlas makers. Since 9/11, Afghanistan and Pakistan have suddenly taken on new importance—and now they are included on maps of the Middle East. After moving west after World War I and

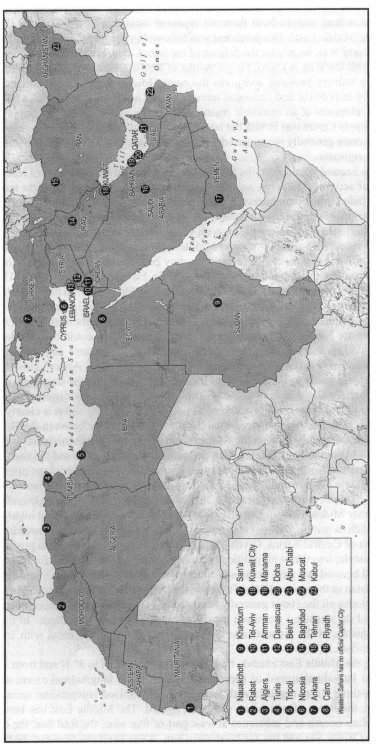

Figure 3.16. The Middle East as defined by Anderson and Anderson, *An Atlas of Middle Eastern Affairs*, 2010. By kind permission of the publisher.

1 Nauakchott	9 Khartoum	17 San'a	
2 Rabat	10 Tel-Aviv	18 Kuwait City	
3 Algiers	11 Amman	19 Manama	
4 Tunis	12 Damascus	20 Doha	
5 Tripoli	13 Beirut	21 Abu Dhabi	
6 Nicosia	14 Baghdad	22 Muscat	
7 Ankara	15 Tehran	23 Kabul	
8 Cairo	16 Riyadh		

Western Sahara has no official Capital City

subsuming the Near East and even part of northwest Africa, the Middle East, which once centered on the Indian subcontinent, is now moving back eastward—incorporating Afghanistan and Pakistan!

But is there a geographer's Middle East? Or should there be a geographer's Middle East? I propose such a region—despite all the problems and inconsistencies that are prevalent in the attempt to identify any world (cultural) region. Certainly, one might make an argument that world cultural regions are somewhat artificial. A cultural region is defined basically in contrast to other artificially defined cultural regions, despite that there are, of course, many similarities across cultural regions and many differences and diversities within a defined cultural region. In order to redefine—or relocate—the Middle East, I return to *The Myth of Continents*.

Lewis and Wigen note that "clearly, the world regional system has some serious flaws. In most presentations, it is contaminated both by the myth of the nation-state and by geographical determinism. Similarly . . . it still bear[s] traces of its origin within a self-centered European geographical tradition."[80] They propose a new set of world regions, which is similar to the standard geographic world cultural regions but with a few subtle and important differences. They "endorse the global architecture that has emerged within the North American academic world."[81] They propose the "Heuristic World Regionalization Scheme," which has fourteen world regions (Figure 3.17). Compared with the many (different) delineations of the Middle East that we have examined, their Middle East (referred to as "Southwest Asia and North Africa") is similar to the broadest definitions. Their southern border in Africa is considerably south of most of the definitions of North Africa, and they include their "Islamic Zone" as part of Central Asia. Lewis and Wigen emphasize that they give "primacy . . . to the spatial contours of assemblages of ideas, practices, and social institutions that give human communities their distinction and coherence."[82]

Now I return to de Blij and Muller's *Geography: Realms, Regions, and Concepts*. It is, in fact, the "realm" that I want to address. Of all the interpretations offered in geographies, maps, and atlases of the Middle East / Southwest Asia (and North Africa), de Blij and Muller's concept of realms is the most intriguing—and closest to my own concept of a wider "cultural region of the Middle East." The difference between a realm and a region is only a matter of semantics—and size, according to de Blij and Muller, who refer to their larger cultural region as a realm. (We might call the realm a region and use

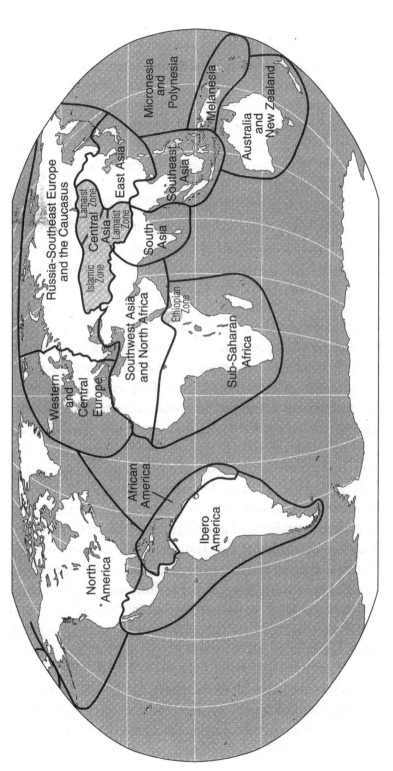

Figure 3.17. A Heuristic World Regionalization Scheme. Lewis and Wigen, *The Myth of Continents*, 1997. By kind permission of the publisher.

subregions as the next lower level as well, of course.) All the various cultural regional delimitations of other authors, as we have seen, have nation-states as the regional boundaries; but what de Blij and Muller propose, similar to what Lewis and Wigen assert, are several "transition zones" rather than sharp boundaries as one cultural area merges into another. Within these transition zones the nation-state is not the unit of definition.

I suggest that de Blij and Muller, indeed, have defined a viable "Middle East," or as they have designated their realm: "North Africa/Southwest Asia" (see Figure 3.11). Their North Africa particularly is more realistic culturally and environmentally: Mauritania, Mali, Niger, and Chad are really not part of "sub-Saharan Africa" (or tropical Africa) and indeed there is a transition zone from the southern parts of these states into the northern parts of Nigeria, Ghana, Ivory Coast, and so forth. Similarly, southern Sudan and the Horn of Africa are cultural transition zones. The addition of Turkestan (Central Asia) is yet another region that seldom is considered part of our region. But, in fact, it is quite relevant to note that the anthropologist Dale Eickelman has incorporated Central Asia into his region (Figure 3.18). The first two editions (1981, 1989) of his popular anthropology of the Middle East textbook are titled *The Middle East: An Anthropological Approach*, whereas the third and fourth editions (1998, 2001) are titled *The Middle East and Central Asia: An Anthropological Approach*.[83]

With de Blij and Muller in mind, let me propose why this realm—this region—makes sense as a cultural region of the "Middle East" (with some small adjustments). There are a number of environmental and cultural characteristics that give this region some coherence, although, again I do not claim exclusivity to any of these specific characteristics. Environmentally, the region, indeed, is characterized mainly as an arid and semi-arid climatic regime—by far the largest such dryland region in the world—from the Sahara and its margins to the deserts of Arabia, Iran, and Central Asia. Certainly, there are exceptions in the region to this dry climate: mainly, the eastern Levantine coast, the coasts of the Black Sea and Caspian Sea, and certain highland areas that garner greater precipitation. Nevertheless, because of this arid environment, throughout much of this region traditional irrigation agriculture and nomadic pastoralism have been significant livelihoods.

However, the Middle East also is a region of cities and urban societies. Whereas some of the world's earliest cities were from "ancient" Mesopotamia, Egypt and Anatolia, later urban conglomerations such as Damascus, Baghdad, Cairo, Istanbul, Jerusalem, Tunis, Rabat, Mecca, and numerous others re-

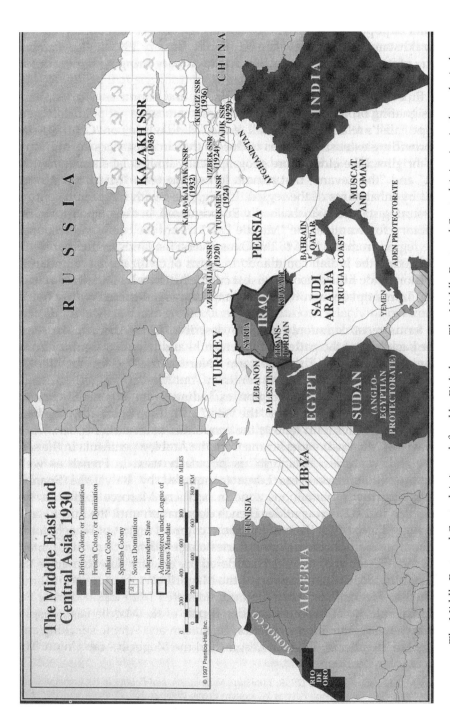

Figure 3.18. The Middle East and Central Asia as defined by Eickelman, *The Middle East and Central Asia: An Anthropological Approach*, 1998. By kind permission of the publisher.

mained significant during much of the Islamic period. The urban was part of an integral interrelationship of the city, agriculture, and nomadism, and this nexus has been noted by Nikki Keddie, who states that after the eleventh century there were "various permutations and combinations of a nomadic-agricultural-urban synthesis."[84] As mentioned above, Paul English also characterized this synthesis of the nomad, villager, and urbanite as the "ecological trilogy."[85]

The Middle East is sometimes identified with Islam, although most Muslims of the world now live outside the Middle East and North Africa (however defined). Nevertheless, this region can be considered not only as the historic core of Islam (and the early Islamic empires) but also as an area in which Islam predominates (knowing, of course, that Bangladesh, Malaysia, Indonesia, and many other nation-states outside our region also have a majority of Muslims). Another issue is oil: certainly some states have it and others do not, but as a region it has over two-thirds of the world's oil reserves and most of its natural gas reserves. From Algeria and Libya to the Sinai and the Persian Gulf and the Caspian region, no other area of the world even comes close to possessing as much of this most valuable, strategic resource.

Finally, in terms of ethnolinguistic groups, the region principally is home to Arab/Semitic, Iranic, and Turkic peoples, although as we merge into the transition zones these designations become less meaningful and useful. There is also the problem of significant minorities within our Middle East, even though most of the languages—and hence the ethnolinguistic groups— are members of one of the principal language families of the peoples of the region: Semitic, Indo-European, or Finno-Ugric languages.

To de Blij and Muller's "North Africa/Southwest Asia," I would add the western part of Pakistan (Baluchistan) and parts of (traditionally) Muslim (and arid) western China (Xinjiang), which often was part of the "Turkestan" of the early European travelers and authors. Hence, in my region—my realm—I place particular emphasis on the combination of climatic characteristics (but not determinism) and language and religious affiliations. Yet, the events of geopolitics often overtake any attempt to freeze in time any regional scheme. The Chinese nation-state, for instance, is very consciously incorporating Xinjiang, and considerable numbers of Han Chinese are being resettled in the region. Southern (Muslim) Spain in the past would have fit into our scheme, but the historical changes in the population and the predominance of a Christian Europe or "Western Europe" has incorporated Spain into another world cultural region. The fact that Central Asia (Turkestan) now can be considered part of a wider Southwest Asia or Middle East is due, of course, mainly to the demise of the Soviet Union, which effectively incorporated those states for decades (and did try to annex Afghanistan into that wider union as well).

Therefore, the point needs to be emphasized that any large world cultural region is constantly undergoing change, and defining specific "boundaries" often only inhibits attempts to understand that region—and its peoples. We must always be aware that our classification schemes and various categories not only help inform but also homogenize and limit our understanding of peoples and the various regions that are devised to define them.

Nevertheless, I maintain that there is indeed a North Africa/Southwest Asia cultural region or realm. Rather, it might—or should be—referred to as the Middle East or perhaps the Middle East and North Africa (and include Central Asia) or Southwest Asia and North Africa, but certainly there is no consensus. However, the various characteristics that in combination define this cultural region lend validity to the notion that, in contrast to its neighbors and other cultural areas or realms, the region possesses sufficient commonality and similar traits to give it enough coherence and uniqueness to affirm that there is indeed a "Middle East"—or perhaps a more accurate designation is "Middle East and North Africa." Even though "Southwest Asia and North Africa" might be the best terminology (incorporating Central Asia into Southwest Asia), the "Middle East" has now become such a significant geopolitical and accepted regional concept that any regional terminology that omits the "Middle East" ends up ignoring the realities of the modern twenty-first century. Hence, I propose that the most appropriate geographer's region is one that has been used by a number of scholars and writers: the "Middle East and North Africa." Yet, even if we agree on that terminology, the exact delimitation of this region continues to be ambiguous and contentious.

4 WHY ARE THERE NO MIDDLE EASTERNERS IN THE MAGHRIB?

Ramzi Rouighi

WHAT IS THE MIDDLE EAST, who is a Middle Easterner, and what does it mean to think of a Middle East and Middle Easterners? This volume offers a number of ways to answer these questions. In this chapter, I propose to look at these categories as products whose social life involves the activities of particular groups that specialize in their production and dissemination. This perspective is attractive because it does not require that those involved fully master or understand the process in which they play an active role. Another aspect of this perspective is that it assumes that without the active production, maintenance, and reproduction of these categories, they would lose the sense that they refer to something in actuality and join the ranks of ideas that have become the hollow reminders of their former social existence. In other words, much as there are particular social sites that confer attributes on the tooth fairy, extraterrestrials, and race, there are particular social sites that specialize in conferring upon the Middle East and Middle Easterners an objective character.

In the Maghrib, it is possible to find the categories and terms "Middle East" and "Middle Easterner."[1] However, Maghribis tend not to use the category "Middle East" very often and use the term "Middle Easterner" even less frequently. When they do employ these categories, however, they do not believe that they refer to themselves. Instead, they believe that the Middle East is to the east and that, although they have ties to Middle Easterners, they consider themselves distinct and separate from them. In other words, as far as Maghribis are concerned, there are no Middle Easterners in the Maghrib. This chapter seeks to explain this peculiar situation by examining the conditions of the emergence of the category "Middle East," the terms of its introduction to the Maghrib, and its subsequent use.[2] Rather than provide a full account of these processes, this chapter limits itself to identifying some of the sites of production, dissemination, and consumption of these two categories.[3]

Although it should be evident to most, it may still be prudent to mention that the Middle East is a category expressed in the English language and that English is not widely used in the Maghrib. Consequently, "Middle East" and "Middle Easterners" rarely appear in English in the Maghrib because few Maghribis speak English; instead, they use the Arabic *al-sharq al-awsat* (the Middle East) and *sharq awsatiyūn* (Middle Easterners) and the French *Moyen-Orient* (Middle East) and *moyen-orientaux* (Middle Easterners) equivalents of these categories. Although the difference between the Arabic, French, and English categories raises a number of potentially interesting questions, there is not sufficient space in this text to delve into this aspect. My intention here is to merely explain why the terms *sharq awsatiyūn* and *moyen-orientaux* rarely occur in the Maghrib and why, when Maghribis use them, they do not mean to refer to other Maghribis.

GRAND BEGINNINGS

As Roger Adelson indicated (Chapter 2), the American naval strategist Alfred Thayer Mahan is commonly held to be the first to use the term the "Middle East," although the term had predecessors in the language of the British India Office,[4] and earlier other languages used it as well, as shown by Huseyin Yilmaz (Chapter 1). However, it was not until the 1940s that the term gained currency when policy makers and advisers began to use it to organize the actions of the U.S. government during the Second World War.

Illustrating the institutional support given this term in the United States, in 1946, Christian Herter cofounded the Middle East Institute, a policy center whose mission was to "promote knowledge of the Middle East in America and strengthen understanding of the United States by the people and governments of the region."[5] Such initiatives helped solidify the Middle East into a region in the minds of government officials, journalists, businessmen, and academics. The category "Middle Easterner" was, however, slower to emerge. In fact, it was not until the 1950s that Middle Easterners began to be regularly imagined as populating a region called the Middle East.[6]

Leading the so-called Herter Committee, Herter contributed to the formulation of what became the Marshall Plan, the U.S. government's plan to consolidate and safeguard its influence in Western Europe. As an official regional category of the U.S. government, the "Middle East" was introduced into use in the newly founded United Nations and became even more widely disseminated and translated. French officials and intellectuals added the term *Moyen-Orient* to preexisting terms such as the *Proche-Orient* (Near East) and began to use the two interchangeably. Regarding the Maghrib, which was still under French rule, they employed the term *Afrique du Nord* (North Africa). The French "Middle East" echoed the original British and American terms, but it was adapted to colonial realities and discourse. However, as far as the inclusion of the Maghrib in the Middle East, there was no doubt that neither Mahan nor those who used the term after him thought that it included the Maghrib. A fortiori, they did not think that "Middle Easterners" included Maghribis.

The integration of the Middle East into the public discourse in France gained momentum after the end of World War II. In 1949, the prominent French sociologist Robert Montagne (1893–1954) used the term "Middle East" in relation to a possible rapprochement between the French and the British.[7] Although foreign policy was not his academic specialty, in his essay Montagne offered advice and council to policy makers based on his expertise. As a noted intellectual, he used references familiar to his target audience. "Why should we not think of settling our differences in the Middle East, in those regions where for exactly a hundred and fifty years since Bonaparte's landing in Egypt, and fifty years after Fashoda, France and Britain have been continually in opposition?"[8] Montagne believed that the French and British should work together to achieve a peace in the Middle East that served their economic and strategic interests, which were being threatened by Arab nationalism. Oil was foremost among these interests. As far as the relation between the Middle East and the Maghrib, Montagne thought that Israel's establishment and victory in 1948 was a positive development that showed Maghribis who had been excited by Arab nationalism that it was the wrong path to follow.[9] And he added: "And why should not this Jewish-Arab conflict continue to be of equally good service to us? As long as conflict goes on in the Middle East, calm will reign in the Maghrib."[10]

Montagne's conception of the Middle East and the Maghrib was not unique. In his memoir published in 1954, and thus before the independence of Tunisia, Morocco, and Algeria from France, Charles de Gaulle defined the *Moyen-Orient* as "the set of countries which stretch from Turkey to India."[11]

For de Gaulle, *Afrique du nord* (or *Afrique du nord française*) belonged with France. It was an integral part of the French colonies and provinces (*départements*). This does not mean that he, and many people in France at the time, did not recognize that North Africa had historical ties with Arabs and Muslims. They most certainly did. However, the idea that those ties could be expressed as one region and through the category "Middle East" was alien to them.

Although de Gaulle clearly excluded the Maghrib from the *Moyen-Orient* and *Proche-Orient*, it is not immediately clear that he was wrong to do so. After all, French colonialism was not the same everywhere. Colonial laws, institutions, and policies differed greatly, owing, in part, to differences in the native customs of rule in those societies prior to French domination and to the manner in which the French imposed their rule. However, scholars and intellectuals did not explain the difference between French North Africa and the Levant in these terms. Settler colonialism in North Africa became a factor only in relation to the degree of modernization or "Frenchification." In other words, the discourse on the difference between North Africa and the Middle East involved a shift away from prevailing local or regional socioeconomic, political, and cultural conditions into idealized, and ideological, conceptions of essential characteristics or historic differences. Examining and comparing the degree of economic development, civilizational attainment, and racial mix were more pertinent than the processes that led to the establishment of these differences.[12]

Under these conditions, the difference between the Middle East and North Africa became an undeniable fact. Maghribis were different from Arab Middle Easterners because they had distinct institutions, customs, practices, dialects, and ultimately, a different past. For men such as Montagne, this irresolvable difference made Arab nationalism an unrealistic dream. Interestingly, Arab nationalists shared this basic vision, even if they expressed it differently. Using premodern conceptions, which distinguished between the Maghrib (West) and the Mashriq (East), they articulated the vision of a unified Arab world.[13] Their imaginary geography conceived of the Maghrib as remote and away from the cultural center. Unlike the secular Arab nationalists, reform-minded religious thinkers saw the Maghrib as an important historical center of Muslim culture. Naturally, when they argued for pan-Islamic revival, they did not insist on long-standing regional differentiation but focused instead on developing a collective response to Western influence.[14]

Another aspect of the discourse on the Maghrib (or North Africa) and the Middle East was that it lumped together Algeria, Morocco, and Tunisia whose national independence was still believed to be preventable. The premodern Maghrib, because it was also prenational, offered the perfect "argument" against nationalists. Maghribi intellectuals found in the Islamic past a way to rally supporters against the French. However, they could find no Morocco, Algeria, or Tunisia in the medieval period. Colonialists used this fact to undermine them, arguing that the idea of an Algerian or Tunisian nation was illegitimate. This phenomenon alone illustrates the importance of regional categories such as "Maghrib" and "Middle East" to the articulation of politics in the modern period. It also demonstrates that the process of political struggle shaped their meanings, connotations, and implications.

In his 1962 *Le Maghreb entre deux guerres* (The Maghrib Between the Two World Wars), Jacques Berque informed his readers that the book was meant to remedy the absence of the Maghrib from his previous study titled *Arabes d'hier à demain* (The Arabs from Yesterday to Tomorrow).[15] Clearly, Berque had thought about including the Maghrib in the history of the Arabs, even though, in fact, he did not. Whereas "Arab" is not the same as "Middle Eastern," for Berque the "Maghrib" is still distinguishable from both. In general, Berque's work highlighted the distinctiveness of North African institutions and insisted on historical specificity. Nonetheless, including the Maghrib in the history of the Arabs would also have preserved them as a distinct entity.[16] The question here is not whether the Arab Maghrib (*al-maghrib al-'arabī*) truly belonged with the Arabs, and thus with the Middle East, but rather why intellectuals failed to explain the distinctiveness of the Maghrib by analyzing the workings of colonialism.

An analysis of French dissertations on Algeria (both in France and Algeria) from 1870 to 1962 shows that the terms *Afrique du nord*, *Arabe*, and *Islam* were the only umbrella categories used that included Algeria.[17] No dissertation about that country conceived of it in terms of the *Moyen-Orient*. Moreover, and although I have not checked every single thesis completed since the independence of Maghribi countries, I have yet to come across a single study that conceives of the *Moyen-Orient* in a way that includes the Maghrib as an integral component and not as an appendix to the Middle East.

Nationalist movements in the Maghrib predated the Second World War and incorporated various tendencies and objectives that ranged from national independence to full French citizenship. However, whether Moroccan,

Algerian, or Tunisian, the earliest nationalist intellectuals did not use the term "Middle East" at all. Since the term only became popular after World War II, this is not surprising. Nationalists articulated their opposition to French colonialism by using categories such as "Muslim," "Berber," "Arab," and "Maghrib / North Africa." In many arenas, they still do so today. However, and as I suggest above, even if these categories were older than French colonialism, they were refitted and remade into new, modern, colonial categories that constituted colonial and then nationalist ideology.[18] This is not to say that colonial discourse was the sole source of the various nationalisms. However, because nationalist intellectuals grew up in a context in which colonial discourse was dominant, quite naturally their thinking reflected some of its elements. One of these was the practice thinking of Maghribis as distinct from Middle Easterners.

Although brief and incomplete, this description of the Middle East and the Maghrib clearly shows that the regional category of the Middle East did not emerge in the Maghrib. Nor was it the result of the concerns of Maghribi intellectuals. However, once it entered the official language of international relations, the "Middle East" made its way through the newspapers and radio broadcasts of the colonial administration. Those who read French-language newspapers could find in the international section references to the Middle East and the actions of the great powers there. Relaying the official language of governments, journalists made the "Middle East" a popular category among the literate public. However, this public in large part consisted of Europeans and a small number of educated Maghribis.

GRAND RE-BEGINNINGS

In 1956, Morocco and Tunisia gained independence from France. In 1962, after a protracted and bloody war, Algeria joined them. The independence of these countries took place at a time of broad geopolitical realignments as part of the Cold War. This international context was particularly important in shaping the economic, political, and ideological orientation of the new Maghribi states. Critically, and in its relations with the broad public, the newly independent governments followed patterns established by the French colonial state. This was especially the case when it came to the content of mass media. Official media dominated and was very active in maintaining the idea that the Middle East was far to the east of the Maghrib and that Maghribis were not Middle Easterners.

An important effect of Cold War rhetoric was that it reinforced and universalized the use of the term "Middle East." For both the U.S. and Soviet governments, this regional category was part of the official language. It described the terrain on which they pursued strategic goals. These governments' activities further consolidated the name, conferring upon it a new layer of objectivity. Cold War politics also explain the appearance of Arab sheikhs, Iranian shahs, radical leftist heroes, and the slew of social statistics that measured the competition for national development. These were the figments of the Cold War Middle East. The "culture industry" in capitalist countries absorbed them and, adding them to the existing repertoire of typified representations, produced new associations and commonplace points of references. This immediately expanded the use of the term beyond governmental circles. Of course, this did not make the new form less political; it merely added an important site of production for the idea of the Middle East. In the socialist bloc, the Middle East remained largely an official category, and pre–Cold War mythologies about the region were similar to Western ones. Significantly, the newly independent Maghribi states did not have culture industries capable of shaping the evolution of the meaning of the "Middle East" on the international scene. Instead, they were clients that more or less purchased finished cultural products and distributed them to their populations. Their input was limited to administering distribution of the idea of a Middle East produced elsewhere.

In contrast to their marginal contribution to the categories and nomenclature of world politics, governments of the newly independent countries of the Maghrib had some say in the ways these ideas were promoted nationally. Through the organization of their bureaucracies, these governments institutionalized a particular vision of the world mostly by compartmentalizing (or perhaps departmentalizing) their actions in it. An analysis of the administrative organization of the foreign ministries in the three countries shows, however, that the term "Middle East" has been consistently absent.[19] There are no Middle East desks and no Middle East specialists at these ministries. Instead, there are specialists of the Arab world, Muslim countries, and international organizations, and there are specialists of individual non-Muslim countries and specific issues such as the Palestinian question. Yet, significantly, the non-Arab countries of the Middle East have garnered little interest on the part of these governments. In this light, the "Middle East" was used as a way to talk about the Palestinian question without directly referring to Israel. For Turkey,

Iran, and other Middle Eastern countries, Maghribi officials simply used the name of the country.

In the same vein, "Middle Easterner" has not been an integral part of the official nomenclature in the Maghrib, and thus has not been necessary to the articulation of foreign policy in any of these countries. This does not mean, however, that Maghribi diplomats have not used the term privately or in discussions with non-Maghribi diplomats. They most certainly have.[20] Although it is difficult to categorize their use of the term in those contexts, it is fairly certain that none of these diplomats would think that he or she was included in the category "Middle Easterner."

In addition to the Foreign Service, the educational systems in the Maghrib sponsored an official understanding of the world. Predictably, curricula and textbooks for geography and history in the three countries do not refer to Middle Easterners. Teachers and other functionaries of the educational system have had no use for the category and have tended to use the names of countries or large umbrella categories such as "Arab world," "Islamic world," or variants thereof. This does not mean that Maghribi governments were trying to prevent their employees from conceiving of the Middle East and Middle Easterners; they did not, and given their inability to control their bureaucracies, they probably would have failed to do so if they had tried. Instead, the Middle East was simply not an official category. Moreover, even when they might have used the term "Middle East" in class, teachers simply did not think of themselves or their students as Middle Easterners. Consequently, high-school graduates were unlikely to have come across these terms in a book and were just as unlikely to have written them in an essay—at least not in school. In this sense, there have been no Middle Easterners in Maghribi schools.

Given the youthfulness of these countries' populations, school-age children represent a large proportion of the total. Only a small portion of students goes on to pursue university-level education, and it is very unlikely that those who did not graduate from secondary school would ever have used the term "Middle Easterner." The reason behind this is very simple: there was no context for them to do so. There is little chance that an agricultural worker in the Atlas Mountains, a maid in Casablanca or Algiers, or a fisherman in Djerba would have ever used the term—or ever uses the term today. Furthermore, with current illiteracy rates equaling 30.1 percent in Algeria, 47.7 percent in Morocco, and 25.7 percent in Tunisia, a sizable portion of these populations still cannot even read or write the term "Middle Easterner."[21] Of course, this alone does not prove that they have never heard the term, that they do not know what it means, or that they do not use it in conversation. However, the likelihood that they would use it differently from newspapers or television newscasts remains rather slim.

Newspapers in the three Maghribi countries have used the terms "Middle East" and "Middle Easterner" on a regular basis. Furthermore, television programs, especially the news broadcasts, have used these terms frequently. This means, at least, that the public has been aware of their existence. However, the adjective "Middle Eastern" (*sharq awsatī/iyūn* and *moyen-oriental/ aux*) appears only rarely, and when it is found, it does not refer to people. For instance, through the entire year of 2008 the two Algerian newspapers *al-Khabar* (Arabic) and *El-Watan* (French) did not once use the adjective to describe people. Instead, the adjectives modified abstractions such as economic and political relations.

At the university level, there are no departments of Middle East studies in the Maghrib, although this may change now that American universities and centers are opening in the region.[22] Within the national university systems, departments of history, Islamic studies, and international policy teach the courses offered by Middle East studies programs in the United States. It is at the university level, however, that it becomes possible to find the terms "Middle East: and "Middle Easterners"—if not in the subject headings and titles of theses and courses, then at least in mostly foreign books read by students and faculty. In other words, whereas schoolteachers do not tend to use the category, university professors, especially those specializing in international affairs are likely to use it on occasion. Again, one is more likely to hear the term "Middle East" than to hear the term "Middle Easterner." In addition, and although it is difficult to establish empirically, "Middle Easterner" is never used to describe an individual person but describes only the inhabitants of the Middle East in general. Even those who might describe Iranians, Turks, and Kurds as Middle Easterners (*sharq awsatiyūn* or *moyen-orientaux*) would not describe the Ayatollah Khomeini as a Middle Easterner.

Adding to the generic, perhaps even disembodied, character the category "Middle Easterner" has in the Maghrib, the description of an individual woman as Middle Eastern (*sharq awsatiya* or *moyen orientale*) is extremely rare. The use of the generic plural, which is masculine in both Arabic and French, and the absence of Middle Eastern women, tends to place Middle

Easterners into a male category. When Middle Eastern women are considered specifically, they tend to be markers of social development. Just as for "Middle Eastern" men, the term "Middle Eastern" is never used to refer to women as individuals. Actual persons such as the famous Egyptian singer Umm Kulthum and the Palestinian politician Hanan Ashrawi are never "Middle Eastern."

Furthermore, and here again it is difficult to show empirically, the term "Middle Easterner" in the Maghrib tends to appear in French rather than Arabic. From my discussion with a great many Maghribis, the term *moyen-orientaux* is used many more times than the term *sharq awsatiyūn*. Even when accounting for bilingual speakers, the number of people who use the French term is much greater than the number of people who use the Arabic one. Those who speak French, even intermittently, are more likely to use these categories, even when they operate in fields other than journalism and government. There is no doubt, however, that whenever Maghribis do so, they do not think of themselves as such. They do not think that they are Middle Easterners as a group or as individuals; consequently no Maghribi would ever describe another Maghribi as a Middle Easterner.

The Maghribi governments' monopolization of the educational systems and their ability to use the media to disseminate their ideas do not help Maghribis feel any more Middle Eastern. Instead, the official production of a discourse on commonality and historical ties with people in the Middle East has not resulted in widespread use of the term by the greater public. For all their opposition to French colonialism, nationalists' discourse in the Maghrib has retained colonial ways of distinguishing between themselves and Middle Easterners. The integration of pan-Arabist rhetoric into official discourse and its gradual and almost complete evisceration over time did little to change the situation.

THE NATIONAL MAGHRIB

If colonial scholars used the premodern history of the Maghrib as a foundation for a discourse on cultural difference, authenticity, and belonging, post-independence intellectuals developed a discourse on the desire to go beyond colonial discourse.[23] In the post-independence period, intellectuals played an important role in the nationalization of society. The newly independent governments proceeded to nationalize the educational systems, the media, and, more generally, the public sphere. Naturally, they also nationalized the past.[24]

By its very nature, nationalist discourse establishes the nation as the main referent and, consequently, identifies distinguishing features that characterize it. For nationalists, the Maghrib is constituted by distinct nations that share a history but are not, and could not be, identical. The idea of a shared history is, however, not simply a polite recognition of one's neighbors. Maghribi nationalist movements trace their evolution back to the L'Étoile Nord Africaine (North African Star), an umbrella organization founded in 1926. And the historical sources that have supported the nationalization of premodern Algerian, Tunisian, and Moroccan history were often the same. Nevertheless, nationalist intellectuals unwittingly maintained a colonial framework by building on its basic epistemological structure and eliminating disparaging references to the populations.[25] Interestingly, when they integrated their nations into broader units, such as the Maghrib, Maghribi intellectuals still did not consider including them in the Middle East. They thought of themselves as Arabs, Muslims, Africans, and as developing nations but not as Middle Easterners.

It is critical here to note that the ideas of an Arab world, Islamic world, Africa, and Third World all shared an important feature: they were ideas whose objective existence was generated by governments and limited to the bureaucratic organizations they created.[26] Of course, the official platforms of these organizations expressed the desire to increase socioeconomic, political, and cultural relations between members. Because they were formed by nation-states, these organizations reinforced the idea of nation among Arabs, Muslims, and Africans. They also made development a national priority.

After independence, the Maghrib was rearticulated based on the idea that nation-states that shared a common historical and cultural heritage would face social, economic, and political difficulties together. In other words, it was based on the thought that national interest would be best served through regional cooperation. Yet, when one analyzes the conditions of the production of the idea of a united or unified Maghrib, it becomes clear that it generally points out the bad faith of neighboring brethren.[27] Officials have produced this Maghrib to reinforce nationalism and the national state. Since the 1960s, they have remade the Maghrib into a national Maghrib whose socioeconomic organization, political direction, and cultural expression express this nationalist, but not regional, orientation. Governments have expended enormous resources to do so. Recognizing the ideological dominance of the national Maghrib explains the reason that Maghribis tend to see themselves primarily as Algerians, Moroccans, and Tunisians. It also explains why they see the Maghrib as an unrealizable pious dream and a myth. Although the creation of the Arab Maghrib Union (AMU) in the late 1980s created an enthusiasm among the populations for this idea, it has since faded. The failure of governments to implement stated goals and projects is nothing new. It is important to see that the idealized Maghrib generated by governments is the outcome of the national Maghrib.

The dominance of the Maghrib of nations should not itself be exaggerated. The long-standing inability of governments to produce the social goods they have promised their populations has chipped away at the broad popular support they had following independence. The idea that those who govern the country should be accountable to the people or that the people should have a say in the direction the country has never truly developed. Instead, governments have behaved much like their colonial predecessors did. In this light, the national Maghrib is the product of the relations between rather limited official circles. For the broader population, official ideas have been both ever-present and beyond reach. It is not the case that official institutions have not relayed official ideology. In spite of their many inadequacies, they generally have performed their function. It is just that there has been no sense that the population should have an input in the matter. As an artifact found in official discourse, the "Middle East" is both familiar and yet alien to most Maghribis. Living in the national Maghrib, they have little use for a term that does not include them. The idea that they might be Middle Easterners does not fit the circumstances of a national Maghrib they experience daily.

STANDING IN THE WAY

There are more than three million French citizens and immigrants of Maghribi origin in France.[28] Beginning in the nineteenth century, Maghribis migrated to France for work. They did again in great numbers after World War II. After the independence of the Maghrib, migration to France continued to involve a great many families on both sides of the Mediterranean. These immigrants are now referred to, among other things, *maghrébins* (Maghribis), a relatively new category in French public discourse.[29]

The experience of Maghribi immigrants in Europe, especially in France, constitutes a basis for solidarity among Maghribis and their distinction from Middle Easterners who are not as numerous in France. In fact, even those Middle Easterners who are present, such as the Lebanese, Turks, and Iranians, tend to espouse markedly different strategies of integration and are seen as properly Middle Eastern.[30] In contrast, West African immigrants, whose socioeconomic and political status have been closer to that of the majority of Maghribis, tend to be closer to Maghribi immigrants than they are to Middle Easterners. Such processes have supported the rearticulation of difference and distance between Maghribis and Mashriqis (Arabs from the lands of the eastern Mediterranean) in France. Of course, the distance between affluent Lebanese professionals, for example, and poor *maghrébins* in the *banlieues* has little to do with the historic differences between Mashriq and Maghrib or the geographic closeness between Northwest Africa and West Africa. However, because these immigrants are tied to their home countries, their experience has further amplified the idea that Maghribis are different from the Arabs and other Middle Easterners. Maghribis, many of whom are French speakers in the Maghrib and in France, thus participate in producing the *Moyen-Orient* as something that does not pertain to them.

An obvious development that illustrates the limited extent of the categories such as "Middle East" and "Middle Eastern" is the very successful deployment by political opposition in the Maghrib of a discourse on Islam. For these opponents, the term "Middle East" has meant very little. Their oppositional discourse posits a completely different map of the world, with its own categories. The participation of supporters of this political movement in conflicts far away from the Maghrib as fighters and organizers connected them and, given their popular appeal, a great number of Maghribis to Muslims who were not necessarily in the Middle East. Indeed, this pan-Islamic discourse was even successful in explaining the closeness between *banlieusards* of Maghribi and West African origins in France itself. By becoming Muslims in this new way, Maghribis did not need to think of themselves as Middle Easterners. The category was simply alien to the vocabulary of that political movement.

In contrast, the political claims made by Berberists in Algeria and Morocco tend to focus on the difference between Berbers and Arabs. These claims are based on the idea that the Berbers are native North Africans whereas Arabs are conquerors who came from the Middle East. Unsurprisingly, Berber nationalism functions in ways that seek to distance the original Maghrib from the Mashriq. However, its ambivalence vis-à-vis Christianity, another Middle Eastern religion, and its pride in figures such as Augustine of Hippo, may lead some to believe that it still operates within French colonial discourse. For, as I have explained above, one of the arguments used to legitimate French colonialism was to bring North Africa back to its place in the Western Christian world. In addition, French missionaries never ceased to try to convert Berbers. Recently, Christian missionaries operating in the Algerian region of al-Qabā'il (Kabylia) have attacked the sacrifice of sheep during 'Īd al-Adhā as a barbaric act, eliciting violent reactions among the population.

Given its francophone, and not always francophile, orientation, it is possible to see reference to Middle Easterners (*moyen-orientaux*) in Berber nationalist discourse. Noticeably, none of these activists ever use the Arabic term (*sharq awsatiyūn*), which is outside of their discourse. Instead, one mostly finds a *Moyen-Orient* tied to Arabs and cast as the other of the Maghrib and its native Berbers. All these factors explain why it is in French that one finds the greatest number of references to Middle Easterners in the Maghrib. However, there is no sense that some Maghribis are Middle Easterners in the same way as those living in the Arabian Peninsula.

In fact, references to the Middle East are used to produce an alienating effect. A militant would say, "We have nothing to do with the Middle East and Middle Easterners, and we want nothing to do with them." This politics of ethnicity sometimes reverts to colonial racialist reflexes and distinguishes between the Arab (Middle Easterner) in the Maghrib from the "European" Berbers.[31] Although it is rare to find serious academics who continue to propound racialist ideas about Middle Easterners, it is striking that most Maghribis refer to Africans as if they were not themselves African. Although explaining this would illuminate the evolution of colonial ideology after independence, it is beyond the scope of this chapter. However, it is worth exploring the conditions that support the absence of Africans from the Maghrib.[32]

POSSIBILITIES

Whether they express themselves in French or Arabic, Maghribis do not believe they are Middle Easterners. Moreover, Maghribis seem familiar enough with the realities of the Middle East and its peoples to refrain from using a concept so devoid of the specificity and nuance afforded by terms such as "Arabs," "Egyptians," "Turks," "Iranians," and "Kurds." They tend to express their commonsense knowledge about the Middle East by using national categories. One should not assume, of course, that because Maghribis have other categories at their disposal that they are in fact knowledgeable about these societies. Modern conditions of mass education, pop culture, and travel restrictions militate against that. However, their familiarity with the Arab world, which is comparable to the knowledge Mashriqis have of the Maghrib, allows them to differentiate between countries and to name a few leaders and some popular singers, past and present. This makes the Mashriq a special region for Maghribis, distinguishing it from Southeast Asia, for example.

Unlike Mashriqis, Maghribis have had regular access to Mashriqi media for the last two decades. Satellite dish technology and Arabic-language channels from the Mashriq have become standard in the Maghrib. Maghribis have found in them new outlets for news and entertainment programs. However, these new media have not changed their basic conceptions about the Middle East and Middle Easterners. On the contrary, they seem to have merely reproduced, perhaps even reinforced, the distinction between Maghrib and Mashriq, even when operating within a diluted version of Arabism supported by the commonality of language. It is important to note here that the Mashriqi media channels, such as al-Jazeera and al-'Arabiya, do not refer to Mashriqis as *sharq awsatiyūn* either. Because their market is linguistically based, these media use the term "Arab world" (*al-watan al-'arabī*) more readily than they use the term "Middle East"—although the latter is not unheard of. Actually, it is also hard to find *sharq awsatiyūn* in the Mashriq, and these media outlets do not use the term to describe people. Naturally then, Maghribi mass viewers do not get to hear about *sharq awsatiyūn* from them. If they do, the term would again not include Maghribis.

A few years ago, some Algerians who took part in international nongovernmental military actions, notably in Iraq and Afghanistan, formed the organization Middle East Warriors (*muhāribū al-sharq al-awsat*), which has not been recognized by the government.[33] The name of the organization may suggest that the term "Middle East" is gaining some use in Maghribi political life. However, this new development still maintains the Middle East as a faraway place that does not include the Maghrib. This *sharq al-awsat* is an indisputable "over there." The reason it is a useful category is that it encompasses those who fought in Arab Iraq as well as those who fought in non-Arab Afghanistan. Because almost everyone in the Maghrib knows that there are non-Muslims in the Mashriq and that these "warriors" fought in these faraway places under the aegis of Islam, neither the Mashriq nor Muslim world fit. Furthermore, given American influence in those countries, these fighters picked up a category that is widely used by the governments and in the media.

Although I have only hinted at it, it should be clear that the integration of the categories of "Middle East" and "Middle Eastern" in the public discourse in

France has to do with institutional mechanisms that guarantee it a sociohistorical existence in that country. These include, but are not limited to, the educational system, the mass media, and various social organizations and parties.

The impact of French public discourse on the way Maghribis conceive of the Middle East and Middle Easterners does not stem only from the experience of immigrants. It stems also from the continued influence France has had on those Maghribis who do in fact use the category. Maghribi rulers, officials, managers, and administrators read French dailies, watch French newscasts, and listen to French radio on a regular basis. Most acquire their information about the world, sometimes including their own country, from French outlets. They send their children who show promise to French schools and universities, and some have French in-laws. The Maghribis who think of Middle Easterners in French, and who translate the term into Arabic when convenient or expedient, are also integrated into the class of international bureaucrats and technocrats. Because nationalist policies have been producing increasingly Arabophone bureaucrats, however, usage of the term is bound to evolve. It is possible that *sharq awsatīyūn* will appear more often in the Maghrib. Nothing, however, suggests that the category will one day include Maghribis.

ENVOI

Categories and terms such as "Middle East" and "Middle Easterner" are not important because they are analytically more useful or precise, or because they more accurately describe social, economic, political, and cultural realities. In this volume, a number of examples of the difficulties that present themselves because of logical inconsistencies and vagueness make this point. Instead, such categories are important because those who use them are important. As such, they become more coherent, or at least they appear to be, thanks to the work of highly educated people who participate in building up conceptions that emanate from centers of power. These intellectuals have done so primarily by expanding the usage of "Middle East" well beyond the strategic circles that originally produced it. Using vehicles including lectures, conferences, articles, and edited volumes such as this one, intellectuals, from scholars and journalists to marketing agents and sportscasters, have made the "Middle East" and "Middle Easterners" intellectually viable, if not coherent, concepts. One of the most important ways they have supported the transformation of the Middle East into a thing—an object of study and a unit of analysis—is by projecting the category back and applying it to a period when the category did not even exist. This anachronistic practice produces the impression that the Middle East has always existed and that it makes sense to analyze various historical periods utilizing this category. Although it is difficult to defend the intentional use of anachronisms intellectually, scholars who commit it do not even try. They just take it for granted.

In another register, and much like train tickets, airplane food, brand names, and industrial pollution, "Middle East" and "Middle Easterners" are artifacts of arrangements in support of which Maghribis have expended much effort and about which they have had little say. Those who use the terms are primarily followers even if they lead their societies in directions, according to conceptual maps, and for reasons they do not choose or even understand. They are mid-level managers in the vast supply chain they are now told to identify as global. Their primary intellectual contribution to the "global community" resides in finding ways to translate and relay the latest directions and orientations.

I end this essay with two anecdotes. Recently, I was at the mechanic waiting for my car to be fixed when a customer who was chatting up one of the mechanics suddenly said, "Well, you know what they say: knowledge is power." I had not followed their conversation up to that point and, just as I was preparing myself to think ill of clichés and those who propagate them, the mechanic replied, "Oh yeah? How come I know so much about cars and all kinds of other things and I still have no power?"

A few months earlier, I used the opportunity of attending a conference to ask Maghribis who were present what they thought about the Middle East (*al-sharq al-awsat*). With a puzzled look in their faces, they all asked, "You mean the newspaper?" (*Al-Sharq al-Awsat* is an Arabic-language daily published in London and controlled by the Saudi royal family).

Part II

HISTORICAL PERSPECTIVES OF
IDENTITIES AND NARRATIVES
IN THE REGION REFERRED
TO AS THE MIDDLE EAST

5 WHEN DID THE HOLY LAND STOP BEING HOLY?
Surveying the Middle East as Sacred Geography

Daniel Martin Varisco

My two fears are distortion and inaccuracy, or rather the kind of
inaccuracy produced by too dogmatic a generality and too
positive a localized focus.
—Edward Said, *Orientalism*

BEFORE THE EAST HAD A MIDDLE, or even nearsighted and far-fetched stretches, it was in principle a convenient relational marker for a world in which some directions were more significant than others. There was nothing absolute about it; as in all perspectives, the view to the east depended on where one was looking from as much as at the object of one's gaze. Of course, as literary critic Edward Said reminded us in his seminal polemic *Orientalism*, it also depended on what one was looking for. For Said, an Anglican Palestinian who wore his crossing-the-border east-to-westness proudly on his rhetorical sleeves, the "Orient" was "almost a European invention."[1] In a loose Foucauldian sense, a discursive tradition that "can accommodate Aeschylus, say, and Victor Hugo, Dante and Karl Marx" is easily imaginable as an easterly ill-wind of the will to dominate given that many men and women looking east considered themselves superior.[2] Rhetoric aside, a shared and power-prone notion that can cross so many centuries, languages, and political contexts must be wholly a European invention, even a phantasm, for how else can it be justified as a unified Western gaze at an inferior Eastern other?

Said's Orientalism thesis, which has achieved sacred status in a secular, literary sense, has received extensive countercriticism even by admirers of the overall thrust of his argument.[3] This criticism centers on two fundamental stumbling blocks that fall out of Said's polemical excess. First, his notion of Orientalism lacks a worldly orientation to the ways in which historically real others in a knowable geographical space have represented themselves. As numerous postcolonial writers have cautioned, there were voices crying out in that discursive wilderness, even if Said chose not to hear or read them. Second, it is arguable that not everyone who looked east did so through the hegemonic lens of a despotic Orientalism writ large. There is more to the gaze than the deconstructable rhetoric of novelists, philologists, and famous travelers. My concern is with this second fault line: the critically acute sine qua non of Said's traveling theory does not account for actual and virtual traveling as a sacred act in which the East as the Holy Land is in fact and devout fancy superior to all other lands and thus to all other directions.

The binary East-vs.-West or Orient-vs.-Occident, given its tropic relevance in many literary texts, the media, and many parts of academia, is indeed problematic, as Said and many other scholars have demonstrated. Such an either-or explanation elides the inevitable nuance that drives all intellectual progress. This is especially the case for analysis of the ways in which a much politicized geographic territory is overlaid with sacred dimensions. The problem with Said's textual genealogy of Orientalist discourse is that he fails to provide a methodological escape from the polemic bind of the binary itself. This results in what Sadiq Jalal al-ʿAzm pointed out just after Said published his argument: an "Ontological Orientalism in reverse."[4] Dueling essentialisms, no matter what directional marker carries the political spin, mire us in a perpetual battle of counter vs. counterpoint, thesis contra antithesis, which prevents arrival at a working synthesis. Said knew this when he warned that the answer to Orientalism was not an equally distorted Occidentalism.[5] To find that answer, or at least to ask the kinds of questions that lead us away from the problems well articulated in Said's *Orientalism*, we must think outside the binary.

I know of no contemporary scholar who would dispute the fact that many Europeans over time created a false idea of the Orient through misrepresentation, but such powerful notions do not arise ex nihilo. It is useful to examine what the term "orient" originally meant to the Greeks themselves. The classical origin of the term "orient" points to an astronomical role: to speak of the orient is to designate where the sun rises or mark a nodal point for coordinating the stars.[6] Greeks used "orient" for the direction of the rising sun rather than a space, real or imagined, for some surrogate other. Later, Roman administrators (those who no doubt would have grown up believing that all roads lead to Rome) spoke of an *oriens-occidens* orientation, but not in the later Christian sense of a civilizational clash of divinely fired proportions. It is highly dubious that a notion of the "Orient" as an inferior other captured a meaningful geopolitical reality for either the phalanxes of Alexander or the legions of Pompey.

The idea of a uniform and inferior "East" was too superficial even for Greek historians. In writing his omnidirectional history, Herodotus described the customs of numerous peoples outside Greece, but those toward the rising sun as he saw it were geographically Asiatic (*Asiatikos*) rather than oriental. The relevant term used in classical Greek to define and at times denigrate the collective pool of non-Greek others is *barbaros*, from which various European languages derived the highly pejorative sense of barbarian and by which the indigenous North Africans were later grouped by outsider logic as Berbers. The origin of *barbaros* as a philological trope is generally accepted as a reference to anyone who could not speak intelligible Greek and thus produced sounds that came across as nonsense, a kind of barbarbarbaristic stuttering.[7] This had not been an important designation in Homer's day, when the Trojans inhabited a joint Grecocentric sphere, even though modern-day geography would locate them in what Said labels the "Near Orient." Usage of *barbaros* appears to have coincided with the sense of a unified Greek people or Hellenes, their joint koine-ing facilitated in part by the invasions of the Persians. As historian James Romm explains, "Once Greeks had faced foreigners in a life-or-death struggle and soundly defeated them, they began to speak of *barbaroi* as peoples naturally or culturally inferior to themselves, not simply 'non-Greek-speakers' but 'barbarians' as well."[8] But, someone did not have to be from some imagined space called an Orient to be a barbarian. The civilizational divide was not determined according to fixed geographical directions but was concentric; Greece was the ethno-concentric focal point for everything, and all others spiraled out as barbarians. As Denys Hay long ago noted, barbarians bothering Greeks were "particularly troublesome in Europe itself."[9]

HOW CAN THERE BE AN ORIENT THAT IS NOT HOLY?

> *"Within thy gates, O Jerusalem"—where everything is wonderful! No other city has a similar place in history, no other has an equally tenacious hold on the heart of the world. Jews, Mohammedans, and Christians, numbering many millions of our race, peoples widely differing in every respect, alike turn their eyes thither with peculiar affection.*
>
> **—Selah Merrill, "Within Thy Gates, O Jerusalem"**

Notably absent from Edward Said's *Orientalism* is the discursive tradition of a "holy land," one that is emphatically not a unique creation of the European imagination.[10] In reviewing the "Near Orient" as the "complementary opposite since antiquity" of the West, Said sums up a "restricted number of typical encapsulations: the journey, the history, the fable, the stereotype, the polemical confrontation."[11] Oddly, but perhaps not ironically so for an avowed secular humanist using clever Whiggish hindsight, the most widespread and arguably the most shared view of this same region is missing: the Holy Land as the devotional focus of Judaism, Christianity, and Islam. Said is so focused on how medieval Christian polemicists, not to mention Renaissance detractors such as Dante, skewed Islam and skewered Muhammad that he neglects both the religious discourse of the devout in the West and the Christian and Jewish populations within the region. Surely the ruins of Solomon's temple and the birthplace of Jesus rather than a Western desire to dominate the Muslim others who gained political control over most of the Holy Land by the end of the seventh century were a greater inspiration and incentive for pilgrims, travelers, and settlers.

My point is not that Said is wrong to identify an ethnocentric, and often blatantly racist, ideology that accompanied European expansion into the Middle East and other parts of Asia, just as it did, *vae victis*, to the departed souls of the New World. His important polemic has facilitated a profound rethinking among scholars across disciplines about the way significant others are represented. In criticizing the excesses of Said's polemic, I do not defend Orientalism as an academic field above the subjective fray of realpolitik, nor do I downplay the discursive complicity that rationalizes oppression under the guise of an imperially minded superiority complex. The problem is that before the Orient was imagined as an inferior surrogate for Western authors, it was discursively appropriated as the Holy Land via the mythical and historical *sacra* articulated in scriptures. The Holy Land served as a religious symbol of origins, a communal utopia, and future apocalypse long before Napoleon's French troops shelled al-Azhar and Englishman William Jones discovered Sanskrit. Indeed for the Christian West, including its Jewish minority, as well as the diversity of inhabitants of the region referred to as the "Near Orient" by Said, the land where God chose to reveal himself and sent his prophets is the ultimate "holy" land. Like it or not, the assumption that this is the Promised Land, Holy Land, *Terra Sancta*, or Armageddon has generated more interest, devotion, travel, and outright bloodshed than any notion of the Orient as inferior or the object of worldly imperial vision.

One thing should be clear from the start: if we assume along with Said that "the essence of Orientalism is the ineradicable distinction between Western superiority and Oriental inferiority," then his thesis cannot account for the Orient as the Holy Land in the eyes of adherents to all three major monotheisms.[12] Whether it is called "Near Orient," "Near East," "Middle East," or simply "Holy Land," this is the sacred geographical space where Yahweh/Almighty God/Allah created Adam and Eve, lifted Enoch into the heavens, suffered Nimrod to build the Tower of Babel, sent the flood to destroy all but Noah and his family, set the Table of Nations, and called Abraham to go to the Land of Promise. Substitute Ishmael for Isaac and much of the subsequent Jewish and Christian history is accepted as real and correctable for Muslims through the Quran. Substitute Jesus of Nazareth for the Jewish Messiah foretold by the Hebrew prophets, and Christianity becomes but a supernatural gentile extension of Judaism. The sacred scriptures of these three faiths all reverberate around a specific geographic region as their point of origin and pivot of final judgment for the whole world.

Throughout much of recorded history this part of the world has been regarded not only as holy but also as the focus of attention. How could it be otherwise?[13] There is little rational terra firma to go on for the claims of Genesis regarding sacred history other than some form of faith in the texts themselves. No earthly paradise, whether referred to as Dilmun, Eden, or simply the "Garden," has been unearthed for historical scrutiny; Noah's ark has not been salvaged, despite the best efforts of an American astronaut who once pranced on the moon. But faith must have something tangible, even if only imagined, to grasp. God showed himself to Moses in a burning bush and revealed the glow of his Shekinah glory in the tabernacle and temple of ancient Israel. Jesus, for Christians, is the word made flesh. Muhammad, for Muslims, was told to recite the literal words of God as recorded in the eternal Arabic Quran. But more than anything else, these faiths have a hallowed section of land still identifiable despite all the artificial man-made borders, and thus it is venerable. In Jerusalem Jews today pray at the Wailing Wall; Christians follow the stations of the cross where Jesus himself is said to have trod; Muslims enact the sacrificial act of Abraham each year at Mecca. For Jews, Jerusalem is Zion in all its anticipated restorative glory; for Christians, Jerusalem is Golgotha and the promise of an empty tomb; and for Muslims, Jerusalem is where Muhammad began his spiritual night journey to commune with God.

HOW DID THE HOLY LAND BECOME HOLY?

> *Whether viewed as the source of our religious faith, or as the most*
> *ancient fountain of our historical knowledge, this singular spot of*
> *earth has at all times been regarded with feelings of the deepest*
> *interest and curiosity. Inhabited for many ages by a people*
> *entitled above all others to the distinction of peculiar, it presents a*
> *record of events such as have not come to pass in any other land,*
> *monuments of a belief denied to all other nations, hopes not*
> *elsewhere cherished, but which, nevertheless, are connected with*
> *the destiny of the whole human race, and stretch forward to the*
> *consummation of all terrestrial things.*
>
> **—Michael Russell,** *Palestine, or the Holy Land from*
> *the Earliest Period to the Present Time*

The importance of Jerusalem and Mecca as the most significant locations on
God's earth for the adherents of the three Abrahamic faiths is so obvious that
the implications of such a truism may escape notice. But myth, for me, is not
credible history. Continental drift and the evolutionary heritage that sent an
early species of *Homo sapiens* into what we now refer to as the Middle East did
not project this region as holy or special from the start. The idea that a certain
area of land, a geographical feature, or even a man-made monument could be
considered holy and special and touched by the gods is not an invention of
Judaism, Christianity, or Islam. Geographical space can become holy whenever a religious rationale accompanies social and political life. Historians and
anthropologists alike can attest to this as essentially true for the entire scope
of human habitation. Holy land does not have to be owned in our modern
sense of private or state control; it simply has to be revered by association with
a highly symbolic event or sacred being.

Here it is useful to return to Said's characterization of Orientalism. If we
were to isolate a distinct discourse around the notion of the "Holy Land," we
would have to admit that it was purely an invention of those who subscribed
to an evolving scriptural corpus and says far more about the one viewing land
as holy than any material aspect of geography or culturally unique characteristic of the human inhabitants. I hesitate to introduce a mangled moniker
such as "Holy Landism" into the crowded ismic sphere of academic linguistic
play, and I do not think a sanctimonious "Terra Sanctism" fits our present
need for a suitable nomenclature. "The Idea of the Holy" has too much reli-

gious baggage and "Biblicity" (a simple but highly biased reduction) misses the point. However, lacking a suitable shorthand term for the notion of the Holy Land as discourse does not excuse the need to define what criteria delineate the notion. A natural wariness of trinities, including Said's own threefold working definition of Orientalism, leads me to propose four criteria that best define my own approach to the contemporary Middle East as the successor of an ascribable "Holy Land" designation in all three relevant faiths.

First, land becomes holy when it is a greater recipient of divine largesse than land elsewhere. The Middle East was made holy by its association with the gods of its conquerors, ultimately the amalgamated universal God of the Abrahamic faiths. Remove the Hebrew scriptures, Christian Bible, and Muslim Quran (and the unwritten lore that informed these sacred texts) and there remains little specifically holy about the area. Whatever the gods touch, that becomes holy. In this sense the Holy Land can be profaned, as its bloody history demonstrates with a vengeance, but it can never be desacralized. Consider the Gospels retort of Jesus to the money changers: "Destroy this temple, and in three days I will raise it up. But he spoke of the temple of his body" (John 2:19–21). In 135 C.E., in retaliation for the Bar Kochba revolt, the Romans plowed over the site of the architecturally sacred temple, relegating the holy site to a dung heap.[14] Neither temple has stayed buried in the minds of the faithful. More pragmatically, the apocalyptic force of a New Jerusalem resonates because of the assumed holy presence of the earthly site. In sum, the Holy Land is what it is because it is the actionable playing field of the God self identified as "I am who I am." (We need not worry here about the meaning of "am.".)

Second, land becomes holy when it is not wholly a matter of mud and bricks, despite the material benefits from exporting wooden bits of the "true" cross or barrels of consumable oil. Like the God whose ascribable presence makes the area holy, the Holy Land's symbolic capital makes the region a matter of historical impact. Being there, in the literal sense, brings one closer to the God who is acknowledged to be everywhere. Here, for example, consider the mental template of the American missionary Reverend William M. Thomson, whose 1859 *The Land and the Book* remains one of the most widely influential Protestant meditations on the illustrative Bible lands (still under the yoke of the unconverted Turks at the time) ever written.[15] "In a word," begins Thomson, "Palestine is one vast tablet whereupon God's messages to men have been drawn, and graven deep in living characters by the Great Publisher of glad tidings, to be seen and read of all to the end of time."[16] The land that gave spiritual birth to the scriptures is the best witness to what God wants the faithful readers to take from the sacred texts. "Broken columns and prostrate temples, cities in ruin, must bear testimony to the inspiration of prophecy; and ravens and sparrows, and cedars and brambles, and fruits and flowers, will preach sermons and utter parables, and we shall not hesitate to listen when they begin to teach."[17] Being in the very land that animates biblical characters was, in a symbolic sense, a foretaste of the kingdom to come.

After rowing on the Sea of Galilee under the "solemn mysteries of night," Reverend Thomson exclaimed:

> Mystery of mysteries! the God-man, the Divine Logos, by whom all things were made which are in heaven and which are on earth, did actually sail over this identical sea in a boat, and by night, as we have done; and not stars only, but angels also beheld and wondered, and still do gaze, and ever will, "designing earnestly to look into those things." This is not fancy, but fact; and shadowy indeed must be his faith in whose breast these sacred shores awaken no holier emotions than such as spring from common earth and ordinary lakes.[18]

Above all else the experience of being in the Holy Land was an emotional journey, one that pilgrims struggled to account for in mere words after the fact. Friar Felix Fabri, whose massive devotional missive followed a pilgrimage in 1483–84, described his rapture at kneeling in the Church of the Holy Sepulchre:

> O my brother! hadst thou been with me in that court at that hour, thou wouldst have seen such plenteous tears, such bitter heartfelt groans, such sweet wailings, such deep sighs, such true sorrow, such sobs from the inmost breast, such peaceful and gladsome silence, that hadst thou a heart of stone it must have melted, and thou wouldst have burst into a flood of tears together with the weeping pilgrims.[19]

A Jew at the Western (Wailing) Wall and a Muslim hurling stones at the pillar of Iblis during the hajj can empathize with the spirit of this devotional rhetoric.[20] Such is the generative imaginative power of this shared Holy Land.

Third, the holiness that infuses the Holy Land in this region is a spiritual panacea for all the ills of the faithful; at the same time it is perhaps more acutely diagnosed by nonbelievers as a communicable disease. That which defines the geographical space of the Holy Land has no fixed rational borders.

Like the Big Bang scenario, this origin point radiates meaning for the expanding generations of believers. In the words of the prophet Ezekiel, redefining Jerusalem from the state of exile, "This is the law of the house: Upon the top of the mountain its whole limit round about shall be most holy" (Ezek. 43:12). Ezekiel's rhetoric cuts no corners, nor does it view east or west as relevant markers of political aspirations. Just as God is present everywhere, even in exile, land can be holy when it is attached to the central point of the faith. Historian of Christianity Robert Wilken considers Ezekiel one of the first instances in which the biblically constituted Holy Land becomes holy in a universally symbolic sense. "Yet, as traditional as much of his language is, there is something new: the land has a center, and God's glory radiates out from its axis to envelop and sanctify everything that surrounds it."[21] Holy land can be extended in a symbolic sense to other geographical areas. Thus the Land of Promise can be conquered as easily in a recently discovered continent, America for instance, as it can be across the trickle of the Jordan River. This does not make the primal Holy Land any less holy, nor prevent partisan politics and economic greed from profaning it any more than the manifest destination of a frontier. However, it does mean that there is never a definable border for the Holy Land, no matter how tall the walls of separation any particular generation may build.

Fourth, but not necessarily a final point of relevance for my working set of definitional criteria, I suggest that the most fertile literary corpus for understanding how the Holy Land has been appropriated across borders is through the narratives of religiously motivated travelers and pilgrims. Texts abound in multiple languages, and examples of relevant rationales for what makes the Middle East especially holy can be chosen almost at random from any time period. The quote above, from Protestant Michael Russell's reflections on an 1830 trip, serves the genre well. The Holy Land, Palestine in particular, is where faith meets history; it is an object of deep curiosity, a distinctively "Promised Land" for the select, and the prophetic site of the ultimate destiny for the human race. I suggest that the writings of the Hebrew prophets (or their redactors), Christian pilgrims, and generations of hajjis about their experience of returning to the physical symbol of their respective faiths are as relevant for unraveling the extensive discourse on "Orient" as are the writings of libertine tourists such as Gustave Flaubert, racist philosophers such as Ernest Renan, swashbuckling rapscallions such as Sir Richard Burton, and historians such as Bernard Lewis.

WHAT MAKES A HOLY LAND TRAVELER HOLY?

> *Now the situation is enriched by the fact that during the entire*
> *nineteenth century the Orient, and especially the Near Orient,*
> *was a favorite place for Europeans to travel in and write about.*
> *Moreover, there developed a fairly large body of Oriental-style*
> *European literature very frequently based on experiences in the*
> *Orient. Flaubert comes to mind immediately as one prominent*
> *source of such literature; Disraeli, Mark Twain, and Kinglake*
> *are three other obvious examples.*
>
> **—Edward Said,** *Orientalism*

Edward Said's estimate, in the statement above, of the volume of Near Orient travel accounts is perhaps too modest. The number of texts in European languages no doubt reaches the tens of thousands, not counting accounts in the indigenous languages.[22] By the fourth century, with the crucial Constantinian conversion of Rome to Christianity, Palestine became a site for ascetic desert fathers, communities of Christian settlers, local bishops, and eventually pilgrims. More than 525 Western-language Christian pilgrimage accounts about Jerusalem, handwritten pre-Gutenberg between 1100 and 1500, have survived.[23] At least two thousand individuals recorded their visits to Palestine between 1800 and 1870, before this area was under European control.[24] Despite the masculine bias of the genre, women also wrote down their experiences. Billy Melman notes that 187 female travelers between 1821 and 1914 published English-language travel accounts on the Holy Land.[25] Not all these accounts revere the space as holy, but all must take account of that unique status.

As a geographic focus, Palestine had long been a primary destination for pilgrims and devouts of holy orders. The first known Latin pilgrim text, the *Itinerarium Burdigalense*, records the itinerary of a Bordeaux Christian who arrived in Palestine in 333 C.E.[26] Some medieval European travel accounts rivaled the famous account of Marco Polo. Among these is the semi-legendary travelogue attributed to Sir John Mandeville, which was first written in French about 1346 C.E. and within half a century became available in every major European language.[27] Allegedly an English knight back from the crusades, the redactable Sir John begins by acknowledging that "the Land of Promise which men call the Holy Land, among all other lands is the most worthy land and mistress over all others."[28] Mandeville as pious narrator, far from being a

Eurocentric or Orientalist dominator, filters his itinerary through a biblical lens that isolates a sacred spot with every step. There is no generic "Oriental" here, but rather there is a mass of diversity. Ironically, his account presents one of the most objective treatments of Islam available up to that time, albeit as a foil for criticizing the lax morals of his own Christian society.[29] Like the many travelers whose accounts are incorporated into this novel travel account, Mandeville comes across as gullible, susceptible to a mania for shrines and relics.

All pilgrims are not the same, and one should not assume that a specific genre of Holy Land travel accounts can be reduced to a shared template apart from the imaginable ways in which the land can be construed as sacred. Some texts are little more than trip logs, others serve as guides for future travelers, and a few are elaborated narrations that tell stories and inspire devotion. My point is that narratives that fix on the Middle East as the physical sign of God's directing of history, all history past and future, do not invariably view the East as inherently inferior to the West. Following the passage quoted above from *Orientalism*, Said insists, "To be a European in the Orient always involves being a consciousness set apart from, and unequal with, its surroundings."[30] His selective choice of travelers, avoiding the vast repertoire of avowedly religious texts, serves his point well.[31] The problem is that none of the examples that come immediately to mind of the literary critic treat the Holy Land as sacred. Flaubert and Disraeli visited the region, but it is their novels rather than their published travel accounts that were influential.[32] Alexander Kinglake, in his pre-tabloid *Eothen*, self-consciously refers to himself as "a headstrong and not very amiable traveller, whose prejudices in favour of other people's notions were then exceedingly slight."[33] In *The Innocents Abroad*, as one of the first steamboat tourists, Mark Twain quite consciously satirized the genre, offering "no apologies for any departure from the usual style of travel writing."[34] These are entertaining accounts to read, but they constitute the exception rather than the rule.

My criticism of Said's conceptual model of Orientalist discourse does not dismiss the obvious ethnocentrism, especially of religiously motivated authors, in all travel texts. "Every interpretation, every structure created for the Orient, then, is a reinterpretation, a rebuilding of it," argues Said.[35] But this is true for travel texts written at any time or about anywhere. Unlike a novel, the author of a travel account cannot escape his necessary presence in the text, which becomes as much a vehicle for memoir as a collection of information, whether geographic facts or romantic farces. There is often a concern, whether fulfilled or not, in these texts to be accurate. Most travelogues, especially those over the past three centuries, are justified as corrections of the mistakes in earlier accounts. This is especially the case for the nineteenth century, which is the focus of Said's interest in Oriental travel writing as a narrative tradition. Thus, Reverend Edward Daniel Clarke in his early nineteenth-century account insists he will not use "monk's eyes" and will correct the misrepresentations of earlier travelers.[36] Nevertheless, the concern for an absolute historical truth, validated in secular, scientific terms rather than rote confirmation of biblical historicity, is a relatively recent phenomenon.[37]

Because the land was holy, there was an extraordinary incentive to experience it firsthand rather than rely on the ambiguity of the sacred scriptures themselves or the inadequacies of earlier accounts. The rationale of Sir Henry Blount, in his *A Voyage in the Levant* (1636), lays bare the common rhetoric: "Wherefore I, desiring somewhat to inform myself of the Turkish nation, would not sit down with a book knowledge thereof, but rather (through all the hazard and endurance of travel), receive it from my own eye, not dazzled with any affection, prejudacy or mist of education, which preoccupate the mind, and delude it with partial ideas, as with a false glass, representing the object in colours, and proportions untrue."[38] Blount was certainly right, in his time, to question book knowledge about the Holy Land. He figured the only rational way to resolve his curiosity was to go there and see the place with his own eyes. Given the travel conditions of the times, Ottoman control of the region, thieves, and the lucrative tourist-gouging guild of the locals, such a trip was indeed a hazard. The hubris, of course, is that seeing the region firsthand with his own eyes dispels error and delusion. Yet, it must be admitted that such travel created the opportunity for more accurate understanding, just as the archaeological exploration of the region has eventually yielded a critical historical lens on the sacred history.

SACRED GROUND: THE LAND AND THE BOOK

> *Our first walk in the Land of Promise. To me a land of promises more numerous and not less interesting than those given to the Father of the Faithful, when the Lord said, "Arise, walk through the land in the length of it and the breadth of it; for I will give it unto thee." It is given to me also, and I mean to make it mine from Dan to Beersheba before I leave it.*
> —William M. Thomson, *The Land and the Book*

To the pilgrim and settler, whether Christian, Muslim, or Jewish, the Holy Land is in the eyes of the beholder. My interest here is not in the overall genre of travel narratives and devotional spinoffs but rather how a given text that appears quintessentially "Orientalist" by default may be probed to reveal an imaginary that is sacred and at the same time must fit into cultural, political, and individual contexts. A key element to Said's *Orientalism* is that Western narratives invariably treat the Orient as "all absence" so that "we must not forget that the Orientalist's presence is enabled by the Orient's effective absence."[39] But what about those texts in which the key objective is presence in the land in order to write the book and in which there is a sacred dimension of that land that transcends the author and those he or she describes? An example is provided by Thomson, the American Protestant missionary who arrived in Syria in 1834 at age twenty-eight. Only fifteen years after the first American missionary activity there in 1819, the Ohio-born Thomson came with a two-fold goal far removed from antebellum American foreign policy at the time. He certainly was commissioned to bring the Gospel as he knew it back to the land of its origin, but he also came to live for the experience itself. He settled in for several decades, a choice made bittersweet by the death of his wife soon after arrival. His goal, as stated at the very start of his book (quoted above) was to walk through the Land of Promise, not just as a pilgrim but in order to make the Holy Land his.

This would seem to be a prime example of the Orientalism Said rightly ascribes to another reverend, William Muir, whose mid-nineteenth-century biography of Muhammad is the epitome of Christian prejudicial dismissal.[40] The obvious rationale for missionary presence was the Great Commission, which prompted Christians over the centuries to spread the message of the Gospel to the ends of the earth. But missionaries to the Holy Land, especially Palestine, faced an ironic fate. They were not bringing news of Jesus to the heathen who had never heard the message, but they were returning to the very land where Jesus had lived. Jerusalem had long contained resident populations of Jews, Christians, and Muslims, each with their holy sites. Reverend Thomson finds a lesson for his own role while musing on an ethnographic datum, a type of wallet that he suggests David would have used to carry the stones for his slingshot and that farmers would carry as a "universal vademecum."[41] "Do you suppose that this wallet, in which they carry their provisions, is the 'scrip' which the disciples were directed *not* to take in their first missionary tours?" he asks.[42] The pragmatic Protestant observer interprets the advice of the disciples' master as a general principle for preaching among one's own brethren. "The best way to get to their hearts and their confidence is to throw yourselves upon their hospitality," he concludes; even the modern Muslim devout is cited as doing this in the same region where Jesus sent his disciples. "Of course," continues Thomson, "such 'instructions' can only have a general application to those who go forth, not to neighbours of the same faith and nation, but to distant climes, and to heathen tribes, and under conditions wholly diverse from those of the fishermen of Galilee."[43]

Thomson is well aware that his mission field is unique, one in which it is important to pay close attention to Jesus' own directives for spreading the word because the Oriental customs are assumed to have remained essentially unchanged. The disciples were admonished to "salute no man by the way." Why? Because, given the Oriental penchant for consuming time with tedious salutations, this would "waste time, distract attention, and in many ways hinder the prompt and faithful discharge of their important mission." Similarly, the disciples were not supposed to go house to house. "They were, therefore, first to seek a becoming habitation to lodge in, and there abide until their work in that city was accomplished," suggests Thomson.[44] Cultural Yankee that he was, Thomson no doubt thought himself following in spirit the directive to travel without a purse simply because he was not gainfully employed (like a fisherman) apart from the Lord's call. As a missionary called to spread the Gospel he should ignore the distractions and otherwise necessary social obligations along the way and secure lodging until his work was done. Yet as a resident in a land where every step conjured sacred history, there was clearly more to his work than this missionary call. This was not a self-imposed exile at the end of the earth among heathens who had no idea of Christianity; as a Christian, Thomson was free to rejoice at returning to the very source of his faith. As sacred turf, the land itself is not inferior, nor are the individuals who need the Gospel easily dismissed or ignored, since in many respects they remain a living testimony to scriptural history.

But who was he called to convert? Local Christians, with whom he finds little common spiritual cause, are set in their ways. Condemning the "buffoonery and the profane orgies of Greek and Latin Christian monks in the Church of the Holy Sepulchre," Thomson concludes, "I doubt whether there is anything more disgraceful to be witnessed in any heathen temple."[45] This was hardly a modern notion in his mind, because Jesus himself upbraided the cities that did not repent and his fellow religionists who were mere whited sepulchers.[46] Thomson observed "how densely the poor Jews can and do pack themselves away in the most wretched hovels" in Jerusalem, but his guided tour of the Holy Land is more concerned with uncovering the spots made famous by biblical Jews. Thomson does not appear to subscribe to the messianic eschatological fervor of some other Protestant missionaries, who thought the remaining Jews must be converted before Christ would return.[47] Converting Muslims in the domain of the Sublime Porte was a suspect act from the start. The fact is that few Muslims ever chose to convert to a distinctly Western mode of Christianity, notwithstanding the theoretical death sentence on the head of an apostate. But acknowledged "heretics" were a different story. On passing by the mysterious Nusayriya sect, Thomson opined that "they were fragments of Syria's most ancient inhabitants—descendants of those sons of Canaan" and that "perhaps many of their brethren, when driven from the south by Joshua, took refuge with them."[48] Here were remnants of the lost from the time of the conquest. Yet Thomson's concern is not so much to bring them to salvation, which they resisted, as it is to be "better acquainted with the origin, history, manners, customs, and religion of this remarkable people."

As a devotional travel guide for the English-speaking Christian, *The Land and the Book* does not leave out the people along the way. The narrative is more than an itinerary of a pilgrim passing through; it is very much the reflections of a stranger who settled and made this Holy Land his own. In the first two pages of his narrative it is the biblical past that comes to life first. Abraham, Moses, the old Phoenicians, Hebrew poets, and Paul enter as the readers' companions before setting off on a ramble "*ala bab Allâh* (towards God's gate), as our Arabs say when they neither know nor care where they are going."[49] Not surprisingly, Thomson is anything but a neutral observer. His ethnocentrically American Protestant views of the local populations drive the narrative. "Have you any curiosity to see a real Arab village?" he asks, after arriving at the Jordan River and halfway through his lengthy narrative. "Will these coarse mat walls and roofs shed rain and defend from cold?" he continues. The response is candid, but ambiguous. "Better than you imagine; still, they are a miserable abode for rational beings. They are the most sinister, ill-conditioned race I have ever seen, and do not begin to fill my *beau ideal* of the free, proud denizen of the desert."[50] The major reason for Thomson's seeming tirade here is the "squalid poverty and inexpressible filth" in a village where there were converts.[51] He experienced this firsthand while stranded there for three days during a major storm. "The good people did what they could to make me comfortable, and were not to blame if my eyes could not bear to be smoked like bacon, nor my nerves endure ceaseless titillation of fleas," Thomson confides.[52]

A modern reader can easily dismiss such rhetoric as racist and dismiss the author as motivated by a latent desire to validate his own superiority. But his text as a whole provides more nuance. The holiness of the "land" in *The Land and the Book* is very much an idyll in which the open country is superior to towns and cities. "The Bible is not a city book; its scenes are mostly laid in the country—its themes suggested by, and its illustrations drawn from the same source; there most of it was thought, felt, spoken, acted, and even written."[53] The very premise of his narrative, as an in situ traveling biblical commentary, is unusual in the genre. This is not a book about the land and the book as much as it is a personalized travel guide extolling the rustic virtues as well as the visible relics. In devotional mode, Thomson concludes, "To reproduce and vitalize all this, we need the country, and best of all, *this* country."

The irony in this idyll is that the land is populated by people worthy of being saved, unlike the Canaanites of old who were wiped out. The current customs of the people encountered along the author's excursions provide illustrations of Bible characters; this is a major theme for *The Land and the Book* and no doubt the most important aspect of its success as a text. Even the author's confrontation with "a troop of the most savage Bedawîn" provides a devotional lesson for the thousands of illusions to robbers in the Bible."[54] Yet Thomson lives to tell the story because he was under the protection of a guide from the tribe of an important sheikh noted for his "dignified manner and intelligence." All Bedouins are not the same. The Bedouins encountered, not surprisingly, fail to fit the author's beau ideal as living testimonies of the biblical patriarchs. "Pshaw!" he humphs, "the Bedawîn are mere barbarians—rough when rational, and in all else coarse and vulgar."[55] Yet Thomson as narrator accepts a contextual rationale that does not view the Bedouin as inferior by nature: "the ancient, generous customs of the Bedawîn were being corrupted by Turkish oppression."[56] Noting the fear of peasants over the insecurity in the region, Thomson turns sympathetic political scientist: "Here is the true explanation of the wide-spread desolations of this beautiful country; and unless some stronger government than the Turkish shall come in to repress these intolerable robbers, the farmers will be driven toward the sea-board, until the whole interior is abandoned and changed to frightful deserts."[57]

Being barbaric does not make the local inhabitants dispensable or less than human as God's creatures that he was sent to minister to, no matter what the results. At several points during his rhetorical journey, Thomson suggests that some of the surviving Arabs before him are the literal descendants of Bible peoples.[58] It is tempting to read *The Land and the Book* and conclude that the local people would be absent in the mind of the author because they are absent in the title. I suggest, however, that the various groups described by Thomson serve as more than foils for biblical history. There is a sincere compassion for the hardships faced by the people as people. This can be seen, without having to read contrapuntally, in Thomson's description of the 1837 earthquake that destroyed Safed. In discussing the Jewish immigrants who repopulated Safed after this earthquake, Thomson reduces them in one passage to "an incredible and grotesque melange of filth and finery, Pharisaic self-righteousness and Sadducean licentiousness."[59] This is a fine example of rhetoric for an isolated quote. But the account of his visit to the scene of the earthquake tells a different story. Arriving with a party to bring medical assistance and supplies, he admits to being "utterly confounded when the reality burst upon our sight." That reality was an entire town in ruin, with hundreds killed by the disaster or buried alive. "Parents heard their little ones crying, Papa! Mamma! fainter and fainter, until hushed in death, while they were struggling to free themselves, or labouring with desperate energy to throw off the fallen rocks and timber from their dying children," he laments. "O God of mercy! my heart even now sickens at the thought of that long black winter's night. Most hideous spectacle, may I never see its like."[60] In such moments the Oriental other strewn throughout the text is humanized.

There is no question that Thomson sees his own values as superior; he is, after all, a missionary who has dedicated his life to spreading these values. But he is neither an imperialist nor an advocate of colonial rule. After describing the difficulties of the local eye-for-an-eye customary law and the difficulties faced by women, he suggests that following his Gospel would alleviate such problems here as he believed it has done in America; yet he warns: "But such large changes in social habits and domestic institutions, to be brought about safely, must begin from within, and develop gradually, and not be rudely forced into society by foreign influence acting from without; and the Christian reformer should be contented to wait for this gradual development."[61] Thomson cites corruption and the weakness of government in providing security as the chief problems: "No wonder people oppressed and robbed as these peasants are, become dishonest and cruel, and even vent their pent-up rage on everything under their control," he concludes, even before Marx had laid out his ideas on exploitation of the masses.[62] My point is that reducing rhetoric to a discourse of bias sacrifices the nuance that salvages the humanity that exists alongside, and at times comes to dominate, the omnipresent bias of ethnocentrism.

EPILOGUE: WHEN DID THE HOLY LAND STOP BEING HOLY?

> *Palestine is desolate and unlovely. And why should it be otherwise? Can the Curse of the Deity beautify a land? Palestine is no more of this workday world. It is sacred to poetry and tradition—it is dreamland.*
>
> **—Mark Twain, *The Innocents Abroad***

> *But for Jerusalem—the city of the Great King, the joy of the whole earth, for many generations the focal point of heavenly light—we can only, like her own captives of old, hang the harp upon the willows and weep. Wherever we turn, the eye seems to rest on desolation. It is a city clothed in pall; and yet our affections cling to it as to the most sacred spot on earth.*
>
> **—J. W. Harding, "The Ruins of Jerusalem"**

In this critical trek through the idea of the Middle East as the Holy Land, I have not attempted to answer the question posed in the title of the essay. The answer is, or should be by now, obvious. The Middle East can never stop being the Holy Land as long as this status is central to Judaism, Christianity, and Islam. In this sense, it has not stopped being holy as an idea, admittedly one that is ever present in the current political turmoil in the region. If Zionism had shifted the homeland for the Jews to Africa, as once envisioned by some, there would probably be no modern state of Israel. If there were no political Israel, the conflict between returning settlers from Europe and other parts of the Middle East versus indigenous Palestinians would have taken a very different trajectory. If American foreign policy had not come to support Israel, within the wider Cold War standoff that embroiled all the nations in the Middle East, it might not have been inevitable that the United States would have taken on the master role that Napoleon and Lord Kitchener had once held. If the United States had not committed its troops to the Arabian Peninsula, Osama bin Laden might still be dreaming of a caliphate in *jihadi* retirement under the Taliban in Afghanistan, and Saddam Hussein conceivably might still be building his palatial mausoleum over the ruins of Nebuchadnezzar's Babylon.

Some might argue that the idea of the Middle East as the Holy Land, whatever that might mean in the real world, would be mere hocus-pocus were it not for the fact that this region holds a large percentage of the world's oil wealth or that it might just be the site of a future nuclear Armageddon. I am far too much a pragmatist to dispute such somber and rational explanations of the way things are. Nevertheless, I am skeptical of the explanatory schema of the social sciences that do not account for the generative force of ideas. The Middle East remains holy in large part because it is thinkable as such, not only because of past association but also because its sacred dimensions, no matter how irrational, unproven, and mythical, motivate actors with real-world consequences and resonate with anyone brought up in Judaism, Christianity, or Islam. Even Mark Twain, anti-pilgrim that he was, recognized that even though Palestine had become desolate and unlovely to his mid-nineteenth-century eyes, it remained a dreamland.

My point in posing a rhetorical question in the title of this chapter is to expand our interpretation of the Middle East as an easily manipulated moniker beyond the East-vs.-West binary repudiated by Said but ironically perpetuated through his polemic excess in the very process of exposing it. Having traced our steps on hallowed discursive ground, it is perhaps fitting to close with a biblical metaphor. "Now Israel loved Joseph more than all his children," reads Genesis 37:3, "because he was the son of his old age: and he made him a coat of many colors." That mosaic, as anthropologist Carlton Coon once styled the Middle East, can be viewed as a geographical imaginary akin to a coat of many colors.[63] Whether the coat is given to Moses as lawgiver, Jesus as savior of the world, or Muhammad as the seal of the prophets, it is seen within each religion as a mark of superiority. But the mark of this divinely sanctioned superiority is one of many colors, dare I say with a multicultural aspect, not a black-and-white distinction. Coloring our interpretation of this region is a mixture of politics, economics, ideologies, and outright individual greed (whether you view that as original sin or hereditary adaptation).

I suggest that texts always have many colors, just as this special coat of privilege has; even seemingly black-and-white images have shades we tend to take for granted. No single text can define a genre as broad and open-ended as travel to the real Middle East, not even by those who approach it, or even reproach it, as the Holy Land. The threads that holds the coat together, like the ethnocentrism that pervades all these texts, is material, no matter how absurd the design imagined. But this authorial bias is such a necessary part for the coat to hold together that we should not let such an objectionable part of reality prevent us from appreciating the full effect of the colors. As shown in the example of William Thomson's *The Land and the Book*, comments by real authors should be seen in contrast to each other within the narrative, like the colors in a coat of many colors are viewed, rather than isolated out as meaningful quote blocks in themselves. Did Thomson construct an Oriental as other? Yes, but he did much more than that. At the same time he redefined himself through the mundane act of traveling through a holy land still inhabited. Few souls were saved, in the usual sense, by his mission, but in the process few were damned and perhaps his own was salvaged. Even as foils for his spiritual pilgrimage back to the Bible lands, the people he encountered came alive in his narrative and in his own life.

Like all good pilgrims, let us have the last word be about Jerusalem, the literal spot venerated by Jews, Christians, and Muslims as sacred outside as well as within time. In mid-nineteenth-century Jerusalem, Reverend Thomson once visited a Jewish synagogue, but the guttural Hebrew of the worshippers was not music to his ears. "The Orientals know nothing of harmony, and cannot appreciate it when heard," laments Thomson, "but they are often spell-bound, or wrought up to transports of ecstasy, by this very music which has tortured your nerves."[64] Shall we stop here and be content to write off such sentiment as typical Orientalist observation? Shall we dismiss the rhetorical bias of the American missionary as yet another example of a Western observer who came, saw what he wanted, and conquered through one-sided representation? Is it enough to label *The Land and the Book* as another manifest text with profane latent malicious intent? The next line should give us pause. "I have never known song more truly effective than among these Orientals," Thomson confides. Immediately after this experience, Thomson's local Arab guide took him to a concert of Muslim musicians. "Thinking it would be a pleasant remembrance to carry away from the Holy City, I went, and was not disappointed," notes the rambling travel guide. Music is always in the ears of the beholder, to be sure, but here is a text in which the Holy Land does not mutatis mutandis mute the voices or the instruments of the Orientals themselves. Analyzing such texts as contemporary critical scholars may be "rough pilgrimizing in the Holy Land," as Twain sarcastically described the process, but the view is well worth the effort.[65]

6 THE RIVER'S EDGE

The Steppes of the Oxus and the Boundaries of the Near/Middle East and Central Asia, c. 1500–1800

Arash Khazeni

The sands of the Oxus, coarse though they be,
Beneath my feet, were soft as silk to me.
—Rudaki, *Chahar Maqala*

IN 'THE VENTURE OF ISLAM' (1958), Marshall Hodgson defined the "Middle East" as the land between "the Nile and Oxus," the historical core of what he called "Islamicate civilization." Hodgson's designation of the Oxus River (Amu Dar'ya) as the eastern boundary of the region suggested the long-standing ecological and cultural connections between the Middle East and Central Asia:

> For this I will not usually use the term "Middle East" but one or another phrase in "Nile to Oxus." The term "Middle East," which seems the best phrase of those more commonly used, has a number of disadvantages. It is of course vague. It can be defined at will; but overtones remain, especially overtones implying an Iran of present-day political bounds. Its principal disadvantage stems from its relatively exact military usage, where it originated. It cuts the Iranian highlands in half—the western half ("Persia") having been assigned to the Mediterranean command, the eastern half ("Afghanistan") to the Indian command. Since the Iranian highlands are of primary importance in the region that is basic to Irano-Semitic and Islamicate history, such a usage is completely unacceptable. Unfortunately, the military usage as to the eastern limits of coverage has become standard in a great many works using the phrase "Middle East," and for many readers it comes to imply an area that is, on balance, more westerly than our history requires.[1]

In Hodgson's view, the region known as the "Middle East" was a modern political construct that detached the Iranian plateau from the Central Asian steppes. The creation of the separate geopolitical units of the Middle East and Central Asia fragmented ecological, economic, and cultural ties that once integrated the regions.[2] For two thousand years, the series of overland trade routes that made up the fabled "Silk Road" connected a "Turko-Persian" civilization across West and Central Asia, linking pastoral nomadic and settled populations.[3] As Martin Lewis and Karen Wigen have contended in *The Myth of Continents: A Critique of Metageography* (1997), the construction of separate world regions such as the "Middle East" and "Central Asia" were figments of the European "geographical imagination" and taxonomies produced for the Western "map of the world."[4] These modern geographic representations, conceived after the turn of the twentieth century, supplanted older geographic notions that integrated Central Asia and the Near / Middle East (see Chapter 1).

This chapter traces the historical processes that led to Central Asia being left off the map of the modern Middle East. Existing studies have offered religious, political, and cultural interpretations of the distance that emerged between the Middle East and Central Asia in modern times. Some have argued, in a tradition dating back to the nineteenth-century explorer Arminius Vambery, that the conversion of Safavid Iran to Shiism created "a barrier of heterodoxy" vis-à-vis a largely Sunni Central Asia. The Sunni-Shi'i sectarian divisions emerging in the region at the time shaped imperial borderlands. At the turn of the sixteenth century, as Shah Isma'il I (1494–1524) established the Safavid dynasty and set out to convert Iran to Shiism, the Shaybanid Uzbeks became the sovereigns of Transoxania, where they staunchly promoted Sunnism. According to Svat Soucek, this "barrier of heterodoxy" resulted in an almost permanent cultural rift "pitting schismatic Iran against orthodox Central Asia for three hundred years, right down to the latter's conquest by Russia in the nineteenth century."[5] Other scholars have highlighted the politics of the "Great Game" and Anglo-Russian imperialism during the nineteenth century in determining the boundaries between the Middle East and Central Asia. With the British consolidating their empire in India, the Russians expanding into Central Asia, and the construction of Afghanistan as a buffer between the two empires, the frontiers between the Middle East and Central Asia were closed. This interpretation has many disciples and has been put forth in Peter Hopkirk's *The Great Game* and the works of various other scholars.[6] More recently, scholars have offered cultural histories of the shaping of the nation or homeland (*vatan*) and its implications for the eastern borderlands of Iran.[7]

Without casting aside these prevailing religious, political, and cultural interpretations, this chapter presents an environmental perspective on the making of the boundary between the Iranian plateau and the Central Asian steppes. The Oxus River, long seen as a border between the two ecological worlds, provides a point of entry for such an approach. The Oxus has long been conceived as marking a frontier. It holds a legendary place in the Persianate geographical imagination, denoting Iran's eastern boundary with Turan (the Persian term for Central Asia), as depicted in the *Shahnama*, the folkloric Persian epic compiled by Firdawsi.[8] Although this frontier was often crossed, it nevertheless represented a natural boundary on the landscape, culturally and geographically separating historic Iran from Turan (and in today's terms the Near and Middle East from Central Asia). Various episodes from the *Shahnama* convey this view of the Oxus River as a frontier. One of the best-known parts of the epic to be set on the Oxus occurs at the end of the tale of Siyavash, as Kay Khusraw, Farangis, and the hero Giv ford the river on horseback, crossing over into Iran, while pursued by the Turanian troops of Afrasiyab. This story and the perception of the river's edge (*lab-i rud-i ab*) as a frontier are beautifully detailed in illustrated manuscripts of the *Shahnama*.[9] Crossing the Oxus as a movement across frontiers is conventional not only in Persian folklore and literature but in geographical histories and chronicles as well. The perception of the Oxus as a frontier was also developed by classical Muslim geographers, who referred to the river by the name Jayhun or al-Nahr ("the River"), and classified it as the edge of civilization, designating the land south of it as the Persian province of Khurasan and the region to the north as Mavaralnahr ("other side of the river"), commonly referred to in the West as Transoxania.[10] The steppes of the Oxus denoted an ecological and cultural frontier ground, renowned as the abode of restless nomads, the "Ghuzz Turkomans."[11] The Oxus was the frontier between the steppe and the sown. The river marked the liminal eastern edges of Islamic empires.

This chapter argues that ecological changes in the early modern period shaped the making of the modern boundary between the Near / Middle East and Central Asia. During the late sixteenth century, the Oxus River changed course, its waters swerving eastward from the Caspian to the Aral Sea. This led to an expansion of the Qara Qum (Black Sands) desert, the arid steppes between the Caspian and the Oxus, which was transformed into an ecological space in between empires.[12] As the Oxus River changed course, Turkmen pastoralists found new possibilities in the expanding arid steppes of the Qara Qum, making it the center of their vast equestrian culture distant from the reach of empires. The Safavid and Qajar dynasties of Iran saw the contours of their imperial frontiers shaped by the ecology of the steppes. The fluctuation in the course of the Oxus River during the sixteenth century spurred ecological changes on the frontiers between the steppe and the sown. Between the sixteenth and nineteenth centuries, the Safavids (1501–1722) and the Qajars (1785–1925) unsuccessfully attempted to reclaim the Central Asian steppes and to reestablish the Oxus region as the eastern borderlands of Iran. These imperial projects to reclaim the steppes coincided with a time when the frontiers of empires in Central Asia were being settled and fixed. Whereas the eastern borderlands of Iran were once impermanent, fluid, and only vaguely known, marked by the nature of an untamed river running through the steppes, by the nineteenth century this frontier came to be permanently fixed by boundary pillars and lines drawn on maps.

FLUID FRONTIER

The Oxus River originates in the Pamir Mountains in modern-day Afghanistan, flows through the Qara Qum and Qizil Qum deserts, and empties into the Aral Sea in the steppes of Central Asia, about sixteen hundred miles from its source (Figure 6.1). From the Pamir Mountains, the stream of the Oxus passes to the north of the oasis of Balkh, and from there it winds through the sun-drenched steppes south of city of Bukhara before reaching the delta of Khvarazm near the end of its course. On its path from the Pamir Mountains to the Aral Sea, it flows through and determines the borders of four states: Afghanistan, Tajikistan, Turkmenistan, and Uzbekistan.

The hydroclimatic history of the Oxus is complicated, and much of it is speculative. The Oxus has flowed northward from the Pamir Mountains since the late Pleistocene (the geological period that ended about ten thousand years ago). The course of its flow, however, has historically been prone to changes and fluctuations carrying environmental consequences for the frontier between the steppe and the sown. During intervals throughout its history, the river is believed to have partially flowed into the Caspian Sea by way of the Uzboy Channel, an ancient bed of the Oxus that is dried up today. In flood years, the Oxus would overflow, emptying into the Sarykamysh depression about 150 miles southwest of the Aral Sea, continuing its westward flow through the Uzboy Channel into the Caspian Sea (Figure 6.2). Thus, the Caspian and the

Figure 6.1. Map of modern-day Uzbekistan, showing Amu Darya (Oxus) through Turkmenistan and Uzbekistan to the Aral Sea (original in color). United Nations, January 2004.

Aral may have episodically been connected through other bodies of water lying between them until the sixteenth century.[13]

Whether the Oxus was changing channels or flowing into both the Aral and Caspian seas during flood years is not entirely clear. Both climatic fluctuations and ancient irrigation works along the Oxus in Khvarazm may have affected the flow and may have dictated which channels were used. What is certain is that since the sixteenth century, there occurred a complete desiccation of the Sarykamysh depression and hence the Oxus has flowed north only into the Aral Sea. Some references to the changing flow of the Oxus may be

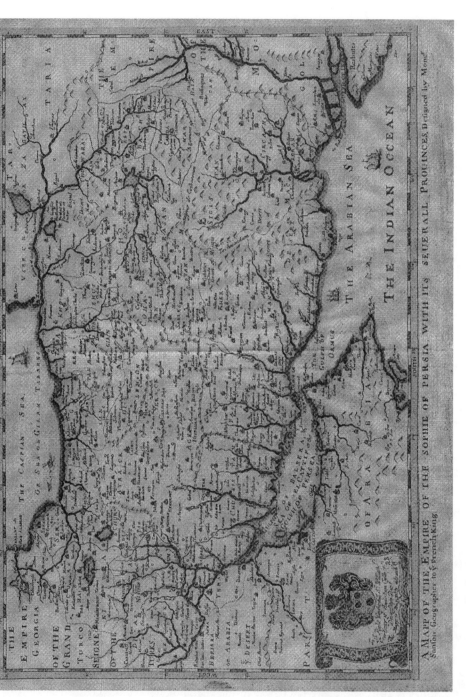

Figure 6.2. Map of Safavid Persia with the Oxus River still depicted as flowing into the Caspian Sea (original in color). Sanson, 1680.

gathered from contemporary written sources, which offer scattered descriptions of the river's changing course. The tenth-century Arab geographer Muqaddasi reported that the Oxus River flowed into the Aral Sea but identified an old bed that led to the Caspian.[14] Writing in the fifteenth century, following the destruction of dams and irrigation works on the Oxus that diverted the river's flow towards the Caspian Sea, Timurid geographer Hafiz Abru claimed that the Aral Sea had nearly disappeared.[15] The main contemporary source detailing the eastward shift of the river in the sixteenth century is Abu'l Ghazi Bahadur (1603–42), khan of Khiva, who writes in *Shajara-yi Tarakima* (Genealogical History of the Turkmen) that around the year 1576, the Oxus River changed channels, swerving toward the Aral Sea and turning the lands between its former bed and the Caspian Sea into a waterless desert.[16] Writing much later in the nineteenth century, Muhammad Hasan Khan Saniʻ al-Dawla Iʻtimad al-Saltana claimed that the shift in the flow and the delta of the Oxus created a significant environmental change (*taghirat-i tabiʻi*) on the eastern frontiers of Iran and added that its drift away from the Caspian and toward the Aral remained clouded in uncertainty, for it occurred over the centuries and went unrecorded in the annals of history.[17]

In the least, there remains substantial evidence to suggest that the Aralo-Caspian lands saw significant environmental changes in the early modern period, including the occurrence of great fluctuations in water channels, with consequences for patterns of settlement and networks of irrigation canals.[18] Some nineteenth-century sources claimed that within the space of one hundred years (1780s–1880s), three hundred lakes disappeared in the Aralo-Caspian region.[19] Similarly, others speculated, as noted above, that that the Aral and Caspian had been separated or disconnected due to the drying up of overflow channels and connections.[20] Along the upper course of the Oxus, the wind-blown "flying sands" and loess of the Qara Qum Desert accumulated over silted, alluvial flood plains, effacing irrigation deltas and riverbeds. The expansion of desert sands in the alluvial plains is thought to have corresponded with an increase in aridity, the shrinkage of seas, the contraction of streams and deltas, the drying of channels, and, lastly, the depopulation of oases.[21] In the early modern period, the process of desertification led to the expansion of the Qara Qum as an ecological zone in between empires. The Black Sands Desert was transformed into a space in between and distant from the Safavid and Qajar dynasties of Iran. Between the sixteenth and nineteenth centuries, the Safavids and Qajar strived, without much success, to reclaim this desert frontier.

THE SETTLEMENT OF THE CENTRAL ASIAN FRONTIER,
C. 1500s–1800s

In 1501, when the Safavid dynasty was established, the Oxus River was still loosely conceived as the eastern boundary of Iran.[22] From the beginning, however, this figurative boundary proved difficult to manifest in reality. The Safavid project to reclaim the Oxus became even more vexed after the river changed course away from the Caspian Sea in the 1570s, leaving behind a desert.

During the early sixteenth century, the steppes of the Oxus were a contested frontier between the armies of the Safavid Shah Isma'il I and those of the Uzbek Muhammad Shaybani Khan (d. 1510). The Uzbeks had risen to power in Mavaralnahr in the 1490s and began their expansion into Khurasan upon the death of Husayn Bayqara, capturing the Timurid capital of Herat in 1507.[23] The pervasiveness of the notion of the Oxus as the frontier between Khurasan and Mavaralnahr, Iran and Central Asia, is suggested by references to the river in Safavid histories, such as the early sixteenth-century chronicle *Tarikh-i Habib al-Siyar* by Ghiyath al-Din Khvandamir. The river was represented as a natural boundary contemplated by the armies that crossed it from both sides. Time and time again, Khvandamir depicted armies passing to and from Iran and Central Asia on their marches across the river, such as in the spring of 1507, when Muhammad Shaybani Khan entered Khurasan and ousted the last Timurid ruler of Iran, Badi' al-Zaman: "And since winter had come to an end and verdure and sweet basil grew on the banks of the river and in the hills and plains . . . Muhammad Shaybani Khan became set on the conquest of the land of Khurasan and crossed the waters of the Oxus."[24]

In response, Shah Isma'il marched his armies into the Qara Qum, capturing the oasis of Marv in 1510, and prepared to take the frontier city of Balkh, near the banks of the Oxus.[25] The Safavids, however, were unable to hold the Oxus frontier, conceding it to two independent Uzbek khanates, one based in Bukhara and Samarqand and another in Khvarazm.[26]

In the years following the death of Shah Tahmasp (1524–76), when the Oxus had turned away from the Caspian Sea, the Safavids increasingly struggled to preserve their Central Asian frontier. With the expansion of the Qara Qum, pastoral nomadic tribes such as the Turkmen found new opportunities, wielding great power and autonomy on the distant borderlands of empires. With their pastoral economy and equestrian culture thriving in the Black Sands Desert, the Turkmen boldly raided the eastern borderlands of Iran, taking Shi'i captives for the slave markets of Khiva and Bukhara.[27] By the late sixteenth century, their raids became so prevalent that the Safavids were forced to mount punitive expeditions. In the 1590s, the Turkmen overran and destroyed the fortress of Mubarakabad (Aq Qal'a), near the shores of the Caspian, which had been designed as a bulwark against their incursions.[28]

The Central Asian frontier was a prime concern for Safavid Shah Abbas I (1588–1629). In 1598, he marched from Isfahan to Khurasan, restoring Mubarakabad, retaking Mashhad and Herat from the Uzbeks, and attempting to stabilize the empire's Central Asian borderlands. The shah attempted to drive the Turkmen from the valleys of the Kopet Dagh and ordered a deep trench to be dug from the foot of the mountains to the shores of the Caspian Sea.[29] Shah Abbas also relocated numerous tribes from the Zagros, where they enjoyed great autonomy and local power, to the Central Asian frontier in order to guard against the raids of the Uzbeks and Turkmen. The forced relocation of the Kurds and other tribes from the western Zagros Mountains to Iran's eastern frontier became a Safavid policy used to bring order to the arid eastern frontier of the empire. Thus, even under Shah Abbas, the Safavids could only assume a defensive policy on the Central Asian frontier. By then, hundreds of miles of the Qara Qum, the homeland of the independent Turkmen tribes, separated Safavid Iran from the Oxus River.[30]

Coming to power in the aftermath of the interregnums and civil wars of the eighteenth century, the Qajar dynasty could only aspire to restore the boundaries of the Safavid Empire before its fall in 1722. On the Central Asian frontier this meant the western margins of the Qara Qum, which became established as the border between the two territories in the nineteenth century. During the Qajar period, the Qara Qum remained distant and beyond the pale of imperial rule. The autonomy of the Turkmen tribes in the Central Asian steppes reached unprecedented proportions; they boldly disregarded the writ of the shah by conducting their slave raids (*alaman: chapu*) into Iran.[31] Numbering between 75,000 to 192,000 yurts, or 375,000 to 960,000 individuals, the Turkmen carved out a loose trading and raiding confederation in the Qara Qum, which the Qajar dynasty perennially struggled to contain.[32] The Turkmen followed clan and tribal authorities, paying only a nominal tribute, if any at all, to the Qajar dynasty and the Khanate of Khiva. They were effectively beyond the control of state power, and their autonomous territory marked the frontiers of surrounding empires. The delimitation of the boundaries between Iran and Central Asia hence became connected to the imperial settlement and reclamation of the Qara Qum. The Qajar dynasty proved incapable of pacifying the Turkmen and reclaiming the steppes at the moment when the Central Asian frontier was becoming fixed.

The demarcation of the boundary between Iran and Central Asia came about in the mid- to late nineteenth century as a result of British and Russian expansion into the region. The boundaries between Iran and Afghanistan were drawn. In 1857, due to British imperial interests in India, Herat was separated from Iran and awarded to Afghanistan.[33] In the 1870s, Major General Frederic Goldsmid of the Indian Telegraphic Department led boundary commissions that established the Helmand River as the border between Iran and Afghanistan in the region of Sistan.[34] As for the Oxus frontier, the Russo-Afghan Boundary Commission established the river as the northern border of the Durrani dynasty in Afghanistan. A nineteenth-century Persian history of Afghanistan acknowledged the extent of the Afghan Durrani kingdom as reaching from the Oxus to the Sind and from Khurasan to Kashmir.[35]

The Qajar project to reclaim the Central Asian frontier effectively came to a disastrous end in 1861 during a military campaign against the Tekke Turkmen stronghold at the oasis of Marv. The Turkmen routed thousands of Qajar troops, capturing their artillery, taking many soldiers into captivity, and proving once and for all that the Qara Qum was a land apart from the guarded domains of Iran.[36] Iran's frontier with Central Asia was subsequently delimited under the shadow of the Trans-Caspian Railway and the Russian expansion into the Eurasian steppes. In 1881, a Russo-Persian boundary commission permanently fixed the border between Russian Central Asia and Iran at the Caspian Sea in a line extending eastward along the lower Atrak River to Darra Gaz, Kalat-i Nadiri, Sarakhs, and the slopes of the Atek on the edge of the Qara Qum, which became the last Persian outposts on the border before the steppes.[37] The treaty was an indication of Iran's diminishing frontiers in the east and a sign of the Russian Empire's expansion into the Central Asian steppes. In his itineraries and reports, ʿAbdallah Khan Qaragazlu, a Qajar frontier agent posted in Sarakhs and Kalat-i Nadiri in the late 1870s and the early 1880s, discusses the creation of the "boundary line" (*khat-i sarhadd*) between Russia and Iran in 1881, commenting that because of the agreement "the subjects (*raʿiyat*) have been unable to freely pass in the valleys and along the rivers as they have in the past.[38]

These fixed boundaries were recorded and published in printed surveys and maps, appearing in such geographic texts as the *Journal of the Royal Geo-*

graphical Society of London (published in fifty volumes in 1831–80), the *Proceedings of the Royal Geographical Society of London* (twenty-two volumes in 1855–78), and the *Proceedings of the Royal Geographical Society and Monthly Record of Geography* (fourteen volumes in 1879–92). In addition, a body of lesser-known nineteenth-century Persian geographic texts also mapped and surveyed the emerging Central Asian frontier.

The genre of Persian travel narratives (*safarnama*) reified the newly formed boundaries between Iran and Central Asia. The border was reaffirmed, for instance, during Nasir al-Din Shah's two tours of the eastern province of Khurasan and pilgrimages to the Shi'i shrine city of Mashhad during the years 1865 and 1882. The shah's pilgrimage tours, and the geographic texts produced during these journeys, reaffirmed that the frontier between Qajar Iran and Central Asia extended little beyond the shrine city of Mashhad.

Nasir al-Din Shah's first journey to Khurasan in 1865 was six months in duration and its itinerary was written by 'Ali Naqi Khan Hakim al-Mamalik as *Ruznama-yi Safar-i Khurasan*.[39] In the opening pages of the work, Hakim al-Mamalik notes that the shah's pilgrimage was also a scientific mission of cartographic exploration on the frontiers:

> A pilgrimage (*ziyarat*) to the threshold of the holy eighth saint and a journey to the eastern parts of the country (*bih janib-i sharq-i mamlikat*) were planned in order to show gratitude and charity, as well as to bring together detailed accounts of that illuminated garden which is a source of blessings. This travel was to also produce solid and reliable information about the frontiers and borderlands (*saghur u sarhaddat*) of the area of Khurasan (*sahat-i mamlikat-i Khurasan*), one of the largest provinces in the guarded domains of Iran.[40]

Subsequently, Hakim al-Mamalik explains the geographical purpose of the *Ruznama*, which was to provide "a summary of the geographical knowledge (*t'alimat-i jughrafiyih-i*), including the condition of roads, terrestrial forms (*hayat-i arzi*), mountains, rivers, villages, and lands."[41] Nasir al-Din Shah's premier journey and pilgrimage to the shrine of Imam Reza at Mashhad in 1865, memorialized in Hakim al-Mamalik's *Ruznama-yi Safar-i Khurasan*, was part of the process through which the Qajar dynasty mapped and measured imperial territories on the Central Asian frontier.

Nasir al-Din Shah followed his Khurasan mission of 1865 seventeen years later with a four-month return journey that he took in 1882. Although shorter in duration than the shah's first mission, the 1882 journey proved to be more prolific in terms of the production of texts. The first of these texts was Nasir al-Din Shah's own *Safarnama-yi Khurasan*, and like its predecessor, it also included numerous lithographed illustrations of landscapes and architectural sites in the province drawn by the artist (*naqqash*) Abu Turab Ghaffari.[42] In the *Safaranama*, the shah left a record of the stages (*manazil*) on the roads between Tehran and Mashhad.[43]

The most substantial of the texts produced in commemoration of the shah's second tour of the eastern frontier was Muhammad Hasan Khan Sani' al-Dawla I'timad al-Saltana's fourteen-hundred-page lithographed regional history *Matla' al-Shams: Tarikh-i Arz-i Aqdas va Mashhad-i Muqaddas, dar Tarikh va Jughrafiya-yi Mashruh-i Balad va Imakan-i Khurasan* [The Place of the Rising Sun: History of the Sacred Land and Sacred City of Mashhad, On the Known History and Geography of the Lands of Khurasan].[44] In *Matla' al-Shams*, I'timad al-Saltana strived to present "a precise geography and history" of the eastern borderlands of Qajar Iran, detailing the environs, monuments, cities, ruins, mosques, tombs, and caravanserais.[45]

Matla' al-Shams is of interest here not simply for what it includes but also for what it leaves out. The text is not without reference to the steppes of the Oxus as Iran's legendary eastern frontier. In one passage, I'timad al-Saltana presents a full explanation of the legend from the *Shahnama* as to how the Oxus came to be designated as Iran's eastern frontier by the flight of an arrow arched eastward from the summit of Damavand: "wherever the arrow (*tir*) falls on the ground is the frontier between Iran and Turan."[46] He continues to recount the flight of the arrow as it "passed over Nayshabur and Sarakhs and Marv, landing on the banks of the river Jayhun [Oxus]."[47] Seeking to explain this myth, he offers several theories as to how an arrow launched from Damavand could reach the Central Asian river, ranging from the idea that there was something magical in the preparation of the arrow to the notion that there was no arrow from a bow but rather a line of sight (*tir-i nazar*): "since in the past the Jayhun used to empty into the Caspian Sea, from the summit of Damavand the line of vision set upon the Shatt-i Jayhun and the river came to be designated as the border between the countries of Iran and Turan."[48]

Despite such allusions to the legendary eastern boundaries of Iran, reference to this greater Khurasan, in *Matla' al-Shams* I'timad al-Saltana sketched the geographical limits of the Qajar's Central Asian frontier far more conservatively. Although he never explicitly defines where the eastern frontier province of

Khurasan begins or ends, he clearly conceives it as a world centered on the Shi'i holy city of Mashhad. Written as a geographical compendium to memorialize Nasir al-Din Shah's pilgrimage to the shrine complex of Imam Reza in Mashhad (*Astan-i Quds-i Razavi*), the chronicle begins by describing the roads from Tehran to Mashhad—one leading from Semnan, Damghan, Shahrud, Sabzevar, and Nayshapur and another leading from Damavand, Firuz Kuh, Bistam, Bujnurd, and Quchan.[49] Gone were the classic oasis cities of the Central Asian frontier: Balkh, Marv, Herat. In *Matla' al-Shams* and other Persian travel narratives from the late nineteenth century, the Shi'i shrine city of Mashhad is represented as the practical and spiritual end of Khurasan, with little mention of what lies beyond it. By the close of the nineteenth century, the steppes had been reclaimed in the Russian conquest of Central Asia, and Iran was gradually absorbed into the nascent geographical category of the Middle East.

CONCLUSION

This chapter has offered an environmental interpretation of the making of the frontier between the Near / Middle East and Central Asia. The Oxus River had long marked the ecological frontier between the steppe and sown, and it marked the figurative border between Central Asia and Iran. During the late sixteenth century, the river changed course away from the Caspian Sea, expanding the desert on the eastern borderlands of Iran. As independent pastoral nomadic populations found new possibilities in the steppes, early modern Islamic empires, including the Safavids and Qajars of Iran, struggled in vain to reclaim the arid Oxus frontier. The Qara Qum was transformed into a borderland desert in between empires, with major consequences for the settlement of the modern boundaries of the Middle East and Central Asia, which occurred in the late nineteenth century under the auspices of imperial boundary commissions and upon the basis of European military dominance. Consequently, the settlement of the Oxus frontier, and the effective division of the Middle East from Central Asia, overlooked the historic ecological and cultural ties between the two regions. The newly determined borders between the Middle East and Central Asia were mapped, inscribed, and made permanent in nineteenth-century European and Persian geographical literature and travel writing about the Eurasian steppes. Someone reading the Persian epic of the *Shahnama* today may find it difficult to understand why the Persian hero Rustam and his horse Rakhsh had ever crossed the distant Oxus at all.

7 AN ISLAMICATE EURASIA
Vernacular Perspectives on the Early Modern World

Gagan D. S. Sood

IN 1748, AS SAYYID MUSTAFA'S SHIP was crossing the Arabian Sea on its way to Iraq, the winds changed direction and he was forced to turn back. While waiting out the monsoon in ports along India's Malabar Coast, this pious Shi'i merchant turned his mind to the problems that were bound to arise from this unexpected detour. Of course, he knew that such vicissitudes were among the inescapable hazards of his age; they simply had to be endured and if possible turned to one's advantage. Knowing this, however, did little to raise his spirits. His journey, which was at once a commercial venture, a pilgrimage to the shrine city of Karbala, and a quest for a family tree, would now be much prolonged, delaying by nearly half a year his return home to Bengal and to his beloved son. Sayyid Mustafa was not alone in experiencing misfortune in 1748. Living close to Basra, where his ship had intended to drop anchor, Sarina was short of money and feeling abandoned. It had been a long, long time since she had last set eyes on her husband. And what was worse, she had also recently had to bid farewell to her eldest son, who was off to India to join his father. Like many wives and mothers of her Armenian community, she belonged to a family of itinerant merchants and brokers. The menfolk were expected to spend much of their lives abroad, often for years at a stretch. But they also were expected, before the onset of old age, to return and stay at home. Sarina was indignant that her husband was refusing to give her what she felt was her due, leaving her at the mercy of others.

The shared world of Sarina and Sayyid Mustafa is the subject of this chapter. They belonged to families and communities that, for their time, were literate, mobile, and cosmopolitan. Though generally excluded from high political office and seldom figuring among the ranks of the recognized cultural elites, such groups were critical in sustaining the polities within which they lived, traveled, and worked. Whether as bankers or scribes, teachers or students, their activities made possible the circulation of goods, tokens, and knowledge, as well as their exchange over many different kinds of political and cultural boundaries. These individuals, and the associations that framed their lives, thus have for us an importance for our understanding of the dynamics of the early modern world (and its differentiated transitions into modern times) that far exceeds their modest numbers. In particular, they offer us a glimpse into the society, culture, and trade of the region before its partitioning into the Middle East and South Asia, and before nation-states arose to redefine preexisting identities.

In the pages that follow, I focus on how the likes of Sayyid Mustafa and Sarina—inhabitants of a region that spanned much of what is known today as the Middle East and South Asia and that, for reasons given below, I call Islamicate Eurasia[1]—conceived of and articulated their mundane world. A sensitive appreciation of the images and ideas that allowed them to approach and make sense of their temporal surroundings is a prerequisite for any deep comprehension of their actions. Only then can we hope to situate them properly within their ambient polities and evaluate their contributions to their period and after. Unfortunately, little that is definitive is known about their everyday views, thoughts, and attitudes. This reflects in part the ongoing tendency in scholarship to stress, on the one hand, the concerns of the region's conspicuous elites, who monopolized the realms of high politics, warfare, state bureaucracy, art, the belles lettres, and formal scholarship, and, on the other hand, the concerns of the Europeans in their diverse guises.[2] But this also reflects the biases of the extant historical record and the challenges that one has to overcome when trying to derive meaningful insights from it.

The vernacular perspectives explored in this chapter are based on a close reading of a collection of documents in Arabic and Persian. Composed between 1745 and 1748 in the commercial, administrative, and spiritual centers of Iraq, the Malabar, and Bengal, it consists of about a hundred personal, business, and official letters; notarized statements; accounts; petitions; contracts; receipts; and certificates of appointment. Originally destined for settlements throughout India, these documents exhibit a wide range of rhetorical conventions and writing styles, combining in varying proportions the local idiom, the spoken vulgate, and the classical form of their writers' language. Their authors and their recipients were indigenous to the region, and include men, women, fathers, sons, wives, mothers, uncles, brothers, sisters, nephews, masters, servants, employees, teachers, students, clerics, pilgrims, and officials. The backgrounds of these individuals reveal a kaleidoscope in which the most prominent were Bengali and Iraqi Shi'is, Iraqi Armenians, Mughal Indians, and Ottoman Turks.

Through this archival miscellany, I elucidate some of the cognitive patterns used by those whose livelihoods were enmeshed in the region's arena of circulation and exchange. These patterns were appropriate and meaningful within the ambit of their daily activities, enabling them to represent, interpret, and explain to their satisfaction their perceived world, at the center of which, as described below, lay places, power, and people. But this world was not to last for much longer; it would witness partial fragmentation and major realignments from the close of the eighteenth century. The main source for these changes was the remarkable growth in Europe's political, economic, and administrative entanglement with India, the Ottoman Empire, and Iran. These produced in time fundamentally new realities. The chapter's final section outlines how these realities interacted with the conceptual repertoire inherited by the region's literate and worldly though mostly inconspicuous residents. It seems that, at around this time, their Islamicate Eurasia started to unravel; it would ultimately be replaced by confessional polities whose rulers were much more conscious of their frontiers and boundaries and were increasingly anxious to police them. As many of the older connections withered away and as new ones were cultivated under the auspices of the emerging global empires, nation-states, and multilateral associations, the gazes of the region's inhabitants shifted to other horizons, and their world in the process was refashioned.

PLACES

Hanna b. 'Abd al-Da'im's appreciation of his larger world was one that was widespread among southern Iraq's population. We can gain a sense of this appreciation because it was invoked as his constant guide in an unfinished quest that was very close to his heart. "For three years," he wrote to his son in 1747, "we have not seen from you a letter. . . . In these three years, I have written nearly a hundred letters. Some I have sent to Basra, some to Misr [Egypt] . . . , some I wrote to places on the Malabar coast, some to Cochin. I am at a loss in the matter of where to write, my son, [because] it is not known where you are."[3] This passage gives us a visceral sense of the great physical expanse over which it was unremarkable for such individuals to travel and to maintain ties, and over which their mind's eye could range with practiced ease. Clearly, their world encompassed territories as far apart as India, Egypt, and Iraq. The main impulses for such a broad outlook were, to be sure, trade and finance. But they were also inextricably bound to pilgrimage, study, and the desire for the most current information. For those who made their living primarily from commerce, transport, or communication, this physical domain was generally treated as a single arena for their activities, woven together by a dense web of continental and maritime routes; for students, teachers, and religious scholars, it was an ecumenism unified and rendered meaningful by their shared commitment to certain ineluctable fundamentals. And what enabled them to come to terms with so many places separated by such large distances was a combination of personal, collective, and inherited experiences, and the existence of a conceptual repertoire made up of a set of images and ideas.

Although there is plenty of evidence that individuals engaged in circulation and exchange were able to conceive of, and operate on, grand scales, and that they were driven to do so by multiple imperatives, there were at the same time frontiers beyond which they seldom ventured. It only requires a glance at the array of places mentioned in their correspondence to see that their affairs were often continental in scope. Closer examination, however, shows that the functional boundaries of their arena of activities never extended beyond mainland Eurasia and the Mediterranean basin, omitting notably those parts of the world incommensurable with Islamicate polities. Thus, there is not a single reference in the documents to a location—whether a region, state, province, district, port, city, town, or village—in, say, sub-Saharan Africa, Christian Europe, Southeast Asia, or East Asia. In other words, the polities within which their authors—and their families and communities—lived were, in a profound sense, always familiar to them. This would suggest that, in practice, their physical world was circumscribed by what was predominantly an Islamicate Eurasia (Figure 7.1).

Within this region, then, how did its inhabitants conceive of settlements? A series of letters written by Sayyid Mustafa, with whose predicament I opened this chapter, gives some useful pointers. While stranded on the Malabar Coast during the monsoon of 1748, he spent much of his time in Cochin. His family and associates at home in Bengal seemingly knew little, if anything, about the settlement. To help them crystallize it in their minds, he

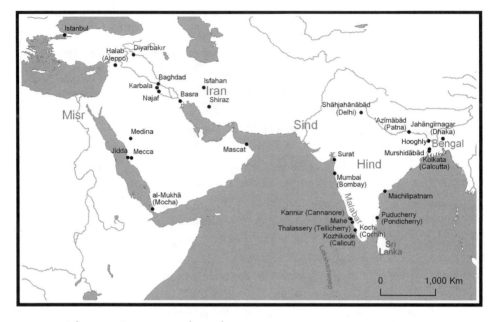

Figure 7.1. Islamicate Eurasia, c. eighteenth century.

provided a few pertinent facts. To describe the settlement, he used several different terms that indicate a definable place.[4] He often prefaced its name with the word for "port."[5] Sayyid Mustafa further noted that it was a "Dutch possession,"[6] and that it was found "half-way to Basra."[7] So we see that settlements such as Cochin were not thought of in terms of their longitude and latitude or in some other technical manner that fixed their absolute location. Rather, they were specified in terms of their surrounding area (in this case, the Malabar region), the basic features of their ambient polity (here, a port under Dutch control), and their position relative to other places that were better known (Cochin as situated between Bengal and Basra).

Cochin is one of more than a dozen settlements explicitly identified in the documents that adjoined or had easy access to the high seas. Alongside these were mentioned a similar number of inland settlements (see Table 7.1). In some cases, such as Aleppo,[8] Diyarbıkr,[9] and Isfahan,[10] the standard practice was to use its bare name on its own. But this was the exception; the toponyms of settlements were usually combined with an attribute that captured something meaningful about the place. Basra, for example, though most often

Table 7.1. Places in Islamicate Eurasia

Settlements	
Littoral	*Inland*
Basra	Azimabad (Patna)
Calcutta	Baghdad
Calicut	Diyarbıkr
Canonore	Halab (Aleppo)
Cochin	Isfahan
Hugli	Jahangirnagar (Dhaka)
Istanbul	Karbala
Jidda	Mecca
Machlipatnam (Machlibandar)	Medina
Mahe	Murshidabad
Mocha	Najaf
Pondicherry	Shahjahanabad (Delhi)
Surat	Shiraz
Suvali	
Tellicherry	

Countries	
Continental	*Maritime*
Anatolia	Lakshadweep
Bengal	Sri Lanka
Hind (India)	
Iran	
Malabar	
Misr (lower Egypt)	
Sind	

invoked without any elaboration whatsoever, was occasionally preceded by the word for "port" or "town," whereas Cochin tended to be prefaced only by the word for "port."[11] More rarely, the settlement's name was denoted not by its unique toponym but rather through a qualification of a more general term, such as the country in which it lay. Thus, *bandar-i Kālī Saylān* (the port of Sri Lanka) was used when referring to Colombo,[12] and major settlements were talked of as *bandar-i Bangālah* (the port of Bengal) or, for those of political import, *mahrūsat al-Hind* ("the guarded city of India").[13] Although the places intended by such names may not be immediately apparent to us today, deciphering them would have posed no problems for contemporaries who were fully aware of the context in which they were being aired (Table 7.1).

The attributes or epithets attached to the names of settlements often served a purpose that went beyond rhetorical adornment or the dictates of etiquette or protocol. They could convey aspects of the place's heritage or history, such as Baghdad *Dār al-salām* (the house of peace),[14] Basra *mubārak* (blessed),[15] Shiraz *Dār al-ʿilm* (the house of knowledge),[16] and Hugli *maftūh* (open or conquered).[17] Others gestured toward its spiritual function, especially if it hosted a mausoleum dedicated to a celebrated figure or a renowned place of worship, or possessed artifacts that bore witness to the central tenets of a religious tradition. Shi'is, for example, always referred to their shrine cities in Iraq as *Najaf-i ashraf* (noble Najaf) and *Karbalā'-yi muʿallā* (exalted Karbala), and Muslims generally referred to their holiest sites in the Hijaz as *Makka al-mukarrama* (revered Mecca) and *al-Madīna al-munawwara* (luminous Medina). By invoking such epithets, the individual signalled his identity and beliefs or displayed consideration for his correspondent's background. There were also terms that flagged the settlement's principal functions or its administrative or political status. Among the most commonplace were words that translate as "port," "protected," "town," and "city." These were useful for highlighting aspects of a place's multifaceted character. So, local officials tended to describe Basra as a "town" or "city,"[18] which was appropriate in view of its status as the provincial seat of government, whereas mariners and merchants—when, that is, they were inclined to use an attribute at all—focused on Basra's role as a "port."[19] Lastly, the qualifiers accompanying toponyms could be invaluable for orienting those, especially couriers and intermediaries, who might not be familiar with the locality. A letter from Iraq written in the 1740s noted that its recipient was living in ʿAzimabad "in the territories of Khan Bahadur Nawwab ʿAbd al-ʿAli Khan."[20] Another letter, dispatched at roughly the same time, stated that its destination was "Jahangirnagar in Bengal."[21]

These littoral and inland settlements are to be contrasted with a group of larger entities, which I term "countries." As with settlements, two broad types of countries may be discerned in the sources: those situated on a continental landmass and those that were islands or formed an island cluster (see Table 7.1). In contrast to settlements, the simple toponym alone normally sufficed, whether in reference to a large portion of the Indian subcontinent, such as Sind or Bengal, or to a big island, such as Sri Lanka. These names communicated a flavor of where the country lay and of its proportions, though its boundaries or frontiers were usually ill-defined and open to interpretation.[22] A case in point is the cluster of islands in the Arabian Sea that are known today as Lakshadweep, which, in testimony to its physical qualities, was occasionally prefaced by the word *hār*, meaning "string" or "necklace" in Hindvi and Persian.[23] What is beyond doubt is that such entities did not coincide with any contemporary state, however it may be defined. Rather, they invoked one or a combination of the area's historical, cultural, and topographical qualities that were known throughout the region, echoing a tradition that, in the Islamic world at least, goes back to human and classical geographers of the ninth and tenth centuries.[24]

Whether speaking of countries or settlements, the letters reveal that relatively few descriptive attributes were in common use, and those that were bore no immediate relation to the sovereign currently exercising formal authority over the place. Instead, they pointed to its history or function or prestige. It would seem, then, that the language deployed for specifying a place's location and character was determined chiefly by inherited, confessional, and practical considerations and not by obeisance to the powers that be. The mental map evinced by this repertoire gives almost no quarter to the political realm. It evokes instead a constellation of brightly shining and distinct ports, towns, and cities, embedded within a country, a kind of hazy nebula, in an otherwise dark background. In the minds of those who lived, worked, and traveled within the region, these places were linked by a dense, crisscrossing network of land and sea routes, conceived in relative, rather than absolute, terms.[25]

POWER

Perhaps the most noteworthy feature of this mental map is the tendency to shun territorial frontiers and boundaries. This runs counter to our present notions of the nation-state or even of larger regions, such as the Middle East. The most popular choices today for demarcating the limits of particular territories are topographical features and political control. In the period that I am discussing, the region's literate, urban, mobile inhabitants certainly had the experiential, conceptual, and lexical wherewithal to imagine and verbalize basic attributes of their physical geography, say, the course of a river or the break between the foothills of a mountain range and the neighboring flood-plain.[26]

But we have found that, with the partial exception of coastlines, physical geography was not a primary filter through which they viewed their world. Similarly, their correspondence dispatched while on the move displays no awareness of passing between districts, crossing into a new province, or traversing the marches of a kingdom. It was as if political markers of separation were fanciful abstractions conjured up by rulers and their courtly bureaucrats with no practical significance for those actually responsible for flows and transactions over long distances.

One way in which politics or, more broadly, sovereign power did impinge on their articulation of the world was in the recognition of a legitimate ruler or his personally delegated representative. The members of this most exclusive of clubs were imagined as embodying the polity over which they exercised their formal jurisdiction. This manifested itself verbally through the absence of direct references to the regimes over which they presided. Instead, the sources show the recurrent and widespread use of regnal titles, such as "sultan," "padishah," "nawab," and "raja." The titles bestowed upon—or, in the eighteenth century, more often wrested by—their representatives varied greatly from polity to polity. Take the case of the Arab territories of the eastern reaches of the Ottoman Empire in the 1740s. The documents note the presence of a governor, provincial governor, deputy, and district chief officer. Accounts of what happened to these officials following the demise in 1747 of Iraq's governor, Ahmad Pasha, give the impression of formal sovereignty as vested in the very person of such individuals. In the midst of the confusion surrounding the succession, a Shi'i living in Basra wrote to his son in Surat that the former "master of the seal" of Diyarbıkr had become the governor of Baghdad and that Basra was now under the rule of its former provincial governor, Muhammad Basha Ilchi.[27] Ahmad Pasha's death was obviously unexpected and resulted in a power vacuum. The letters convey the speed with which the Porte strove to make new appointments to the high-level posts necessary for maintaining order and imperial rule. Moreover, our observer describes these men as "the companions of the sultan."[28] This harmonizes with the idea that a select group of leading officials were vital for the functioning of government and their authority was in direct proportion to the strength of their personal ties to the distant sultan in Istanbul. In this conception, formal sovereignty over the polity is conflated with the sultan and his ruling companions, and it is deemed to have no viable existence independently of them.

A second way in which the realm of such elite individuals was evoked was in terms of territoriality demarcated units. These units were primarily for the purposes of extracting revenue and bureaucratic control, exemplified by the *parganah* in India.[29] But they could also refer more generally to settled areas over which the sovereign exercised full authority. In these cases, we see the use of terms such as "rule," "sovereignty," "possession,"[30] "protected,"[31] and *sarkār*.[32] What all these have in common is that they represent part of the larger entities over which the supreme rulers claimed jurisdiction. But interestingly there is no evidence in the language used by the arena's participants of the existence of such larger entities in abstraction, which, in today's parlance, we would refer to as "states" or "empires." If such entities did in fact exist as meaningful, integrated, and self-perpetuating phenomena, then the closest that these contemporaries came to recognizing them was in terms of their constitutive units. Furthermore, as these units were grounded in land that was cultivated, settled, and taxable, they presumably had clear and fixed boundaries. The sources, however, offer no direct evidence for these.

Territoriality per se is less prominent in the third way in which the arena's participants articulated legitimate and universal temporal authority. In addition to homing in on individuals or units of governance, there was the option of tapping a lexicon that may be described as canonically imperial (*rūm*) or folkloric (*ʿarab, ʿajam*) or some combination of the two—*Īrān*.[33] All of these terms functioned as synecdoches, pointing rhetorically to large, ill-defined entities, with contemporaries fully cognizant of the fact that the whole referred to that part of it invested with agency. The differences between these terms lie in the location of this agency, be it in a people, a tribal confederation, or an imperial legacy, each with its own distinctive historical and cultural associations.

The image of sovereign power that emerges on the basis of these modes of thinking is that of a supreme but far-off individual who resided in his well-guarded capital surrounded by territory that was under his sway nearby, but over which his authority gradually waned with increasing distance until a kind of no-man's-land was reached, separating formally adjacent polities. The sharply curtailed authority of the ruler and his inaccessibility that this picture highlights is in keeping with the lack of concern shown by the documents' authors for their ambient political structures or the everyday machinations of the political elites. Only when sovereign acts directly impinged on their everyday affairs, such as changes to Nadir Shah's taxation policies or a decree compelling the merchants of Baghdad to loan money to the governor's treasury, were they moved to comment on the political situation.[34] Even so, the discussions were usually anecdotal and brief, with no serious attempt made to place the events in a broader context or to interpret them from the viewpoint of their possible ramifications for their future prospects. Participants in the region's arena of circulation and exchange generally behaved as if sovereign power were far removed from the realities of their daily lives. This may appear surprising in view of the exceptionally acute political upheavals that characterised the region over much of the eighteenth century.[35]

PEOPLE

In a region as diverse as Islamicate Eurasia, it was perhaps inevitable that a counterpart of the conceptual repertoire described above was an approach toward people that was broadly tolerant and pragmatic. This is reflected in the letters' vocabulary and idiom. It suggests that the people with whom their authors dealt on a daily basis were viewed primarily through their markers of personal identity and through the collectives to which they belonged.

Personal identity was conceived mainly along cultural, relational, and social lines (see Table 7.2). By far the most widespread of the cultural markers were ethnicity, described by terms such as "Persian," "Arab," and "Abyssinian," and subjecthood, indicated by terms such as "French" and "Dutch."[36] In contrast, the religious markers deployed in these documents were essentially limited to "Muslim" and "Christian."[37] On this matter, it is worth adding that, though an individual's religious affiliation was without doubt a crucial aspect of his persona in public, this was usually left unstated. Religion, it seems, was subsidiary to ethnicity and subjecthood as a marker of difference.[38] The second category of identifiers used to differentiate individuals was relational. These were chiefly intimate or respectful in nature and included terms such as "sir," "the most generous," "venerated," "lord," "spirit," "soul," and "life." They reflected or asserted what the ties meant to those involved, and they were especially useful for signaling their—factual or imagined or desired—relationship and degree of proximity. Commonly, writers gestured to these ties not directly, with the focus primarily on the addressee, but more self-referentially, for example, by using phrases like "the one who prays [for you]" or "[your] servant." As for social markers, terms such as "the presence," "agent," "haji," and "viceroy" constituted the third (and very diverse) category of personal identifiers. They designated an individual's formal status and function in the polity by means of his titles, occupation, rank, or office.

No less foundational in conceptualizing people were terms that denoted collectives (see Table 7.3). Normally bounded in number and self-aware as coherent groupings, they were expressed by means of a lexicon and rhetorical techniques that, notwithstanding their spare character, were flexible enough to capture the salient features of the pluralistic environment. The simplicity of this language resulted in part from the remarkable paucity in everyday par-

Table 7.2. Markers of personal identity in Islamicate Eurasia

Cultural markers of identity		
Indigenous	*Foreign*	*Religious*
Abyssinian (*habashī*)	Dutch (*falamankī/walandīz*)	Christian (*masīhī*)
Angria (*angrīyah*)	English (*ankrīzī*)	Muslim (*muslim/muwahhid*)
Arab (*'arab*)	European (*farangī*)	
Armenian (*armanī/julfānī*)	French (*farānsīsī*)	
Persian (*'ajam*)	Portuguese (*purtakīsh*)	

Relational markers of identity			
Direct		Indirect	
Complimentary	*Affective*	*Devotional*	*Deferential*
āqā (sir)	*anīs* (close friend)	*dā'in* or *du'āgū* (one who prays)	*ahqar* (humblest)
mūsā (monsieur, mister)	*'azīz* (dear)		*bandah* (servant)
khātūn (lady)	*akh* (brother)		*faqīr-i dūr uftādah* (uncomprehending pauper)
sāhib (lord)	*mukarram* or *akram* (most generous, venerated)		
mawlā, khudāwand, sayyid (master, lord)	*ghālī* (precious)		*rūsīyā* (black-faced)
khwājā (man of distinction, generally applied to non-Muslim merchants)	*muhabb* (loved)		*jārīyatak* (your female slave)
	jān (spirit, soul, life)		
mihrbān or *mushfiq* (compassionate, kind)	*rūh* (spirit)		
qiblah-i qadrdān (pivot of appreciation)	*nūrchashm* (light of the eye, darling)		
qiblah-i dū jahān (pivot of the two worlds)	*barkhurdār* (successful, prosperous, for referring to juniors)		
faydbakhsh or *faydrisānah* (bestower of bounty)	*bābā* (for referring to juniors)		

(continued)

Table 7.2. (continued)

Social markers of identity		
Titles	*Occupations*	*Ranks/offices*
Honorific	**Commerce**	**Ottoman Empire**
janāb (threshold)	*tājir* or *savdāgar* (merchant)	*hākim* (governor)
bahādur (valiant)	*dallāl* (broker)	*mutassalim* (provincial governor)
hadra (presence)	*turjumān* (interpreter)	
For accomplishments	*gumāshtah* (agent)	*nā'ib* (deputy, viceroy, representative)
muqaddasī (holy)		
al-hājj or *hājjī* (one who has performed the pilgrimage to Mecca)	*khidmatkār* (servant, employee)	*kāhiya* (chief officer of a district or province)
'umdat al-tujjār (the chief of the merchants)	**Shipping and maritime**	*qādī* (judge)
fakhr al-tujjār (the pride of the merchants)	*tandīl* (head of a body of men, boatswain)	**Iran**
	sārang or *sarhang* (boat-swain, chief of lascar crew)	*pādishāh* (shah)
By birth		**India**
sayyid (descendent of the Prophet Muhammad)	*nākhudā* (skipper, master)	*nawwāb* (governor)
mīyān (nobleman)	*mu'allim* (pilot, sailing-master, mate)	*rājah* (king)
mīrzā (prince, son of great lord)	*kirānī* or *karānī* (clerk, accountant)	*qādī* (judge)
khān-sahib (nobleman)	**Writing and bookkeeping**	**Eastern Christianity**
	hafiz al-kitāb or *kātib* (scribe, secretary)	*qassīs* (priest)
	munshī (clerk, scribe)	*shammās* (deacon)
	nivīsandah (writer)	**Islamic tradition**
	kirānī or *karānī* (clerk, accountant)	*shaykh*
	Communication	*qādī* (judge)
	qāsid or *sā'in* (messenger, courier, runner)	*murīd* (Sufi novice or disciple)
	Religion and education	*mullā* (theologian)
	kāhin (diviner, priest)	**Maritime Asia**
	mullā (theologian)	*gūrnar ganral* (the British governor general in Calcutta)
		qansul (the Compagnie des Indes' Consul in Basra)
		daraktūr (the VOC's governor on the Malabar, based in Cochin)

Table 7.3. Collectives in Islamicate Eurasia

Generic nouns	Specialized terminology	Nominal phrases
tā'ifa	mahājan	all of the relatives
ahl	sinf	people [or inhabitants] of the house
bayt		the people of [or from] Shirāz
khānah		all the merchants
		the group of the people of the ship
		the men [or people] of the ship

lance of specialized terms that referred to specific corporations or groups, such as the family firm, the *mahājanī* or the trade guild. This is despite the fact that collectives of these types were vital, and known to be so, for sustaining activities that had to do with circulation and exchange. Instead, a handful of generic nouns were tapped in order to signify a wide spectrum of collectives. So, for example, the basic meaning of *tā'ifa* is "people." Depending on the context, however, it could stand for "clan," "tribe," "extended family," "religious minority," or "nation."[39] The term *ahl* is synonymous with *tā'ifa* when used in the sense of "people." But in other scenarios, it might mean "inhabitants," "followers," or, more commonly, "kin," "relatives," or "local community."[40] Furthermore, the household and the family, the social constellations that exerted the greatest influence on the daily lives of the region's inhabitants, were very often denoted by *bayt* and *khānah*.[41]

Although generic nouns such as *tā'ifa* and *ahl* were certainly not absent, it was much more common to deploy nominal phrases to articulate the region's collectives. In these constructions, to one of several words that mean "inhabitants" or "collection" or "people" or "gathering" was attached the quality shared by each of its members. This could be residence, occupation, degree of intimacy, or religious affiliation (see Table 7.3). The resulting expression then functioned as a noun. Examples of these abound. In southern Iraq, one might talk about the extended family as "all of the relatives."[42] It was more frequent, however, to convey the idea of the family through the phrase "the people [or inhabitants] of the house."[43] When describing individuals from a certain place, *ahl* was used again, but in the form of "the people of [or from] Shiraz."[44] Similarly, "all the merchants" stood for the body of recognized traders who resided locally,[45] whereas on board a ship the officers and passengers (though not the ordinary crewmen) were designated by constructions such as "the group of the people of the ship" or "the men [or people] of the ship."[46] There were exceptions, such as the phrases "the great and little" and "the old and young," which, in context, pointed to the extended family or the immediate community at home.[47] Even so, these constructions, like all the others, acknowledged explicitly that social collectives were composed of individuals.

What the everyday lexicon of these residents of Islamicate Eurasia shows is that the individuals whom they met in the course of their ordinary lives were generally identified by publicly visible personal attributes—cultural, relational, social—and by the collectives that laid bare their most pertinent biographical qualities. This lexicon's great advantage was its precision and flexibility. It allowed the region's inhabitants to distinguish effectively their arena's many varied associations and at the same time account for the great diversity in the backgrounds of their individual participants.

CONCLUSION: ISLAMICATE EURASIA IN THE AGE OF GLOBAL EMPIRES

The preceding sections examine the ideas and images that had wide currency in Islamicate Eurasia in the mid-eighteenth century. These ideas and images were regularly invoked by a historically crucial segment of the population to generate what was for them a satisfactory outlook on their world. Although their conceptual repertoire reflected their everyday reality, it also powerfully moulded the arena of circulation of exchange within which their working lives were largely played out. The feature of this arena that today we can perhaps most readily appreciate is the prevalence of large distances. This was particularly visible wherever communication or transport was at issue. The state of technology at the time—essentially confined to a choice between foot, beasts of burden, and sail—imposed fundamental constraints. Long periods of silence commonly punctuated relations between correspondents; consignments of luxury and bulk goods often took weeks or months to reach their destination; the latest news from a far-off place might have been overtaken by events since its dispatch.

Due to the timescales involved, seasons mattered and major uncertainties were endemic to a great many prosaic though formative transactions. This had two immediate consequences. The first was that boundaries between spheres that are nowadays often viewed as distinct—notably, the private, public, economic, political, and social—were highly porous or, as is more likely, nonexistent. In other words, the signal divisions in everyday life were constructed on a set of foundations entirely different from those that are familiar to us. This may be seen, for example, in the morphology of letters typically exchanged among the arena's participants. The operative distinction that they made in accounts of their daily affairs seems to have been between the personal realm and the realms that were accessible by external authoritative bodies, sovereign or otherwise. This follows quite naturally from the need to situate their activities within sufficiently broad parameters so that the information received by their correspondents was still of relevance on arrival. Thus, those who participated in the arena of circulation and exchange depicted a world shaped at once by social, political, economic, private, and public dynamics which, in their minds, could not be disentangled from one another.

The second direct consequence of the timescales that marked circulation and exchanges within the arena was the stress placed, as evidenced by their lexicon, on tolerance and pragmatism. These formed part of a troika of which the third member was trust.[48] These three qualities were critical for enabling many of the transactions that made up the stuff of daily life. Given the distances typically involved, the arena's plurality, and the prevalence of limited sovereignty, the significance accorded to tolerance, pragmatism, and trust is only to be expected. They introduced the flexibility, and facilitated access to the resources, necessary for bringing deferred, complex transactions within the reach of humble associations and even of individuals acting for their own account. Without adherence to this troika of values, the operations of the arena would have been greatly curtailed.

The arena's plurality that this troika suggests, however, was far from comprehensive. Sovereign power was, at least formally, the preserve of a tiny portion of the region's population, invariably determined by lineage. Moreover, ethnic and communal boundaries were rarely breached when it came to marriage or adoption. So there was little in the way of political and cultural plurality. There was, however, considerable plurality in economic and logistical dealings and in urban living arrangements. Many different types of associations, rooted in a remarkably diverse array of traditions, were in continuous interaction for purposes of trade, finance, communication, travel, and transport. Similarly, many different ethnic groups resided together in the region's urban settlements, even if they tended to cluster in their own quarters. It is in these senses that the word "plural" is used when describing the arena of activities of those who were mobile, literate, and worldly.

At the same time, it should not be thought that this plurality, even in its qualified form, extended to all groups. There were absences, and perhaps the most prominent were the region's conspicuous elites. Although happy to make use of the services offered by the arena, members of the ruling dynasties and government officials, as well as establishment clerics and intellectuals, were seldom involved as active participants. This separation was reinforced by the tendency of those in political authority to adopt a laissez-faire posture in relation to the arena of circulation and exchange. The vernacular mental maps conformed to this reality by ignoring political divisions in favor of ties that spanned the region. Thus, what gave this region coherence was not a unifying sovereign ideal or the existence of a single political community but rather a socioeconomic and sociocultural complex of structural connections and parallels that, respectively, linked together and were held in common by Eurasia's Islamicate polities. Important examples of these include networks sustained by various Sufi orders, families, and family firms; the rhetorics of long-distance correspondence; and the art of negotiation and contract making. Pulling together all these strands, it is because of its qualified plurality, its Islamicate character, and its physical dimensions that the region within which the arena of circulation and exchange was embedded is best labeled, so I argue, an Islamicate Eurasia.

Though the present state of research into Islamicate Eurasia's economic, social, and cultural history means that views on its formation are mostly at the stage of conjecture, there is much less doubt about its unravelling from the latter half of the eighteenth century. This coincided with the broadening and intensification of Europe's engagement with the region. What had been since the sixteenth century a relationship based primarily on economic interests, especially trade in spices and textiles, maritime transport, and credit transactions, later became enmeshed with growing concerns over security, territorial control, and direct administration. Led by Russia in the north and Britain in the south, those presiding over the region's polities became much more aware of their frontiers and were impelled as never before to police them. In the nineteenth century, these developments were reinforced by industrialization in Europe, speedier communication and travel, and the consolidation of Europe's global empires. This occurred in step with the fall of Islamic dominion throughout much of the region, the emergence of well-defined sovereign borders, and the diffusion and internalization of previously unfamiliar categories promoted by regimes increasingly assertive at all levels of their polity. The result was a simultaneous contraction and reorientation of the everyday world of those who made their living through the circulation and exchange of people, tokens, knowledge, and goods.

The convergence of these events and trends had a transformative effect on the shared ideas and images that are the subject of this chapter. The deepening involvement in the region of centralizing regimes and the growing saliency of territoriality intersected with a more restricted plurality and with heightened religious and political dogma to produce a reconfigured ecumenism. Much of the conceptual repertoire of earlier times proved incompatible with this environment. The result was cognitive rupture. Islamicate Eurasia as a region was ultimately supplanted by global empires, nation-states, and multilateral associations and was divided between a Middle East and a South Asia. Faced with this, the descendants of Sayyid Mustafa and Sarina had no realistic choice but to craft and learn a fresh language more in keeping with the new, emerging world order.

8 SCORCHED EARTH

The Problematic Environmental History That Defines
the Middle East

Diana K. Davis

> *Nowhere in all the waste around was there a foot of shade, and*
> *we were scorched to death . . . in this blistering, naked, treeless*
> *land [Palestine].*
> —**Mark Twain, *The Innocents Abroad*, 1869**

> *[In Algeria] . . . the resplendent sun . . . the almost imperceptible*
> *vibrating of the air above the scorched earth.*
> —**Gustave Guillaumet, "Tableaux Algériens," 1879**

> *The Negeb is barren and sun-scorched, . . . [and] marauding*
> *nomads . . . swoop down . . . killing . . . destroying . . . [and]*
> *contribut[ing] to the creation of "man-made" deserts.*
> —**Walter Lowdermilk, *Palestine: Land of Promise*, 1944**

NO OTHER REGION ON THE PLANET, except, perhaps, the polar zones, has been
more strongly defined by its environment than the Middle East. From Morocco to Afghanistan, many writings on the Middle East, penned today and in
the past, contain detailed descriptions of the profound aridity and dearth of
vegetation in most of the region. Phrases such as "the highest percentage of
land at high risk for desertification in the world" are all too commonly applied to the Middle East. Such descriptions are also nearly inevitably accompanied by histories of environmental degradation wrought over centuries or
millennia by ignorant and destructive indigenous populations. Deforestation,
overgrazing, and over-irrigation by humans are most commonly blamed for
ruining what is often claimed to have been a much lusher, more forested, and
more fertile environment in the past (Figure 8.1). Such long-standing environmental histories of the Middle East, though, were largely constructed by European colonial (and Mandate) powers in the nineteenth and early twentieth
centuries and were based on questionable evidence.

Figure 8.1. Camel bones in southern Morocco. Photo by the author.

Recent scientific research has questioned the rate and extent of deforestation and desertification in the region as well as the assumed destructiveness of
grazing. This new research argues that much of the arid environment of the
Middle East is remarkably resilient rather than fragile, as it has been portrayed for a long time.[1] The extensive grazing systems of nomadic pastoralists,
in fact, have been shown to be the most environmentally appropriate and
sustainable land uses for large areas of the Middle East. Despite this new evidence, the conventional environmental history of a desertified landscape persists, in large part because it is frequently politically expedient. Such environmental crisis narratives are very useful to raise international funds, to justify
the control of local populations (the sedentarization of nomads, for example),
and to help shape national development plans.[2] This chapter provides an overview of several of the mainstream environmental histories of the Middle East
and explores the primary documentation on which they are based. It argues
that such conventional environmental narratives were constructed and used
by colonial powers in large part to dominate many states in the Middle East,
to justify the appropriation and extraction of resources (especially land), and
to control local populations. The continued use of this environmental narrative by Western and Middle Eastern powers today raises interesting geopolitical and geoeconomic questions.

Before the technology was developed in the mid-twentieth century to sci-
entifically reconstruct past vegetation through the analysis of proxy data such

Figure 8.2. Fords of the Jordan by A. W. Calcott. Horne, *Landscape Illustrations of the Bible: Consisting of the Most Remarkable Places Mentioned in the Old and New Testaments,* 1836, p. 17.

as fossil pollen, environmental history relied primarily on the written word. It was very common, therefore, for Europeans in foreign lands, especially in the Mediterranean basin and the Middle East, to compare what they saw in the landscape with what they had read about in the works of the ancient authors of the classical world and in holy books or to what they had seen rendered in paintings and sketches (Figure 8.2). They incorrectly interpreted widespread and often splendid ruins from earlier times as proof that larger populations had enjoyed a much more fertile and productive environment in the past. They then assumed that destructive practices of local populations had ruined the environment.

The fact that the idea of geologic time, spanning millions of years, was not widespread until the mid- to late nineteenth century meant that past climate changes were grossly misunderstood. The Sahara desert, for example, we know now was indeed much wetter between 6500 B.C.E. and 4500 B.C.E., during which time it supported a great deal of savanna woodland vegetation, many lakes, and large mammals such as hippopotami. After this period, however, a drying trend occurred, and the Sahara gradually transformed into the great desert it is today by about 1500 B.C.E.[3] In a worldview constrained by the conception of biblical time, however, these huge shifts in climate appeared to have taken place in only a few thousand, or a few hundred, years because the world was believed to be only about six thousand years old. The publication of Charles Lyell's *Principles of Geology* in 1830 and then Charles Darwin's *On the Origin of Species* in 1859, of course, helped to change this conception of time, making it possible to consider a significantly longer history of the planet by the end of the nineteenth century.

The framework for the conventional environmental narrative of ruin and decay in the region had already been formed by the mid-nineteenth century, though, and it was not much changed by this new knowledge and these important intellectual innovations. Thus, in 1909, it is not surprising that T. E. Lawrence could write to his mother from Palestine that "it is such a comfort to know that the country was not a bit like this in the time of our Lord. The Renaissance painters were right who drew him and his disciples feasting in a pillared hall, or sunning themselves on marble staircases: everywhere one finds the remains of splendid Roman roads and houses and public buildings. . . . [T]he country was well-peopled, and well-watered . . . [and] . . . they did not come upon dirty, dilapidated Bedouin tents. . . . Palestine was a decent country then, and so could easily be made so again."[4] (See Figure 8.3.)

The idea that the Mediterranean region and the Middle East were ruined landscapes in need of resurrection became very popular among Europeans in the nineteenth century. By constructing the environmental history of an environment degraded by centuries or millennia of neglect and abuse, European powers also frequently concocted justifications for colonial policies and laws in many of these lands. What I call here a declensionist environmental narrative, that is, an environmental history of degradation, was one of the central leitmotifs in the discourse of European imperialism during the nineteenth and early twentieth centuries. Cyprus, for example, came under the control of the British in 1878 in part because the British claimed they could manage the island better than the Cypriots and, in particular, save the forests.[5]

Figure 8.3. Bedouin tents. Elmendorf, *A Camera Crusade Through the Holy Land*, 1912, plate lxiv.

Most of the arguments for a ruined, deforested, and desertified landscape in the Middle East rested on the assumption that about two thousand to three thousand years ago the region was substantially more forested, and therefore more fertile, and less eroded. What the paleoecological evidence shows, however, is that the most significant changes in vegetation, especially arboreal vegetation, took place six thousand to ten thousand years ago, millennia before the period most commonly identified as the one during which the local peoples destroyed the land.

In the Levant, for example, existing evidence shows that the most significant changes in vegetation took place between eight thousand and twelve thousand years ago as the climate warmed.[6] In this part of the Middle East, tree cover declined abruptly after the end of the last ice age and then fluctuated, sometimes greatly, for the next several thousand years. Some species, such as deciduous oak, appear to have declined fairly consistently, whereas others, such as evergreen oak and pine, have experienced large increases and de- creases periodically and an overall increase in the last couple of thousand years. Cedar, however, declined dramatically at the end of the Pleistocene and never recovered, leading some to argue that it is a relict species from the last glacial period. And yet the presumed destruction of cedar forests has pro- voked some of the most woeful lamentations and vitriolic condemnations of local peoples in discussions of environmental history in the Levant since the nineteenth century.[7]

Some of these changes in tree species may have been influenced by human activity to a certain degree, but they were also certainly influenced by changes in climate over the last ten thousand years. The climate in the Mediterranean basin has experienced a slow warming and drying trend since the last ice age, but it has also experienced several significant wet periods during this time. The overall pattern was of oscillating humid and dry conditions until about 1000 B.C.E. or 1500 B.C.E. when it is widely agreed that the climate and most vegetation conditions stabilized in the more arid pattern still found today (see Figure 8.4).[8] The changes in vegetation over the last two thousand to three thousand years, therefore, are not nearly as significant as they were believed to have been during the colonial period.

In the Maghreb, where more paleoecological evidence is available, pollen core analysis shows that the significant changes in vegetation occurred about eight thousand years ago when trees and some shrubs increased dramatically after the end of the last ice age.[9] Although there have been declines and in- creases in various species over the last several thousand years, the evidence does not support the widespread belief, as commonly claimed during the French colonial period, that between 50 percent and 80 percent of North Africa's original forest cover has been deforested since the Roman era.

DESERT WASTES OF THE MAGHREB

One of the earliest examples of the construction and utilization of a declen- sionist environmental narrative to justify and facilitate colonial rule is found in French North Africa. Algeria, Tunisia, and Morocco were well known to many in France and the rest of Europe as fertile lands long before the 1830

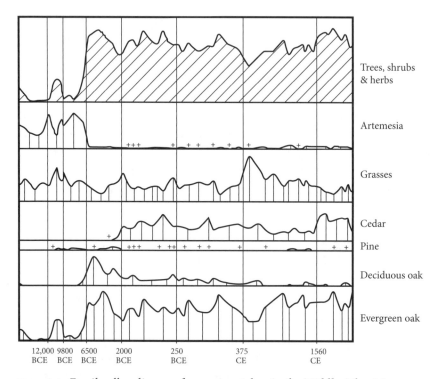

Figure 8.4. Fossil pollen diagram from a core taken in the Middle Atlas, Morocco, showing the changing levels of plant pollen over the last 14,000 years. Diagram by the author after Lamb, Eicher, and Switsur, "An 18,000-Year Record of Vegetation" (1989), 65–74.

conquest of Algiers inaugurated the French colonial project in North Africa. Until the mid-1830s, the most common environmental narrative of North Africa was a benign one of a lapsed fertility blamed on local negligence and Ottoman ineptitude rather than a narrative of willful destruction by local peoples. By the time the French had conquered Algeria and incorporated it as a province of France in 1848, however, this narrative began to change to one of environmental destruction, and subsequent desiccation, by the "natives," especially by the nomadic pastoralists who formed the majority of the population in the early nineteenth century. This declensionist narrative was refined over the course of the nineteenth century and used widely, not only in Algeria but also in Tunisia and Morocco as they were occupied by the French, to execute many imperial goals.[10]

Both the precolonial and the colonial narratives commonly assumed that in the past North Africa had been "the most fertile region of the world," a belief instilled primarily by familiar French readings of classical sources.[11] Many authors claimed that North Africa had been the granary of Rome. Partisans supported this interpretation by arguing that the numerous Roman ruins found in North Africa proved that large populations had thrived in a more fertile environment (Figure 8.5).[12] Such a view was given official sanction and became very widespread by its repeated iteration in such official government publications as, among many others, the monumental and highly influential *Exploration scientifique de l'Algérie*. In 1847, for instance, one of the contributing authors to this compendium, a physician, wrote that "this land, once the object of intensive cultivation, was neither deforested nor depopulated as today. . . . [I]t was the abundant granary of Rome."[13] This particular quote also reveals some of the key negative changes that began to be made to the narrative early in the colonial period.

The colonial environmental narrative, by the 1860s, had evolved to place the blame for the assumed deforestation and desertification of North Africa on the "hordes" of Arab nomads and their ravenous herds. From mid-century onward, the most common version of the colonial narrative attributed the onset of environmental destruction to the "Arab invasions" of the seventh and eleventh centuries. The Hillalian "tribal invasion" of the eleventh century was especially condemned for the presumed destruction it wreaked on cities and the natural environment alike. The French drew selectively on medieval Arab historians for their evidence of the devastation of North Africa's environment by Arab nomads and their flocks over the previous eight centuries. Carefully chosen parts of the writings of Ibn Khaldun, in particular, were used to portray negatively Arab nomads and their "destruction," despite the fact that Ibn Khaldun actually wrote about nomads in a very complex way, praising them as well as condemning them. As a result, Ibn Khaldun was widely and frequently cited as proof that, in the words of the influential geographer Augustin Bernard, "the Arabs have been fatal . . . by their way of life and their habits; it is their sheep, their camels, their goats that have ruined North Africa."[14]

The contemporary pastoralists that the French encountered when they occupied North Africa were assumed to be the direct descendants of these eleventh-century "invaders," and their "destructive habits" were said to have been passed down with each generation, further damaging the environment during the intervening centuries. This narrative became ubiquitous and

Figure 8.5. Photo of Roman ruins at Cuicul, Djemila, Algeria. The original caption reads, "Numerous monumental arches mark the ruins of the ancient Cuicul, Djemila, magnificent evidence of Roman power in Africa. In the midst of a country then wooded, it was a vacation and summer holiday town." Alzonne, *Clément L'Algérie*, 1937, p. 6. Courtesy of the author.

very powerful in Algeria by 1870 and was applied liberally in both Tunisia and Morocco, as they were occupied in 1881 and 1912, respectively. The narrative remained influential into the independence period of the mid-twentieth century. During the centennial celebrations of France's victory over Algeria, for example, a government publication on the history of Tunisia proclaimed that "the profound convulsions that since the Roman era have upset the country: the passage of the Arab armies and later the Hillalian tribal invasion . . . have made of this country a desert strewn with ruins which, however, attest to its ancient prosperity."[15]

Just as historical research has shown that the land in North Africa produced no more, and in fact less, grain during the Roman period than it did during the colonial period, contemporary research in arid lands ecology and pastoral studies highlights the fact that traditional land uses, particularly extensive grazing, are not inherently destructive.[16] Many experts have concluded, contrary to colonial claims, that Roman overcultivation was followed by "a phase of relative soil conservation and vegetative regeneration with the more nomadic land use system of the Arabs."[17] Equally important, paleo-ecological studies have not provided evidence of massive deforestation over the last two millennia, as was commonly claimed during the colonial period.[18] Rather, the majority of deforestation that has been documented in fact resulted from European activities during the colonial period itself, especially from 1880 to 1930 when the colonial narrative was at its apogee.

This declensionist environmental narrative was constructed slowly beginning in the early part of the colonial period primarily to facilitate particular colonial objectives such as the acquisition of land and resources as well as to control the local populations. As the pastoralists and their herds were increasingly blamed for irrationally destroying forests and for creating deserts, it became easier for the administration and colonists to justify the confiscation of much of their land, including forests, in the name of environmental protection or increased productivity. One of the most important and effective ways this was accomplished was through the passage of new forestry, land use, and land tenure laws.

As early as 1838, for example, new laws were passed in Algeria that outlawed, for environmental reasons, the burning of any trees or scrub. By 1846 this law was expanded to include the burning of any agricultural land, and the fines and penalties were raised steeply.[19] Criminalizing these ecologically appropriate land uses severely curtailed the livelihoods of many Algerians who depended on the traditional technique of burning in and near forests to prepare agricultural land as well as to create better pastures for livestock. Increasingly draconian forest laws, justified with the declensionist narrative, were passed in 1874 and 1885 that criminalized nearly all indigenous uses of the forests. The colonial environmental narrative itself was actually incorporated into the 1903 Algerian Forest Law, the earliest and most comprehensive of the French colonial forest laws.[20] Similarly wide-ranging and socially detrimental laws invoking the declensionist narrative were passed in the name of environmental protection in all of the Maghreb territories until the end of the colonial period.

Land tenure laws also depended heavily on the colonial environmental narrative for their justification and passage. One of the most infamous of these laws was the 1873 Warnier Law, although earlier laws had also invoked all or part of the narrative, including the 1851 land law. The Warnier Law utilized the declensionist narrative for much of its justification, claiming that nomads (and all those who held collective property) wreaked environmental destruction wherever they went. This law provided the mechanism that allowed collective property of the nomadic pastoralists and others to be transformed into private property and thereby made into a commodity to be easily sold.[21] As a result of this law, most of what remained of "collective tribal land" in Algeria was dismembered. Much of this land was sold to settlers, but a substantial amount was also confiscated by the state on the grounds that it was being "wasted." This law provided the precedent for several subsequent land tenure laws in Algeria, and as a result of these laws, the Algerians lost about 75 percent of the best agricultural land to European colonists and the state by the end of the colonial period. Very similar laws, using the same justifications based on the declensionist narrative, that were passed in Tunisia and Morocco had comparable effects. These laws, and others that invoked the environmental narrative, also led to the pauperization and immiseration of a large portion of the North African population, profoundly disrupting their traditional livelihoods and resulting in their proletarianization.[22]

This colonial environmental narrative of the Maghreb became deeply entrenched in many official publications written during the colonial period, including forestry and agricultural manuals, histories, and botanical treatises, not only in Algeria but also in Tunisia and Morocco. By the 1930s and 1940s, the declensionist narrative had been formalized, quantified, and institutionalized in the science of plant ecology across the Maghreb.[23] These publications ensured the long legacy of the colonial narrative because much subsequent education, research, and policy formulation relied heavily on these ecological and historical works imbued with the declensionist narrative, including, for example, inaccurate deforestation statistics. The resulting environmental history was widely accepted by the postcolonial governments of North Africa and has become the dominant environmental history of the region still in widespread use today.

DEGRADED EDEN: THE LEVANT

A similar environmental story was told for the Levant, at the opposite end of the Mediterranean basin. Although official European imperial rule did not begin until the twentieth century, the French and British were involved in the Levant in various capacities during the nineteenth century, as were missionaries from these and other countries including Americans.[24] The environmental narrative of deforestation and desertification is as strong in several ways in the Levant as it is in the Maghreb. Similarly, it is often the nomads, here called Bedouin, who were blamed for presumed environmental destruction by commentators during the nineteenth and twentieth centuries. This story is somewhat more complicated, however, due to the number of countries with vested interests active in the region since the nineteenth century.

From early in the nineteenth century, a common Western perception of the Levant was that it was largely a fertile region, although it had some areas of desert where agriculture was difficult.[25] A Western traveler wrote in 1859, for example, that "the whole country [Palestine] is thickly studded with villages, the plains clothed with grass or grain, and the rounded hills with orchards of olive, fig, pomegranate, and other trees."[26] Such early writings did not contain many descriptions of the destruction of forests or the degradation of land by overgrazing.

By the end of the century, though, this narrative of fertility changed to one of lapsed fertility and environmental overuse (timber harvesting), and for some, to one of environmental ruin. There were those concerned with perceived deforestation, such as the French diplomat who wrote that "the magnificent woods in the Aleppo district . . . are being destroyed by charcoal burners and oak-bark strippers. . . . In Syria and Palestine forests no longer exist."[27] Others lamented the loss of vineyards saying that "the disappearance of vineyards and not of forests is the difference with which we have to reckon in the landscape of Palestine."[28]

Some with an interest in settling the region perceived the environment as full of potential but sadly mismanaged. If only the "curse of the country, . . . bad government and oppression" could be lifted, "Palestine would become once more a land of corn, vines, and olives, rivaling in fertility and in wealth its ancient condition, as deduced from careful study of such notices as remain to us in the Bible and in the later Jewish writings," wrote a member of the Palestine Exploration Fund (PEF) in the 1870s.[29] Another member of the PEF, however, Professor Edward Palmer, blamed the Arab nomad "invaders" and their descendants, the contemporary Bedouin, for ruining the environment and creating the desert.[30] His is one of the earliest iterations of what would become one of the dominant declensionist environmental narratives in the twentieth century. Palmer was murdered in 1882 by Bedouins in the Sinai.[31]

During this period, Western interest in Palestine grew steadily and included an increasing number of people who wanted to settle in Palestine. Not surprisingly, the Ottoman administration received a lot of blame for environmentally destructive policies from the late nineteenth century to well into the British Mandate period (1920–48). One of many policies blamed for the destruction was the so-called Ottoman tree tax. Many tales recount how villagers cut down fruit trees, and even entire orchards, in order to avoid this tax. Estelle Blyth, the daughter of the Anglican bishop of Jerusalem and secretary for the Palestine Exploration Fund, wrote that "to escape the tree tax, the men from a village in the Hebron district one winter cut down some five hundred trees, in all stages of growth and promise, and left them lying where they fell."[32] It appears that this tax was limited to agricultural (fruit and nut) trees and not forest trees, because the tax seems to have been levied on the potential products harvested from the trees. It likely had little effect, therefore, on the natural vegetation of the region. Such stories, moreover, may have been exaggerated due to many writers' bias against the Ottoman administration. In fact, the Ottomans had invited the French to help them develop a forest law in the 1860s, which resulted in the 1870 Réglements des Forêts.[33] This law later informed the British forest law in Palestine during the Mandate period.

By the early twentieth century, Jewish settlers in Palestine took advantage of the narrative of deforestation to justify tree planting that had as its primary aim the appropriation of rural land. The Jewish National Fund, for example, planted forest trees on land bought from local peoples "in order to hold the land purchased," although the publicized purpose was "the provision of jobs and the improvement of Palestine's landscape and environment."[34] Tree planting was a particularly good way to claim land and thus to prevent Arab pastoralists from having access to traditional grazing land under the machinations of Ottoman law.[35] Competition for land between Zionist settlers and Palestinians became more frequent and more intense after the 1880s and motivated questionable actions by both groups. Afforestation by the settlers continued into the Mandate period, although not over significantly large areas. Hence, the declensionist narrative was used to help appropriate land for the new immigrants.

A forest service was established under the British in 1920, and its mission was, in part, to try to repair the "centuries of neglect" under the Ottomans that had resulted in the "denudation of Palestine's forests."[36] The narrative of deforestation and desertification in Palestine and the Transjordan was made official during the British Mandate period in several ways. The forest department reported in 1936, for example, that half the habitable area had become "an artificial desert due to overgrazing."[37] The Peel Report of 1937 stated that although Palestine now had no "real" forests, it should be (and was in the past) at least 15 percent forested. The forest law in Mandate Palestine, known as the Woods and Forest Ordinance (1920), was based on the forest law of Cyprus developed under the British and the 1870 forestry law developed for the Ottomans by the French.[38] The primary goal of the Woods and Forest ordinance was to "protect the remaining areas of woodland and scrub from unauthorized cultivation, cutting or burning and the depredations of grazing animals."[39] The Forestry Ordinance of 1926 went further and defined forest resources as state forests and state reserves, thereby officially protecting about 72,000 hectares of forest, scrubland, and potential forest.[40]

Livestock grazing, particularly that conducted by Arab villagers and Bedouin, came under special attack for causing (and having caused for centuries) deforestation and desertification during the Mandate period. The forest service strongly recommended that grazing be curtailed and restricted and that an ambitious program of reforestation be implemented. Overgrazing was blamed, incorrectly for the most part, for preventing forest and other plant growth and causing erosion and thus for water loss and dune mobilization. The Arab pastoralists were deemed such a threat by the forest department that in 1936 it strongly recommended that fully half of the pasture lands in Palestine should be permanently protected from grazing and be reforested.[41] Up to that point, only about 700,000 *dunums* of Palestinian land (2.5 percent) actually had been designated as forest reserves. After the Arab Rebellion of 1936–39, however, the activities of the forest department were curtailed and those in the high levels of administration referred to the department as a "dummy department."[42] The administration feared that restricting the Arabs' rights to grazing with aggressive forestry policies might provoke more unrest.

The demonization of grazing, and thus of the humans who owned the livestock, mostly Arab pastoralists, also played a part in the justification of two significant laws in the 1940s: the Bedouin Control Ordinance of 1942 and the Shepherds Ordinance of 1946.[43] Both of these laws aimed to control and curtail the movement of livestock and people, in part in the name of environmental protection. The actual effect that these two laws had in the 1940s, though, was likely small, coming as they did late in the Mandate period. The importance of these laws lies, rather, in the institutionalization of the declensionist environmental narrative that blamed the Arab pastoralists for the majority of the presumed deforestation and desertification down through the centuries. They also illustrate the utilization of the declensionist narrative for the social control of "undesirable" populations. By 1947, the narrative was found even in influential botanical treatises of the region, such as Paul Mouterde's *The Arborescent Vegetation of the Levant*. This botanist stated that the mountains were "covered nearly entirely [in trees] two thousand years before our era, in the Bronze age. But, since antiquity, to establish agriculture and make livestock pastures, humans have attacked the dense cover and reduced it to these meager relicts."[44]

With the creation of the state of Israel in 1948, the declensionist narrative was enshrined, and it has been used for decades to justify forestry, agricultural, and social policies (Figure 8.6). Prime Minister David Ben-Gurion proclaimed in an opening session of the Knesset in 1951 that "we are a state at the beginning of repairing the corruption of generations, corruption which was done to the nation and corruption which was done to the land. . . . [W]e must plant hundreds of thousands of trees . . . [comprising] a quarter of the area of the state. We must wrap all the mountains . . . and their slopes in trees . . . [and] the dry lands of the Negev."[45] As Shaul Cohen has pointed out, the new politics of planting in Israel had several purposes including security for the military, memorials for special persons, and, perhaps most important, "as a method for the prevention of grazing or cultivation on the land that the government did not want to fall into or return to the hands of the Arab[s]."[46]

Likely as a result of this rhetoric, the old narrative of the ruin of the Levantine environment by the Arab (nomad) conquests was revived and found its way into the writings of many in the 1940s, 1950s, and 1960s. It was assumed that environmental destruction during the Islamic conquests had been exacerbated by the overgrazing of Arab nomads' livestock over the intervening centuries, especially in the southern parts of Israel. American Walter Lowdermilk helped to highlight and spread this narrative in his many writings on soil erosion in the Middle East. His 1944 *Palestine, Land of Promise* is replete with accusations of destruction wrought by the Arab invaders in the seventh and thirteenth centuries and by pastoral nomads in the region since. He blamed them for deforestation, overgrazing, erosion, and desertification. He visited Palestine to make his three-month study at the end of the "Arab

Figure 8.6. The Balfour Forest above the Jezreel Valley, 1947. The Balfour Forest was planted on rocky land near Kibbutz Ginegar purchased by the Jewish National Fund in the 1920s to commemorate Lord Balfour, author of the Balfour Declaration. Photograph by Zoltan Kluger. Reproduced with the kind permission of the National Photo Collection, the Government Press Office, Israel.

Revolt" in 1939, and he displays a very negative and biased opinion of Arabs, and especially nomads, throughout this book.[47]

This declensionist narrative was incorporated, in large part, into Israeli histories of the Levant and may still be found today. Professor Adolf Reifenberg of the Hebrew University recounted this narrative, blaming the Arab invasions and subsequent Arab nomads for the deforestation and desertification of large parts of Israel and Transjordan in his 1955 *The Struggle Between the Desert and the Sown*, as have more contemporary Israeli scholars.[48] Recent research in the Negev, however, demonstrates that this claim is not true. The ruined and abandoned settlements that for so long have been blamed on the destructiveness of the Arab conquests, overgrazing, and subsequent desertification were in fact abandoned because of profound changes in regional politics and economics. The erosion present in the region "cannot be linked to the over-grazing that is often tied to . . . pastoral incursions. . . . In short, the Islamic conquests . . . did not bring any desertification."[49] The author of this work, Steve Rosen, professor at Ben-Gurion University, warns in the conclusion of his article that claims of overgrazing have been used to legitimize the "expropriation of Bedouin grazing lands. . . . The notion of Islamic invasions . . . in fact, masks political agendas."[50]

CONCLUSION

Similar long-standing arguments claiming desertification due to centuries of overgrazing by Arab nomads in Libya and southern Jordan likewise recently have been shown to be false.[51] Other narratives of ruined environments exist in other parts of the Middle East, the analysis of which is not possible in the space of this chapter. The story of the over-irrigation and ruin of Iraqi agricultural land, for example, needs closer scrutiny due to recent research on sea level and coastline changes associated with the end of the last ice age. Egypt has at least two primary declensionist environmental narratives worthy of investigation: one of deforestation, desiccation, and desertification, and the other of squandered irrigation expertise and thus lost agricultural lands. Such narratives have been used to implement large water and other development projects as well as to relocate sizable marginalized populations.

What is clear, even from this brief survey of parts of the Middle East, is that the dominant environmental narrative of the region is one of a ruined, desertified environment. The examination presented here of the basis for such a conclusion, however, suggests that much of this declensionist narrative is unfounded, and moreover, it is largely a social construction closely associated with imperialism. By interrogating such stories, one of my aims is to redeem the "desert wastes" of the Middle East. Only when the Middle East environment is seen without the mutually reinforcing lenses of imperialism and Orientalism can appropriate, sustainable, and socially just development in these "naturally" arid regions be possible. The continued use of the declensionist narrative has resulted in too many environment and development projects such as the "green dam" in Algeria and the accidental creation of "green deserts" in some nature reserves in Israel that have done more social and environmental harm than good.[52]

For the most part, scholars have yet to explore these complex topics and their contemporary implications for the Middle East and North Africa, despite a thriving and growing literature in critical environmental history for other regions such as sub-Saharan Africa and South Asia.[53] Much of this work demonstrates the relevance, even urgency, of understanding environmental narratives that often reach back to the colonial period for contemporary efforts toward economic development and environmental conservation that is socially just. This lacuna has been noted by recent scholarship in environmental history, although few have begun to analyze the environmental history of the Middle East from a critical perspective.[54] Even fewer researchers have examined the important relationship between environmental narratives and European imperialism (and proto-imperialism) that is so important to understanding the Middle East and North Africa, which this chapter has begun to explore.

Because so much "scientific" research on the Middle East has been conducted by Europeans (and Americans) steeped in the declensionist narrative, this inaccurate narrative has been incorporated into the educational and research systems of the postcolonial Middle East just as it has in much of the global north. Many people in the region, from researchers to government administrators to average citizens, subscribe to it. If the majority of people in the Middle East hold a common identity as inhabitants of a degraded environment, what, then, are the political, economic, and social ramifications of this? One answer is the type of environmental development exemplified by the United Arab Emirates in recent years, which overexploits groundwater reserves in a highly unsustainable manner to "roll back the desert" with a variety of afforestation and other "greening" projects.[55] A second result is the sort of agricultural/social development currently being implemented in Egypt's Western Desert with the building of the Toshka canal. This "New Valley Project" aims to restore the "ancient fertility" of the region and to produce modern organic produce in the pristine desert environment for the "new, clean" model Egyptian citizen.[56] A third outcome is the kind of economic development typified by the hugely expensive indoor ski resort in Dubai that has prompted local people to comment that "now it is Europe here too."[57] Exploration of such questions for the Middle East holds promise for meaningful research that may well help to bring about more appropriate, sustainable, and less socially exploitative development in these splendid desert spaces in the future.

CHALLENGING EXCEPTIONALISM:
THE CONTEMPORARY MIDDLE EAST
IN GLOBAL PERSPECTIVE

Part III

9 AMERICAN GLOBAL ECONOMIC POLICY AND THE CIVIC ORDER IN THE MIDDLE EAST

James L. Gelvin

FROM THE PERSPECTIVE of twentieth-century political economy, the notion of a Middle East provides an analytical vantage point that is useful but incomplete. It is useful because it highlights the characteristics shared by a number of contiguous states in Southwest Asia and North Africa, although, admittedly, those characteristics are not necessarily exclusive to the region, and the borders demarcating the region are not necessarily consistent (e.g., see Chapter 3). It is incomplete because the trajectory of the political economy of any set of contiguous states is constrained by the broader global and extra-regional political economic systems in which it is situated. Political economic histories must, therefore, take account of those systems, as well as their effects on constituent subsystems. The purpose of this chapter is to reconstruct the political economic history of the Middle East in the twentieth century, keeping these caveats in mind.

A NEW CIVIC ORDER FOR THE MIDDLE EAST

In the aftermath of the economic crisis spawned by the Great Depression and industrial growth spawned by World War II, increasing numbers of Middle Easterners moved to cities, sold their labor, and became integrated into the political process. Although postwar governments in the region were hardly democratic, they did have to respond to the aspirations and needs of newly urbanized and politicized populations to survive. Some—not all—Middle Eastern states responded by adopting an increasingly popular-nationalist rhetoric that appealed to those populations. More important, all states throughout the region responded to popular demands and expectations by taking on many of the trappings of post–World War II welfare states in Europe and North America. Over time, they introduced new economic planning boards, labor laws, and educational and welfare benefits for their citizens. In return, they expected compliance and support. Overall, then, there was a transformation of what a number of historians have called the "civic order"— the "norms and institutions that govern relations among citizens and between citizens and the state."[1] The concept of civic order enables us to unite the so-called populist/authoritarian states and others within a common framework.

Four factors encouraged the broadening and deepening of the new civic order. The first was the heritage of defensive developmentalism and imperialism in the region. During the nineteenth century, the Ottoman Empire, the semi-autonomous Ottoman province of Egypt, and, to a lesser (but perhaps underappreciated) extent, Persia began experimenting with institutions and structures designed to expand the reach of the state and more effectively mobilize and harness the social power of their populations. Whatever the efficacy of individual programs initiated by Middle Eastern states, the overall result was a fundamental shift in attitudes about statecraft and social practice among both political elites and populations upon which later generations of statesmen and politicians might build.[2]

During the post–World War I period, independent states in the region based the institutions and structures they needed to construct on prevailing international and regional models, whereas territories that remained under colonial occupation or mandatory control found those institutions and structures imposed upon them. Thus, in the case of Turkey, ruling elites consciously drew their post–World War I developmental strategies and ruling bargains from Western models popular at the time of regime consolidation and, in the case of Iran, the example of Turkey was thrown into the mix as well. In the Levant and Egypt, France, Britain, and, during World War II, the United States imposed developmental strategies and ruling bargains directly, drawing on their own experiences with wartime mobilization and Depression-era statism. For example, during the 1930s, the French government attempted to maintain social peace in its increasingly restive mandatory territories by exporting Popular Front–style welfare policies to Syria and Lebanon. During World War II, Britain and the United States imposed New Deal–style regulatory and industrial development policies in Egypt and the Levant under the auspices of the Middle East Supply Center.[3] Over time, the governments of other states—Jordan and Saudi Arabia, for example—initiated similar programs in response to challenges posed by their revolutionary neighbors, strictures imposed by international financial institutions, or the spirit of the times.[4]

The second factor that secured the new civic order in the region was the nurturing environment created by the postwar international economic system, the Bretton Woods system. Two aspects of the system are important here. First, the Bretton Woods system established a global economic structure marked by what political scientist John Gerard Ruggie has termed "embedded liberalism."[5] This is a system in which economic decision making on issues such as trade and tariffs were handled multilaterally whereas individual states were free to pursue Keynesian principles in their domestic economy. This enabled states to set economic policies and goals, such as full employment or industrial expansion, independently. As Fred L. Block puts it, "It is one of the stranger ironies of international monetary history that the men who actually dominated U.S. international monetary policy during World War II were far more sympathetic to national capitalism than to the idea of an open world economy. In fact, the International Monetary Fund, designed to be the central institution of the postwar monetary order, was shaped initially by national capitalist assumptions."[6]

This brings us to the second aspect of the Bretton Woods system that is important for our argument: the two Bretton Woods institutions, the International Monetary Fund and the World Bank. The initial role of the IMF was to ensure the overall stability of the system. The initial role of the World Bank was to promote development by funding large-scale infrastructural projects. "Initial" is the key word here—the role of the IMF was enlarged during the 1980s; the role of the World Bank shifted during the late sixties. The World Bank was, of course, active in the Middle East, as it was in much of the developing world. For example, between 1957 and 1974, the bank lent Iran $1.2 billion.[7] More important than the loans it made, however, was the fact that the bank's very existence ensured that "development" would be enshrined as an international norm.

Initially, the new international economic dispensation was more a blueprint for a new international economic dispensation than the realization of one that was truly global in scope. Although forty-four nations attended the Bretton Woods Conference, most—lumped together by the American and British delegations under the rubric "the smaller powers"—had little input into the deliberations (at a follow-up meeting, American representative Harry

Dexter White joked that the main function of the Cuban delegation was to bring cigars).[8] And not only was the attention of the delegates and their immediate successors directed toward the recovery and stabilization of the Atlantic economy, but also the undercapitalized Bretton Woods institutions were initially bypassed by the Marshall Planners. The IMF remained dormant through the 1950s.[9]

Nevertheless, as Craig N. Murphy and Enrico Augelli argue, the effects of the new international economic dispensation would be felt worldwide because of its underlying logic, which linked decolonization, development, a liberal economic order, and peace and prosperity inextricably together.[10] According to their argument, the chief guarantor and underwriter of the system, the United States, did everything in its power to replace the system of imperial trade preferences, the primary rationale for formal empire, with one that guaranteed an open door. Thus, although in practice the American commitment to free trade was spotty at best, the United States backed decolonization, as far as Cold War imperatives allowed.[11] The promise of decolonization could only be realized if the postwar economic system abetted economic development for new nations. But the strategy to promote development had another function as well: development was to be the key to guaranteeing former colonies a stake in a peaceful community of nations and an expanding global trade system. "Peace through mutual prosperity," inscribed as a guiding principle in the two foundational documents of the postwar period, the Atlantic Charter and the Charter of the United Nations, became watchwords of the postwar order.

American policy toward the Middle East is the third factor that was instrumental in promoting both development and the civic order development was intended to sustain. Consider, for example, the core problem of national economic planning—a problem that went to the heart of America's first real foray into development assistance, Truman's Point Four Program. Deploying the latest instruments of economic and social science theory, American experts, sometimes acting alone, sometimes acting with their similarly disposed colleagues associated with UN agencies or the World Bank, intervened throughout the Middle East to create "planning councils," "councils for the development of national production," "development boards," and the like.[12] "The history of development in the post–World War II period," Arturo Escobar asserts, "is, in many ways, the history of the institutionalization and ever more pervasive deployment of planning. . . . From the emphasis on growth and national planning in the 1950s, to the Green Revolution and sectoral and regional planning of the 1960s and '70s . . . the scope and vaulting ambitions of planning have not ceased to grow."[13]

American intervention in national economic development in the Middle East did not end with national economic planning. American policy makers championed the empowerment of the developmentally oriented "new middle classes" and, to an extent that is still debated, at times encouraged the "vanguard" of those middle classes—"modernizing" military officers—to force the hand of history.[14] American policy makers backed the construction of large-scale public works projects (the Unified Plan for the Development of the Jordan River Basin, the Litani River Valley electrification plan, the Aswan High Dam project before things got out of hand), which, they believed, would provide the foundation for national economic development.[15] Finally, from the late 1940s through the White Revolution of the 1960s in Iran, American policy makers urged governments to undertake land reform. The crusade for land reform perfectly encapsulates the obsessions of American policy makers, who believed that land reform would eliminate the most vexing example of economic and social stratification in the developing world; solidify the bond between non-communist reformers and the bulk of the population, which lived in rural areas; take the wind out of the sails of communist-inspired revolutionary movements; destroy the economic and political base of "traditional" elites who blocked "modernization"; and stimulate national economies by creating a market for domestically produced goods among newly enriched peasant consumers.[16]

The final factor that secured the new civic order in the region was the fact that the gospel of development found receptive ears throughout the periphery of the world economy and inspired common imperatives and approaches to that end for nations located there. Throughout the developing world, governments took advantage of the system of embedded liberalism to introduce policies— state-led economic development, centralized economic planning, import substitution industrialization—designed to support the new civic order. The consistency of their choices is not surprising. Having adopted the same internationally recognized diagnosis for the causes of their underdevelopment[17]—lack of capital, infrastructure, a skilled and motivated workforce—governments throughout the region adopted many of the same, standard-issue solutions to confront that underdevelopment.[18] Thus it was that Nasser's first point man on land reform cited the influence of British development economist Doreen Warriner on his work. Nasser himself was not immune from thinking within the box, even during his foray into Arab Socialism: Having read a serialized version of W. W. Rostow's *The Stages of Economic Growth: A Non-Communist Manifesto* in the journal *al-Ahram al-Iqtisadi*, Nasser invited the Kennedy/Johnson adviser and modernization guru to Cairo to discuss the problem of constructing an internal market in Egypt.[19] When it came to core assumptions about how societies are constructed and how social evolution works, modernization theorists and Third Worldists drank from the same well.[20] In the Middle East as elsewhere, the leadership of some states—post-1952 Egypt, post-independence Algeria, Iraq and Syria at various times—linked economic nationalism to the new civic order through a populist discourse that extolled anticolonialism and the virtues of the revolutionary masses.[21] Other states—Jordan, Saudi Arabia—did not.[22] Whether "revolutionary" or reactionary, however, Middle Eastern governments came to the same conclusion, albeit via different routes.

THE REVOLT FROM BELOW

If the immediate postwar period was one marked by optimistic visions of a civic order supported by economic nationalism in what became known as the "Third World," by the end of the 1960s that optimism had soured. As early as 1960, the General Agreement on Tariffs and Trade (GATT) statistics indicated the Third World's declining share of both world trade and world income. Although historically minded economists liked to point out that GNP in the Third World was rising faster than GNP had risen in the developed world during the first industrial revolution, over the course of the decade the economic gap between industrialized and industrializing states had become a chasm.[23] Little wonder, then, that the notion that the developmental promise of decolonization could not be realized within a liberal economic order became an increasingly popular idea among political elites in the Third World

The fact that political elites defined this problem as a trade problem—specifically, a "terms of trade" problem—might be attributed to four factors. First, although the Korean War (1950–53) had driven commodity prices through the roof, throughout the 1950s and 1960s those prices steadily declined in real terms.[24] Second, over the course of the decade, nations that had undertaken an import substitution industrialization path to development increasingly found themselves confronting shortfalls in foreign exchange—a natural pitfall when basic commodities are exchanged for technology. Third, Raul Prebisch and others of the dependency school proposed and disseminated through channels associated with international development agencies a co-herent theoretical framework that supported the terms of trade argument. Whatever the validity of the framework, the argument proved popular among Third World development experts and their allies, in no small measure be-cause it shifted the responsibility for developmental setbacks from a state to a systemic level.[25]

Finally, beginning in 1961 with the Belgrade Summit, the nonaligned move-ment increasingly came to view the world through the lens of a North-South polarization, rather than an East-West one, and representatives to the confer-ences held under the movement's auspices shifted the movement's focus from Cold War politics to the problem of global economic inequity. To address that inequity and the terms of trade problem, representatives put forward a num-ber of interconnected proposals, including those dealing with commodity pricing arrangements, compensation mechanisms to make up for shortfalls in export income, foreign aid goals for donor nations, preferential tariffs for pri-mary goods, and special aid for the least developed nations. By the time of the Algiers Non-Aligned Summit in 1973, the nonaligned movement had effec-tively become the Group of 77, the piecemeal approach to correcting what was widely perceived to be a systemic problem had been all but abandoned, and the call for an entirely New International Economic Order (NIEO) had come to replace the so-called reform agenda.[26]

Although the NIEO included a wide-ranging list of specific demands and grievances drawn from the reform agenda—from debt relief and the right to form commodity-producer cartels to increased aid to and investment in de-veloping countries by industrialized nations—it differed from the reform agenda in terms of its scope and ambitions. The gist of the NIEO boiled down to two sets of demands.[27] First, the Third World sought to supplant the liberal regime that was the foundation for international economic relations and over-haul global economic structures to make them more responsive to Third World needs. One principal strategy for achieving that aim concerned the weighted voting mechanisms that favored the core industrialized nations within international organizations such as the IMF. Instead of basing the al-location of votes on the relative financial power of the nations participating in those organizations, the Group of 77 pushed for a "one nation, one vote" sys-tem that would reflect the numerical primacy of Third World states. Second, the Third World sought to expand the legal norms associated with sovereign rights. Although this affected a vast array of subjects, from the right to define population policy to the establishment of a "new world information order," that which concerns us here are those related to economic nationalism. They included greater authority over multinational corporations and greater control over the exploitation of a nation's natural wealth.

The demands made by the Third World would have constituted little more than a minor irritant to industrialized nations in general and the United States in particular had they not been given salience by two events that took place in the early 1970s. On August 15, 1971, the United States unilaterally severed the link between the dollar and gold. Because under the Bretton Woods system the dollar had been tacked to gold at a fixed price, and because the United States had run up a huge balance of payments deficit, this act was undertaken to prevent a run on American gold reserves. It also struck at the very foundation of the Bretton Woods regime and eventually led to the devaluation of the dollar and a system of floating exchange rates.[28] The so-called Nixon shock and subsequent developments provided the advocates of a NIEO with both an opportunity and an incentive for action: an opportunity insofar as disagreements among industrialized nations about how to go about reordering the international system left a vacuum only partially filled by crisis-management-driven summitry; an incentive insofar as dollars paid in aid and for exported commodities did not go as far.[29]

The second event that bolstered the Third World's bargaining position was the oil shock of 1973–74. Although the roots of the shock might be traced far back—from the oil nationalization movement in Iran in 1953, Iraq's 1961 Public Law 80, the Tripoli and Tehran Agreements, and a host of other actions through which, over the years, oil producers had gained increasing control over the exploitation and marketing of their product—OPEC actions from October 1973 through January 1974 marked an unprecedented assertion on the part of a group of Third World countries of sovereign rights, market power, and unity of purpose. And although the proximate trigger for the nearly 400 percent rise in oil prices might have been the October War, it is no coincidence that the oil shock came on the immediate heels of the Algiers summit.[30] After the onset of the shock, the United Nations General Assembly acted to establish a legal precedent endorsing OPEC's action by approving the Algerian-sponsored Charter of Economic Rights and Duties of States. Article 5 of the charter asserted "the right [of states] to associate in organizations of primary commodity producers in order to develop their national economies." The remaining articles affirmed the General Assembly's support for the much of the rest of the NIEO program.[31]

The developed world—and in particular the United States—watched with both horror and panic at this betrayal of every assumption around which the postwar international order had been constructed. In a series of articles published during the early and mid-1970s, C. Fred Bergsten, who coordinated international economic affairs for Henry Kissinger's National Security Council from 1969 to 1971, articulated the dominant position held by American policy elites toward the economic instability of the era and the ensuing Third World assertion.[32] For Bergsten, the shift in the balance of power between the industrialized world and the Third World, embodied in the oil crisis and the proliferation of Third World demands, represented an existential threat to the United States. What was to prevent Third World nations, working alone, in groups, or en masse, from using their power to provoke competitive scrambles for raw materials and markets among industrialized nations, upset international capital markets, or act discriminatorily toward the United States? What was to prevent the exporters of copper, tin, rubber, bauxite, coffee, and even timber from taking their cue from OPEC and organizing producer cartels?[33] For Bergsten, the choice for the United States was clear:

> As a result of their shabby treatment in the past, and skepticism about meaningful change in the attitudes of the rich, the countries of the Third World are unlikely to recant quickly the policies based on that new power which has so sharply boosted their pocketbooks and prestige. Indeed, it may be impossible to persuade them to do so even with the most forthcoming measures. . . .
>
> The United States must therefore prepare to defend itself through new national policies, including efforts to break up the solidarity of the Third World itself, and seek to coordinate those policies with the other industrialized countries to reduce the threat of increasing tension with them.[34]

In place of a NIEO, Bergsten asserted, the industrialized nations should work to reform the international system in a manner that would facilitate the exchange between raw material producers and raw material consumers for the benefit of both:

> The basic issue of international relationships for the foreseeable future is the tension between the imperatives of international interdependence and the quest to retain adequate degrees of national autonomy. The overriding goal is to make the world safe for interdependence, by protecting the benefits which it provides for each country against the external and internal threats to those

benefits which will constantly emerge from those willing to pay the price of more autonomy for individual nations. This may sometimes require slowing the pace at which interdependence proceeds, and checking some aspects of it. More frequently, however, it calls for checking national intrusions into the international exchange of both economic and non-economic goods.[35]

In other words, the liberal order was to be preserved and those who were "willing to pay the price of more autonomy for individual nations"—economic nationalist/developmentalist regimes that refused "to take systemic concerns into account in formulating their own national policies"[36]—would be marginalized. For most of Europe, this meant preserving the embedded liberalism aspect of the Bretton Woods system. The new buzzword became "global interdependence."[37] The Americans, however, crossed the line separating "interdependence" from a (proto-) neoliberal "globalization" early.

THE EMPIRE STRIKES BACK

Bergsten's reading of the problem and its solution was, of course, no more or less unreasonable than the Third World's reading of the problem and its solution. Proponents of the NIEO had looked at the growing gap between rich and poor and diagnosed the problem as one of systemic failure. Increasingly, opponents of the NIEO looked at the growing gap between rich and poor and diagnosed the problem as one of paradigmatic failure—the development strategy itself was flawed, meaning, of course, the developmental state was flawed as was the social compact on which that state rested. Symptomatic of this new line of attack was the abandonment by donor governments and aid agencies of the developmental model they had embraced since the 1950s, citing problems with its urban/industrial bias, its so-called trickle-down premise (i.e., the assumption that an expanding industrial sector would eventually raise the living standards of the entire population), and its rising GNP yardstick. In its stead, they embraced the "basic needs" approach to aid delivery, adopted as World Bank policy in 1972, which focused instead on the direct targeting of poverty and hunger, particularly among the rural populations of the Third World. Earlier developmental models, it was argued, had not only failed to alleviate poverty, they had increased "absolute poverty" by as much as 20 percent to 40 percent. Even worse, development strategies were thinly disguised delivery systems to reward those included in the social compact—bureaucrats, industrial workers, "consumers," and so forth—at the expense of the truly poor.[38] Thus, in a bizarre and ironic twist, proponents of the new approach advocated for it in the name of "equity," the very term developmentally minded economic nationalists had used to argue against the injustices of domestic liberalism since the 1950s.[39] And just as the World Bank's existence had ensured that development would be enshrined as an international norm in the early days of the Bretton Woods system, the bank's imprimatur ensured the same for the basic needs approach after the system's collapse.

The adoption of the basic needs model was but one manifestation of what might be termed a counterattack against both the NIEO and the policy assumptions and paradigm of political economy on which the developmentalist state rested. Some states in the industrialized world had initially been prepared to adopt a conciliatory stance toward the Third World, an approach later endorsed by the Brandt Report.[40] Others attempted to temporize with its demands through bilateral arrangements.[41] The American reaction, however, was confrontational. As the former American ambassador to the United Nations, Daniel Patrick Moynihan, put it, the time was ripe for the United States to "go into opposition."[42] Henry Kissinger was even more direct. "The United States, better than almost any other nation, could survive a period of economic warfare," he warned the Third World leaders in 1976. "We can resist confrontation and rhetorical attacks if other nations choose that path. And we can ignore unrealistic proposals and peremptory demands."[43]

Ultimately, the United States could turn the tables on the Third World and play the major role in defining the international economic agenda for years to come for a number of reasons. First, there was the international economic crisis of 1979–82 which was, in reality, two crises that erupted in tandem: the first as a result of a second round of oil price hikes; the second as a result of the so-called Volcker shock of 1979, when Paul Volcker, then the chairman of the U.S. Federal Reserve, decided that fighting inflation was more important than assuring high rates of employment and hiked interest rates to unprecedented levels.[44] America's tight monetary policy simultaneously raised the value of the dollar and precipitated a global liquidity shortage. In the West, the economic downturn of the 1980s replaced the "stagflation" of the 1970s. In the Third World, states faced higher debt servicing costs, collapsing commodity prices, and diminishing markets—the result of the global recession sparked by the liquidity crisis.[45] More than at any previous time since the establishment of the Bretton Woods System, Third World states found their economic fate in the hands of "creditor clubs."[46]

The United States launched a series of initiatives as well, designed to splinter Third World solidarity and shift the international economic agenda away from the NIEO (and out of the United Nations). The United States wielded its influence successfully in international institutions, such as the IMF and World Bank, and in international venues where it confronted Third World claims and succeeded in dividing what turned out to be a fragile coalition.[47] It also used its weighted voting powers to encourage the transformation of the Bretton Woods institutions, expanding the breadth and scope of their operations, rendering them such effective enforcers of the "Washington consensus" through the application of conditionalities and structural adjustment programs that even the official historian of the IMF would later write, "By the turn of the century, the phrase 'Washington Consensus' had become a synonym for a narrow-minded and excessive zeal for laissez faire market economics."[48] American-trained economists of the Chicago school not only dominated these institutions, but came to dominate ministries throughout the Third World as well, replacing those with more dirigiste inclinations. Finally, the United States could turn the tables on the Third World and play the major role in defining the international economic agenda for years to come through just plain bullying, such as by withdrawing or threatening to withdraw from international treaties or agencies, cutting assistance, or tying American assistance to "policy-dialogues," described by one analyst as "coercive diplomacy."[49]

The combination of oil price hikes, the Volcker Shock, and policy decisions made in Washington, D.C., took the wind out of the sails of the NIEO. The international economic agenda was not to be set by what the Reagan administration dismissed as the "so-called Third World," nor would that administration engage with what Secretary of State Alexander Haig called "sterile debates and unrealistic demands."[50] There would be a new order, for sure, but it would not be like the one envisioned by advocates of the NIEO; instead, it would be an order that extended the realm of the liberal in "embedded liberalism" into the domestic economies of states. Within a decade, this new order had replaced the NIEO at the top of the international economic agenda.

In 1987, C. Fred Bergsten wrote another article for *Foreign Affairs* titled "Economic Imbalances and World Politics."[51] Just a few years prior, it might logically have been assumed that the "imbalances" referred to in the title were those that fed North-South friction, as well as Bergsten's apocalyptic vision of a South triumphant. But by this time Bergsten had moved on, as had his audience; instead of the South, it was now America's debt obligations to the rest of the world that was the stuff of apocalyptic economic visions.

THE MIDDLE EAST PIECE IN THE THIRD WORLD PUZZLE

This, then, provides the context for understanding the fate of the civic order among states in the Middle East, as well as the fate of the economic nationalism that was to support it. Some Middle Eastern states—Algeria, Libya, Iraq, and even Iran[52]—had played key roles in designing and promoting the NIEO; others—Algeria, Egypt—had provided models of state-led economic development, centralized economic planning, and import substitution industrialization emulated elsewhere. Nevertheless, they, like states throughout the world, found themselves enmeshed in the same three-part dialectical process:1944–71, when the global economic system created an environment conducive to economic nationalism in the South; 1971–80, when the South deployed the power derived from economic nationalism to challenge the system; and 1980–2008, when a reinvigorated system effectively vanquished economic nationalism in the South—through which the present order achieved dominance and the civic order of those states was put to the test.

The decade of the 1970s was a time of prosperity for most states in the Middle East, as it was for many states in the developing world.[53] From 1973 to 1982 about $400 billion flooded into the coffers of OPEC. About half of that went to Saudi Arabia and another quarter to Kuwait and the UAE. Anywhere from $96 billion to $124 billion found its way to the Eurodollar market, where it was "recycled" for investment in public industries and development banks of "credit-worthy"—hydrocarbon exporting, newly industrializing, or both—developing nations. About $76 billion in oil money went to less credit-worthy nations, mostly in the form of grants.[54] It is here that the trajectory of states in the Middle East veers slightly from that of states in other parts of the world: During the same period, most OPEC grants went to Muslim states, with the largest sum going to states in the Middle East. Thus, OPEC money played a significant role in underwriting the civic order in Egypt (until 1979), Syria, Jordan, Lebanon, and the Yemen Arab Republic.[55] In addition, non-oil exporting states in the region benefitted indirectly from oil wealth through remittances sent home by their expatriate citizens working in the Gulf. Remittances enabled some beleaguered governments in the region to at least partially fulfill the promise of full employment, and it acted as a safety valve for others. In addition, remittances added to states' coffers by increasing the amounts they collected through import duties and provided states with the foreign exchange necessary for industrial expansion. The export of labor to the Gulf was not negligible: at its peak, Gulf countries provided employment for 5 million Arab workers, contributing anywhere from an estimated $5.2 billion to $7.2 billion to the Egyptian economy alone.[56]

When the rug was pulled out from under the international economy in 1979, states in the Middle East found themselves left with some of the highest ratios of debt obligation to GDP in the Third World.[57] In addition, the stagflation in the North, induced by the oil price revolution of 1973–74, along with conservation and competition, wreaked havoc on the overheated economies of the oil producers, who passed their shortfalls along to those states dependent on earnings from remittances and financial aid. Producers found no relief from the 1980–81 price hike, whose effect was short lived.[58] The economies of the states in the Middle East, already reeling from the inherent contradictions of import substitution industrialization, never recovered from the Volcker shock. As summed up by one observer:

> Economic decline has plagued the Middle East since the mid-1980s. . . . Overall growth rates have stagnated. In most countries of the region, gross national product (GNP) has barely kept pace with population growth, and in some, such as Saudi Arabia and Iran, per capita GNP has registered an absolute decline. Unemployment continues to climb. The jobless rate is officially estimated at 25 percent regionwide, and the failure of job creation to keep pace with demographic trends projects even higher levels of unemployment in the years ahead. Investment levels have declined. Fiscally strapped states have dramatically cut back on public investment, and the private sector has not stepped in sufficiently to pick up the slack. Capital flight is endemic. Middle East residents hold an estimated $100–500 billion in savings abroad, and the region has been unsuccessful in attracting foreign direct investment (FDI) in sectors other than tourism and petroleum. Productivity levels are down. Middle East products and labor have become progressively less competitive in the global market and this has spelled worsening trade imbalances, rising international indebtedness, and increased debt overhang. Finally, poverty remains a challenge. More than 30 percent of the population is estimated to live below the human poverty line despite the MENA's reputation for admirably extensive family-sponsored and state-sponsored safety nets. Overall, the Middle East and North Africa is a region of deteriorating living standards and

persistent economic anemia—a pale shadow of the promise it held in the 1960s and 1970s.[59]

This bleak environment has been apposite for IMF-induced stabilization and structural adjustment programs, which have been applied from Morocco to Jordan. States not compelled by IMF conditionalities—Algeria, Iraq, Syria, Saudi Arabia, Iran—followed many of the same policy prescriptions as those that were, to greater or lesser effect. In some of these cases, governments viewed neoliberal policy prescriptions as a quick fix to economies ravaged by the recession of the 1980s, or, in the case of Iran and Iraq, as the means to relieve the stresses induced by war mobilization. For Syria and Saudi Arabia, however, institutional reform was made a prerequisite for participation in the Euro-Mediterranean Free Trade Area and the World Trade Organization, respectively.[60] The neoliberal agenda thus became virtually ubiquitous in the region, although its application remained spotty in practice.

At first, the introduction of neo-liberal policies was met with resistance on the street, particularly when those policies entailed cuts in consumer subsidies—a concrete example of the unilateral attempt on the part of states to redefine the civic order.[61] The first "IMF riot" took place in Egypt in 1977, when the government, at that time in negotiations with the IMF, announced plans to cut subsidies for a number of basic goods, an act that would have raised their overall price by 50 percent. After two days—during which time seventy-nine protesters were killed—the government backed down (ultimately, the IMF advised the government to withdraw the subsidies but to do it gradually). Comparable IMF riots took place in Turkey (1980, 2000), Morocco (1983), Tunisia (1984), Sudan (1982, 1985), Algeria (1988), Jordan (1989, 1996), and Lebanon (1987).[62]

By the decade of the 1990s, however, it appeared that the austerity-induced riot in the Middle East was mostly a thing of the past.[63] More effective repression and a slower, more judicious application of structural adjustment policies certainly played a role in this.[64] But other factors were at work as well, especially the dismantling of the structures and institutions with which the post–World War II civic order had articulated. This altered social and political practice and, it might be argued, the moral economy such practice validated.

Throughout much of the Middle East, for example, the state had created categories of collective identity—peasants, workers, syndicates, and so forth—for both functional and symbolic reasons. In terms of function, it was through these categories of collective identity that organized interests were represented to governments. At the same time, states laid out a framework of rights and privileges of citizenship which, for all its inherent biases, operated as the playing field for those organized interests.[65] The functionalist categories that states had used to define those with claims to rights and privileges are now gone or empty, as are the guarantees for those rights and privileges. For example, the Egyptian constitution of 1971 defined the state as a "socialist democracy," described employment as "a right, a duty, and an honor guaranteed by the state," promised education and health care to all, and gave the state "the lead role in managing and allocating resources." In 2007, the constitution was amended: no longer was it the responsibility of the state to allocate resources, ensure equity, and guarantee outcomes; rather, the market was to take the lead, with the state merely taking responsibility for regulating the market.[66] The beneficiaries of the contemporary state's munificence—members of the ruling cohort or their cronies—are linked to the government through privileged ties of access, not through shared ideology or corporatist structures as they had been.[67] Mobilizational parties, where they still exist, have been severed from their populist/developmentalist context, are functionally anachronistic, and have also ceded ideological space to groupings representing so-called primordial bonds, such as religion or sect. At the same time, smaller service-providing associations have colonized abandoned spaces in the urban economy.[68]

All this seems to point to the end of the postwar civic order in the Middle East. But it just might be the case that, as with Mark Twain, reports of its death are greatly exaggerated. Two pieces of evidence point in this direction. First, the upsurge in labor activism targeting issues of political economy— and not just shop issues—indicates that resistance to the new dispensation has not disappeared; it has merely assumed a new shape.[69] Second, the global economic meltdown of 2008 has once again put the Keynesian option on the table. In other words, there may be yet a fourth moment in the dialectical process that encapsulates global and regional political economy since 1929.

10 THE MIDDLE EAST THROUGH THE LENS OF CRITICAL GEOPOLITICS
Globalization, Terrorism, and the Iraq War

Waleed Hazbun

UNLIKE TERMS FOR AMERICA, Asia, Europe, or Africa, the "Middle East" denotes a region of the globe defined from the point of view of the north Atlantic states and is devoid of geographic or cultural referents. As a result, plenty of confusion and imprecision surrounds the question of the precise location and boundaries of the Middle East.[1] Nevertheless, as with the term "the West," the American public and news media often associate the Middle East with particular political, economic, and cultural characteristics. Among these associations is that the Middle East represents a territorial exception to globalization. Regardless of how globalization is defined or understood, the Middle East is often referred to as disconnected from its processes and resisting its effects. More specifically, the region is commonly viewed as having been excluded from the post–Cold War trends toward economic liberalization, global market integration, and democratization that have more closely integrated the West with other regions of the globe.

To explain this exception, some suggest that access to oil resources created "rentier states" able to forgo globally competitive production and political accountability.[2] Others emphasize what they consider to be a distinct Arab-Islamic political culture as the causal factor.[3] Most notably, historian Bernard Lewis places blame on what he sees as the Islamic world's historic failure to adapt to the economic and political practices of Western modernity.[4] In making their claims these views all evoke the notion of Middle East exceptionalism (also referred to as Arab exceptionalism). Although one can easily compile tables of data and charts that show the Middle East, or more specifically the Arab-Muslim world, as a region, to be "less globalized" and "less democratic" than most other regions of the globe, this chapter warns of the dangers of thinking about the region in exceptionalist terms. The notion of Middle East exceptionalism generalizes across a very diverse collection of peoples, states, and economies. For example, it may refer to oil resources in one context and the role of religion in politics in another, and furthermore, such characteristics differ widely across the region. It nevertheless often refers to an undifferentiated entity, the Middle East or the Arab-Muslim world, where politics and economics seemingly function according to a unitary logic. Most critically, Middle East exceptionalism also suffers the faults of other exceptionalist notions, such as American exceptionalism. As historian Daniel Rogers argues, "When difference is put in exceptionalist terms, in short, the referent is universalized."[5] Rogers points out that notions of exceptionalism beg the question, "Different from what?" and imply the answer, "Different from the universal tendencies of history, the 'normal' fate of nations, the laws of historical mechanics itself."[6] In other words, notions of Middle East exceptionalism avoid analyzing the diverse peoples and states across the Middle East in terms of dynamics found elsewhere and perpetrate the notion that the rest of the world can be understood as variations of a common type or that all societies, except those in the Middle East, are evolving toward a common political and economic system.

Rather than contest the data and observations that sustain portrayals of Middle East exceptionalism, this chapter views this discourse through the lens of critical geopolitics. As an approach to the study of global politics, critical geopolitics questions models and representations that claim to be objective, disinterested portrayals of reality. It argues that language used in these geopolitical discourses tends to reflect particular political as well as cultural attitudes and interests.[7] This chapter shows how notions such as Middle East exceptionalism do more than represent objective data; they sustain what I refer to as a particular "geopolitical imaginary." In contrast to geopolitical maps, which are defined by criteria such as borders, topography, and population, geopolitical imaginaries refer to the territorial terms of reference, or the mental maps, that policy makers, academics, popular media, and the general public use to translate aspects of geography—such as location, distance, and space—and the impact of mobility and flows into geopolitical terms.

As an approach to the study of international politics, critical geopolitics can be understood as similar to constructivist international relations theory.[8] In contrast to rationalist approaches, such as neorealism and neoliberalism, constructivism denies that state interests and security (including notions of threat) can be objectively determined by an assessment of material resources and relative power capabilities. Constructivists argue that identities and intersubjective understandings help define, for example, whether or not a powerful neighbor with nuclear weapons is viewed as a threat. The approach also shows how geopolitical change generally occurs as part of the process of shifting identities and relationships between states. By a similar logic, the political importance of geopolitical imaginaries is that they shape discourses and mobilize ideological power, rhetorical force, and political affect to promote certain notions of threat, geopolitical goals, and forms of authority over territory. In doing so, they often shape the policies and behaviors of states.

This chapter shows how notions such as Middle East exceptionalism operate as a geopolitical imaginary similar to the geopolitical maps that define state interests and threats in global politics. But unlike geopolitical maps—which offer a complex mapping of political, economic, and geographic features—the geopolitical imaginary of Middle East exceptionalism divides the world into two by limiting its vision to a binary register defined by the presence or absence of a range of characteristics associated with globalization. The result is a mapping that flattens topographies and leaves a hole in the space where patterns do not match. That space is viewed in exceptionalist terms, that is, it is regarded as not following historical patterns elsewhere, and the binary lens of this imaginary fails to register, let alone understand, viable alternative patterns. This chapter shows how, especially after the end of the Cold War, Middle East exceptionalism came to operate as an imagined geography similar to those, as Edward Said argued, developed within Western scholarship of the Arab and Muslim Middle East during the era of colonialism.[9] As geographer Derek Gregory explains:

> These are constructions that fold distance into difference through a series of spatializations. They work, Said argued, by multiplying partitions and enclosures that serve to demarcate "the same" from "the other," at once constructing and calibrating a gap between the two by "designating in one's mind a familiar space which is 'ours' and an unfamiliar space beyond 'ours' which is 'theirs'." "Their" space is often seen as the inverse of "our" space: a sort of negative, in the photographic sense that "they" might "develop" into something like "us," but also the site of an absence, because "they" are seen as somehow to lack the positive tonalities that supposedly distinguish "us."[10]

As discussed below, some of the most influential commentators about the Middle East within the American media view the region through the geopolitical imaginary of Middle East exceptionalism. In doing so, they tend to portray the politics and economics of the Middle East as defined by factors distinct from those found in other countries and other regions of the world. As a consequence, in the wake of the September 11, 2001, attacks on the United States, they came to view the rise of security threats emanating from the Middle East as a product of the region's failure to embrace globalization. This view led them to argue that American policy toward the Middle East should set out to "fix" the region, as it lacked sufficient internal forces for change and reform. This discourse naturalized the notion that the United States can and should play a role in advancing that progress by unblocking the internal obstacles standing in the way of the region "joining the rest of the world." Although the factors that led to the American invasion of Iraq are numerous and complex, this chapter argues that these exceptionalist discourses framed both public and official understandings of Bush administration policy toward the Middle East in the wake of 9/11. The depiction of Iraq as the archetype of the most dangerous form of exceptionalism facilitated the Bush administration's efforts to use force as part of a broader effort to transform the political and economic landscape of the Middle East. This chapter concludes by noting that even though the Bush administration sought to justify its policies by portraying them as a break from what it termed "Middle East exceptionalism," such an approach was blind to the diverse ways that globalization is experienced and imagined in the region, and it simultaneously embraced the notion of American exceptionalism: that the United States is uniquely endowed with a mission to define the fate of other nations.

CARTOGRAPHIES OF GEOPOLITICS AND GLOBALIZATION

When American naval strategist Alfred Thayer Mahan invoked the term "the Middle East" in 1902, he was seeking a geographically defined label to mark the strategic value of the region around the Persian Gulf.[11] In his essay "The Persian Gulf and International Relations," published in London's *National Review*, Mahan emphasized the need for Britain to establish naval bases in the region to secure its trade and communication lines between British-controlled Egypt and India, which he viewed as under threat from Russian expansion southward and German development of the Berlin-Baghdad railway. As such, the early use of the term "Middle East" somewhat differs from—though is not inconsistent with—the contemporary usage of the term "the Orient" that defined a linguistic and cultural object. Oriental studies, or Orientalism, was concerned not directly with geopolitics but rather with the culture, languages, and history of the Arab and Muslim Middle East. According to Said, Orientalism "was ultimately a political vision of reality whose structure promoted the difference between the familiar (Europe, the West, 'us') and the strange (the Orient, the East, 'them.')."[12] In contrast, Mahan's use of the term "Middle East" was a product of the distinctive genre of strategic analysis known as geopolitics. Broadly defined, geopolitics refers to the territorial dimensions of international politics.

The study of geopolitics focuses on the implications of nature, geography, and material factors on patterns of international politics defined primarily in terms of territorial competition between great powers.[13] The development of "classical" geopolitical reasoning in the late nineteenth century was largely a product of technological changes and colonial territorial expansion that led great powers to view their interests within the framework of a "closed system" at the global geographical scale. As geographer John Agnew explains, geopolitics "framed world politics in terms of an overarching global context in which states vie for power outside their boundaries, gain control (formally and informally) over less modern regions (and their resources) and overtake other major states in a worldwide pursuit of global primacy."[14] Both Mahan and fellow geopolitical strategist Halford J. Mackinder—who emphasized the advantages of land power over sea power—measured the strategic value of the Middle East region in terms of its geographic position in the global system over which great powers competed for mastery.[15]

For its practitioners, geopolitics operated as a seemingly scientific description of the material environment that defined the conditions for international politics. In the wake of World War II, classical geopolitics as a field was generally viewed as increasingly irrelevant due to technological changes, decolonization, and the rise of a liberal economic order in which states gained relative power through trade, increased economic efficiency, and alliances rather than through territorial control.[16] In the United States, the academic study of international politics was soon dominated by realist international relations theory. American international relations theory helped reframe the language of global politics and foreign policy in terms of an anarchic system of sovereign territorial nation-states, each with different degrees of material power.[17] Whereas the United States sought to forge a negotiated, but U.S.-led, liberal international economic order and security community amongst its democratic, capitalist allies, foreign policy doctrines and policies continued to be profoundly shaped by geopolitical features, such as the containment of communism and the fear of "falling dominoes" or the spread of communism across the developing world.[18] In this system, the Middle East remained a region of critical strategic importance. Not only did it retain important maritime communications and trade routes and was situated between the spheres of influence of great powers, but it also expanded its strategic value considerably due to the presence of massive oil reserves and the global development of petrol-based economies and militaries. Throughout the Cold War, rival superpowers competed for influence in the region, leading to complex patterns of shifting alliances.

With the end of the Cold War and the rise of globalization in the 1990s, the saliency of classical geopolitics seemed to decline as international relations became increasingly defined by global markets, electronic communications, free trade, capital flows, and the erosion of borders. Many observers noted the seeming decline of distance and some even pronounced the "end of geography."[19] A critical feature of American foreign policy under Presidents George H. W. Bush and Bill Clinton was the goal of "enlargement," that is, the effort to expand the scope of the liberal international order across formerly communist East Europe and the newly democratic, emerging markets of Latin America and Asia. As Agnew argues, "This views powerful states, above all the United States, as sponsoring a new global 'market access' regime that is producing a new geopolitics of power in which control over the flows of goods, capital, and innovation increasingly substitutes for fixed or static control over the resources of bounded territories."[20]

In this context, the state-dominated economies and authoritarian regimes of the Middle East looked out of step and they posed a challenge to the extension of a U.S.-dominated post–Cold War order. Beginning with the 1990–91 Gulf War, the U.S. advanced its interests through the projection of military power, directed mostly at containing Iraq and Iran and providing security for Saudi Arabia and the smaller Gulf states. As the phenomenon of globalization dominated academic and policy debates, the Middle East appeared excluded from the post–Cold War trends toward economic liberalization and global market integration as well as democratization. Rather than adjusting to become "trading states" competing for capital and markets in the global economy, Middle Eastern states were viewed as remaining territorially oriented— guarding borders, territorial resources, and state control over their closed national economies—and Middle Eastern societies and political culture were commonly viewed as resisting global trends and unwilling to "confront the age of globalization." In this context, many scholars of the contemporary Middle East, often marginalized from the ongoing globalization debates, focused on compiling explanations for why the region was being "left behind" by globalization. When the Middle East was mentioned in the globalization literature, it was usually to note, by contrast, the region's failure to follow these "global" trends. As such, it has not been uncommon to find references to "the region's status as eternally out of step with history and immune to the trends affecting other parts of the world."[21]

POPULARIZING MIDDLE EAST EXCEPTIONALISM

Although the notion of Middle East exceptionalism is well represented in academic portrayals of the region, it finds its most prolific representations in American popular media and commentary. One of the most influential popularizers of the geopolitical imaginary of Middle East exceptionalism is *New York Times* columnist Thomas Friedman, who gained fame for his prize-winning coverage of the Middle East in the 1980s. In the 1990s he began to frame his reporting, in the form of a widely syndicated twice-weekly foreign affairs column, around the concept of globalization. In 1999, he published the first edition of his bestseller, *The Lexus and the Olive Tree*, a textbook that is often taught in high school and college classrooms. As exhibited in its title, Friedman presents contemporary politics, economics, and culture through a binary framework defined in terms of the integrating and freedom-expanding forces of global capitalism ("the Lexus") that are uprooting the territorial attachments and borders ("the olive tree") that have sustained nationalism and authoritarianism.[22]

Friedman contends these transformations are driven primarily by technological change, such as the spread of the Internet, and are making economic liberalization and market integration nearly unavoidable while creating pressures for democratization. In the new emerging order, Friedman contends, all economies will become integrated into a single, global economic system disciplined by the need to attract the "electronic herd" of unregulated global financial flows. As a result, all governments will have no choice but to don the "golden straitjacket" and implement neoliberal economic policies or else they will fall to discontented societies demanding economic and political freedoms and be weakened by economic decline and international isolation.

In Friedman's world, the American policy of promoting enlargement and neoliberal globalization may be viewed as an adaptation to technological changes and market forces that no one controls rather than understood as a geopolitical strategy for expanding American hegemonic power.[23] With a similar lack of nuance, Friedman equates globalization with Americanization and celebrates its spread.

With his background and enduring interest in the Middle East, Friedman continued to report on political and economic developments in the region. But in his books and columns, references to the Middle East and his numerous anecdotes from the region often serve as "exceptions" that highlight his putative "rules" about global change. These writings illustrate Rogers's observation that "when difference is put in exceptionalist terms . . . the referent is universalized."[24] In Friedman's depiction, the Middle East is the last great battleground where the forces of globalization have yet to claim victory, and he sees this struggle as the key to understanding all major political changes and processes in the region. He often tells his readers, "If you want to see this war between the protected and the globalizers at its sharpest today, go to the Arab world."[25] Tracking political change in the region, he announces that "the internet and globalization are acting like nutcrackers to open societies and empower Arab democrats."[26]

Friedman collapses the politics of the Israeli-Palestinian conflict, the rise of political Islam, and growing challenges to the American projection of power in the region into the same binary struggle between neoliberal economic policies and statist economic systems. Through this lens, Arab supporters of peace with Israel and democracy advocates are understood as motivated by the same logic as economic globalization. He repeatedly explains the widespread opposition to a broad set of trends (mostly American policy objectives) as a reflection of the endemic Middle Eastern resistance to globalization. When he encounters Arabs who challenge or disagree with his ideas about globalization or the peace process, he declares that they suffer from "systematic misunderstanding" because they follow a framework of understanding that fails to correct itself when exposed to more information.[27] In a similar fashion, however, Friedman with little imagination seems to view all processes and struggles in terms of a binary framework defined by a vision of a universal future with no room for alternative possibilities.

Although Friedman sometimes blames access to oil resources for the lack of globalization in the region, suggesting that when the oil runs out there will be no further resistance to economic reform and democratization, he constantly invokes a cultural basis to the region's exceptionalism. For no other region does he make claims such as in "the Arab-Muslim world . . . cultural attitudes . . . have become a barrier to development" and constantly observe how "there is huge resistance to . . . modernization from the authoritarian and religiously obscurest forces within the Arab-Muslim world."[28] He often returns to the notion that "traditional societies" as found in the Middle East cannot cope with the freedom that globalization offers. He also complains that people in the Arab world fail to correctly understand globalization; for them "it is a challenge that is devoid of any redemptive or inspirational force."[29]

When discussing the cultural backlash against globalization, Friedman notes it is "most apparent in the Middle East" where people are still caught up in fights over territorially rooted symbols and resist globalization under the battle cry of "I don't want to be global. I want to be local."[30] These people are "ready to go to war to protect their culture from the global."[31] Along with the French, he asserts that Arab culture is "intuitively hostile to the whole phenomena" of globalization.[32] Writing an imagined memo from Bill Clinton, he complains that "what troubles me most about the mood on the Arab street today is the hostility I detect there to modernization, globalization, democratization and the information revolution."[33] In 2001, as the Oslo peace process collapsed (an event that had little to do with globalization), he viewed its decline and the rise of regional opposition to the post-9/11 policies of the George W. Bush administration as signs of the failure of the forces of globalization to transform the region. Rather than recognize these trends as the product of local political forces with rival interests, he cites his friend Stephen P. Cohen and announces that "we are heading back to . . . an era characterized by . . . the Arab world's isolation from the dominant trends in global economics and politics."[34]

AFTER 9/11: THE MIDDLE EAST, GLOBALIZATION, AND TERRORISM

With the help of Friedman and others, in the wake of September 11, 2001, the geopolitical imaginary of Middle East exceptionalism shaped popular images and policy options largely because it offered a ready lens that seemed to explain the causes of the attacks and suggest what the United States should do to prevent future ones. The popularity and pervasiveness of this lens are enhanced for most Americans because it does not require specific knowledge of the

Middle East. It claims the Middle East generates abnormal threats because its political, social, and economic conditions are abnormal. This imaginary operates without any reference to U.S. policies and interests in the region.

In American post-9/11 debates, efforts to explain the attacks and consider appropriate American responses often ignore geopolitical issues, such as American alliances and its military presence in the Arab-Muslim world. Instead, American media commentators, think-tank scholars, and policy makers quickly come to argue that the attacks of September 11 were due primarily to the failure of the states of the Middle East to globalize and expand economic opportunities and political liberties for their peoples. Although these are, to a large degree, fair characterizations, they do not in themselves explain Middle East politics and the rise of international terrorism networks. These observers portray the Middle East as a region of dysfunctional states, economies, and societies with little awareness or appreciation of the geopolitical factors that may account for such conditions.

Although the belief in Middle East exceptionalism certainly does not explain all facets of American post-9/11 policy under George W. Bush, it does help to account for the way American policy makers and much of the American public came to think about the threat 9/11 represented. We can read back to Friedman's reporting before 9/11 to trace how the logic of Middle East exceptionalism came to define much of the public debate and policy making in the post-9/11 era. In a 1998 column, Friedman explains that one "can't understand [the American standoff with Iraq] without reference to . . . U.S. hegemony after the cold war and globalization." By this Friedman meant to suggest that "America's economic success" was "brewing" "deep resentment against the U.S." and, more broadly, Americanization-globalization was a "destabilizing force, challenging every traditional society." At the same time, he warned that "globalization empowers the haters" and, referring to the 1993 bombing of the World Trade Center, he expressed fear that the threat the United States now faced was the "super-empowered individual—the super-empowered angry man."[35] Thus even before 9/11, Friedman's theory of globalization had led him to a rethinking of the geopolitics of America's relationship with the Middle East. He argued that the United States faced a threat from the Middle East primarily because the Middle East failed to embrace globalization.

In his post-9/11 book on globalization, *The World Is Flat*, Friedman represents the Middle East as the exceptional space that has remained unflat.[36]

He argues that the failure of the region to embrace globalization produces not only some "super-haters" but also many passive supporters of terrorism. These men are often the young living in a "state of half-flatness" who "see that the Arab-Muslim world . . . has fallen behind the rest of the planet."[37] Friedman explains to his readers that "the flattening of the world only sharpens that dissonance by making the backwardness of the Arab-Muslim region, compared to others, impossible to ignore."[38] This logic ignores popular opposition to the projection of American military power in the region since the 1990–91 Gulf War, the primary stated grievance of Osama bin Laden, and portrays various aspects of the American presence in the Middle East—including political, economic, cultural, and military—as simply facets of globalization's inescapable process of transforming the world and spreading freedom, democracy, and prosperity.

At the same time, another component of American post-9/11 discourse that Friedman articulated years prior to the event was that as globalization collapses distance it gives the forces that oppose both the United States and the forces of globalization new capabilities to threaten the American homeland. Prior to 9/11, most Americans considered the primary regional threat to U.S. interests to be "rogue states" such as Iran and Iraq, which were subject to strategic containment, political isolation, and economic sanctions. After the 9/11 attacks, however, many scholars and analysts in the United States hastily suggested that globalization was refining geopolitics. International relations scholar Robert O. Keohane, for example, concluded, "Globalization means, among other things, that threats of violence to our homeland can occur from anywhere. The barrier conception of geographic space . . . was finally shown to be thoroughly obsolete on September 11."[39] These new threats could only be contained, in Friedman's view, by ending "the state of half-flatness" in the Middle East. Within the discourse of Middle East exceptionalism, this goal required the elimination of the obstacles that have hampered the forces of globalization from transforming the Middle East and allowing its people to experience globalization and its effects. Friedman not only supported American efforts to bring economic and political transformation to the region but also clearly articulated an influential rationale for the American invasion of Iraq based not on the threat of nuclear, biological, or chemical weapons but rather on the need for socioeconomic and political reform.

MAKING THE MIDDLE EAST SAFE FOR GLOBALIZATION

A defining moment in the evolution of American support for the Iraq war came in 2002, just as the Bush administration was articulating a new global strategy based on "preventative war," termed the Bush Doctrine, that would lead eventually to the invasion of Iraq. In the midst of an ongoing debate about the threat that Iraq posed to the United States, the United Nations published the first in a series of annual Arab Human Development Reports (AHDRs) drafted by a team of well-known social scientists, development planners, and intellectuals from the Arab world.[40] American officials, media commentators, and academics broadly approved the report. They read it as a sign that some Arabs had finally correctly diagnosed the maladies of the Arab world. Chapter by chapter, the report surveys topics including economic, political, demographic, health, and educational conditions across the Arab world, noting the vast range of differences between the rich and poor countries of the region. Most American commentators, however, focused on aggregate comparisons between collective data for the Arab states and data for other regions.

Whereas the region does not usually rank the lowest globally in these cross-regional comparisons, it often does on political freedom indicators—such as political and civil rights, independent media, and accountability of rulers to the ruled. And most American commentators focused on this image to view the whole report through the lens of Middle East exceptionalism and suggested that the report explains the reasons that the Middle East is a generator of terrorism and threats to the United States, even though no such claims are made in the report. More critically, although the authors of the report called for internal reform in the realms of human rights, effective governance, women's empowerment, and improved educational systems, many in the United States, from Friedman to the Bush administration, used this report to justify American policies in the Middle East—from invading Iraq to financing microcredit schemes—claiming they are in the interest of the Arab peoples and would have their backing.

Friedman and others focused on the lack of freedom, with little sense of its historical and geopolitical causes, and read the document as proof of their Middle East exceptionalist narratives, which collapsed notions of the Middle East's absence from globalization, modernity, and history into a binary framework. In Friedman's words, the report analyzes the "main reasons the Arab world is falling off the globe."[41] Suggesting that the 9/11 attacks can be explained by reference to internal regional conditions rather than geopolitical struggles or the breakdown of the central state in Afghanistan, Friedman tells his readers that "if you want to understand the milieu that produced bin Ladenism, and will reproduce it if nothing changes, read this report."[42]

By the fall of 2002, Friedman had evolved from opining that the United States should care about socioeconomic conditions in the Middle East (because they "produce bin Ladenism") to arguing that the only way to stop the threat of terrorism "is by administering some shock therapy to the whole region."[43] Suggesting that "replacing Saddam Hussein with a progressive Iraqi regime" might be such a shock, he declares, "If America made clear that it was going into Iraq, not just to disarm Iraq but to empower Iraq's people to implement the Arab Human Development Report, well, [Arab terrorists] still wouldn't be with us" but, referring to the broad mass of public opinion, he suggests "the Arab street just might."[44] When time came to take a definitive stand in support of the invasion of Iraq, Friedman explains that though a nuclear-armed Iraq could be deterred, the real threat to American interests was the "undeterrables—the boys who did 9/11, who hate us more than they love life."[45] Friedman goes on to reason:

> So then the question is: What is the cement mixer that is churning out these undeterrables—these angry, humiliated and often unemployed Muslim youth? That cement mixer is a collection of faltering Arab states, which, as the U.N.'s Arab Human Development Report noted, have fallen so far behind the world their combined G.D.P. does not equal that of Spain. And the reason they have fallen behind can be traced to their lack of three things: freedom, modern education and women's empowerment. If we don't help transform these Arab states—which are also experiencing population explosions—to create better governance, to build more open and productive economies, to empower their women and to develop responsible media that won't blame all their ills on others, we will never begin to see the political, educational and religious reformations they need to shrink their output of undeterrables.[46]

Although Friedman's support for the AHDR goals may be laudable, by justifying this support as an anti-terrorism strategy he ignores the means the AHDR authors suggested for promoting *internally driven* reform, to be supported by intraregional cooperation, increased education spending, a restructuring of the nature of the global economic order, and peacefully ending military occupations over Arab territories. Instead, Friedman portrays the peoples of the region as terrorists and captives in need of liberation, noting "in today's globalized world, if you don't visit a bad neighborhood, it will visit you."[47] Even after the invasion, when the war was losing support in America, Friedman explains: "The right reason for this war . . . was to oust Saddam's regime and partner with the Iraqi people to try to implement the Arab Human Development Report's prescriptions in the heart of the Arab world. . . . The real reason for this war—which was never stated—was to burst what I would call the "terrorism bubble," which had built up during the 1990s."[48] Friedman's "terrorism bubble" lumps together disparate events such as the 1993 World Trade Center attack in New York and the suicide bombers unleashed in Israel by the Palestinian militant group Hamas. He explains them all in terms of the Arab youth whose "governments and society have left them unprepared for modernity." [49]

A similar logic drove the thinking of Johns Hopkins professor Fouad Ajami. In early 2003, writing in *Foreign Affairs*, one of the most influential Middle East experts in American media and inside White House policy circles, explains:

> For a while, the failures of [the Arab world] were confined to its own terrain, but migration and transnational terror altered all that. The fire that began in the Arab world spread to other shores, with the United States itself the principal target of an aggrieved people who no longer believed that justice could be secured in one's own land, from one's own rulers. It was September 11 and its shattering surprise, in turn, that tipped the balance on Iraq away from containment and toward regime change and "rollback."[50]

Although concerned about Iraq's "deadly weapons," Ajami argues that "the driving motivation of a new American endeavor in Iraq and in neighboring Arab lands should be modernizing the Arab World."[51]

THE GEOPOLITICAL IMAGINARY OF "THE PENTAGON'S NEW MAP"

In early 2003, while diplomats at the United Nations debated weapons inspections regimes and American and British officials presented frightening images of the threat Iraq posed, a broader discourse defined by Middle East exceptionalism was igniting support for a war with Iraq. Adding to the writings of Friedman, Ajami, and others, security analyst and former Pentagon strategist Thomas P. M. Barnett published a brief essay and a map that graphically depicted a version of this emerging geopolitical imaginary in the March 2003 issue of *Esquire*.[52] Although the specific influence of his iteration of Middle East exceptionalism might be hard to assess, his popular writings clearly represented the ongoing rethinking and redrawing of geopolitical strategies that folded the ideals of neoliberal capitalism into geopolitics and military affairs.[53] Barnett argues that the American post-9/11 grand strategy should be defined by the notion that "disconnectedness defines danger." His vision of a U.S. grand strategy calls for an explicit connection between the muscular use of military power and the promotion of globalization in the Middle East. According to Barnett, his ideas germinated while working at the U.S. Naval War College in the year before 9/11, when he was tapped to join a Pentagon strategic planning team. In the years since, he has disseminated his ideas first through his briefings of government officials and then through his public writings.

The power of his map is in its simplicity. Barnett graphically defines what he terms his "horizontal" way of thinking by mapping out the locations of major American military operations since the end of the Cold War. These zones fall almost entirely within the region of what he refers to as the "nonintegrating gap." This vast region, he contends, is disconnected from the global flows of people, capital, and security that sustain mutually assured dependence across "the core." The resulting territorial division of the globe is what Barnett describes as "the Pentagon's new map" defining American security challenges in the twenty-first century (Figure 10.1).[54] Rather than read this ordering of the planet as a legacy of colonialism, structural inequality, or underdevelopment, Barnett writes: "September 11 told me that globalization's uneven spread around the planet delineated more than just a frontier separating the connected from the disconnected—it marks the front lines in a struggle of historic proportions. The combatants in this conflict harbor very different dreams about the future."[55]

Barnett notes that "the true enemy" is "neither a religion (Islam) nor a place (the Middle East), but a condition—disconnectedness." He continues: "To be disconnected in this world is to be kept isolated, deprived, repressed, and uneducated. For the masses, being disconnected means a lack of choice and scarce access to ideas, capital, travel, entertainment, and loved ones overseas. For the elite, maintaining disconnectedness means control and the ability

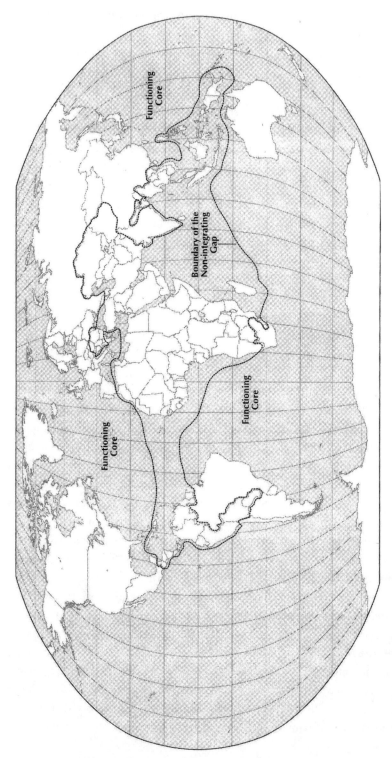

Figure 10.1. Barnett's "Core" and "Gap." "The Pentagon's new map" as redrawn in Roberts, Secord, and Sparke, "Neoliberal Geopolitics," 2003.

to hoard wealth, especially that generated by the exportation of valued raw materials."[56] Although he notes the enemy is a condition, not a place, his map of the "gap" region results in a territorially contiguous space where he claims globalization has not reached (note Figure 10.1). "These are the world's bad neighborhoods . . . the enter-at-your-own risk regions."[57]

Barnett views globalization as a process in which the local dissolves into the emerging global mosaic, but like Friedman, he worries that the Middle East is resisting such integration. Due to its vast oil resources as well as its religious and cultural proclivities, Barnett argues that the Middle East continues to be the region "most disconnected from the global economy by many measures and it's getting worse with time. . . . Simply put, the Middle East exports oil and terrorism and virtually nothing else of significance to the global economy."[58] In his view, Middle Eastern societies tend to "harbor very different dreams about the future." He notes that "Saddam Hussein's outlaw regime was dangerously disconnected from the globalizing world. . . . He was the Demon of Disconnectedness."[59]

Such views of the Middle East have provided the basis for claims by American and other Western policy makers, development experts, and business elites that to make the West safe, the Middle East must be transformed in order to integrate it into the global economic order. Barnett argues for a military strategy beginning with Iraq, suggesting that "America's use of military power in this war has to be guided towards strategic ends: the destruction of those who would wage war against global connectivity and the freedoms it unleashes."[60] By breaking Saddam's hold on power, Barnett enthusiastically claims, the American invasion of Iraq in 2003 "could be the first step towards a larger goal: true globalization."[61] He views the war through the lens of what he refers to as the "big bang theory": an American strategy to radically shrink the spaces across the globe that remain disconnected from globalization by reconnecting Iraq and demonstrating to the people of the Middle East that the mission of the United States is to offer what he refers to as "connectivity." Barnett's vision seeks to redefine the American grand strategy in a manner akin to Henry Luce's vision of "the American Century," which similarly argues that the United States should become the guarantor of global trade and mobility.[62]

"A FORWARD STRATEGY OF FREEDOM"

We can show, based on their own statements, that scholars such as Lewis and Ajami, who supported both the Iraq war and notions of Middle East exceptionalism, influenced the Bush administration's thinking about the Middle East.[63] Barnett claims that "senior military officials began citing [his] brief as a Rosetta stone for the Bush Administrations' new national security strategy."[64] Nevertheless, the above survey of the post-9/11 discourse about globalization, the Middle East, and security cannot offer a complete explanation for the American invasion of Iraq. It does, however, suggest its important contributions. For one, these perspectives helped build support for the war among some "liberal hawks," such as Friedman, who found the case for war based on the supposed threat of Iraqi "weapons of mass destruction" not fully convincing.[65] At the same time, Middle East exceptionalism both bolstered claims that Iraq was undeterrable and depicted for the American public a view of the Middle East as a region of dysfunctional states, economies, and societies, which was devoid of any awareness or appreciation of the geopolitical factors that may account for such conditions. Moreover, this discourse helped frame the Bush administration's break from policies based on realist balance of power calculations and its embrace of an ambitious vision for using military force to launch a radical transformation of the political, economic, and social conditions in the region. Although we cannot fully account for all the factors that determined Bush administration policies, we can show that Middle East exceptionalism provided a logic the administration used to publicly justify its policies.

This logic found its clearest expression in a November 2003 speech that President Bush made as American troops occupying Iraq, who had failed to discover stockpiled "weapons of mass destruction," were facing domestic resistance from Iraqi nationalists and struggling to bring order to a country that now lacked a functioning state and was plagued by deadly bombings perpetrated by foreign terrorists. Extending a theme previously developed, President Bush boldly announced that "the United States has adopted a new policy, a forward strategy of freedom" for transforming the political and economic landscape of the Middle East. Whereas the United States had long sought to promote reform and modernization in the Middle East, mostly to help ensure the stability of allied regimes, President Bush now defined the lack of reform as a security threat to the United States: "As long as the Middle East remains a place where freedom does not flourish, it will remain a place of stagnation, resentment, and violence ready for export [as experienced on September 11, 2001]."[66]

Though the articulation of a "forward strategy of freedom" was developed and promoted most forcefully in the weeks and months after the fall of the Baathist regime in Iraq, the policy was a core element of the "Bush doctrine" developed in the wake of 9/11. In his January 2002 "axis of evil" State of the Union address Bush called for "sweeping political change in the Arab world."[67] He pledged that "America will take the side" of those "around the world, including the Islamic world," "who advocate" American values of freedom.[68] Although the case for promoting economic and political reform was often presented without direct reference to the Iraq war, the discourse resonated in ways that likely increased support for the war as it projects the geopolitical imaginary of Middle East exceptionalism and defined domestic conditions in the Arab world as the basis of the most pressing security threat facing America. In December 2002, as Bush was beginning to promote his vision for "regime change" in Iraq, Secretary of State Colin Powell announced the Middle East Partnership Initiative (MEPI) to promote political, economic, and educational development in the Middle East. In his speech Powell noted, "The spread of democracy and free markets, fueled by the wonders of the technological revolution, has created a dynamo that can generate prosperity and human well-being on an unprecedented scale. But this revolution has left much of the Middle East behind."[69] The MEPI was one of the first major American policy initiatives to explicitly seek to redress the "job gap," "freedom gap," and "knowledge gap" between the Arab world and global trends.[70] Powell emphasized that these "gaps" are the ones defined by the UN-sponsored Arab Human Development Reports.[71] Powell did not make the case for war based on the AHDR, but as noted above, influential pundits such as Thomas Friedman were doing so at the time.

To build public support for the war in Iraq, Bush administration officials often blended the logics of promoting reform into their case for regime change in Iraq. They evoked the notion of Middle East exceptionalism, which suggested the need to eliminate the conditions that fostered support for international terrorism, and exaggerated the "gathering threat" Iraq posed by evoking images of deterritorialized dangers, such as international terrorism. In doing so, they associated the threat of international terrorism with the threat of Iraq, though the two were not connected. In his speech announcing the "forward strategy of freedom," after invoking the notion that the Middle East, due to lack of freedom, was generating "violence ready for export" as experienced on 9/11, Bush notes, "And with the spread of weapons that can bring catastrophic harm to our country and to our friends, it would be reckless to accept the status quo."[72] Bush also indirectly depicts the war as one that will convert Iraq into a developed, liberal democratic state. Bush then implies that by bringing political and economic freedom to the Middle East through the projection of U.S. power in the region—as it did previously in Europe and Asia (with the defeat of totalitarian regimes during World War II and then with its triumph in the Cold War)—the United States would be able to establish peace and diminish threats to U.S. interests. Regime change in Iraq lay at the center of this strategy that was to transform the political and economic landscape of the Middle East. As U.S. trade representative Robert Zoellick wrote in the summer of 2003: "The reconstruction and reopening of Iraq presents an opportunity for change—a chance for the people of the Arab world to ask why their region, once a nucleus of trade, has been largely excluded from the gains of this modern era of globalization."[73]

REDEFINING THE MIDDLE EAST

In the aftermath of 9/11, the Bush administration even tried to invent a new geographical moniker, the "Greater Middle East," to refer to the countries of the Arab world, plus Pakistan, Afghanistan, Iran, Turkey, and Israel. This exercise in naming follows that of Mahan as it defines its object in reference to Western security interests rather than any regional conceptions, identities, or geographical features. A draft memo outlining the American proposal for a "Greater Middle East Partnership Initiative" (GMEPI) to be discussed at a G-8 summit explains: "The Greater Middle East region poses a unique challenge and opportunity for the international community. . . . So long as the region's pool of politically and economically disenfranchised individuals grows, we will witness an increase in extremism, terrorism, international crimes and illegal migration."[74] The memo supports its vision with a review of data drawn from the Arab Human Development Reports that starkly illustrates the various "gaps" between conditions in the Arab states and the rest of the world. The GMEPI announces the region is at a crossroads and must choose between continuing on the same path of "adding every year to its population of underemployed, undereducated, and politically disenfranchised youth" or, instead, taking the "alternative . . . route to reform."[75] To stem the tide of the threatening flows emanating from the Middle East, the GMEPI called for counterflows of expert advice and joint programs to help promote institutional reform across the region. It offers a long list of reform projects, guidelines, and institutions that cover education, finance, governance, media, and elections. The goals are less striking than the impression that the memo's authors seem to want to micromanage the process of change within these societies bypassing the authority and sovereignty of regional governments. Although the document does not link reform with the American rationale for the invasion of Iraq, it does state that "the liberation of Afghanistan and Iraq from oppressive regimes" is one of the factors that has presented Western countries with "a historic opportunity" to "forge a long-term partnership with the Greater Middle East's reform leaders and launch a coordinated response to promote political, economic, and social reform in the region."[76] Moreover, the GMEPI specifically mentions as its model the experience of East Europe whose inclusion into the global economy was initiated by the collapse of the Soviet Union and the end of the Cold War. The "fall" of the Baathist regime in Iraq is seemingly viewed as providing an analogous impetus expected to ignite a similar regional transition to free market democracy.

AGAINST EXCEPTIONALISM: UNMAPPING THE MIDDLE EAST

By incorporating reference to the Arab Human Development Reports, the GMEPI sought to suggest that its script for reform was a universal one and that it should be supported by Arabs who want to diminish the "gaps" separating Arab countries from the rest of the world. Defined by the binary logic of Middle East exceptionalism, this discourse erases the geopolitical context and tries to depoliticize the notion of reform. The GMEPI memo and similar American plans for reform in the Middle East, however, fail to recognize the diverse ways states and societies in the region understand and seek to engage in their own processes of defining reform and globalization and addressing their forms and impact. Joseph Samahah, then the Beirut-based editor for *Al Safir* newspaper, wrote about the original 2002 MEPI that its purpose was "to link the ambitions of some people in the Arab world to the objectives of the United States, not the objectives of the United States to the ambitions of people in the Arab world."[77] When the draft memo was leaked to the London-based, pan-Arab daily *Al Hayat*, it caused a firestorm of criticism from not only leftist, nationalist, and Islamist critics of U.S. policy but also the political leaders of America's allies in the Middle East and Europe as well as the drafters of the AHDR themselves. Marwan Muasher, the foreign minister of Jordan—one of America's closest allies in the region—publicly criticized the GMEPI, arguing that "reform is important and needed in the Arab world . . . but for it to work we need ownership of the process, not a one-for-all blueprint from Washington."[78] Nader Fergany, a principal author of the AHDR, was also critical of what he referred to as the American administration's "arrogant attitude in respect to the rest of the world, which causes it to behave as if it can decide the fate of states and peoples."[79] Most critically, the Bush administration's approach to reform in the Middle East clearly failed to imagine that in a few years' time Arab regimes might fall to popular, locally driven protest movements calling for democracy and the rule of law.

The Bush administration's project for transforming the Middle East was first scaled back, and then it eventually petered out due to the failure to convert Iraq into a model for the region, the success of Islamists opposed to American policy in elections in Palestine and Lebanon, and the unwillingness of the United States to impose reforms on its moderate allies Egypt, Jordan, and Saudi Arabia. In 2006, with Iraq engulfed in what seemed to be the verge of a sectarian civil war, a new wave of exceptionalist notions entered into American discourse about Iraq. Most Americans converted from expecting the new Iraq to become the model for a new Middle East to blaming the Iraqis and the nature of Iraqi society for the failure of the American project and the ongoing violence.[80] Many argued that Americans were only then coming to understand the "true" nature of Iraqi society and history—an artificial nation, where ethics and religious identities left no room for liberal democratic norms and a love of freedom.

The failure of this project should not be understood as rooted in the belief that democracy and reform are not possible in the Middle East, but as with modernization theory, it is due to the conceit of viewing its task as fostering an inevitable outcome as well as assuming that the United States had the capability to succeed in bringing it about.[81] In an insightful critique of the influence of modernization theory on U.S. policy toward the Middle East since the 1950s, historian Richard Bulliet notes that one reason for the failure of modernization theory as a guide for U.S. policy in the Middle East is that American "policy circles seem incapable of imagining a Muslim model of modernity."[82] The rise of Middle East exceptionalism in American policy debates can trace its origins to the failures of modernization theory to understand

and embrace the agency, imagination, and interests of diverse communities across the Middle East who did not have the same dreams as American policy makers. Likewise the Bush administration was also unwilling to ever consider "whether there might be merit in some of those other ways of looking at reality."[83] The notion of Middle East exceptionalism fails to recognize such alternatives because they challenge its binary structure, which views the differences between the Middle East and the rest of the world in exceptional terms. It is more profitable to approach the range of diversity found across the Middle East in terms of variations across the same multiple registers experienced elsewhere.

Oddly, the Bush administration often sought to argue that its project for regional transformation represented a rejection of the notion of Middle East exceptionalism. By this they did not mean they rejected what I have analyzed as Middle East exceptionalism, but rather they rejected simpleminded "skepticism about the capacity or even the desire of the Middle Eastern peoples for self-government."[84] Secretary of State Condoleezza Rice often tried to defend the Bush doctrine by arguing that the Bush administration had rejected past American policies that followed "so-called Middle East exceptionalism," meaning pursuing "stability at the expense of democracy."[85] Journalist David Brooks, a strong supporter of the Bush doctrine, defines the notion of "Arab exceptionalism" as follows: "This is the belief that while most of the world is chugging toward a globally integrated future, the Arab world remains caught in its own medieval whirlpool of horror. The Arab countries cannot become quickly democratic; their people aren't ready for pluralistic modernity; they just have to be walled off so they don't hurt us again."[86] Brooks claims President George W. Bush stands against this view, because the latter believes that "the Arabs aren't very different from anybody else, and *can be brought* into the family of democratic nations."[87]

Although Brooks seems to reject a cultural determinist view of Middle East exceptionalism, he nevertheless suggests that it is America's role to "bring" the Arabs into modernity, implying that they are incapable of bringing themselves due to their societies' own internal characteristics. Such a view still relies on the binary logic of Middle East exceptionalism, and it can only really be understood through the lens of "American exceptionalism." In other words, the Bush administration viewed itself as capable of negating the region's exceptional status due to the exceptional capacities and universal values of the United States. As a senior adviser to President Bush explained to journalist Ron Suskind: "We're an empire now, and when we act, we create our own reality. And while you're studying that reality—judiciously, as you will—we'll act again, creating other new realities, which you can study too, and that's how things will sort out. We're history's actors . . . and you, all of you, will be left to just study what we do."[88]

CONCLUSION: THERE *IS* A MIDDLE EAST!

Michael Ezekiel Gasper

> *The Middle East has become . . . a geographical expression*
> *for countries whose current orientations show more diversity*
> *than unity.*
>
> **—Nikki Keddie, *Is There a Middle East?***

SO, *IS* THERE A MIDDLE EAST? And if so, *where* is it? Is it a particular place? If not, *what* is it? This volume shows the ways in which the term "Middle East" seems to evoke a set of questions, or often a set of problems, more than it does a clearly delineated geographical location. These essays show how the concept of the Middle East was and is constructed and reconstructed from a variety of sources that include political/strategic, religious, and ideological elements that often have little relation to the region's geography, culture, or history. Accordingly, this collection suggests that rather than try to define or redefine or not define the Middle East it is perhaps more fruitful to investigate the effects that this abstract category has had, and continues to have, on the way that many people in the world think and act with respect to the region. In this sense these chapters enumerate some of the links between the production of knowledge and the categories used to arrange that knowledge and their impact on the lives of the people who live there. Thus, in the main this diverse collection of essays by historians, geographers, anthropologists, and political scientists shares a concern with the effects of geographic categories on the lives that people lead and the ways that scholars depict them.[1]

The contributors take the question "Is there a Middle East?" as a starting point to explore how the production of knowledge has consequences in the ways people think and have thought about the region both inside and outside of it. For example, Diana Davis argues that the environmental history of the region is based on assumptions derived in part from biblical imagery of a land of milk and honey. Her chapter charts the emergence of the "declensionist environmental narrative," which asserts that livestock overgrazing, careless deforestation, and general mismanagement caused the land to lose its putative "biblical" lushness. She then shows how this assumption became foundational for narratives of Middle Eastern environmental history and even more perversely for land management strategies of both local states and of the international development community.

Perhaps the primary question that comes to mind in reading these chapters is first and foremost, *is* there a Middle East? Too often laypeople, influential commentators, policy experts, and even scholars speak confidently about "the Middle East" without clearly defining the object to which they are referring. The essays in the volume have attempted to speak to this paradox from a variety of different perspectives that take into account geographical, historical, and ideological factors. These chapters explore the reception and evolution of the imaginative power of the West. They explicate how outsiders—Europeans and Americans—have delineated and defined the region geographically and conceptually. We have learned that the outlines of the Middle East changed according to strategic and professional concerns lying outside of the region. We have also glimpsed the perhaps unwitting collusion on the part of the academy in the making and remaking of the modern Middle East.[2] In their contributions, Hüseyin Yılmaz, Roger Adelson, and Michael Bonine describe some of the myriad permutations of the term among experts and laypeople and the dizzying array of political and professional considerations that went into their making.

Yılmaz begins this discussion by identifying the discursive antecedents that came to underpin the term in its early development. He shows that after World War I the term "Middle East" inherited much of the politics and the sense of absolute Otherness that underlay the "Eastern Question" in the nineteenth century. As a consequence, during the twentieth century the Middle East, including the lands of the Ottoman Empire and its successor states, which was formerly the referent territory for the "Eastern Question," continued to signify all that the West was not. In some of the recent debates about the appropriateness of the modern Turkish Republic joining the European Union, one detects traces of these same arguments. For example, a French parliamentarian responding to a question about Turkish ascension to the EU remarked that the "integration of Turkey is the breakdown of the European project. . . . We don't have a common history, culture or vision. . . . European identity is built on a common history, a Judeo-Christian culture, a culture of human rights and the enlightenment ideas."[3]

Adelson adds another dimension to this discussion as he examines the history and use (and "misuse") of the term by British and American figures in the early twentieth century. Then he traces how experts in a number of disciplines and fields of endeavor transformed the "Middle East" into a mainstay of policy discussions and public discourse. Bonine focuses more narrowly on how professional geographers conceptualized the region and examines the way they have aggregated, and in some cases disaggregated, the Middle East (and North Africa). While Adelson and Bonine look at the rise of expertise and specialization on the Middle East in the Anglophone world, Ramzi Rouighi provides much-needed insight into how this process unfolded in Francophone discourses on North Africa. In his contribution to the volume Rouighi explicates how the idea of "the Middle East" was and was *not* translated into the discursive practices of Francophone North Africans.

In the volumes of writing on the Middle East, one discovers that some do not hesitate to define it as the Arab world plus Iran, Turkey, and Israel. However, one can find others who include Morocco, Algeria, Tunisia, Libya, Turkey, Iran, Mauritania, Sudan, and Somalia. Others insist on excluding Morocco, Algeria, Tunisia, and Libya, while some append the Central Asian nations of the former Soviet Union to their Middle East. In addition, in more recent days it is fairly common to find references to Afghanistan and Pakistan as Middle Eastern states. As Bonine has shown, even for professional geographers the geographical ambiguity of the region is perhaps most clearly manifested in the fact that there is neither consistency nor even a clear consensus on the outlines of the region.

One may suggest that the term "Middle East" is often so imprecisely or variously defined that it becomes almost meaningless. Similarly, one may put forth many warranted criticisms about the political nature of the concept, or one may readily accept that delineating regions such as the Middle East inevitably entails political questions. However, pointing out that our geographical concepts are informed by our politics hardly ranks as a major theoretical insight. Indeed, a variety of decisions factor into the production of categories, definitions and concepts that we use to make sense of the world. No one can doubt that the decision on what to include or exclude within a regional rubric inevitably involves some political considerations, and this book has explored the politics of geography in the term "Middle East."

If a standard geographical description eludes us, perhaps some other way that the region is commonly represented as a single unit provides a criterion by which to better grasp the nature of the Middle East. While no doubt an incomplete list, some of the more familiar themes that are often said to unite the Middle East range from religion to language to ethnicity to political identity.

Over the decades many of those writing about the Middle East began with the assumption that Islam is the linchpin for understanding the region. There are a number of reasons why this is a fallacy. The most basic problem is that Islam by itself does not provide a coherent frame of analysis for students of the region, which contains significant minorities of non-Muslims such as Christians, Jews, Bahi'is, and Zoroastrians. To privilege Islam as the primary social and cultural marker effectively excludes many millions of people from consideration. Second, and even more obvious, the Muslim world does not correspond to the Middle East; the vast majority of Muslims live outside the region—however one defines it. Thus, the term "Muslim" tells us very little that is specific to the Middle East. It is an open question as to what kinds of specific insights for one region may be garnered from the designation "Muslim," since it applies to a fifth of the world's population. Why should we presume that being a Muslim in the Middle East differs from being a Muslim *qua* Muslim in Pakistan or Chile? That a large segment of the population self-identifies as Muslim would tell a researcher very little that is specific to the Middle East. At the same time, while it is true that in the contemporary Middle East one encounters a host of self-described Islamic social and political organizations, charity and welfare societies, and a range of piety movements, this is hardly unique to the region. One can find similar organizations, associations, and movements among Muslims in many other parts of the world, including the United States and Europe.

One can find stacks of dusty books that no one reads anymore that argue that to come to grips with Middle Eastern society, politics, and history one must begin and end with an emphasis on Islam. All of these books lost their sheen when some shift in Middle Eastern politics or society demonstrated the fallacy of this supposition. This happened during the Nassar era when a "dangerous" form of assertive nationalism inspired by atheistic communism was said to be displacing Islam as the primary sociopolitical force in Middle Eastern society. It happened again after the Iranian Revolution and the assassination of Anwar Sadat, when books about Islamic quietism were replaced with books about resurgent and revolutionary Islam. We saw this after the events of September 11, 2001, and we have seen this once again in the wake of the political convulsions that began in Tunisia in early 2011 and then spread throughout much of the Arab world, and we will no doubt continue to see this occur. The simple fact is that "Islam" is too broad a signifier to provide any useful insight into a society's politics, culture, or history. Indeed, in studying the diversity of cultural and social phenomena, to say nothing of the political dynamics of the Middle East, one is severely handicapped by using "Islam" as the primary investigative instrument. Imagine trying to use the rubric "Christianity" to understand the breath of European culture, politics, and history throughout the entire modern period!

Another common iteration of the term "Middle East" has it roughly interchangeable with the Arab world. The Arab world is a collection of about twenty-five countries where a single language (Arabic) and a single "ethnicity" (Arab) ostensibly dominate. This Middle East / Arab world would necessarily include all of North Africa, the Arabian Peninsula, the Persian Gulf, the eastern Mediterranean, and several states in northeast Africa, and would exclude Israel, Cyprus, Turkey, and Iran. However, great linguistic heterogeneity exists within this area, as significant minorities of non-Arabic speakers reside in both North Africa and the Arab states of the East. In addition, there are significant differences between Arabic dialects themselves. And as for "Arabs" being an ethnic group, this is a misnomer. An Arab is simply a designation for a person whose mother tongue is Arabic, regardless of one's "ethnic" origin. Even if we ignore these issues, the more basic problem, of course, is that if the term "Middle East" is to denote an entity larger than the Arab world we are faced with including the many millions of Turkic and Persianate language speakers. However one looks at it, the Arab world is linguistically heterogeneous, and the larger Middle East is even more so.

Just as they speak many languages, the region's peoples are comprised of many different ethnicities. Nevertheless, the idea that somehow the Middle East is where one finds only Arabs still persists. In any case, as mentioned above, the term "Arab" itself is fraught in many ways. "Arab" is little more than an approximate linguistic designation. Just as the Arabic language has many dialects (even if generally mutually comprehensible), Arabic speakers come in all sizes, shapes, and colors. This can lead to much confusion. For example, one often reads that the conflict between northern and southern Sudan pits "Africans" against "Arabs" as if this were some kind of race conflict. Obviously, all Sudanese are Africans, and moreover, the partisans of both sides often do not differ significantly from one another with regard to physical appearance. If the ethnic term "Arab" is so encumbered, how are we to size up the even more general category, Middle Easterner? Rouighi examines this question from the perspective of the people of the Maghrib (Morocco, Algeria, and Tunisia). He explains why the people of the Maghrib do not see their countries as part of the Middle East or consider themselves Middle Easterners.

Just as these frameworks fail to capture the diversity of the Middle East, one is hard pressed to uncover a single comprehensive and exclusive political formation that is distinct from the rest of the world. For example, Middle Eastern states are organized in ways familiar to political scientists studying any other region of the world. Nor is the range of ideological orientations particularly unique. Liberal, statist, corporatist, and socialist trends vie with Islam-inspired political movements and organizations that have counterparts throughout the wider Muslim world and, indeed, across the globe. There exist few political ideologies—besides an array of garden variety particularist nationalisms—that are singularly "Middle Eastern." This is not to deny that powerful ideological currents have transcended the region's national borders over the last 150 years (the various Arab nationalisms are perhaps the most obvious) and that for periods these have been very important. Nevertheless, however successful these movements might have been at particular moments, they faced both strong internal and external obstacles that frustrated their full crystallization. This is one reason observers were equally surprised and hard pressed to explain the obvious similarities between the protests and upheavals that began in the Tunisian town of Sidi Bouzid in December 2010 and then spread through much of the rest of the Arab world in winter and spring 2011. First in Tunisia, and then in Egypt, Yemen, Morocco, Jordan, Bahrain, Oman, Libya, and Syria, protesters called for democratic reform by strengthening the rule of law. In addition, they called for an end to the corruption and cronyism that had marked these countries' economic life for decades. People throughout the entire region even took up the same chant coined by demonstrators in Tunisia, "The people want the downfall of the regime."

In the face of the above observations, some are willing to accept that the complicated human geography of the Middle East frustrates almost any conceivable cultural, religious, or political framework for defining the region even while they suggest a negative framework for understanding it as a single unit. For them Middle Easterners have isolation from global economic and political trends in common. Similarly, one of the stereotypical commonplaces one encounters in best-selling nonfiction, newspaper commentary, and late-night comedy shows is that "the people in the Middle East have been killing one another since the beginning of time and will continue to do so." This view echoes one found surprisingly often in more serious commentary and even among some in policy circles. It is so pernicious because it displaces the role of history, that is, the agency of human beings, with this odd amalgam of geopolitical folklore. The most troubling effect of this is that the Middle East seems to stand outside the rules of history and rationality. Unfortunately, it is not hyperbole to suggest that the Middle East, in so much of what is written today, is represented as the quintessential exception to the human experience.

Despite the obvious parallels with the rest of the postcolonial world, many specialists and influential media figures continue to see the region through this lens of "exceptionalism." The basic idea of exceptionalism is that the social, political, and economic life of Middle East society operates according to criteria different than those found elsewhere in the world. This is the starting point for Waleed Hazbun's chapter. In it he analyzes the production and husbanding of the idea of Middle East exceptionalism in the face of globalization in Western academia and media. In his critical intervention he shows how the "geopolitical imaginary" of Middle East exceptionalism supports a "mental map" for a particular kind of political geography. In the post-9/11 world this mental map has been translated into American-led efforts to "fix" the Middle East by making it unexceptional. This would be accomplished through a range of indirect and direct interventions, including the use of military force. Hazbun provocatively concludes that Middle East exceptionalism has ultimately served the imperial aims of the West.

Here one might interject that there are indeed things that are exceptional to the contemporary Middle East. For example, some states in the region control vast petroleum resources. Doesn't the wealth derived from these resources insulate these states and indeed the entire region from the forces of the global economic order? Historian James Gelvin's contribution speaks directly to this question. His chapter looks at developments in Middle Eastern political economy from the Great Depression to the present. Specifically, it explicates how transformations in the regional "civil order" (the relations among citizens and those between citizens and state) were the result of both local and global forces, and in so doing he too casts grave doubt on the Middle East exceptionalist narrative. His chapter situates major shifts in the regional political economy solidly within global developments.

Across the Middle East a number of states enacted social programs resembling the welfare states of Western Europe and North America beginning in the mid-twentieth century. The states promoting this new "civic order" drawing on populist nationalist rhetoric pledged a minimum of material support in return for loyalty and compliance from its citizens. The Middle Eastern states espousing these ideas were intimately involved in the emergence of the nonaligned movement and then the Group of 77 and their call for a New International Economic Order that challenged the post–World War II Bretton Woods system. The West, led by the United States, hit back aggressively at this challenge to the status quo of economic liberalism. Gelvin's chapter shows how this civic order began to unravel toward the end of the twentieth century due to economic and political pressures exerted by the major Western powers. Gelvin concludes with the caveat that the economic crisis of 2008 may open yet another avenue for regional agency. The recent political developments in Tunisia, Egypt, and elsewhere in the region may be the first signs of the opening of just such "another avenue." In any case, the lesson one can draw from Gelvin's contribution is that large-scale shifts in the international political economy reverberated in the Middle East, and that Middle Eastern states were major players in contestation over the global economic order over the last seventy-five years or more.

Is there some kind of common history that impels us to accept the Middle East as a single analytical unit? Over thirty years ago the historian Nikki Keddie took up this question in her essay "Is There a Middle East?"[4] She concluded that the term had concrete analytical value for those looking at the period after the rise of Islam and before 1500 C.E. She argued that historians of the early centuries of Muslim rule were justified in considering the Middle East (comprised of the Umayyad, early Abbasid, and Ottoman empires) as a single unit of study because after the rise of Islam these lands came to share a common fate. However, citing the divergence between Ottoman and Persian (Iranian) experiences for the period after 1500, she doubted whether there is historical justification for thinking of this entire area as a single unit of study. In addition, while much of the territory that is often considered the Middle East was at times nominally part of the Ottoman Empire, that experience differed greatly from place to place and from one era to another. Ottoman power was sporadic and had limited reach in many hinterland areas of North Africa and the Arabian Peninsula. Another complicating issue is the fact that large portions of the Ottoman Empire, such as Egypt, were nearly independent by the eighteenth century and had begun to develop historical trajectories increasingly independent of their Ottoman pasts.

Historiographical issues aside, people in the area did have their own conceptions of the geography before the notion of the "Middle East" was imposed on them by the West. The contributions of three historians, Arash Khazeni, Gagan D. S. Sood, and Huseyin Yilmaz, shed light on alternative geographies that once marked the imaginative frontiers for some living in the region, while Daniel Varisco examines how Western pilgrims viewed the Holy Land before there was a Middle East. Khazeni and Yilmaz also go one step further and chronicle the beginning of the end of these older imaginative geographies. They describe the processes by which European power obliged a new geographical reckoning upon the populations of the Eurasian and African lands that eventually became the Middle East.

In his chapter on the history of the frontier between Iran and Central Asia, Khazeni explicates the relationship between emergent forms of state power, the new science of map-making, and the geographical imagination of people in the area. He narrates how changes in state power paralleled the ways in which the frontier was represented and understood. Taking a different approach, Sood explores the socioeconomic worlds that produced what he calls a "cosmopolitan Islamic Eurasia." His history of everyday life recalls the vibrant "arena of circulation and exchange" that incorporated the lands around the Indian Ocean that eventually were to give way to centralized states with fixed territorial borders. Taken together, these historians demonstrate the vitality of geographic-historical imaginaries that were eventually displaced by the Eurocentric notions of the Near and Middle East that were supported by the considerable military, economic, and ideological power of the West.

Lastly, Varisco writes about the complicated relationship between the idea of the Holy Land and visitors to the region. His chapter critiques an account of the binary relationship between Europe and Orient, which he attributes to the late Edward Said, that was predicated on the assumptions of "Western superiority" and "Oriental inferiority." Varisco reverses this as he argues that in thinking of the Orient-as–Holy Land, Western pilgrims often viewed the region in sacral and ideal terms. As a consequence, the binary conception that overlay their representations was punctuated with a view of the region as a utopia rather than as a site of degradation and misery for which colonial administrators such as Lord Cromer later became famous.

· · ·

This volume has offered a number of perspectives on the history, evolution, and use of the term "Middle East" in Europe and North America. We have also seen some of the ways that people in the region came to adopt, adapt, or reject the term. The essays have shown how the definition of the region has shifted with various paradigms of inquiry and research whose roots can, at least in part, be traced to the rise and fall of various strategic and political calculations of Western powers. Europe's colonial and imperial past, the imperatives of the Cold War, and more recently, the so-called war on terror have each played their part in producing contingent incarnations of the Middle East. Consequently, we have come to understand that the idea of the Middle East cannot be separated from the power to create and impose categories of knowledge on the rest of the world. The Middle East exists because the West has possessed sufficient power to give the idea substance. In this regard the colonial past and the imperial present are parts of the equation that make the Middle East real. For it is as real as any other geopolitical abstraction in use today. There is no small irony that the Middle East is an inescapable fact for those who live in the countries of the eastern and southern Mediterranean and southwest Asia even if the mental map on which it depends is imported.

In reflecting on the essays in this book we are left with two basic suppositions. First, despite the pretensions of scientific geography, many subjective elements figure into geographic calculations. Just as these subjective factors are liable to change, so too are the calculations based on them. In this sense geography is neither fixed nor permanent. We have seen that one's geographical horizons can be imagined in more than one way. These chapters have offered glimpses of alternative geographies that existed before the extension of Western power to the region. Second, the Middle East belongs to a geographic imaginary that is in part built on the general alignment of contemporary geostrategic power. Accordingly, it will inextricably accumulate new meaning until some major strategic realignment occurs and the geographical paradigms that have been in place for more than a century give way to something new. Until that time, despite the difficulties, the inconsistencies, and the contradictions, we have to say that, indeed, there *is* a Middle East.

REFERENCE MATTER

NOTES

Chapter 1

1. Marx, *Eastern Question*, 2.

2. For a detailed discussion of the British role in the making of the Middle East, see Adelson, *London and the Invention of the Middle East*, as well as his chapter in this volume. For the Middle East as a security concept, see Bilgin, "Inventing Middle Easts," 10–37. For a geopolitical analysis of the Middle East, see Davutoğlu, *Stratejik Derinlik*, 129–43, 323–455, as well as the chapter by Waleed Hazbun in this volume.

3. For a fairly recent designs of the region, see Lewis, "Rethinking the Middle East," 99–119; "G8-Greater Middle East Partnership," *Al-Hayat* (February 13, 2004).

4. For the variability and indefinability of the region, see Pearcy, *The Middle East—An Indefinable Region*, 407–16; Keddie, "Is There a Middle East?" 255–71; Achcar, "Fantasy of a Region That Does Not Exist"; and the chapter in this volume by Michael E. Bonine, "Of Maps and Regions: Where Is the Geographer's Middle East?"

5. Argyll, *Eastern Question*, xv.

6. Millard, *Our Eastern Question*.

7. Duruy, *Abrégé d'histoire universelle*, 601–14.

8. Fysh, *Time of the End*, 19.

9. Weethe, *Eastern Question in Its Various Phases*, x.

10. Marriott, *Eastern Question*, 1.

11. Sorel, *Eastern Question in the Eighteenth Century*, 9.

12. Pepin, *Deux ans de règne, 1830–1832*, 362; "France," *Morning Chronicle* (London) (May 18, 1833); "German Papers," *Morning Chronicle* (London) (June 17, 1833); "Foreign Intelligence," *Caledonian Mercury* (December 15, 1834); "Foreign Intelligence," *Bell's Life in London and Sporting Chronicle* (February 2, 1834); "Egypt and Mohammed Ali, or Travel in the Valley of the Nile, by James Augustus Saint-John," *La*

France littéraire 13 (1834): 416–17; Bucquet, *Compte-rendu des sessions législatives, session de 1834*, 275.

13. Cobden, *England and Russia* (London: James Ridgway & Sons, 1835), 154; Urquhart, *Portfolio*, 533; Urquhart, "Turkey, Egypt, and the Affairs of the East," 100–115.

14. Von Ranke, *Historisch-politische Zeitschrift*, 233.

15. Carl Brown, for example, would still define the Middle East as the Afro-Asian lands of the former Ottoman Empire. See Brown, *International Politics and the Middle East*, 3–18.

16. For a critique of modern studies on the subject, see Brummett, "Imagining the Early Modern Ottoman Space," 15–58.

17. Suyuti, for example, thought that the middle of the earth was Jerusalem on the authority of reports he attributed to Prophet Muhammad. See al-Suyuti, *History of the Temple of Jerusalem*, 2, 15, 20. For other views see Collins, *Al-Muqaddasi*, 7.

18. Yücesoy, "Ancient Imperial Heritage and Islamic Universal Historiography," 135–55.

19. Al-Mes'udi, *Meadows of Gold and Mines of Gems*, 76.

20. Ibid., 200.

21. Ibid., 334.

22. For medieval Muslim views on Babil, see Janssen, *Babil, the City of Witchcraft and Wine*, 114–15.

23. Ibn al-Jawzi, *Al-muntazam fi al-tarikh*, 70.

24. Ibn al-Wardi, *Ajaib al-buldan*, 77.

25. Ibid., 78.

26. Ibn Khordâdhbeh, *Kitâb al-masâlik wa'l-mamâlik*, 234.

27. *Wasat al-mashriq* literally means "the middle of the East"; see Ibn Khordâdhbeh, *Kitâb al-masâlik*, 4.

28. al-Dhahabi, *Tarikh al-Islam*, 249. I am grateful to Hayrettin Yücesoy of Saint Louis University for providing me with this reference.

29. Ibn al-Wardi, *Ajaib al-buldan*, 15, 29, 107. For the Ottoman adoption of this designation, see Âlî, *Künhü'l Ahbar*, 218–30. For classical views in Islamic geography, see İbrahim Harekat, "Mağrib," in *Türkiye Diyanet Vakfı İslam ansiklopedisi*, vol. 27 (Istanbul: Türkiye Diyanet Vakfı, 1988–).

30. "Al-Maghrib," in *Encyclopedia of Islam*, 2nd ed., vol. 5 (Leiden: Brill, 1960–2009),

31. Ibn Khaldun, *Tarikh Ibn Khaldun*.

32. Hegel, *Vorlesungen über die Philosophie der Geschichte*, 211. For an English translation, see Hegel, *The Philosophy of History*, 242.

33. Franzos, *Aus Halb-Asien Culturbilder aus Galizien, der Bukowina, Südrußland und Rumänien*. For an analysis of European views on Eastern Jewry, see Saposnik, "Europe and Its Orients in Zionist Culture Before the First World War," 1105–23, and Levesque, "Mapping the Other," 145–65.

34. Sowards, *Moderne Geschichte des Balkans: Der Balkan im Zeitalter des Nationalismus*, 42.

35. Tyler, *European Powers and the Near East, 1875–1908*; Scheffler, " 'Fertile Crescent,' 'Oriens,' 'Middle East,' " 253–72.

36. Von Ranke, *Historisch-politische Zeitschrift*, 236.

37. Desprez, "Souvenirs de l'Europe orientale: La grande Illyrie et le mouvement illyrien," 1007–1029.

38. Ferret, *Voyage en Abyssinie dans les provinces du Tigré, du Samen et de l'Amhara*, 44.

39. Julius Fürst, "Oesterreichische Nebenländer," *Der Orient*, 9/40 (1848): 315–18.

40. Alletz, *De la démocratie nouvelle*, 359.

41. Wright and Reid, *Malay Peninsula*; Wright and Reid, "Near East," 904–7.

42. Meadows, *Chinese and Their Rebellions*, 188; Meadows, "Communications with the Far East," 574–81.

43. Rubbi, *Poesie ebraiche*, 19.

44. Canovai, *Panegirici di Stanislao Canovai delle scuole pie*, 214.

45. Tenca, "Della litteratura Slava," 53–67.

46. "L'Obolo per la fede," *La Civiltà cattolica* 6 (1857): 385–400.

47. Kanne, *Erste Urkunden der Geschichte oder allgemeine Mythologie*, 459; Wagner, *Der Staat*, 384; Wagner, "Einige vorläufige Angaben und Bemerkungen," 172–76; Wagner, *Jahrbücher der Literatur*, 41; Rosen, *Mesnewi oder doppelverse des Scheich Mewlânâ Dschelâl-ed-dîn Rûmî*, 41; von Rumohr, *Italienische Forschungen*, 311; Donop, *Das magusanische Europa*, 140; Dirckinck-Holmfeld, ed., *Politisches Journal, nebst Anzeige von Gelehrten und andern Sachen*, 281; Vámbéry, *Der Islam im neunzehnten Jahrhundert*, 18.

48. Townshend, *A Cruise in Greek Waters with a Hunting Excursion in Tunis*, 285.

49. Meadows, *Chinese and Their Rebellions*, 188; Meadows, "Communications with the Far East," 574–81. For similar examples of this Far East-based perception of the Near East, see "The Fleets at Cherbourgh," *Littel's Living Age* 30 (1865): 571–73; Sala, *Echoes of the Year Eighteen Hundred and Eighty-three*, 238–39; Lowell, *Chosön*, 164; *The Parliamentary Debates*, ser. 4, vol. 19 (London: Reuter's Telegram Co., 1893), 1899; "Want to Aid China," *Chicago Daily Tribune* (January 30, 1898); "Why Not China Conference?" *Daily News* (March 12, 1898); Sladen, *Queer Things About Persia*, xii.

50. Mitchell, *History of Ancient Sculpture*, 274.

51. For a representative sample, see *Graphic* (December 28, 1895); *Penny Illustrated Paper and Illustrated Times* (August 10, 1895); *Belfast News-Letter* (September 6, 1895); *Derby Mercury* (September 11, 1895); *Ipswich Journal* (November 9, 1895); *Pall Mall Gazette* (November 13, 1895); *Birmingham Daily Post* (November 20, 1895); *Northern Echo* (November 20, 1895); *Western Mail* (November 20, 1895); *Manchester Times* (November 22, 1895); *Leeds Mercury* (December 19, 1895); *Glasgow Herald* (December 23, 1895).

52. Rycaut, *Present State of the Ottoman Empire*.

53. Mitchell, *History of Ancient Sculpture*, 274.

54. Flügel, *Geschichte der Araber bis auf den Sturz des Chalifats von Bagdad*, 143; National Liberal Federation, *Proceedings in Connection with the Twentieth Annual Meeting*, 27.

55. It seldom appears in other European languages. For French uses of the term *l'Orient plus proche* around the turn of the twentieth century, see Bérard, "Angleterre et Russie, 865–86; Waliszewski, *Ivan le Terrible*, 132.

56. Richard Burton, *Personal Narrative of a Pilgrimage to El Medinah and Meccah*, 62; Richard Burton, "Unexplored Syria," 217–19; Isabel Burton, *Inner Life of Syria, Palestine, and the Holy Land*, 199.

57. Lamport, "Levantine Sects," 268–76.

58. *Pall Mall Gazette* (October 15, 1878; April 7, 1879); *Newcastle Courant* (September 14, 1883).

59. *Manchester Times* (October 18, 1895); *Birmingham Daily Post* (October 28, 1895); *Northern Echo* (October 28, 1895); *Leeds Mercury* (February 3, 1896); *Daily News* (February 20, 1896); *Bristol Mercury and Daily Post* (April 15, 1896); *Glasgow Herald* (March 25, 1897).

60. "Christianity in Ceylon," 66–90.

61. "The New Essayists: Dr. Williams and Others," 240–60.

62. Wilson, "Séances historiques de Genève," 281.

63. Upham, "Upham on the Star of the Nativity," 437–51. For Upham, see Adams, *Dictionary of American Authors*, 394.

64. Upham, "Upham on the Star of the Nativity," 437–51.

65. Peloubet, *Select Notes on the International Sabbath School Lessons*, 16; Besant and Palmer, "Jerusalem, the City of Herod and Saladin," 235; Richard Burton, "The Long Wall of Salona and the Ruined Cities of Pharia and Gelsa di Lesina," 262–96; "Van Lennep's Bible Lands," 502–4.

66. Gower, *My Reminiscences*, 365; Fairbairn, *Religion in History and in the Life of Today*, 156; Lowell, *Chosön: The Land of the Morning Calm*, 378; Beazley, *The Dawn of Modern Geography*, 211.

67. Griffith, "Egypt and Assyria," 155; Bancroft, *New Pacific*, 407; McCarthy, *Story of Gladstone's Life*, 459.

68. Hogarth, *Nearer East*, 1–2.

69. Ibid., 285.

70. Ibid., 279–80.

71. Allen, *European Tour*, 118; Strong, *Story of the American Board*, 393.

72. Wheeler, "The Old World in the New," 145–53; Wheeler, "Alexander's Invasion of India," 525–39.

73. Renton, "Changing Languages of Empire and the Orient," 645–67; Scheffler, "'Fertile Crescent,' 'Orient,' 'Middle East,'" 253–72; Barbir, "Alfred Thayer Mahan, Theodore Roosevelt, the Middle East, and the Twentieth Century"; Lewis and Wigen,

The Myth of Continents, 65; Davison, "Where Is the Middle East?" 665–75; Chammou, "Near or Middle East? Choice of Name," 105–20; Koppes, "Captain Mahan, General Gordon and the Origins of the Term 'Middle East,'" 95–98.

74. Akbari, "Alexander in the Orient," 105–26.

75. Reinaud, "Mémoire sur les relations politiques et commerciales de l'Empire romain avec l'Asie orientale," 93–297.

76. Kayserling, "Richelieu, Buxtorf père et fils et Jacob Roman," 74–95.

77. Lamport, "Légende Ateniénne," 402–4; "Flora Orientalis," *La Rivista Europea* (1873): 423–24; Amadori-Virgilj, *La questione Rumeliota (Macedonia, Vecchia Serbia, Albania, Epiro) e la politica Italiana*, 639; Fernández y González, *Historia general de España*, 58.

78. Goethe, *West-oestlicher Divan*, 301.

79. For the reception of Goethe's conceptualization, see, for example, Michelet, *Das System der Philosophie*, 258.

80. Laffitte, *Les grands types de l'humanité*, 345; Ludlow, *Age of the Crusades*, 60; "Talk About New Books," *Catholic World* 64 (February 1897): 700; Bernard, *De Toulon au Tonkin*, 88; Stanley, "New Books of Travels," 330–38; Beazley, *Dawn of Modern Geography*, 6; Morey, *Outlines of Ancient History*, 25.

81. Curzon, *Problems of the Far East*, 6–7.

82. "Problems of the Far East," *Book News* 13 (November 1895): 85.

83. *Pall Mall Gazette* (October 30, 1895); *Blackwood's Edinburgh Magazine* 158 (December 1895): 930.

84. Gordon, "Problem of the Middle East," 413–24.

85. Mahan, "Persian Gulf and International Relations," 237.

86. Chirol, *Middle Eastern Question*.

87. Vambéry, *Western Culture in Eastern Lands*.

88. Dickins, "The Far East," 577–78; Eliot, *Letters from the Far East*, 91; Wilser, "Weltbetrachtung eines Ariers," 409–29; Steed, "Quintessence of Austria," 225–47; Dyer, *Japan in World Politics*, 6; Seymour, *Diplomatic Background of the War*, 85, 122–25, 159–62; "A Missionary Survey of the Year 1917," *The Biblical World* 51 (March, 1918), 170; Holdich, *Boundaries in Europe and the Near East*, 1.

89. Toynbee, *Western Question in Greece and Turkey*, 5–10.

90. Ibid.; see the map at the end of the book.

91. "The Near Eastern Question" *Review of Reviews* 12 (December 1895), 475; "The Near Eastern Question," *Review of Reviews* 13 (January 1896), 4; Miller, "Europe and the Ottoman Power Before the Nineteenth Century," 452–72; Monroe, *Turkey and the Turks*, 301; Courtney, *Nationalism and War in the Near East*, 1; Gibbons, *Introduction to World Politics*, 96.

92. Hart, "Reservations as to the Near Eastern Question," 120–24.

93. McCarthy, *Story of Gladstone's Life*, 459; Daubeny, *Strength and Decay of Nations*, 29; Phillips, *Modern Europe*, 341.

94. The number of writings on the conceptual transition from the Eastern Question to the region-based conception of the Question is simply overwhelming; the following provides a representative selection. For the Nearer Eastern Question, see McCarthy, *Story of Gladstone's Life*, 459; Daubeny, *Strength and Decay of Nations*, 29. For the Near Eastern Question, see Perris, *Eastern Crisis of 1897*, 46; Williams, "Russian Advance in Asia," 306–19; Miller, "Europe and the Ottoman Power Before the Nineteenth Century," 452–72; Monroe, *Turkey and the Turks*, 301; Courtney, *Nationalism and War in the Near East*, 1; Gibbons, *Introduction to World Politics*, 96. For the Middle Eastern Question, see Gordon, "Problem of the Middle East," 413–24; Chirol, *Middle Eastern Question*; Birdwood, "Province of Sind," 593–610; Kawakami, *What Japan Thinks*, 176. For the Far Eastern Question, see Faber, *Mind of Mencius*, 3; O'Donovan, *The Merv Oasis*, 448; Duncan, *Corea and the Powers*.

95. Turhan, *Other Empire*, 4.

96. The sick man metaphor became the staple of the Eastern Question debate after the Ottoman victory against Russia in the Crimean War, and it has a colorful conceptual history of its own in Western imagination. It could be attributed to the sultan himself or to the Ottoman Empire in association with a geographical location, a civilizational entity, or some abstraction. It was mainly used with respect to the Near East. For the sick man of the Near East, see Meadows, *Chinese and Their Rebellions*, 188; Adler, *Voice of America on Kishineff*, 283; Barrett, *Russia's New Era*, 40. For the sick man of the Orient, see "Geography and Travels," *Christian Examiner* 64 (1858), 139–42. For the sick man of the East, see Comte de Montalembert, "Sardinia and Rome," *Brownson's Quarterly Review* 2 (July 1861): 403–16. For the sick man of the Bosporus, see Cook, *Biology*, 137. For the sick man of the Golden Horne, see Gilpin, *Cosmopolitan Railway*, 147. For the sick man of Europe, see Hulburt, "The Mexican Question," *Knickerbocker* 53 (March 1859): 224–33. For the sick man of the Balkan Peninsula, see "Slav and Moslem," *Critic* 21 (March, 1894), 321. For the sick man of nations, see W. H. Allen, "From Advance Shifts of the Protectionist Theory of Money," *American Economist* 54 (September 1914), 152.

97. *Brockhaus' Konversations-Lexikon*, 14th ed., vol. 17 (Leipzig: F. A. Brockhaus, 1892–1897), 818a, s.v. "Historische Karte zur Orientalischen Frage."

98. İsmail Hami's understanding of "the Near East" (*Şark-ı Karib*) consisted of the Ottoman Empire and Iran. See his essays "İran İhtilafnamesi," 10–15, and "Avrupa'nın Beyhude Teşebbüsleri," 214–16.

99. Başbakanlık Osmanlı Arşivi (1919–20) MV 217/45, 219/35, 219/70, 221/257, 223/48, 252/1, 253/74, 256/122, 256/34; İ.DUİT 12/41, 71/97, 71/111, 71/127, 100/1-7.

100. The association was founded in 1921 in İzmir while the city was under Greek occupation; it pleaded with the Greek government for recognition of their rights as a nationality. See Gingeras, "Notorious Subjects, Invisible Citizens," 89–108.

101. See, for example, "Şark-ı Karîb Buhranı ve İçinden Çıkmanın Çaresi" [The Crisis of the Near East and the Way Out of It], *İrşad Dergisi* 19 (Aralık 1921).

102. Aydın, *Politics of Anti-Westernism in Asia*, 71–93.

103. Toynbee, *Murderous Tyranny of the Turks*, 7.

104. St. Clair and Brophy, *Twelve Years' Study of the Eastern Question in Bulgaria*, v.

105. Urquhart mocks this attitude of his generation further: "These prejudices, all dictated by self-love, hinder him from seeing what is different from himself; diversities offend him. He discovers that a Turk believes that a public debt is a bad thing. 'The ignoramus!' he exclaims. That a Turk regards this debt as contrary to religion. 'Ah, the fanatic!' He discovers again that a Turk has a repugnance to the idea of an assembly which makes laws. 'Ah, the slave!' That a Turk despises a representative chamber. 'Ah, the tool of despotism!'" Urquhart, "Islam and the Constitutional System," 177–82.

106. See, for example, Kemal, *Renan müdaafanamesi*.

Chapter 2

1. The expansion of the Middle East may be traced in recent U.S. college textbooks: Aroian and Mitchell, *Modern Middle East and North Africa*; Eickelman, *The Middle East and Central Asia*; Cleveland, *History of the Modern Middle East*; Cleveland's second edition (2000) included "Expanding the Middle East: The Regional Reintegration of Central Asia and Transcaucasia," 517–23, which was dropped in his third and fourth editions. For a similar expansion of the region among geography textbooks, see Bonine, Chapter 3, this volume.

2. Yapp, *Making of the Modern Near East*, 47–265.

3. Adelson, *London and the Invention of the Middle East*, 24–25.

4. Hogarth, *Nearer East*. Hogarth's "Nearer East" included the Balkans, Southwest Asia, and Northeast Africa (Egypt). See the map that accompanies this chapter.

5. Mahan, "The Persian Gulf and International Relations," 39.

6. Adelson, *London and the Invention of the Middle East*, 24–25.

7. Mahan, "The Persian Gulf and International Relations," 39.

8. Ibid.

9. For an excellent biography of Valentine Chirol, showing his influence and work as the foreign editor of the *Times* of London, see Fritzinger, *Diplomat Without Portfolio*.

10. Chirol, *Far Eastern Question*.

11. Chirol, *Middle East Question*.

12. Ibid., 176.

13. Mackinder, "Geographical Pivot of History," 421–44.

14. Adelson, *London and the Invention of the Middle East*, 27–108.

15. Adelson, "Winston Churchill and the Middle East," 138; Adelson, *London and the Invention of the Middle East*, 96–100.

16. Adelson, *London and the Invention of the Middle East*, 31–34, 56, 92–93.

17. Ibid., 59–62.

18. Adelson, *Mark Sykes*, 249–55.

19. Adelson, *London and the Invention of the Middle East*, 190–97.

20. Ibid., 197–201; Dodge, *Inventing Iraq*, 5–41; Polk, *Understanding Iraq*, 67–101.

21. Davison, "Where Is the Middle East?" 668.

22. Balakian, *Burning Tigris*, 354–72; Khalidi, *Resurrecting Empire*, 9–36.

23. Yergen, *Prize*, 303–88; Yapp, *Near East Since the First World War*, 1–47.

24. Satia, "Defense of Inhumanity." 34; Monroe, *Britain's Moment in the Middle East*, 71–95.

25. Davison, "Where Is the Middle East?" 669; Kirk, *Middle East in the War*, v; Adelson, *Churchill, British Power, and the Middle East*.

26. Davison, "Where Is the Middle East?" 669–70.

27. McAlister, *Epic Encounters*, 31–42.

28. However, Bonine notes in Chapter 3 (this volume) that the November 1947 U.S. conference on the study of world regions designated this region as the "Near East," although by the time the Middle East Studies Association of North America had been founded in 1966, the term "Middle East" was being used by academics studying the contemporary and Islamic world.

29. Monroe, *Britain's Moment in the Middle East*, 151–206; see also Kirk, *Middle East in the War*.

30. Yergen, *The Prize*, 563–744.

31. Sick, "The United States in the Persian Gulf," 315–31.

32. Smith, *Palestine and the Arab-Israeli Conflict*, 270–538.

33. Quandt, "New Policies for a New Middle East?" 493–503.[0]

Chapter 3

1. Bonine, "Where Is the Geography of the Middle East?"

2. Marston, Knox, and Liverman, *World Regions in Global Context*, 2.

3. Ibid., emphasis in the original.

4. Ibid.

5. Lewis and Wigen, *Myth of Continents*, 8.

6. Ibid.

7. Ibid.

8. Ibid., 14.

9. *Survival on Land and Sea*, prepared by the Ethnographical Board and the Staff of the Smithsonian Institution.

10. See Bennett, *Ethnogeographic Board*; Price, *Anthropological Intelligence*, 97–106.

11. Lewis and Wigen, *Myth of Continents*, 166.

12. Ibid., 167.

13. Wagley, *Area Research and Training*.

14. Ibid., 28.

15. Ibid., 29–31.

16. Ibid., 29.

17. Ibid., 30.

18. Ibid.

19. Cressey, *Asia's Lands and Peoples*.

20. Ibid., 373.

21. Ibid., viii.

22. Ginsburg, *Pattern of Asia*.

23. Ibid., 700.

24. Fisher, *Middle East*, 1950.

25. Fisher, *Middle East*, 7th rev.ed.,1.

26. Ibid., 3

27. Ibid., 3, 5, my emphasis.

28. Ibid., 5

29. Fisher, *Middle East*, 6th rev. ed., xi.

30. *The Middle East and North Africa*, Handbook 2008, vol. 54 (London: Europa Publications, 2007).

31. Brice, *South-West Asia*.

32. Ibid., 5.

33. Beaumont, Blake, and Wagstaff, *Middle East*.

34. Ibid., 3.

35. Ibid.

36. Held, *Middle East Patterns*.

37. Ibid., xix.

38. Held and Cummings, *Middle East Patterns*. The 2011 fifth edition has nineteen chapters compared with the twenty-two chapters in the first edition; it has fewer chapters in the "Physical and Cultural Geography" section, although there are the same divisions and number of chapters under the section "Regional Geography." The fifth edition has 659 pages whereas the first edition has 442 pages, an indication of the amount of material added to some chapters.

39. Pearcy, *Middle East—An Indefinable Region*.

40. Held, *Middle East Patterns*, 7. In later editions because of the unification of North and South Yemen, there are sixteen rather than seventeen states.

41. Ibid., 3.

42. Ibid., 7. Held's (and Held and Cummings's) definition does not change in any of the editions; the Middle East remains Pearcy's "core" of Southwest Asia and Egypt.

43. Drysdale and Blake, *Middle East and North Africa*.

44. Ibid., 5.

45. Ibid., 11.

46. A more recent (2000) political geography textbook is *The Middle East: Geography and Geopolitics* by Ewan Anderson, a professor of geopolitics at the University of Durham. Anderson uses the same definition of the Middle East that W. B. Fisher uses (Iran on the east and Libya, Egypt, and Sudan in Africa), and, in fact, his book is specifically a revision and reorientation of Fisher's last (1978) edition of *The Middle East*. It also lacks a theoretical framework such as Drysdale and Blake's.

47. Marston, Knox, and Liverman, *World Regions in Global Context.*

48. De Blij and Muller, *Geography.*

49. De Blij and Muller, *Geography*, 10th ed., 282.

50. Ibid., 297, emphasis in original.

51. Ibid.

52. See the brief discussion on Southwest Asia by Martin Kramer, posted on Middle East Strategy at Harvard (MESH), a project of the John M. Olin Institute for Strategic Studies at the Weatherhead Center for International Affairs at Harvard University. Martin Kramer, "Southwest Asia," Middle East Strategy at Harvard, March 2, 2009, http://blogs.law.harvard.edu/mesh/2009/03/southwest-asia/.

53. English and Miller, *World Regional Geography: A Question of Place.*

54. Paul English, who taught at the University of Texas at Austin, conducted research in Iran in the 1960s and is author of the now classic *City and Village in Iran: Settlement and Economy in the Kirman Basin* (Madison: University of Wisconsin Press, 1966). James Miller was a student of Paul English (his second Ph.D. student; I was his first), who conducted research in Morocco and wrote *Imlil: A Moroccan Mountain Community in Change* (Boulder, CO: Westview Press, 1984).

55. English and Miller, *World Regional Geography*, 3rd ed., 469.

56. English, "Geographical Perspectives on the Middle East."

57. Hepner and McKee, *World Regional Geography.*

58. Cole, *Geography of the World's Major Regions.*

59. Pulsipher, *World Regional Geography.*

60. Ibid., 269.

61. Rand, McNally and Co., *Indexed Atlas of the World*, 177.

62. Ibid., 221.

63. Ibid.

64. Rand McNally, *Goode's World Atlas.*

65. Rand McNally, *Quick Reference World Atlas.*

66. Rand McNally, *New International Atlas.*

67. National Geographic Society, *National Geographic Atlas of the World.*

68. Bartholomew, *World Atlas.*

69. Encyclopaedia Britannica, *Encyclopaedia Britannica World Atlas.*

70. Times Books, *Times Atlas of the World.*

71. National Geographic Society, *National Geographic Atlas of the Middle East.*

72. Ibid., 6.

73. Ibid., 10.

74. Central Intelligence Agency, *Atlas: Issues in the Middle East*.

75. Ibid., 2.

76. Blake, Dewdney, and Mitchell, *Cambridge Atlas of the Middle East and North Africa*.

77. Ibid., 3.

78. Anderson and Anderson, *Atlas of Middle Eastern Affairs*.

79. Ibid.

80. Lewis and Wigen, *Myth of Continents*, 186.

81. Ibid.

82. Ibid.,188.

83. Eickelman, *Middle East*; Eickelman, *Middle East and Central Asia*.

84. Keddie, "Is There a Middle East?" 273.

85. English, "Geographical Perspectives on the Middle East."

Chapter 4

1. In this chapter, the Maghrib refers to Morocco, Algeria, and Tunisia. Although Libya and Mauritania are sometimes included in the Maghrib, I have limited the scope of this chapter to these three countries. Maghribis are the people of the Maghrib.

2. In order to highlight the fact that I do not presume a particular definition of these terms, I first put them in quotation marks. This is particularly useful because I do not intend to shed light on what the categories referred to and focus only on what it means for Maghribis to use them in the way they do. Although I stop using quotation marks after this point, I do so only to suggest that the reader is responsible for not taking the categories for granted.

3. Both the Middle East and the Maghrib are products of specific historical conditions. See Brown, "Maghrib Historiography," 4–16; Burke "Towards a History of the Maghrib," 306–23; Seddon, "Dreams and Disappointments," 197–231.

4. Adelson, *London and the Invention of the Middle East*, 22–23. The term "Middle East" appears in newspapers in the first decade of the twentieth century. Its earliest appearance in the *New York Times* was in 1903; see "The Persian Riddle," *New York Times*, March 21, 1903, BR9.

5. Middle East Institute, "Mission and History," http://www.mei.edu/Home/MissionandHistory.aspx, accessed April 10, 2011. The institute was originally associated with the School of Advanced International Studies (SAIS) at the Johns Hopkins University. This future secretary of state also cofounded SAIS with Paul Nitze in 1943.

6. *The Oxford English Dictionary* cites a 1952 article in *The Public Opinion Quarterly* as the earliest occurrence of "Middle Easterner," although reference to Middle

Easterners occurs slightly earlier. See Roosevelt, "Middle East and the Prospect for World Government," 57.

7. Edmund Burke remarked that it was "striking how historians of the colonial Maghrib as different as Julien, Ageron, Berque, and Montagne all accepted the basic legitimacy of the colonial system." Burke, "Theorizing the Histories of Colonialism and Nationalism in the Arab Maghrib," 20.

8. Montagne, "France, England, and the Arab States," 286–87. "Fashoda" refers to the 1898 Fashoda Incident, which brought the imperial designs of France in East Africa against those of Britain and almost led to a war between the two.

9. "As soon as the motley armies of the Arab countries of the Middle East had been defeated by Israel, and the Arab League had broken up, *all our people of the Maghrib*, who are men of common sense, understood that the great renaissance movement of the Arab countries was only an illusion, talk, and political incitement." Ibid., 288 (italics added).

10. Ibid. Montagne attributes this sentiment to "the French man in the street."

11. De Gaulle, *Mémoires de Guerre*, 1:112.

12. Brown, "Many Faces of Colonial Rule in French North Africa," 171–91; Burke, "Morocco and the Middle East," 70–94.

13. Mashriq refers to Arab countries east of Libya, starting with Egypt, and hence the Arab states of the eastern Mediterranean.

14. See McDougall, *History and the Culture of Nationalism in Algeria*; Touati, "Algerian Historiography in the Nineteenth and Early Twentieth Centuries," 84–94.

15. Jacques Berque, *Le Maghreb entre deux guerres*, 9. Also see Berque's *Arabes d'hier à demain*.

16. See for instance Berque, "Qu'est-ce qu'une tribu nord-africaine?" 22–34.

17. Leimdorfer, *Discours académique et colonisation*.

18. See for example Lorcin, *Imperial Identities*.

19. See *Journal Officiel de la République Algérienne* 79 (December 1, 2002): 6. For Moroccan and Tunisian foreign ministries, see http://www.maec.gov.ma; http://www.diplomatie.gov.tn/site/index.php, both accessed April 10, 2011.

20. See "La Banque mondiale disposée à consolider sa coopération avec la Tunisie," *La Presse* (April 30, 2006); "Mabʿūth rubāʿī al-wisāta li al-sharq al-awsat yuqarrir al-tanahhī," *al-Sahāfa* (April 30, 2006).

21. The illiteracy rate has been steadily decreasing since independence. Central Intelligence Agency, *2008 World Factbook* .

22. For instance, in 1995, al-Akhawayn University in Ifrane (Morocco) opened its doors. Its curriculum stands out as having a more Anglo-American orientation than any other university in the Maghrib. I counted three courses with "Middle East" in their titles.

23. See Brett, "Colonial Period in the Maghrib and Its Aftermath," 291–305; Johnson, "Algeria," 221–42; Laroui, *L'histoire du Maghreb*; Sahli, *Décoloniser l'histoire*; Wansbrough, "Decolonization of North African History," 643–50.

24. See *Histoire Générale de la Tunisie*; Slim, Mahjoubi, Belkhodja, and Ennabli, *L'Antiquité*; Djaït, Talbi, Dachraoui, Dhouib, M'Rabet, and Mahfoudh, vol. 2, *Le moyen-âge*; Guellouz, Masmoudi, and Smida, vol. 3, *Les temps modernes, 941–1247 H./1534–1881*; Kaddache, *L'Algérie médievale*.

25. For example, see Julien, *Histoire de l'Afrique du Nord: Tunisie, Algérie, Maroc*.

26. I refer here to the Arab League (1945–), the Organization of the Islamic Conference (1971–), the Organization of African Unity (1963–2002), and the Non-Aligned Movement (1955–). Morocco left the OAU in 1984, and it is the only country in Africa that is not a member of the African Union (2002–).

27. Filali, *Le Maroc et le monde Arabe*. The book, which put the blame for the failure to build the Maghrib on Algerian leaders, elicited a vigorous response in Algeria. See, for instance, Mohamed Said, "Oui l'Algérie est en droit de revendiquer un rôle regional," *El-Watan*, Part I, September 10, 2008, and Part II, September 12, 2008. Both authors are former high-level diplomats.

28. French statisticians tend to collapse the two, especially when they evaluate the number of "Muslims" in France.

29. Not all French citizens who migrated there are able to be reminded of their place of origin as a group. For instance the Italians, Poles, Portuguese, and Hungarians are generally treated as individuals. Their "group identity" seldom is remembered in public discourse. The *maghrébins* seem to have benefited from the rise of power of the socialists with François Mitterrand and the formation of associations such as "SOS Racisme."

30. The concept of integration informs French social and political discourse and policies. It is based on an insistence on notions of difference, which produce the cultural otherness of immigrants and their French-born children (theoretically full citizens) as a way of explaining their socioeconomic and political disenfranchisement.

31. See Hannoum, *Colonial Histories, Post-Colonial Memories*.

32. The Maghribi media has tended to describe the mostly West African migrants who cross the Maghrib on their way to Europe as Africans.

33. See the article "Middle East Warriors Renew Demand to Recognize their Organization" in the Algerian newspaper *Al-Khabar*, August 14, 2008.

Chapter 5

1. Said, *Orientalism*, 1.

2. Ibid., 3.

3. I provide a review of the three-decade-old debate in Varisco, *Reading Orientalism*. See also Irwin, *For Lust of Knowing*.

4. al-'Azm, "Orientalism and Orientalism in Reverse," 376.

5. Said, *Orientalism*, 328.

6. Goldammer, *Der Mythus von Ost und West*, 10–11.

7. Such repetition of nonsense syllables is used in a number of languages to indicate people who cannot be understood. In the highland valley of al-Ahjur in Yemen, villagers would refer to those who spoke another language or difficult dialect as *laghallaghallaghal*.

8. Romm, *Herodotus*, 95–96.

9. Hay, *Europe*, 4.

10. Said recognizes the importance of the "revolution in Biblical studies" but chooses not to focus on this. In his list of possible Orients, he gives precedence to Freud, Spengler, and Darwin (none of whom said very much about the Orient) without any mention of pilgrims, saints, or theologians. Said, *Orientalism*, 17, 22.

11. Ibid., 58.

12. Ibid., 42.

13. Of course I am talking about mainly the Mediterranean World, Europe, and Western Asia in the earlier periods, as there were other ecumenisms in East Asia and South Asia. With the later spread of peoples and of these monotheistic religions, the Holy Land becomes a center for adherents throughout the world.

14. It is reported by the patriarch Sophronius that he personally took Umar ibn al-Khattab, whose Muslim army has just conquered Jerusalem, to the dung heap where the temple had been and this is where Umar determined a mosque should be built. See Wilken, *Land Called Holy*, 237.

15. Obenzinger, *American Palestine*, 4, cites this text as "one of the most popular books ever written by a missionary."

16. Thomson, *Land and the Book*, xvi.

17. Ibid., xiii.

18. Ibid., 403.

19. Howard, *Writers and Pilgrims*, 43.

20. For a Muslim perspective on the holiness of Jerusalem, see the discussion in Matthews, "Palestine, Holy Land of Islam," 171–78, of a work by Burhan al-din Ibn al-Firka in 1477 C.E. Although some later Muslim writers, such as Ibn Taymiyya, denigrated Christian Jerusalem as a site for Muslim worship, there was earlier an entire literature on the merits (*fadâ'il*) of the holy city for Muslims; see Frankel, "Muslim Pilgrimage to Jerusalem in the Mamluk Period," 63–87.

21. Wilken, *Land Called Holy*, 11.

22. Interest in Holy Land travel has been keen by scholars and bibliographers over the past two centuries. For general bibliographic information on travelers, see Bevis, *Bibliotheca Cisorientalia*; Röhricht, *Bibliotheca Geographica Palaestinae*; and Weber, *Voyages and Travels in Greece*. For accounts of early Christian pilgrims, see Hunt,

Holy Land Pilgrimage in the Later Roman Empire, A.D. 312–460; Maraval, *Lieux saints et pèlerinages d'Orient*; Wilken, *Land Called Holy*; and Wilkinson, *Egeria's Travels*. Hachicho, "English Travel Books About the Arab Near East in the Eighteenth Century," provides an excellent starting point for English texts from the eighteenth century. For British travel accounts of the nineteenth century, see Damiani, *Enlightened Observers* and Tibawi, *British Interests in Palestine*; American travelers are discussed in Moshe Davis, *American and the Holy Land*; Finnie, *Pioneers East*; Obenzinger, *American Palestine*; Schueller, *U.S. Orientalisms*; and Tibawi, *American Interests in Syria*. For female Western travelers, see Melman, *Women's Orients*; Yoshihara[o], *Embracing the East*.

23. This is reported in Röhricht, *Bibliotheca Geographica Palaestinae* in 1890, so the number is no doubt higher today after a century of research.

24. Ben-Arieh, "Geographical Exploration of the Holy Land," 83.

25. Melman, *Women's Orients*, 7.

26. Wilkinson, *Egeria's Travels*.

27. It is clear that the work is a compilation of sources, many from eyewitness accounts. Howard, argues that this text is a "new kind of work, a summa of travel lore which combined the authority of learned books and guidebooks with the eyewitness manner of pilgrim and travel writers." Howard, *Writers and Pilgrims*, 58.

28. Mandeville, *Travels of Sir John Mandeville*, 43.

29. The sultan, who was said to be fluent in French, speaks to Mandeville: "You ought to be simple, meek and truthful, and ready to give charity and alms, as Christ was, in whom you say you believe. But it is quite otherwise. For Christians are so proud, so envious, such great gluttons, so lecherous, and moreover so full of covetousness, that for a little silver they will sell their daughters, their sisters, even their own wives, and no one keeps his faith to another: and you so wickedly and evilly despite and break the Law that Christ gave you." Ibid., 107–8. The contrast between lax local Christians and admirably devout Muslims is also found in the pilgrimage account of the thirteenth century Brocardus; see Howard, *Writers and Pilgrims*, 32.

30. Said, *Orientalism*, 157.

31. The two nineteenth-century French Holy Land travel accounts, those of Chateaubriand and Lamartine, are driven by ego more than by devotion and are atypical of the genre even for the nineteenth century. See Said, *Orientalism*, 169–79. As Murphey remarks in critique of Said's assumptions about pre-nineteenth-century noncolonialist authors, they "drank at Pierian springs of another description." Murphey, "Bigots or Informed Observers?" 291.

32. The first edition of Flaubert's notes on his travels appeared in 1910, but this was expurgated; see Flaubert, *Voyage en Égypte* for a recent edition of the original letters. Lockman wrongly assumes that Flaubert wrote one of the "influential accounts of travel in the Levant." Lockman, *Contending Visions of the Middle East*, 69.

33. Kinglake, *Eothen*, 3.

34. Twain, *Innocents Abroad*, xvii.

35. Said, *Orientalism*, 158.

36. Clarke, *Travels in Various Countries of Europe, Asia, and Africa*, vol. 2, p. x.

37. Varisco, "Archaeologist's Spade and the Apologist's Stacked Deck."

38. Quoted in Parker, *Early Modern Tales of Orient*, 177.

39. Said, *Orientalism*, 208.

40. Said (ibid., 151) wrongly states that Muir's two major works "are still considered reliable monuments of scholarship." In fact twentieth-century scholars such as Gibb, Watt, and even Lewis had repudiated the missionary bias of Muir. For a critique of Muir's ethnocentric cleansing of Muhammad, see Varisco, *Islam Obscured*, 81–113.

41. Thomson, *Land and the Book*, 345.

42. The reference is to the Gospel account, for example, Matthew 10:10, where the twelve disciples are sent out to "the lost sheep of Israel."

43. Thomson, *Land and the Book*, 346.

44. Ibid., 347.

45. Ibid., 679.

46. Other travelers expressed similar sentiments. Taylor states that "Jerusalem is the last place on the world where an intelligent heathen would be converted to Christianity," adding for emphasis that he would "at once turn Mussulman." Taylor, *Lands of the Saracen*, 19.

47. James Turner Barclay, a Disciples of Christ missionary who lived in Jerusalem in the 1850s, explicitly targeted (without much success) Palestinian Jews. Barclay focused on converting Jews as eschatological fulfillment. See Blowers, "'Living in a Land of Prophets,'" 498–99. In Barclay's 1860 "The Welfare of the World Bound Up in the Destiny of Israel," he predicted a *novus ordo seclorum* in which the total conversion of Israel was imminent. As Obenzinger notes, "The millennialist mania to appropriate Palestine was at the farthest, most radical end of a continuum of reading and writing sacred geography, but the impulse to seize 'my undying property' was also embodied by less feverish travelers." Obenzinger, *American Palestine*, 56–57.

48. Thomson, *Land and the Book*, 228.

49. Ibid., 20.

50. Ibid., 255.

51. The operative word "filth" is common in Western accounts of nineteenth-century Palestine. For example, Taylor complains, "Jerusalem, internally, gives no impression but that of filth, rain, poverty, and degeneration." Taylor, *Lands of the Saracen*, 77.

52. Thomson, *Land and the Book*, 388.

53. Ibid., 27.

54. Ibid., 369.

55. Ibid., 255.

56. Ibid., 369.

57. Ibid., 370. For further perspectives on the belief that the Bedouins were the cause for desertification in the region, see Diana Davis, Chapter 8, this volume.

58. In addition to the Nusayriya mentioned above, Thomson believes that the villagers of Alma may stem from the Kenites. Thomson, *Land and the Book*, 272.

59. Ibid., 275.

60. Ibid., 278.

61. Ibid., 294.

62. Ibid., 322.

63. Coon, *Story of the Middle East*.

64. Thomson, *Land and the Book*, 683.

65. Twain, *Innocents Abroad*, 24.

Chapter 6

1. Hodgson, *Venture of Islam*, 60–61.

2. Fernand Braudel similarly noted the ecological and economic exchanges linking the arid lands from Central Asia to the eastern Mediterranean, claiming: "The chain of deserts between the Atlantic and China is divided in two by the high Iranian plateaux; to the west lie the warm deserts; to the north and east the cold deserts. But there is a continuity between these barren spaces and their caravan traffic." See Braudel, *The Mediterranean and the Mediterranean World in the Age of Philip II*, 171. The pioneering work of Joseph Fletcher on Islamic networks likewise emphasized the cultural exchanges that integrated Central Asia and the Middle East. See Fletcher, *Studies on Chinese and Islamic Inner Asia*.

3. Here I refer to the world Robert Canfield has called "Turko-Persia." See Canfield, *Turko-Persia in Historical Perspective*.

4. Lewis and Wigen, *Myth of Continents*, 177.

5. Soucek, *History of Inner Asia*, 150. For an excellent critique of this perspective, see McChesney, "'Barrier of Heterodoxy'?" 231–67.

6. See Hopkirk, *Great Game*; Hopkins, "Bounds of Identity," 233–54; Mojtahed-Zadeh, *Small Players of the Great Game*.

7. See Najmabadi, *Story of the Daughters of Quchan*; Kashani-Sabet, *Frontier Fictions*.

8. Turan is supposedly derived from Tur and according to the *Shahnama*, Tur was the name of emperor Faridun's eldest son, and hence, Turan was the land ruled by Tur.

9. Firdawsi, *Shahnama*.

10. Le Strange, *Lands of the Eastern Caliphate*, 433. Also see, Frye, *Heritage of Central Asia*, 243.

11. Crossing the Oxus was a difficult task not to be taken lightly. The thirteenth-century Muslim geographer Yaqut recounted in his voluminous geographical dictionary,

Muʿjam al-Buldan, how on a journey from Marv, he and his companions nearly died from the cold, the snow, and the ice they endured on the river. See Le Strange, *Lands of the Eastern Caliphate*, 444–45. See for instance the sixteenth-century illustrated manuscript page of Mirkhvand's *Rawzat al-Safa* showing Mirza Abu'l Qasim crossing the Oxus with a sense of fear and caution.

12. Other common English spellings for Qara Qum (Black Sands) are Kara-Kum, Karakum, and Kara Kum.

13. Létolle, "Histoire de l'Ouzboi, cours fossile de l'Amou Darya," 195–240; Létolle, Micklin, Aladin, and Plotnikov, "Uzboy and the Aral regressions," 125–36. Also see Konchin, "La Question de l'Oxus," *Annales de Géographie*, 496–504.

14. Le Strange, *Lands of the Eastern Caliphate*, 455.

15. Ibid., 456–57.

16. See Bahadur Khan, *Shajara-yi Tarakima*, vol.1, 221, 312, vol.2, 207, 291.

17. I'timad al-Saltana, *Tatbiq-i Lughat-i Jughrafiyihi-yi Qadim va Jadid-i Iran*, 24.

18. Konchin, "La Question de l'Oxus," 496–504.

19. Reclus, *Earth and Its Inhabitants*, 193–219. Also see Raphael Pumpelly Papers (1864–1912), MSS Pumpelly, Part 1, Box 2, Transcaspian and Turkestan Notebooks, the Huntington Library; Pumpelly, *Explorations in Turkestan*, 291–98.

20. Pumpelly, *Explorations in Turkestan*, 294.

21. Ibid., 295.

22. As Palmira Brummett has noted in a recent essay on the Ottoman Empire, "In the early modern era conceptual divisions of space and time were not primarily linear and did not lend themselves to precise territorial demarcation." See Brummett, "Imagining the Early Modern Ottoman Space," 26.

23. Roemer, "Safavid Period," 217.

24. Khvandamir, *Tarikh-i Habib al-Siyar*, 294.

25. Ibid., 36. Balk is located in northern Afghanistan.

26. Barthold, *Four Studies on the History of Central Asia*, 136; Roemer, "Successors of Timur," 126–27. On the little explored subject of the Safavids and Uzbeks, see Dickson, "Shah Tahmasp and the Uzbeks."

27. Soucek, *History of Inner Asia*, 182.

28. Barthold, *Four Studies on the History of Central Asia*, 144.

29. Hidayat, *Sifaratnama-yi Khvarazm*, 27.

30. In the early seventeenth century, the task of administering and preserving order on this imperial frontier was entrusted to Faridun Khan (d. 1621), the governor of Astarabad. Faridun Khan's campaigns against the Turkmen during this time are related in a *fathnama* (book of victory) penned by Muhammad Tahir Bistami with the title *Futuhat-i Fariduniya*. Interestingly, the author of *Futuhat-i Fariduniya* makes no mention of the Oxus or Ab-i Amuya and instead provides a more modest view of the Atrak and Gurgan rivers as the boundaries and eastern frontiers of Iran. See Bistami,

Futuhat-i Fariduniya. See also, Barthold, *Four Studies on the History of Central Asia*, 146.

31. In 1841, Major James Abbott estimated that there were 700,000 slaves in the Khanate of Khiva, roughly one-third of the total population. In the city of Khiva alone there were 30,000 Persian and 12,000 Herati slaves. See Marvin, *Merv, the Queen of the World*, 181.

32. The yurt, the traditional dwelling of Central Asian nomads, usually is a round structure of wooden poles covered by felt. Nineteenth-century European and Persian sources offer varying estimates of Turkmen populations according to the number of tents or yurts. Population figures may be found in Fraser, *Narrative of a Journey into Khorasan in 1821 and 1822*; Burnes, *Travels into Bokhara*; Anonymous, "Safarnama-yi Bukhara;" Arminius Vámbéry, *Travels in Central Asia*; FO 60/379, "Report by Ronald Thomson on the Toorkoman Tribes Occupying Districts Between the Caspian and the Oxus," Tehran, February 29, 1876; Marvin, *Merv, the Queen of the Word*; Moser, *Travers l'Asie Centrale*.

33. On the "Herat Question," see Amanat, *Pivot of the Universe*; Amanat, "Herat Question."

34. On the Helmand River, the Goldsmid Mission, and the Sistan Boundary, see Hopkins, "Bounds of Identity," 233–54; Khazeni, "Helmand," 173–76.

35. al-Saltana, *Tarikh-i Vaqa'i'[o] va Savana-yi Afghanistan*, 47.

36. For a narrative of the disastrous Persian campaign on Marv in 1861, see de Blocqueville, "Quatorze mois de captivité, chez les Turcomans aux frontieres du Turkestan et de la Perse," 225–72.

37. For the text of this agreement and a facsimile of the original document, see Mirniya, *Vaqa'i'[o]-yi Khavar-i Iran dar Dawra-yi Qajar*, 179–90.

38. Qaragazlu, *Majmu'a[o]-yi Asar*, 142–43.

39. al-Mamalik, *Ruznama-yi Safar-i Khurasan*. This travel book was written in the *nastaliq* script of Persian by a scribe in the service of Hakim al-Mamalik by the name of Ali Asghar. The 485-page text was completed and lithographed in the printing house of Aqa Mir Baqir Tehrani in 1868.

40. Ibid., 4–5.

41. Ibid., 6.

42. Nasir al-Din Shah Qajar, *Safarnama-yi Khurasan*. This work is also referred to as *Safarnama-yi Duvvum-i Khurasan*, an oral travel narrative by the shah that was written down by Muhammad Hasan Khan Sani' al-Dawla I'timad al-Saltana during the course of the journey. The final 227-page text was written in *nastaliq* script in the hand of Mirza Riza Kalhur and printed in lithograph form.

43. In addition to the shah's own journal of his second pilgrimage and journey to Khurasan, the *safarnama* of Mirza Qahraman Amin Lashkar, who accompanied the 1882 pilgrimage and mission to the eastern borderlands, also deserves mention. See Lashkar, *Ruznama-yi Safar-i Khurasan*.

44. I'timad al-Saltana, *Matla' al-Shams: Tarikh-i Arz-i Aqdas va Mashhad-i Muqaddas, dar Tarikh va Jughrafiya-yi-Mashruh-i Balad va Imakan-i Khurasan*. I'timad al-Saltana (1843–1896), a graduate of the Dar al-Funun, was Nasir al-Din Shah's "dragoman in royal attendance" and minister of publications. In the late 1870s, he compiled a geographical chronicle of Iran in four volumes, titled *Mir'at al-Buldan*, but the project was never completed, the fourth volume ending with the letter jim (before the entry for Khurasan). This geographical interest continued with *Matla' al-Shams*, which was lithographed in three books between 1882 and 1884. For a reference to this text and its purported author, see Browne, *Literary History of Persia*, 453–56.

45. I'timad al-Saltana, *Matla' al-Shams*, vol. 1, 4.

46. In Persian: *"Har ja ki tir bar zamin aftad anja sarhadd-i Iran va Turan bashad."* Ibid., 18.

47. Ibid.

48. Ibid.

49. Ibid., 7.

Chapter 7

1. As is well known, Marshall G. S. Hodgson originally coined the word "Islamicate" in the 1960s. For his definition, together with a discussion of the surrounding terminological issues, see his *Venture of Islam*, vol. 1, 56–60. Hodgson justified the neologism on the grounds that the default term "Islamic" is so closely associated in modern scholarship with the religious traditions of Islam and with the doings of Muslims that it cannot be readily extended to other aspects of the more capacious polities of which they were part. "Islamicate," however, is relatively free of such associations, which makes it appropriate for emphasising, in contrast, the everyday social and cultural complexes typically found in premodern polities that were under one form of Islamic dominion or another. This was Hodgson's approach, and, as the situation has not changed much in the interim, his is my approach too. For my purposes, the chief analytical value of "Islamicate" is that it not only acknowledges the significance of Islam and of Muslims but also permits (a) meaningful involvement in the life of the region's polities of non-Muslim individuals, corporations, and groups, and (b) polities to be interpreted as Islamicate without themselves being under direct Islamic rule. This flexibility is essential if we are to take full account of the empirical findings that follow.

2. Perhaps the best-known work to escape such constraints is Goitein's *Mediterranean Society*. This is complemented by his *Studies in Islamic History and Institutions* and (with Mordechai A. Friedman) *India Traders of the Middle Ages*. Also see Guo's *Commerce, Culture and Community in a Red Sea Port in the Thirteenth Century*.

3. British Library, London (hereafter BL)/Lansdowne/1046, doc. 68.

4. Ibid., docs. 40, 56, 60.

5. Ibid., docs. 37, 38, 39, 49, 50, 54, 58.

6. Ibid., docs. 39, 40, 60.

7. Ibid., docs.39, 40, 49, 50, 58.

8. Ibid., docs. 65, 66, 70, 71, 78.

9. Ibid., doc. 74.

10. Ibid., doc. 26.

11. In a sample of 44 documents, Basra is mentioned 68 times. The frequency distribution of attributes used with the toponym, which on occasion is qualified by more than one simultaneously, is: no attribute, 57; *bandar* (port), 8; *madīna* (town), 2; *balda* (town), 1; *mahrūsa* (protected), 1; *mubārak* (blessed), 1;. Cochin in the same sample is mentioned 31 times, and the frequency distribution of attributes used is: *bandar*, 18; *makān* (place), 5; *jā* (place), 3; *mulk* (possession, estate), 2; *mahrūsa*, 1; *maqām* (place), 1; no attribute, 1.

12. BL/Lansdowne/1046, doc. 8.

13. Ibid., doc. 77.

14. Ibid., doc. 63.

15. Ibid., doc. 2.

16. Ibid., doc. 14.

17. Ibid., doc. 8; The National Archives, Kew, Richmond, Surrey, UK (hereafter NA) /HCA/32/1833.

18. Ibid., docs. 63, 64.

19. Ibid., docs. 2, 4, 5, 6, 49, 54, 71.

20. NA/HCA/32/1833.

21. Ibid.

22. The partial exceptions to this were the outer limits of islands and, more generally, transitions between land and sea. These were sometimes noted explicitly. Thus, a Shi'i trader mentioned that his ship on a recent voyage had reached the frontier (*sar hadd*) of Lakshadweep before it was surrounded by Angria pirates. BL/Lansdowne/1046, doc. 11.

23. BL/Lansdowne/1046, doc. 13.

24. On these genres, see Young, Latham, and Serjeant, *Religion, Learning and Science in the 'Abbasid Period*, 307-19.

25. Compare this mental map with what is currently known about indigenous cartography in the region in premodern times: Harley and Woodward, *History of Cartography*; Gole, *Indian Maps and Plans*.

26. This is discussed for an earlier period in Bonner, "The naming of the frontier: 'Awāsim, thughūr, and the Arab geographers," 17-24 and Brauer, *Boundaries and Frontiers in Medieval Muslim Geography*.

27. He also noted that Salaymā Kāhīya had gained control of Adana.

28. BL/Lansdowne/1046, docs. 73, 74.

29. BL/Lansdowne/1046, doc. 8.

30. BL/Lansdowne/1046, docs. 39, 40, 60. In the documents, the word is written as ملك. There are two possible readings of this: *mulk* and *milk*. The latter has a more specialized meaning than *mulk*. It is a legal concept in Sharia that refers to ownership in the sense of "the right to the complete and exclusive disposal of a thing" and is to be distinguished from "possession" (*yad* or *mulk*). Schacht, *Introduction to Islamic Law*, 136–39. Of course, both meanings might have been intended.

31. BL/Lansdowne/1046, docs. 12, 67, 68.

32. NA/HCA/32/1833.

33. BL/Lansdowne/1046, docs. 14, 26.

34. For commentary on Nadir Shah's taxation policies, see NA/HCA/30/682(undated) and BL/Lansdowne/1046, doc. 32; for commentary on the decree to merchants, see BL/Lansdowne/1046, docs. 73, 76.

35. Interestingly, this approach to politics and the state is in marked contrast to the practice of western Europeans residing in the region and that of their close associates. As shown by the records of the European trading companies and the papers of European merchant-officials and private traders of the time, it was commonplace and, indeed, expected for correspondents to discuss systematically and in detail political goings-on, both near and far. This information was considered an invaluable asset to be exploited if necessary to tilt local circumstances in their favor.

36. Subjecthood here refers narrowly to exclusive political allegiance to a single sovereign. With regard to ethnicity, I follow Frederik Barth in taking an ethnic group to be defined by "self-ascription." In other words, the members of a group select and use a handful of cultural attributes, such as dress, language, general style of life, and house form, as "overt signals or signs" of their distinctiveness. Barth, *Ethnic Groups and Boundaries*, 14.

37. I have yet to chance across any explicit reference to the Hindu or Jewish religious traditions, even though their followers resided in urban settlements throughout the region in noticeable communities. When individuals who belonged to these faiths do crop up, which is a frequent occurrence, they are invariably denoted by their given names or the occupations typically associated with them.

38. This is to be contrasted to jurists in the Islamic tradition for whom the socio-cultural world was defined first and foremost in religio-civilizational terms.

39. BL/Lansdowne/1046, docs 67, 68, 70.

40. Ibid., doc. 67.

41. Ibid., docs. 13, 49, 71.

42. Ibid., docs. 67, 68, 71.

43. Ibid., docs. 12, 65, 69, 70, 71, 73, 74, 76.

44. Ibid., doc. 14.

45. Ibid.

46. Ibid., docs. 4, 5.

47. For "the great and little," see ibid., doc. 49. Elsewhere, the standard pattern reasserts itself: "all of the young and old gentlemen" (*jamīʻah-yi khwurd o kalān-i sāhibān, hamah-yi khwurd o kalān, jamīʻah-yi khwurd o kalān*). Ibid., docs. 13, 23. For "the old and young," see ibid., doc. 68. In other documents, this phrase is prefaced by a general collective: 'people of the house, young and old' (*ahl bayt sighār wa kibār*). Ibid., doc. 73.

48. Before any transaction can take place, it is necessary that (a) the total level of trust between the parties exceeds a certain threshold; and (b) the expected costs of undertaking the transaction be affordable. If these requirements are not met, then, in a situation where free choice prevails, the transaction will not be deemed viable. Trust in this context is understood to be a quality innate to relationships between individuals. It is a concept that is, in effect, a label for the nexus of mechanisms that facilitate one or more desired ends. Depending on the nature of these mechanisms, trust may be separated into the personal and impersonal types. The first is rooted mainly in the personal relationship between the individuals concerned; it is a function of the strength of their kinship ties and their ties of sentiment, as well as their knowledge of each other's character. The second results primarily from public knowledge about each other, usually in the form of reputation, and from the available institutions, such as couriers and arbitration forums, through which they might monitor and verify one another's activities and enforce their agreement. Though both types were in play throughout history, there was relatively more emphasis on personal trust in the kind of arena treated in this chapter in comparison with analogous arenas in modern times.

Chapter 8

1. Adams, *Green Development*, chap. 8; Blumler, "Biogeography of Land-Use Impacts in the Near East"; Perevolotsky and Seligman, "Role of Grazing in Mediterranean Rangeland Ecosystems"; Davis, "Indigenous Knowledge and the Desertification Debate"; and Olsvig-Whittaker et al., "Grazing, Overgrazing and Conservation."

2. Swift, "Desertification"; Davis, "Neoliberalism, Environmentalism and Agricultural Restructuring Morocco."

3. Messerli and Winiger, "Climate, Environmental Change, and Resources of the African Mountains from the Mediterranean to the Equator"; Roberts, *Holocene*, 115–17, 162–63.

4. J. Wilson, *Lawrence of Arabia*, 57–58.

5. See Grove and Rackham, *Nature of Mediterranean Europe*; Thirgood, *Man and the Mediterranean Forest*. Thirgood provides a particularly well-articulated version of the declensionist environmental narrative for the Mediterranean basin, whereas Grove and Rackham systematically and successfully rebut it in their important and well-documented book.

6. Meadows, "The Younger Dryas Episode and the Radiocarbon Chronologies of the Lake Huleh and Ghab Valley Pollen Diagrams, Israel and Syria"; Yasuda, Kitagawa, and Nakagawa, "The Earliest Record of Major Anthropogenic Deforestation in the Ghab Valley, Northwest Syria."

7. See, for example, Mikesell, "Deforestation of Mount Lebanon."

8. Blumler, "Biogeography of Land-Use Impacts in the Near East"; Wengler and Vernet, " Vegetation, Sedimentary Deposits and Climates During the Late Pleistocene and Holocene in Eastern Morocco."

9. Lamb, Damblon, and Maxted, "Human Impact on the Vegetation of the Middle Atlas"; Lamb, Eichner, and Switsur, "An 18,000-Year Record of Vegetation"; Ritchie, "Analyse pollinique de sédiments holocènes"; Rognon, "Late Quaternary Climatic Reconstruction."

10. For a detailed discussion of this French colonial environmental narrative and its construction and application in the occupation and administration of the Maghreb, see Davis, *Resurrecting the Granary of Rome*.

11. Christian, *L'Afrique française, l'empire de Maroc et les déserts de Sahara*, 315.

12. Although it is true that significant quantities of grain were produced and exported from North Africa during the Roman period, even larger amounts were produced during the French colonial period using primarily indigenous agricultural methods, and these amounts were surpassed easily by the mid-twentieth century. See Davis, *Resurrecting the Granary*, 5. The amounts of grain produced during the Roman period, therefore, were not spectacular or unusual as they were portrayed during the colonial period.

13. Périer, *Exploration scientifique de l'Algérie*, 29.

14. Bernard and Lacroix, *L'Évolution du nomadisme en Algérie*, 26. See Davis, *Resurrecting the Granary of Rome*, chap. 3, for a fuller discussion of the use and misuse of the work of Ibn Khaldun during the French colonial period.

15. Résidence Générale de France à Tunis, *Historique de l'annexe des affaires indigènes de Ben-Gardane*, 13.

16. Ballais, "Conquests and Land Degradation in the Eastern Maghreb During Classical Antiquity and the Middle Ages." See also Milchunas and Lauenroth, "Quantitative Effects of Grazing on Vegetation and Soils over a Global Range of Environments"; Niamir-Fuller, "Resilience of Pastoral Herding in Sahelian Africa;" Davis, "Indigenous Knowledge and the Desertification Debate"; Swift, "Dynamic Ecological Systems and the Administration of Pastoral Development;" Westoby, Walker, and Noy-Meir, "Opportunistic Management of Rangelands Not at Equilibrium"; Olsvig-Whittaker et al., "Grazing, Overgrazing and Conservation."

17. Messerli and Winiger, "Climate, Environmental Change, and Resources of the African Mountains," 332.

18. Lamb, Damblon, and Maxted, "Human Impact on the Vegetation of the Middle Atlas"; Lamb, Eichner, and Switsur, "An 18,000-Year Record of Vegetation"; Ritchie,

"Analyse pollinique de sédiments holocènes"; Rognon, "Late Quaternary Climatic Reconstruction."

19. Davis, *Resurrecting the Granary of Rome*, 32–33.

20. Ibid., 120–23.

21. Ibid., 96–99.

22. This process included the massive sedentarization of nomads who were forced out of their traditional livelihoods for lack of extensive grazing lands. Their sedentarization had been a primary goal of the colonial administration since the early days of occupation because they were deemed a threat to security as well as a threat to the environment.

23. See Davis, *Resurrecting the Granary of Rome*, chap. 5.

24. I am not dealing here with Ottoman rule, although policies impacting the environment, such as the "tree tax," were instituted during the Ottoman period.

25. W. Browne, *Travels in Africa, Egypt, and Syria from the Year 1792 to 1798*, especially chaps. 22, 23.

26. Thomson, *The Land and the Book*, 1859, quoted in Thirgood, *Man and the Mediterranean Forest*, 113.

27. "Note sur la situation économique de la Syrie," 1897, quoted in Shaul Cohen, *Politics of Planting*, 45.

28. G. Smith, *Historical Geography of the Holy Land*, 83.

29. Conder, "Fertility of Ancient Palestine," 207.

30. Ben-Arieh, *Rediscovery of the Holy Land*, 206; S. Rosen, "Decline of Desert Agriculture," 46.

31. Ben-Arieh, *Rediscovery of the Holy Land*, 211.

32. Blyth, *When We Lived in Jerusalem*, 1927, quoted in Thirgood, *Man and the Mediterranean Forest*, 113.

33. El-Eini,[o] "British Forestry Policy in Mandate Palestine," 79.

34. Shaul Cohen, *Politics of Planting*, 49.

35. Ibid.

36. El-Eini,[o] "British Forestry Policy in Mandate Palestine," 75.

37. Ibid., 79.

38. Thirgood, *Man and the Mediterranean Forest*, 53, 115. The 1870 Ottoman forest law had been applied to Palestine before the Mandate period. See also Goadby and Doukhan, *Land Law of Palestine*, 51, 58, 66.

39. Tyler, *State Lands and Rural Development in Mandatory Palestine*, 22.

40. Amir and Rechtman, "Development of Forest Policy in Israel in the 20th Century," 42, 47.

41. El-Eini, "British forestry," 90.

42. Ibid., 91.

43. Abu-Rabia, *A Bedouin Century*, 39; El-Eini,[o] "British Forestry Policy in Mandate Palestine," 118, 122. The Bedouin Control Ordinance was not repealed until 1973.

44. See Mouterde, *La végétation arborescente des pays du Levant*, 7.

45. Ben-Gurion quoted in Shaul Cohen, *Politics of Planting*, 62.

46. Shaul Cohen, *Politics of Planting*, 63.

47. Lowdermilk, *Palestine*.

48. Reifenberg, *Struggle Between the Desert and the Sown*, 30–31, 98–100. See also Evenari, Shanan, and Tadmor, *Negev* and Avraham Negev, "The Nabatean Cities in the Negev," *Ariel* 62–63 (1988): 1–157, in Hebrew, cited in S. Rosen, "Decline of Desert Agriculture."

49. S. Rosen, "Decline of Desert Agriculture," 54.

50. Ibid., 58. For more details of this argument, see S. Rosen, "Desertification and Pastoralism."

51. Barker, "A Tale of Two Deserts." Barker explains that Roman smelting, rather than overgrazing by Bedouin as commonly claimed, degraded Wadi Faynan in Southern Jordan.

52. See Perevolotsky and Seligman, "Role of Grazing in Mediterranean Rangeland Ecosystems" and Ballais, "Aeolian Activity, Desertification and the 'Green Dam' in the Ziban Range, Algeria."

53. Anderson, *Eroding the Commons*; Arnold, *Tropics and the Traveling Gaze*; Arnold and Guha, *Nature, Culture and Imperialism*; Bassett and Crummey, *African Savannas*; Grove, Damodaran ,and Sangwan, *Nature and the Orient*; Grove, *Green Imperialism*; Kull, *Isle of Fire*; Leach and Mearns, *Lie of the Land*; McCann, *Green Land, Brown Land, Black Land*; Neumann, *Imposing Wilderness*; Rajan, *Modernizing Nature*; Showers, *Imperial Gullies*; Tiffen, Mortimore, and Gichuki, *More People, Less Erosion*.

54. McNeill, "Observations on the Nature and Culture of Environmental History." A recent book, however, does explore the environmental history of the Middle East and North Africa from a critical perspective; see Davis and Burke, *Environmental Imaginaries of the Middle East and North Africa*.

55. For details of the extent of these projects, see Ouis, " 'Greening the Emirates.' "

56. See Sowers, *Allocation and Accountability*.

57. Quote from a story on the BBC World News television broadcast, February 16, 2006.

Chapter 9

1. Thompson, *Colonial Citizens*, 1.

2. The effects of defensive developmentalist policies in the Middle East are summed up in Gelvin, *Modern Middle East*, 73–87.

3. See Gelvin, "Developmentalism, Revolution, and Freedom in the Arab Middle East," 62–96; Thompson, "Climax and Crisis of the Colonial Welfare State in Syria

and Lebanon During World War II," 59–99; Vitalis and Heydemann, "War, Keynes-ianism, and Colonialism," 100–148.

4. Economic Nationalism in the post-1952 Middle East is well known. For the pre-1952 period, see Weinryb, "Industrial Development of the Near East," 471–99; Sayigh, *Economies of the Arab World*, 323–25; Franck, "Economic Nationalism in the Middle East," 429–54.

5. Ruggie, "International Regimes, Transactions, and Change," 379–415.

6. Block, *Origins of International Economic Disorder*, 32. See also Frieden, *Global Capitalism*, 279.

7. Woods, *Globalizers*, 33.

8. Borgwardt, *New Deal for the World*, 112.

9. Ruggie, "International Regimes, Transactions, and Change," 398.

10. Murphy and Augelli, "International Institutions, Decolonization, and Develop-ment," 71–85. See also U.S. State Department, "Interim Report of Special Committee on Relaxation of Trade Barriers," December 8, 1943, RG 59/Lot 1/Box 7, National Archives.:

11. Newsom, *Imperial Mantle*, 50; Borgwardt, *New Deal for the World*, 254. Ac-cording to a position paper issued by the Colonialism Working Group of the State Department,

We must attempt to convince the colonial powers that the growth of nationalism in dependent territories is inevitable and irreversible and to persuade them that the continuing close relationships between them and their present dependencies re-quired by our interests as well as theirs can best be assured by moving with or, better, anticipating this trend. The fact that some dependencies have not yet been signifi-cantly affected by nationalism should be regarded by the metropoles as an opportu-nity to prepare for an enlightened and moderate nationalism, not as a cause for complacency. We should make it clear that except in extraordinary circumstances we cannot support or assist them in suppressing *bona fide* nationalist movements.

U.S. State Department S/P Colonialism Working Group, "A Reconsideration of US Policy Toward Colonialism," June 6, 1956, RG59/LF 66D 487/Box 106, Na-tional Archives. For a more nuanced view of British interests in the Middle East the United States might want to support, see "The British Position in the Middle East" (n.d., n.a.), RG 59/Lot 61D214/Box58, National Archives.

12. See Alterman, *Egypt and American Foreign Assistance*, 46–50; "Saudi Arabia—An Economic and Financial Survey," April 20, 1965, RG59/DM/65/24: 254074, National Archives; "Development Projects and Planning in the Arab States and Is-rael," RG 59/Lot 55D643/Box 3, December 29, 1949, National Archives.

13. Escobar, "Planning," 137. See also "Development Projects and Planning in the Arab States and Israel," December 29, 1949, USNA RG 59/Lot 55D643/Box 3, National Archives.

14. In the words of Manfred Halpern, perhaps the most vigorous promoter of this view, "In this century, army coups have ceased to mirror merely the ambitions of individuals. Instead, they reflect larger forces and issues than were once involved in the frequent changing of the guard. The army has become the instrument of the new middle class." *Politics of Social Change in the Middle East and North Africa*, 253. See also Pye, "Military Development in the New Countries."

15. See Abdel-Razek to Gardiner, November 23, 1953, RG 59/Lot 57D298/Box 4, National Archives; "Development Projects and Planning in the Arab States and Israel," December 29, 1949, RG 59/Lot 55D643/Box 3, National Archives; Sayigh, *Economies of the Arab World*, 364.

16. For general discussions of the place of land reform in American policy toward the developing world, see Loftus to McGhee, "Some Notes on Agrarian Reform," December 7, 1950, RG 59/55D643/Box 6, National Archives; Baran, *Political Economy of Growth*, 167–70, 263–36; Alterman, *Egypt and American Foreign Assistance*, 30, 42–43; Tannous, "Land Reform," 1–20.

17. See Packenham, *Liberal America and the Third World*; Brown and Opie, *American Foreign Assistance*, 383–85; Streeten, "Development Ideas in Historical Perspective," 21–52; Frankel, "United Nations Primer for Development." 301–26.

18. For an overview, see Girvan, "Economic Nationalism,"149.

19. el-Barawy, *Military Coup in Egypt*, 83; el-Barawy, *Economic Development in the United Arab Republic (Egypt)*, 20–21; Polk to Rostow, November 15, 1965, RG59/Lot 71D139/Box 302, National Archives.

20. For those core assumptions, see Gelvin, "Politics of Notables Forty Years After," 19–31. For a good overview of the influence of modernization theorists and their theories, see Gilman, *Mandarins of the Future*; Weiner, *Modernization*. For Third Worldism, see Malley, *Call from Algeria*.

21. For the isomorphism of the civic order constructed in the revolutionary republics, see Heydemann, "Social Pacts and the Persistence of Authoritarianism in the Middle East," 34.

22. For an excellent discussion of the first and fourth factors leading to the civic order but within a different analytical framework, see ibid., 29–34.

23. Murphy, *Emergence of the NIEO Ideology*, 60; Girvan, "Economic Nationalism," 149; Grant, "Development," 44–45.

24. Nesadurai, "Bandung and the Political Economy of North-South Relations, 13–14.

25. Murphy, *Emergence of the NIEO Ideology*, 93–94.

26. Ibid., 60–65; Krasner, *Structural Conflict*, 85–86.

27. Akinsanya, "Third World Quest for a New International Economic Order," 208–17; Krasner, *Structural Conflict*, 6–7.

28. For a good overview of the breakdown of the Bretton Woods system and its causes, see Solomon, *International Monetary System*. According to Joel Krieger, the

American share of the total manufacturing goods in the West had declined from 60 percent to 30 percent in the thirty years between the founding of the Bretton Woods system and the breakdown of that system in 1971. Krieger, *Reagan, Thatcher, and the Politics of Decline*, 116.

29. Murphy, *Emergence of the NIEO Ideology*, 92–93, 98–99; Murphy, "What the Third World Wants," 62–63, 67–68.

30. See Mikdashi, "The OPEC Process," 205.

31. Cooper, "Developed Country Reactions to Calls for a New International Economic Order," 245–46; Murphy, *Emergence of the NIEO Ideology*, 112–14.

32. For a more extended discussion of how this occurred, see Cohen, "Approaches to the International Economic Policy-Making Process," 147–74. See also Solomon, *International Monetary System*, 291.

33. Bergsten, "The Threat from the Third World," 106–10.

34. Bergsten, "The Response to the Third World," 6–7.

35. Bergsten, "Interdependence and the Reform of International Institutions," 363–64.

36. Ibid., 365.

37. See Cooper, "Economic Interdependence and Foreign Policy in the Seventies," 159–81.

38. Tickner, "Reaganomics and the Third World, 56–60; Feinberg, "Reaganomics and the Third World," 151–52; Alissa, "Political Economy of Reform in Egypt: 13–14; Rist, *History of Development*, 162–69.

39. See Esteva, "Development," 14–15; Murphy, *Emergence of the NIEO Ideology*, 131–39; Paolillo, "Development Assistance," 108–12; Grant, "Development," 43–45; Streeten, "Development Ideas in Historical Perspective."

40. Krasner, *Structural Conflict*, 26–27. The report itself can be found at Share the World's Resources, "The Brandt Report," http://www.stwr.org/special-features/the-brandt-report.html, accessed May 3, 2010.

41. "NSSM 174 Report: National Security and US Energy Policy: Executive Summary," August 1974, Nixon Archive/NSC/H-174-5, National Archives; van Lennep, "Interdependence of Nations," 16–18.

42. Sewall and Mathieson, "United States and the Third World," 86.

43. Quoted in Newsom, *Imperial Mantle*, 142.

44. Augelli and Murphy, *America's Quest for Supremacy and the Third World*, 161. For a historical overview, see James M. Boughton, "From Suez to Tequila: The IMF as Crisis Manager," WP/97/90, Doc. #213834, IMF Archives.

45. Boughton, "From Suez to Tequila"; Tickner, "Reaganomics & the Third World," 67; Augelli and Murphy, *America's Quest for Supremacy and the Third World*, 160–61.

46. "Survey of Multilateral Debt Renegotiations Undertaken within the Framework of Creditor Clubs, 1975–80," December 22, 1980, SM/80/274, Doc. #174836, IMF

Archives; "Developing Countries' Indebtedness to Official Creditors - Supplementary Information," 1 March 1, 1985, SM/85/62, Doc. #98852, IMF Archives.

47. See Nau, "Where Reaganomics Works," 14–37; Livingston, "Politics of International Agenda-Setting," 313–30.

48. James M. Boughton, "The IMF and the Force of History: Ten Events and Ten Ideas That Have Shaped the Institution," May 2004, Doc #216230, IMF Archives.

49. Augelli and Murphy, *America's Quest for Supremacy and the Third World*, 182–83; Oye, "International Systems Structure," 26; Feinberg, "Reaganomics and the Third World."

50. Feinberg, "The Reagan Administration's Economic Policies and the Third World," 20, 22.

51. Bergsten, "Economic Imbalances and World Politics," 770–94.

52. For Iran's participation, see Murphy, *Emergence of the NIEO Ideology*, 112–14.

53. States whose economies were dependent on the export of basic commodities such as cotton fell victim to the stagflation in the industrialized North, as did those whose overseas citizens had found employment there as guestworkers. Turkey, for example, fits in both categories. See "Turkey—Use of Fund Resources," November 3, 1975, EBS/75/394, Doc. #230271, IMF Archives; "Turkey—Recent Economic Developments," March 17, 1976, SM/76/51, Doc. #172301, IMF Archives; "Morocco—Use of Fund Resources—Compensatory Financing," March 29, 1976, EBS/76/152, Doc #230794, IMF Archives; "People's Democratic Republic of Yemen—Use of Fund Resources—Compensatory Financing (Reclassification)," April 20, 1976, EBS/76/178, Doc #230519, IMF Archives.

54. Spiro, *Hidden Hand of American Hegemony*, 69–74, 128; Frieden, "International Finance and the Third World," 4, 6–7; Frieden, *Global Capitalism*, 369–70; Tina Rosenberg, "Reverse Foreign Aid," *New York Times Sunday Magazine*, March 25, 2007, 16. The lower figure for Euromarket holdings of OPEC deposits comes from Spiro, the higher from Frieden (1983).

55. Krasner, *Structural Conflict*, 106–7. For the effects of oil wealth on the Syrian economy and state, see Richards, "Economic Reform in the Middle East," 57–128. For its effects on Jordan, see Satloff, "Jordan's Great Gamble," 129–52.

56. Beinin, *Workers and Peasants in the Modern Middle East*, 150–51.

57. Richards, "Economic Reform in the Middle East," 76–77; Henry, *Mediterranean Debt Crescent*, 3.

58. Karl, *Paradox of Plenty*, 25–31; Clawson, "What's So Good About Stability?" 214–15.

59. Bellin, "The Political Economic Conundrum, 6.

60. Henry and Springborg, *Globalization and the Politics of Development*, 35; Charlene Barshefsky, "The Middle East Belongs in the World Economy," *New York*

Times, February 22, 2003, 17; Chaudhry, "Economic Liberalization and the Lineages of the Rentier State," 8–9.

61. Boris Bernstein and James M. Boughton, "Adjusting to Development: The IMF and the Poor," March 1993, PPAA/93/4, Doc. #58017, IMF Archives. From 1980 to1984, 41 percent of recommended adjustment programs capped or reduced consumer subsidies. Amuzegar, "IMF Under Fire," 103.

62. Bernstein and Boughton, "Adjusting to Development," 6; Sadiki, "Popular Uprisings and Arab Democratization," 71–95; Brumberg, "Survival Strategies vs. Democratic Bargains", 73–74; Ryan, "Peace, Bread and Riots."

63. Such protests continued in Iran which, in the wake of eight years of war, followed logic of its own. Bayat, "Activism and Social Development in the Middle East," 4.

64. See Richter, "Political Economy of Regime Maintenance in Egypt," 186–88; Bernstein and Boughton, "Adjusting to Development," 6.

65. Heydemann, "Social Pacts," 30–31.

66. Alissa, "Political Economy of Reform," 7.

67. Alissa, "Rethinking Economic Reform in Jordan;" Lawson, "Domestic Transformation," 51–53; Sfakianakis, "Whales of the Nile," 77–100.

68. Richards, "Economic Reform in the Middle East," 87.

69. Bayat, "Activism and Social Development in the Middle East," 4. *Note*: I completed this chapter in April 2010. Subsequent developments in the region have more than borne out this conclusion.

Chapter 10

1. Davison, "Where Is the Middle East?" Also, see the discussions in various chapters in this volume.

2. Thomas L. Friedman, "Drowning Freedom in Oil," *New York Times*, August 25, 2002; Friedman, "First Law of Petropolitics"; Luciani, "Economic Foundations of Democracy and Authoritarianism." See also Ross, "Does Oil Hinder Democracy?"

3. Ajami, *Arab Predicament*; Kedourie, *Democracy and Arab Political Culture*.

4. Lewis, *What Went Wrong?*

5. Rogers, "Exceptionalism," 7.

6. Ibid., 23.

7. Dodds, *Geopolitics*, 42–49. See also Ó Tuathail, *Critical Geopolitics*.

8. Wendt, *Social Theory of International Politics*.

9. See Said, *Orientalism*.

10. Gregory, *Colonial Present*, 17. See also Said, *Orientalism*, 54.

11. See Adelson, *London and the Invention of the Middle East*, 22–23.

12. Said, *Orientalism*, 43. On Mahan's cultural reading of the region, see Barbir, "Alfred Thayer Mahan, Theodore Roosevelt, the Middle East, and the Twentieth Century."

13. See Deudney, "Geopolitics and Change."

14. Agnew, *Geopolitics*, 1.

15. See Jones, "Global Strategic Views."

16. See Blouet, *Geopolitics and Globalization in the Twentieth Century.*

17. Waltz, *Theory of International Politics*; Mearsheimer, *Tragedy of Great Power Politics.*

18. Dodds, "Cold War Geopolitics."

19. Cairncross, *Death of Distance*; O'Brien, *Global Financial Integration.*

20. Agnew, "New Global Economy," 135.

21. Aarts, "Middle East," 911.

22. Friedman, *Lexus and the Olive Tree.*

23. See Agnew, *Hegemony.*

24. Rogers "Exceptionalism," 23, as cited in Vitalis, *America's Kingdom*, 7.

25. Friedman, *Lexus and the Olive Tree*, 324.

26. Thomas L. Friedman, "Censors Beware," *New York Times*, July 25, 2000.

27. Friedman, *Lexus and the Olive Tree*, 325.

28. Friedman, *World Is Flat*, 412, 493.

29. Friedman, *Lexus and the Olive Tree*, 325–26.

30. Ibid., 329.

31. Ibid.

32. Ibid., 325, 375.

33. Thomas L. Friedman, "Clinton's Last Memo," *New York Times*, January 12, 2001.

34. Thomas L. Friedman, "Don't Look Back," *New York Times*, July 17, 2001.

35. Thomas L. Friedman, "Iraq of Ages," *New York Times*, February 28, 1998.

36. Friedman, *World Is Flat.*

37. Ibid., 485.

38. Ibid.

39. Keohane, *Power and Governance in a Partially Globalized World*, 275.

40. UNDP, *Arab Human Development Report 2002*; UNDP, *Arab Human Development Report 2003.*

41. Thomas L. Friedman, "Arabs at the Crossroads," *New York Times*, July 3, 2002.

42. Ibid.

43. Thomas L. Friedman, "Under the Arab Street," *New York Times*, October 23, 2002.

44. Ibid.

45. Thomas L. Friedman, "Thinking About Iraq (I)," *New York Times*, January 22, 2003.

46. Ibid.

47. Ibid.

48. Thomas Friedman, "Four Reasons to Invade Iraq," *Slate.com*, January 12, 2004, http://www.slate.com/id/2093620/entry/2093763/.

49. Ibid.

50. Ajami, "Iraq and the Arabs' Future," 3.

51. Ibid., 2.

52. Barnett, "Pentagon's New Map."

53. See Roberts, Secord, and Sparke, "Neoliberal Geopolitics."

54. See Barnett, *Pentagon's New Map.*

55. Ibid., 48.

56. Ibid., 49.

57. Ibid., 150.

58. Ibid., 217–18.

59. Ibid., 286.

60. Ibid., 48.

61. Thomas P.M. Barnett and Henry H. Gaffney Jr., "Global Transaction Strategy," *Military Officer,* May 2003.

62. See Luce, "American Century."

63. See Peter Waldman, "A Historian's Take on Islam Steers U.S. in Terrorism Fight," *Wall Street Journal,* February 3, 2004.

64. Barnett, *Pentagon's New Map,* 6.

65. Jacob Weisberg, Paul Berman, Thomas Friedman, Christopher Hitchens, Fred Kaplan, George Packer, Kenneth M. Pollack, and Fareed Zakaria, "Liberal Hawks Reconsider the Iraq War," January 12, 2004, http://www.slate.com/id/2093620/entry/2093641/.

66. White House, Office of the Press Secretary, "President Bush Discusses Freedom in Iraq and Middle East."

67. Philip H. Gordon, "Bush's Middle East Vision," 160.

68. As cited in ibid.

69. Powell, "U.S.–Middle East Partnership Initiative."

70. Sharp, "Middle East Partnership Initiative"; Powell, "U.S.–Middle East Partnership Initiative."

71. UNDP, *Arab Human Development Report 2002;* UNDP, *Arab Human Development Report 2003.*

72. White House, Office of the Press Secretary, "President Bush Discusses Freedom in Iraq and Middle East."

73. Robert B. Zoellick, "A Return to the Cradle of Free Trade," *Washington Post,* June 23 2003.

74. Dar al Hayat, "U.S. Working Paper for G-8 Sherpas: G-8 Greater Middle East Partnership," *al Hayat,* February 13, 2003, http://www.pogar.org/publications/reforms/documents/greater-middleeast.pdf.

75. Ibid.

76. Ibid.

77. As cited in David Isenberg, "Pennywise Commitment to Arab Democracy," *Asian Times Online*, January 9, 2003, http://www.atimes.com/atimes/Middle_East/EA09Ak01.html. See also Sharp, "Middle East Partnership Initiative," 6.

78. As cited in Steven R. Weisman, "U.S. Muffles Sweeping Call to Democracy in Mideast," *New York Times*, March 12, 2004.

79. As cited in International Crisis Group, "Broader Middle East and North Africa Initiative," 6.

80. Thomas E. Ricks and Robin Wright, "As Iraq Deteriorates, Iraqis Get More Blame," *Washington Post*, November 29, 2006.

81. See Heydemann, "In the Shadow of Democracy," 123.

82. Bulliet, *Case for Islamo-Christian Civilization*, 116.

83. Ibid., 118.

84. President Bush's speech at the Royal Banqueting House in London, November 19, 2003, cited in Neep, "Dilemmas of Democratization in the Middle East," 78.

85. White House, Office of the Press Secretary, "Press Briefing: Situation in the Middle East." http://georgewbush-whitehouse.archives.gov/news/releases/2006/07/20060716-2.html.

86. David Brooks, "It's Not Isolationism, but It's Not Attractive," *New York Times*, March 5, 2006.

87. Ibid. (emphasis added).

88. Suskind, "Without a Doubt."

Conclusion

1. Todorova, in her *Imagining the Balkans*, has described something quite similar occurring in the Balkans. Building on the work of Edward Said, she argues that the accumulation of knowledge about the Balkans gave birth to a discourse she terms "Balkanism." Subsequently, this discourse has had significant repercussions on the politics and society of the nations of the peninsula as well as on how the rest of the world has conceived of, and interacts with, the area.

2. For more on this question, see Lockman, *Contending Visions of the Middle East*.

3. Keith B. Richburg, "E.U., Turkey Agree to Membership Talks," *Washington Post*, December 18, 2004, A22.

4. Keddie, "Is There a Middle East?" 255–71.

BIBLIOGRAPHY

Aarts, Paul. "The Middle East: A Region Without Regionalism or the End of Exceptionalism?" *Third World Quarterly* 20, no. 5 (1999): 911–25.

Abu-Rabia, 'Aref. *A Bedouin Century: Education and Development Among the Negev Tribes in the 20th Century.* New York: Berghahn Books, 2001.

Achcar, Gilbert. "Fantasy of a Region That Does Not Exist: Greater Middle East, the US Plan." *Le monde diplomatique* (April 2004). http://mondediplo.com/2004/04/04world.

Adams, Oscar F. *A Dictionary of American Authors.* Boston and New York: Houghton Mifflin, 1904.

Adams, William M. *Green Development: Environment and Sustainability in a Developing World.* London: Routledge, 2009.

Adelson, Roger. *Churchill, British Power, and the Middle East.* Forthcoming.

———. *London and the Invention of the Middle East: Money, Power and War, 1902–1922.* New Haven, CT: Yale University Press, 1995.

———. *Mark Sykes: Portrait of an Amateur.* London: Jonathan Cape, 1975.

———. "Winston Churchill and the Middle East." In *Telling Lives: From W. B. Yeats to Bruce Chatwin,* ed. Alistair Horne, 135–48. London: Macmillan, 2000.

Adler, Cyrus. *The Voice of America on Kishineff.* Philadelphia: Jewish Publication Society of America, 1904.

Agnew, John. *Geopolitics: Re-visioning World Politics.* 2nd ed. London: Routledge, 2003.

———. *Hegemony: The New Shape of Global Power.* Philadelphia: Temple University Press, 2005.

———. "The New Global Economy: Time-Space Compression, Geopolitics, and Global Uneven Development." *Journal of World-Systems Research* 7, no. 2 (Fall 2001): 133–54.

Ahmida, Ali Abdullatif, ed. *Beyond Colonialism and Nationalism in the Maghrib: History, Culture, and Politics.* New York: Palgrave, 2000.

Ajami, Fouad. *The Arab Predicament: Arab Political Thought and Practice Since 1967.* 2nd ed. Cambridge: Cambridge University Press, 1992.

———. "Iraq and the Arabs' Future." *Foreign Affairs* 82, no. 1 (January/February 2003): 2–18.

Akbari, Suzanne Conklin. "Alexander in the Orient: Bodies and Boundaries in the *Roman de toute chevalerie.*" In Ananya Jahanara Kabir and Deanne Williams, eds., *Postcolonial Approaches to the European Middle Ages: Translating Cultures,* 105–26. Cambridge: Cambridge University Press, 2005.

Akinsanya, Adeoye, and Arthur Davies. "Third World Quest for a New International Economic Order: An Overview." *International and Comparative Law Quarterly* 33, no.1 (1984): 208–17.

Âlî, Mustafa. *Künhü'l Ahbar,* vol. 1 (Istanbul: 1277), 218–30.

Alissa, Sufyan. "The Political Economy of Reform in Egypt: Understanding the Role of Institutions." *Carnegie Papers* 5 (October 2007).

———. "Rethinking Economic Reform in Jordan: Confronting Socioeconomic Realities." *Carnegie Papers* 4 (July 2007).

Allen, Grant. *The European Tour: A Handbook for Americans and Colonists.* London: G. Richards, 1899.

Allen, W. H. "From Advance Shifts of the Protectionist Theory of Money." *American Economist* 54 (September 1914): 152.

Alletz, Edouard. *De la démocratie nouvelle.* 2nd ed., vol. 2. Paris: F. Lequien, 1838.

Alterman, Jon B. *Egypt and American Foreign Assistance, 1952–1956: Hopes Dashed.* New York: Palgrave Macmillan, 2002.

Amadori-Virgilj, Giovanni. *La questione Rumeliota (Macedonia, Vecchia Serbia, Albania, Epiro) e la politica Italiana* [The Rumelian Question (Macedonia, Old Serbia, Albania, Epirus) and Italian Politics]. Bitonto: N. Garofalo, 1908.

Amanat, Abbas. "The Herat Question." *Encyclopaedia Iranica* 12/2, 2003.

———. *Pivot of the Universe: Nasir al-Din Shah and the Iranian Monarchy.* Berkeley: University of California Press, 1997.

Amir, Shaul, and Orly Rechtman. "The Development of Forest Policy in Israel in the 20th Century: Implications for the Future." *Forest Policy and Economics* 8, no. 1 (2006): 35–51.

Amuzegar, Jahangir. "The IMF Under Fire." *Foreign Policy* 64 (Autumn 1986): 98–119.

Anderson, David M. *Eroding the Commons: The Politics of Ecology in Baringo, Kenya, 1890–1963.* Oxford: James Currey, in collaboration with the Ohio University Press, 2002.

Anderson, Ewan W. *The Middle East: Geography and Geopolitics.* London: Routledge, 2000.

Anderson, Ewan W., and Liam D. Anderson. *An Atlas of Middle Eastern Affairs*. London: Routledge, 2010.

Anonymous. *"Safarnama-yi Bukhara"* [1259–1260/1844], Kitabkhana-yi Majlis, Tehran, ms. 2860, published as *Safarnama-yi Bukhara*, by Husayn Zamani (Tehran: Vizarat-i Farhang, 1373/1994).

Argyll, George D. C. *The Eastern Question from the Treaty of Paris 1856 to the Treaty of Berlin 1878 and to the Second Afghan War*, vol. 1. London: Strahan & Co., 1879.

Arnold, David. *The Tropics and the Traveling Gaze: India, Landscape and Science, 1800–1856*. Delhi: Permanent Black, 2005.

Arnold, David, and Ramachandra Guha, eds. *Nature, Culture and Imperialism: Essays on the Environmental History of South Asia*. Delhi: Oxford University Press, 1998.

Aroian, Lois A., and Richard P. Mitchell. *The Modern Middle East and North Africa*. New York: Macmillan, 1984.

Augelli, Enrico, and Craig Murphy. *America's Quest for Supremacy and the Third World: A Gramscian Analysis*. London: Pinter Publishers, 1988.

Aydın, Cemil. *The Politics of Anti-Westernism in Asia: Visions of World Order in Pan-Islamic and Pan-Asian Thought*. New York: Columbia University Press, 2007.

Al-'Azm, Sadiq Jalal. "Orientalism and Orientalism in Reverse." In *Forbidden Agendas: Intolerance and Defiance in the Middle East*, ed. Jon Rothschild, 349–76. London: AlSaqi Books, 1984.

Bahadur Khan, Abu'l Ghazi. *Shajara-yi Tarakima*, trans. Baron Desmaisons, *Histoire des Mogols et des Tatares*. St. Petersbourg: Imprimerie de l'Académie Impériale des sciences, 1871, vols. 1 and 2.

Balakian, Peter. *The Burning Tigris: The Armenian Genocide and America's Response*. New York: Perennial Press, 2003.

Ballais, Jean-Louis. "Aeolian Activity, Desertification and the 'Green Dam' in the Ziban Range, Algeria." In *Environmental Change in Drylands: Biogeographical and Geomorphological Perspectives*, ed. Andrew Millington and Ken Pye, 177–98. New York: John Wiley & Sons, 1994.

———. "Conquests and Land Degradation in the Eastern Maghreb During Classical Antiquity and the Middle Ages." In *The Archaeology of Drylands*, ed. Graeme Barker and David Gilbertson, 125–36. London: Routledge, 2000.

Bancroft, Hubert Howe. *The New Pacific*. New York: Bancroft Co., 1900.

Baran, Paul A. *The Political Economy of Growth*. New York: Monthly Review, 1957.

El-Barawy, Rashed. *Economic Development in the United Arab Republic (Egypt)*. Cairo: Anglo-Egyptian Bookshop, 1970.

———. *The Military Coup in Egypt: An Analytic Study*. Cairo: Renaissance Bookshop, 1952.

Barbir, Karl K. "Alfred Thayer Mahan, Theodore Roosevelt, the Middle East, and the Twentieth Century." *Journal of Middle Eastern and North African Intellectual and*

Cultural Studies 2, no. 1 (Spring 2004), http://bingdev.binghamton.edu/mena/karlkbarbir.htm.

Barclay, James T. "The Welfare of the World Bound Up in the Destiny of Israel." *Millennial Harbinger* (1860): 661–68.

Barker, Graeme. "A Tale of Two Deserts: Contrasting Desertification Histories on Rome's Desert Frontiers." *World Archaeology* 33, no. 3 (2002): 488–507.

Barnett, Thomas P. M. "The Pentagon's New Map." *Esquire*, March 2003.

Barrett, Robert John. *Russia's New Era*. London: Financier and Bullionist Ltd., 1908.

Barth, Frederik. *Ethnic Groups and Boundaries: The Social Organization of Culture Difference*. Boston: Little, Brown and Co., 1969.

Barthold, Vasily V. *Four Studies on the History of Central Asia*, vol. 3. Leiden: E. J. Brill, 1962.

Bartholomew, John C. *The World Atlas*. 10th ed. Edinburgh: John Bartholomew & Sons, 1975.

Bassett, Thomas J., and Donald Crummey, eds. *African Savannas: Global Narratives and Local Knowledge of Environmental Change*. Oxford: James Currey, 2003.

Bayat, Asef. "Activism and Social Development in the Middle East." *International Journal of Middle East Studies* 34, no. 1 (February 2002): 1–28.

Beaumont, Peter, Gerald H. Blake, and J. Malcolm Wagstaff. *The Middle East: A Geographical Study*. London: John Wiley & Sons, 1976.

Beazley, Charles Raymond. *The Dawn of Modern Geography: A History of Exploration and Geographical Science*, vol. 2. London: H. Frowde, 1901.

Beinin, Joel. *Workers and Peasants in the Modern Middle East*. Cambridge: Cambridge University Press, 2001.

Bellin, Eva. "The Political Economic Conundrum: The Affinity of Economic and Political Reform in the Middle East and North Africa." *Carnegie Papers* 53 (November 2004).

Ben-Arieh, Yehoshua. "The Geographical Exploration of the Holy Land." *Palestine Exploration Quarterly* 104 (1972): 81–92.

———. *The Rediscovery of the Holy Land in the Nineteenth Century*. Jerusalem and Detroit: Hebrew University Magnes Press, 1979.

Bennett, Windell Clark. *The Ethnogeographic Board*. Washington, DC: Smithsonian Institution, 1947.

Bérard, Victor. "Angleterre et Russie." *La revue de Paris*, 16 August 1904, 865–86.

Bergsten, C. Fred. "Economic Imbalances and World Politics." *Foreign Affairs* 65, no. 4 (Spring 1987): 770–94.

———. "Interdependence and the Reform of International Institutions." *International Organization* 30 (Spring 1976): 361–72.

———. "The Response to the Third World." *Foreign Policy* 17 (Winter 1974–1975): 3–34.

———. "The Threat from the Third World." *Foreign Policy* 11 (Summer 1973): 102–24.

Bernard, Augustin, and Napoleon Lacroix. *L'évolution du nomadisme en Algérie*. Algiers: Adolphe Jourdan, 1906.

Bernard, Marius. *De Toulon au Tonkin (Itinéraire d'un transport)*. Paris: Laplace, Sanchez, 1885.

Berque, Jacques. *Les Arabes d'hier à demain*. Paris: Éditions du Seuil, 1960.

———. *Le Maghreb entre deux guerres*. 2nd ed. Paris: Éditions du Seuil, [1962] 1970.

———. "Qu'est-ce qu'une tribu nord-africaine?" In *Maghreb: Histoire et sociétés*. Algiers: SNED, 1974, 22–34.

Besant, Walter, and E. H. Palmer. *Jerusalem, the City of Herod and Saladin*. London: E. Bentley and Son, 1871.

Bevis, Richard W., ed. *Bibliotheca Cisorientalia*. Boston: Hall and Co., 1973.

Bilgin, Pinar. "Inventing Middle Easts: The Making of Regions Through Security Discourses." In *The Middle East in a Globalized World*, ed. Bjorn Ulav Utvik and Knut S. Vikor, 10–37. Bergen: Nordic Society for Middle Eastern Studies, 2000.

Birdwood, H. M. "The Province of Sind." *Journal of the Society of Arts* 51 (May 1903): 593–610.

Bistami, Muhammad Tahir. *Futuhat-i Fariduniya: Sharh-i Jangha-yi Faridun Khan ChariksAmir al-Mara yi Shah 'Abbas-i Avval* [The Victory Book of Faridun: Account of the Wars of Faridun Khan Chariks in the Reign of Shah 'Abbas I], ed. Mir Muhammad Sadiq and Muhammad Nadir Nasiri-Muqaddam. Tehran: Nashr-i Nuqta, 1380/2001.

Blake, Gerald, John Dewdney, and Jonathan Mitchell. *The Cambridge Atlas of the Middle East and North Africa*. Cambridge: Cambridge University Press, 1987.

Block, Fred L. *The Origins of International Economic Disorder: A Study of United States International Monetary Policy from World War II to the Present*. Berkeley: University of California Press, 1977.

Blocqueville, Henri de Couliboeuf de. "Quatorze mois de captivité, chez les Turcomans aux frontières du Turkestan et de la Perse, 1860–1861 (Frontières du Turkestan et de la Perse)." *Le tour du monde* (1866): 225–72.

Blouet, Brian W. *Geopolitics and Globalization in the Twentieth Century*. London: Reaktion, 2001.

Blowers, Paul M. "'Living in a Land of Prophets': James T. Barclay and an Early Disciples ofChrist Mission to Jews in the Holy Land." *Church History* 62, no.4 (1993): 494–513.

Blumler, Mark A. "Biogeography of Land-Use Impacts in the Near East." In *Nature's Geography: New Lessons for Conservation in Developing Countries*, ed. Karl S. Zimmerer and Kenneth R. Young, 215–36. Madison: University of Wisconsin Press, 1998.

Bonine, Michael E. "Where Is the Geography of the Middle East?" *Professional Geographer* 28, no. 2 (1976): 190–95.

Bonner, Michael D. "The Naming of the Frontier: Awāsim, Thughūr, and the Arab Geographers." *Bulletin of the School of Oriental and African Studies* 57, no. 1 (1994): 17–24.

Borgwardt, Elizabeth. *A New Deal for the World: America's Vision for Human Rights.* Cambridge, MA: Belknap Press, 2005.

Braudel, Fernand. *The Mediterranean and the Mediterranean World in the Age of Philip II.* 2 vols. Berkeley: University of California Press, 1995.

Brauer, Ralph W. *Boundaries and Frontiers in Medieval Muslim Geography.* Philadelphia: American Philosophical Society, 1995.

Brett, Michael. "The Colonial Period in the Maghrib and Its Aftermath: The Present State of Historical Writing." *Journal of African History* 17, no. 2 (1976): 291–305.

Brice, William C. *South-West Asia.* Vol. 8, *A Systematic Regional Geography.* London: University of London Press, 1966.

Brown, Carl L. *International Politics and the Middle East: Old Rules, Dangerous Game.* London: I. B. Tauris, 1984.

———. "Maghrib Historiography: The Unit of Analysis Problem." In *The Maghrib in Question: Essays in History and Historiography,* ed. Michel Le Gall and Kenneth Perkins, 4–16. Austin: University of Texas Press, 1997.

———. "The Many Faces of Colonial Rule in French North Africa." *Revue de l'Occident musulman et de la Méditerranée* 13–14 (1973) : 171–79.

Brown, William Adams, Jr., and Redvers Opie. *American Foreign Assistance.* Washington, DC: Brookings Institution, 1953.

Browne, Edward G. *A Literary History of Persia,* vol. 4. Cambridge: Cambridge University Press, 1930.

Browne, William G. *Travels in Africa, Egypt, and Syria from the Year 1792 to 1798.* 2nd ed. London: T. Cadell and W. Davies, and Longman Hurst Rees and Orme, 1806.

Brumberg, Daniel. "Survival Strategies vs. Democratic Bargains: The Politics of Economic Reform in Contemporary Egypt." In *The Politics of Economic Reform in the Middle East,* ed. Henri J. Barkey, 73–104. New York: St. Martin's Press, 1992.

Brummett, Palmira. "Imagining the Early Modern Ottoman Space, from World History to Piri Reis." In *The Early Modern Ottomans: Remapping the Empire,* ed. Virginia Aksan and Daniel Goffman, 15–58. Cambridge: Cambridge University Press, 2007.

Bucquet, Edouard, ed. *Compte-rendu des sessions législatives, session de 1834.* Paris: E. Bucquet, 1834.

Bulliet, Richard W. *The Case for Islamo-Christian Civilization.* New York: Columbia University Press, 2006.

Burke, Edmund, III. "Morocco and the Middle East: Reflections on Some Basic Differences." *Archives européennes de sociologie* 10 (1980): 70–94.

———. "Theorizing the Histories of Colonialism and Nationalism in the Arab Maghrib." In *Beyond Colonialism and Nationalism in the Maghrib: History, Culture, and Politics*, ed. Ali Abdullatif Ahmida, 17–34. New York: Palgrave, 2000.

———. "Towards a History of the Maghrib." *Middle Eastern Studies* 11, no. 3 (October 1975): 306–23.

Burnes, Alexander. *Travels into Bokhara: Being the Account of a Journey from India to Cabool, Tartary, and Persia.* 3 vols. London: John Murray, 1834.

Burton, Isabel. *The Inner Life of Syria, Palestine, and the Holy Land*, vol. 1. London: H. S. King and Co., 1875.

Burton, Richard Francis. "The Long Wall of Salona and the Ruined Cities of Pharia and Gelsa di Lesina." *Journal of the Anthropological Institute* 5 (1876): 262–96.

———. *Personal Narrative of a Pilgrimage to El Medinah and Meccah*, vol. 2. London: Longman, 1957.

———. "Unexplored Syria." *The Academy* 4 (1873): 217–19

Cairncross, Frances. *The Death of Distance: How the Communications Revolution Will Change Our Lives.* Cambridge, MA: Harvard Business School Press, 1997.

Canfield, Robert, ed. *Turko-Persia in Historical Perspective.* Cambridge: Cambridge University Press, 1991.

Canovai, Stanislao. *Panegirici di Stanislao Canovai delle scuole pie* [Stanislaus Canovai's Panegyrics of the Pious Schools]. Florence: S. G. Calasanzio, 1817.

Cartographica. *Middle East.* 1:400,000. Budapest, 2003.

Central Intelligence Agency. *Atlas: Issues in the Middle East.* Washington, DC: U.S. Government Printing Office, 1973.

———. *The 2008 World Factbook.* https://www.cia.gov/library/publications/the-world-factbook/.

Chammou, Eliezer. "Near or Middle East? Choice of Name." *Cataloging and Classification Quarterly* 7 (1987): 105–20.

Chaudhry, Kiren Aziz. "Economic Liberalization and the Lineages of the Rentier State." *Comparative Politics* 27 (October 1994): 1–25.

Chirol, Valentine. *The Far Eastern Question.* London: Macmillan, 1896.

———. *The Middle East Question; or, Some Political Problems of Indian Defence.* London: J. Murray, 1903.

Christian, Pierre. *L'Afrique française, l'empire de Maroc et les déserts de Sahara.* Paris: A. Barbier, 1846.

"Christianity in Ceylon." *Westminster Review* 17 (1860): 66–90.

Clarke, Edward Daniel. *Travels in Various Countries of Europe, Asia, and Africa.* 4th ed. New York: D. Huntington, 1814.

Clawson, Patrick. "What's So Good About Stability?" In *The Politics of Economic Reform of the Middle East*, ed. Henry J. Barkey, 213–36. New York: St. Martin's Press, 1992.

Cleveland, William. *A History of the Modern Middle East.* 3rd ed. Boulder, CO: Westview Press, 2004.

Cobden, Richard. *England and Russia.* London: James Ridgway & Sons, 1835

Cohen, Shaul E. *The Politics of Planting: Jewish-Palestinian Competition for Control of Land in the Jerusalem Periphery.* Chicago: University of Chicago Press, 1993.

Cohen, Stephen D. "Approaches to the International Economic Policy-Making Process." In *America in a Changing World Political Economy,* ed. William P. Avery and David P. Rapkin, 147–74. New York: Longman, 1982.

Cole, John. *Geography of the World's Major Regions.* London: Routledge, 1966.

Collins, Basil Anthony, trans. *Al-Muqaddasi: The Man and His Work.* Ann Arbor: Department of Geography, University of Michigan, 1974.

Conder, Claude R. "The Fertility of Ancient Palestine." In *The Survey of Western Palestine: Special Papers on Topography, Archaeology, Manners and Customs, etc.,* ed. Anonymous. London: Committee of the Palestine Exploration Fund, 1881.

Cook, Joseph. *Biology.* London: Richard D. Dickinson, 1879.

Coon, Carlton S. *The Story of the Middle East.* New York: Henry Holt, 1951.

Cooper, Richard N. "Developed Country Reactions to Calls for a New International Economic Order." In *Toward a New Strategy for Development: A Rothko Chapel Colloquium,* ed. Rothko Chapel, 243–74. New York: Pergamon Press, 1979.

———. "Economic Interdependence and Foreign Policy in the Seventies." *World Politics* 24 (January 1972): 159–81.

Courtney, Leonard Henry, ed. *Nationalism and War in the Near East.* Oxford: Clarendon Press, 1915.

Cressey, George B. *Asia's Lands and Peoples: A Geography of One-Third the Earth and Two-Thirds Its People.* New York: Whittlesey House, McGraw-Hill, 1944.

Curzon, George N. *Problems of the Far East.* London and New York: Longmans, Green, and Co., 1894.

Damiani, Anita. *Enlightened Observers: British Travelers to the Near East, 1715–1850.* Beirut:American University of Beirut, 1979.

Daubeny, Giles Andrew. *The Strength and Decay of Nations: Being Two Essays with Notes.* London: N.p., 1899.

Davis, Diana K. "Indigenous Knowledge and the Desertification Debate: Problematising Expert Knowledge in North Africa." *Geoforum* 36, no. 4 (2005): 509–24.

———. "Neoliberalism, Environmentalism and Agricultural Restructuring in Morocco." *Geographical Journal* 172, no. 2 (2006): 88–105.

———. *Resurrecting the Granary of Rome: Environmental History and French Colonial Expansion in North Africa.* Athens: Ohio University Press, 2007.

Davis, Diana K., and Edmund Burke III, eds. *Environmental Imaginaries of the Middle East and North Africa: History, Policy, Power and Practice.* Athens: Ohio University Press, 2011. .

Davis, Moshe. *America and the Holy Land: With Eyes Toward Zion*. Westport: Praeger, 1995.

Davison, Roderic H. "Where Is the Middle East?" *Foreign Affairs* 38, no. 4 (July 1960): 665–75.

Davutoğlu, Ahmet. *Stratejik Derinlik*. Istanbul: Küre Yayınları, 2001.

De Blij, H. J., and Peter O. Muller. *Geography: Realms, Regions, and Concepts*. New York: John Wiley & Sons, 1971. 10th ed., 2002; 14th ed., 2010.

Desprez, Hippolyte. "Souvenirs de l'Europe orientale: La grande Illyrie et le mouvement illyrien." *Revue des deux mondes* 17 (1847): 1007–1029.

Deudney, Daniel. "Geopolitics and Change." In *New Thinking in International Relations Theory*, ed. Michael W. Doyle and G. John Ikenberry, 91–123. Boulder, CO: Westview Press, 1997.

Al-Dhahabi. *Tarikh al-Islam* [The History of Islam], vol. 34, ed. Umar Abd al-Salam Tadmuri. Beirut: Dar al-Kitab al-Arabi, 1987.

Dickins, F. Victor. "The Far East." *Journal of the Royal Asiatic Society* (1903): 577–78.

Dickson, Martin B. "Shah Tahmasp and the Uzbeks." Ph.D. dissertation, Princeton University, Princeton, New Jersey, 1958.

Al-Din Shah, Nasir. *Safarnama-yi Khurasan* [Travel Book of Khurasan]. Tehran: Intisharat-i Kavvash, 1363/1984.

Dirckinck-Holmfeld, Constant, ed. *Politisches Journal, nebst Anzeige von Gelehrten und andern Sachen*, vol. 2. Hamburg: H. G. Voigt's Buchdruckerey, 1838.

Dodds, Klaus. "Cold War Geopolitics." In *A Companion to Political Geography*, ed. John Agnew, Katharyne Mitchell, and Gerard Toal, 204–18. London: Blackwell, 2003.

———. *Geopolitics: A Very Short Introduction*. Oxford: Oxford University Press, 2007.

Dodge, Toby. *Inventing Iraq: The Failure of Nation Building and a History Denied*. New York: Columbia University Press, 2003.

Donop, Georg Carl Wilhelm Philipp. *Das magusanische Europa, oder: Phönizier in den innen-landen des europäischen Westens bis zur Weser und Werra*. Hildburghausen and New York: Bibliographischen Institut, 1834.

Drysdale, Alasdair, and Gerald H. Blake. *The Middle East and North Africa: A Political Geography*. Oxford: Oxford University Press, 1985.

Duncan, Chesney. *Corea and the Powers: A Review of the Far Eastern Question, with Appendices*. Shanghai: Shanghai Mercury Office, 1889.

Duruy, Victor. *Abrégé d'histoire universelle*. Paris: Librairie Hachette et Cie., 1878.

Dyer, Henry. *Japan in World Politics: A Study in International Dynamics*. London: Blackie & Son Ltd., 1909.

Eickelman, Dale F. *The Middle East: An Anthropological Approach*. Englewood Cliffs, NJ: Prentice Hall, 1981. 2nd ed., 1989.

———. *The Middle East and Central Asia: An Anthropological Approach*. 3rd ed. Englewood Cliffs, NJ: Prentice Hall, 1998. 4th ed., 2001.

El-Eini, Roza. "British Forestry Policy in Mandate Palestine, 1929–48: Aims and Realities." *Middle Eastern Studies* 35, no. 3 (1999): 72–155.

Eliot, Charles. *Letters from the Far East.* London: Edward Arnold, 1907.

Encyclopaedia Britannica. *Encyclopaedia Britannica World Atlas.* 20th ed. Chicago: Encyclopaedia Britannica, 1966.

English, Paul Ward. *City and Village in Iran: Settlement and Economy in the Kirman Basin.* Madison: University of Wisconsin Press, 1966.

———. "Geographical Perspectives on the Middle East: The Passing of the Ecological Trilogy." In *Geographers Abroad: Essays on the Problems and Prospects of Research in Foreign Areas,* ed. M. V. Mikesell. Chicago: University of Chicago, Department of Geography, Research Paper no. 152, pp. 134–64.

———. *World Regional Geography: A Question of Place.* New York: Harper & Row, 1977.

English, Paul Ward, and James A. Miller. *World Regional Geography: A Question of Place.* 2nd ed. New York: John Wiley & Sons, 1984. 3rd ed., 1989; 4th ed., 1993.

Escobar, Arturo. "Planning." In *The Development Dictionary: A Guide to Knowledge as Power,* ed. Wolfgang Sachs, 132–45. London: Zed, 1993.

Esteva, Gustavo. "Development." In *The Development Dictionary: A Guide to Knowledge as Power,* ed. Wolfgang Sachs, 7–25. London: Zed, 1993.

Evenari, Michael, Leslie Shanan, and Naphtali Tadmor. *The Negev: The Challenge of a Desert.* Cambridge, MA: Harvard University Press, 1982.

Faber, Ernst. *The Mind of Mencius; or, Political Economy Founded upon Moral Philosophy,* trans. Arthur B. Hutchinson. Boston: Houghton Mifflin, 1882.

Fairbairn, Andrew Martin. *Religion in History and in the Life of Today.* London: Hodder & Stoughton, 1884.

Feinberg, Richard E. "The Reagan Administration's Economic Policies and the Third World." *Development Policy Review* A15, no. 2 (October 1982): 20–45.

———. "Reaganomics and the Third World." In *Eagle Defiant: United States Foreign Policy in the 1980s,* ed. Kenneth A. Oye et al., 131–66. Boston: Little, Brown and Co., 1983.

Fernández y González, Francisco. *Historia general de España,* vol. 1. Madrid: El Progreso, 1891.

Ferret, Pierre Victor Ad. *Voyage en Abyssinie dans les provinces du Tigré, du Samen et de l'Amhara,* vol. 1. Paris: Paulin, 1848.

Filali, Abdellatif. *Le Maroc et le monde arabe.* Paris: Scali, 2008.

Finnie, David H. *Pioneers East: The Early American Experience in the Middle East.* Cambridge, MA: Harvard University Press, 1967.

Firdawsi. *Shahnama,* "Crossing the Oxus," British Library, India Office Or. 12688, folio 180.

Fisher, W. B. *The Middle East: A Physical, Social and Regional Geography.* London: Methuen, 1950. 2nd ed., 1952; 3rd ed., 1956; 4th ed., 1961; 5th ed., 1963; 6th rev. ed., 1971; 7th rev. ed., 1978.

Flaubert, Gustave. *Voyage en Egypte*. Édition intégrale du manuscrit original, établie et présentée par Pierre-Marc de Biasi. Paris: Grasset, 1991.

Fletcher, Joseph. *Studies on Chinese and Islamic Inner Asia*. Aldershot: Ashgate/Variorum, 1995.

Flügel, Gustav. *Geschichte der Araber bis auf den Sturz des Chalifats von Bagdad*. Leipzig: W. Baensch, 1864.

Franck, Peter G. "Economic Nationalism in the Middle East." *Middle East Journal* 6 (1952): 429–54.

Frankel, S. Herbert. "United Nations Primer for Development." *Quarterly Journal of Economics* 66, no. 3 (August 1952): 301–26.

Franzos, Karl Emil. *Aus Halb-Asien Culturbilder aus Galizien, der Bukowina, Südrußland und Rumänien*. 2 vols. Leipzig: Duncker & Humblot, 1876.

Fraser, James Baillie. *Narrative of a Journey into Khorasan in the Years 1821 and 1822*. London: Longman, Hurst, Rees, Orme, Brown, and Green, 1825.

Frenkel, Yehoshua. "Muslim Pilgrimage to Jerusalem in the Mamluk Period." In *Pilgrims and Travelers to the Holy Land*, ed. Bryan F. Le Beau and Menachem Mor, 63–87. Omaha, NB: Creighton University Press, 1996.

Frieden, Jeffry A. *Global Capitalism: Its Fall and Rise in the Twentieth Century*. New York: W. W. Norton, 2006.

———. "International Finance and the Third World." *MERIP Reports* 117 (September 1983): 3–11.

Friedman, Thomas L. "The First Law of Petropolitics." *Foreign Policy*, no. 154 (May/June 2006): 28–36.

———. *The Lexus and the Olive Tree*. Rev. ed. New York: Farrar, Straus and Giroux, 2000.

———. *The World Is Flat: A Brief History of the Twenty-first Century*, updated and expanded ed. New York: Farrar, Straus and Giroux, 2006.

Fritzinger, Linda. *Diplomat Without Portfolio: Valentine Chirol, His Life and "The Times."* London: I. B. Tauris, 2006.

Frye, Richard N. *The Heritage of Central Asia: From Antiquity to the Turkish Expansion*. Princeton, NJ: Markus Weiner, 1996.

Fysh, Frederic. *The Time of the End; or, The Sultan of Turkey the Wilful King, and Mehemet Ali the King of the South Pushing at Him, as Foretold by Daniel*. London: Binns and Goodwin, 1839.

Gaulle, Charles de. *Mémoires de guerre*. 3 vols. Paris: Plon, 1954.

Gelvin, James L. "Developmentalism, Revolution, and Freedom in the Arab Middle East: The Cases of Egypt, Syria, and Iraq." In *The Idea of Freedom in Asia and Africa*, ed. Robert H. Taylor, 62–96. Stanford: Stanford University Press, 2002.

———. *The Modern Middle East: A History*. New York: Oxford University Press, 2007.

———. "The Politics of Notables Forty Years After." *Middle East Studies Association Bulletin* 40 (June 2006): 19–31.

Gibbons, Herbert Adams. *An Introduction to World Politics.* New York: Century Co., 1922.

Gilman, Niels. *Mandarins of the Future: Modernization Theory in Cold War America.* Baltimore: Johns Hopkins University Press, 2003.

Gilpin, William. *The Cosmopolitan Railway: Compacting and Fusing Together All the World's Continents.* San Francisco: History Company, 1890.

Gingeras, Ryan. "Notorious Subjects, Invisible Citizens: North Caucasian Resistance to the Turkish National Movement in Northwestern Anatolia, 1919–23." *International Journal of Middle East Studies* 40 (2008): 89–108.

Ginsburg, Norton, ed. *The Pattern of Asia.* Englewood Cliffs, NJ: Prentice-Hall, 1958.

Girvan, Norman. "Economic Nationalism." *Daedalus* 104 (Fall 1975): 145–58.

Goadby, Frederic M., and Moses J. Doukhan. *The Land Law of Palestine.* Tel-Aviv: Shoshany's Printing Co., 1935.

Goethe, Johann Wolfgang von. *West-oestlicher Divan.* Stuttgart: Cottaischen Buchhandlung, 1819.

Goitein, Shelomo D. *Mediterranean Society: The Jewish Communities of the Arab World as Portrayed in the Documents of the Cairo Genize.* 6 vols. Berkeley: University of California Press, 1967–1993.

———. *Studies in Islamic History and Institutions.* Leiden: E. J. Brill, 1966.

Goitein, Shelomo D., and Mordechai A. Friedman. *India Traders of the Middle Ages: Documents from the Cairo Geniza "India Book."* Leiden: Brill, 2007.

Goldammer, Kurt. *Der Mythus von Ost und West: Eine kultur-und religionsgeschichtliche Betrachtung,* 1962.

Gole, Susan. *Indian Maps and Plans: From Earliest Times to the Advent of European Surveys.* N.p: South Asia Books, 2010.

Gordon, Philip H. "Bush's Middle East Vision." *Survival* 45, no. 1 (Spring 2003): 155–65.

Gordon, General Sir Thomas. "The Problem of the Middle East." *Nineteenth Century* 277 (March 1900): 413–24.

Gower, Ronald Sutherland. *My Reminiscences.* New York: Charles Scribner's Sons, 1884.

Grant, James P. "Development: The End of Trickle Down?" *Foreign Policy* 12 (Autumn 1973): 43–65.

Gregory, Derek. *The Colonial Present: Afghanistan, Iraq, Palestine.* Malden, MA: Blackwell, 2004.

Griffith, Francis L. L. "Egypt and Assyria." In *Authority and Archaeology, Sacred and Profane: Essays on the Relation of Monuments to Biblical and Classical Literature,* ed. David George Hogarth, Samuel Rolles Driver, Francis Llewellyn Griffin, Arthur Cayley Headlam, Ernest Arthur Gardner, and Francis Haverfield, 155–253. London: J. Murray, 1899.

Grove, Alfred T., and Oliver Rackham. *The Nature of Mediterranean Europe: An Ecological History*. New Haven, CT: Yale University Press, 2001.

Grove, Richard H. *Green Imperialism: Colonial Expansion, Tropical Island Edens and the Origins of Environmentalism, 1600–1860*. Cambridge: Cambridge University Press, 2005.

Grove, Richard H., Vinita Damodaran, and Saptal Sangwan, eds. *Nature and the Orient: The Environmental History of South and Southeast Asia*. Delhi: Oxford University Press, 1998.

Guillaumet, Gustave. "Tableaux algériens." *La nouvelle revue* 1 (1879): 144–58.

Guo, Li. *Commerce, Culture and Community in a Red Sea Port in the Thirteenth Century: The Arabic Documents from Quseir*. Leiden: Brill, 2004.

Hachicho, Mohamed Ali. "English Travel Books About the Arab Near East in the Eighteenth Century." *Die Welt des Islam* 9 (1964): 1–206.

Halpern, Manfred. *The Politics of Social Change in the Middle East and North Africa*. Princeton, NJ: Princeton University Press, 1963.

Hami, İsmail. "Avrupa'nın Beyhude Teşebbüsleri" [Futile Efforts of Europe]. *Edebiyat-ı Umumiye Mecmuası* 1 (1335/1917): 214–16.

———. "İran İhtilafnamesi" [The Iranian Conflict]. *Edebiyat-ı Umumiye Mecmuası* 1 (1335/1917): 10–15.

Hammond International. *Near and Middle East*. Munich: Geographic Publishers, 2006.

Hannoum, Abdelmajid. *Colonial Histories, Post-Colonial Memories: The Legend of the Kahina, A North African Heroine*. Portsmouth: Heinemen, 2001.

Harding, J. W. "The Ruins of Jerusalem." In *Sacred Biography and History, Containing Descriptions of Palestine, Ancient and Modern*, ed. Tiffany Osmand, 597–609. Chicago: Hugh Heron, 1875.

Harley, John B., and David Woodward, eds. *The History of Cartography*, vol. 2, bk. 1, *Cartography in the Traditional Islamic and South Asian Societies*. Chicago: University of Chicago Press, 1992.

Hart, Albert Bushnell. "Reservations as to the Near Eastern Question." *Annals of the American Academy of Political and Social Science* 108 (1923): 120–24.

Hay, Denys. *Europe: The Emergence of an Idea*. Edinburgh: Edinburgh University Press, 1957.

Hegel, Georg Wilhelm Friedrich. *The Philosophy of History*, trans. John Sibree. New York: P. F. Collier, 1902.

———. *Vorlesungen über die Philosophie der Geschichte*, ed. Eduard Gans. Berlin: Duncker & Humblot, 1848.

Held, Colbert C. *Middle East Patterns: Places, Peoples, and Politics.* Boulder, CO: Westview Press, 1989. 2nd ed., 1994; 3rd ed., 2000; 4th ed., 2005; 5th ed. (with John Thomas Cummings), 2011.

Henry, Clement M. *The Mediterranean Debt Crescent: Money and Power in Algeria, Egypt, Morocco, Tunisia, and Turkey.* Gainesville: University of Florida Press, 1996.

Henry, Clement M., and Robert Springborg, *Globalization and the Politics of Development in the Middle East.* Cambridge: Cambridge University Press, 2001.

Hepner, George F., and Jesse O. McKee, eds. *World Regional Geography: A Global Approach.* St. Paul: West Publishing Co., 1992.

Heydemann, Steven. "In the Shadow of Democracy." *Middle East Journal* 60, no. 1 (Winter 2006): 146–57.

———. "Social Pacts and the Persistence of Authoritarianism in the Middle East." In *Debating Arab Authoritarianism Dynamics and Durability in Nondemocratic Regimes,* ed. Oliver Schlumberger, 21–38. Stanford: Stanford University Press, 2007.

Hidayat, Riza Quli Khan. *Sifaratnama-yi Khvarazm* [Relation de l'Ambassade au Kharezm (Khiva) De Riza Qouly Khan. Texte Persan], ed. Charles Schefer. Paris: Ernest Leroux, 1876.

Histoire Générale de la Tunisie. Vol. 1, *L'antiquité,* by Hédi Slim, Ammar Mahjoubi, Khaled Belkhodja, and Abdelmajid Ennabli (Tunis: Sud Editions, 2003); Vol. 2, *Le moyen-âge,* by Hichem Djaït, Mohamed Talbi, Farhat Dachraoui, Abdelmajid Dhouib, M'hamed Ali M'Rabet, and Faouzi Mahfoudh (Tunis: Sud Editions, 2008); Vol. 3, *Les temps modernes, 941–1247 H./1534–1881,* by Azzedine Guellouz, Abdelkader Masmoudi, and Mongi Smida (Tunis: Sud Editions, 2007).

Hodgson, Marshall G. S. *The Venture of Islam: Conscience and History in a World Civilization,* vol. 1. Chicago: University of Chicago Press, 1958.

Hogarth, David George. *The Nearer East.* London: W. Heinemann, 1902; H. Froude, 1905. Appleton's World Series: The Regions of the World, ed. H. J. Mackinder.

Holdich, Thomas Hungerford. *Boundaries in Europe and the Near East.* London, Macmillan, 1918.

Hopkins, B. D. "The Bounds of Identity: The Goldsmid Mission and the Delineation of the Perso-Afghan Border in the Nineteenth Century." *Journal of Global History* 2 (2007): 233–54.

Hopkirk, Peter. *The Great Game: On Secret Service in Asia.* London: John Murray, 1991.

Howard, Donald R. *Writers and Pilgrims: Medieval Pilgrimmage Narratives and Their Posterity.* Berkeley: University of California Press, 1980.

Hulburt, W. H. "The Mexican Question." *Knickerbocker* 53 (March 1859): 224–33.

Hunt, E. D. *Holy Land Pilgrimage in the Later Roman Empire,* A.D. 312–460. Oxford: Oxford University Press, 1982.

International Crisis Group. *The Broader Middle East and North Africa Initiative: Imperiled at Birth*. Brussels: International Crisis Group, 2004.

Irwin, Robert. *For Lust of Knowing: The Orientalists and Their Enemies*. London: Penguin Books, 2006.

I'timad al-Saltana, Muhammad Hasan Khan Sani' al-Dawla. *Matla' al-Shams: Tarikh-i Arz-i Aqdas va Mashhad-i Muqaddas, dar Tarikh va Jughrafiya-yi Mashruh-i Balad va Imakan-i Khurasan* [The Place of the Rising Sun: History of the Sacred Land and Sacred City of Mashhad, on the Known History and Geography of the Lands of Khurasan]. 2 vols. Tehran: Farhangsara, 1362/1983.

———. *Tatbiq-i Lughat-i Jughrafiyihi-yi Qadim va Jadid-i Iran*, ed. Mir Hashim Muhaddas. Tehran: Amir Kabir, 1363/1984.

Janssen, Caroline. *Babil, the City of Witchcraft and Wine: The Name and Fame of Babylon in Medieval Arabic Geographical Texts*. Ghent: University of Ghent, 1995.

Ibn al-Jawzi. *Al-muntazam fi al-tarikh* [A Categorical Collection of History], vol. 8. Beirut: Dar Sadr, 1939.

Johnson, Douglas. "Algeria: Some Problems of Modern History." *Journal of African History* 5, no. 1 (1964): 221–42.

Jones, Stephen B. "Global Strategic Views." *Geographical Review* 45, no. 4 (October 1955): 492–508.

Julien, Charles-Andre. *Histoire de l'Afrique du Nord: Tunisie, Algérie, Maroc*. 2 vols. 2nd ed. Paris: Payot, 1968–69.

Kabir, Ananya Jahanara, and Deanne Williams. *Postcolonial Approaches to the European Middle Ages: Translating Cultures*. Cambridge: Cambridge University Press, 2005.

Kaddache, Mahfoud. *L'Algérie medieval*. Algiers: Société nationale d'édition et de diffusion, 1982.

Kanne, Johann Arnold. *Erste Urkunden der Geschichte oder allgemeine Mythologie*. Bayreuth: J. A. Lübecks Erben, 1808, 1813.

Karl, Lynn. *The Paradox of Plenty: Oil Booms and Petro-States*. Berkeley: University of California Press, 1997.

Kashani-Sabet, Firoozeh. *Frontier Fictions: Shaping the Iranian Nation, 1804–1946*. Princeton, NJ: Princeton University Press, 1999.

Kawakami, Kiyoshi Karl. *What Japan Thinks*. New York: Macmillan, 1921.

Kayserling, M. "Richelieu, Buxtorf père et fils et Jacob Roman." *Revue des études juives* 8 (1884): 74–95.

Keddie, Nikki. "Is There a Middle East?" *International Journal of Middle East Studies* 4, no. 3 (1973): 255–71.

Kedourie, Elie. *Democracy and Arab Political Culture*. London: Routledge, 1994.

Kemal, Namık. *Renan müdaafanamesi* [Written Defense Against Renan], ed. M. Fuad Köprülü. Ankara: Güven Matbaası, 1962.

Keohane, Robert O. *Power and Governance in a Partially Globalized World.* London: Routledge, 2002.

Ibn Khaldun. *Tarikh Ibn Khaldun: Al-musamma bi-kitab al-Ibar wa Diwan al-Mubtada wa al-Khabar fi Ayyam al-Arab wa al-Ajam wa al-Barbar wa man Asarahum min Dhawi al-Sultan al-Akbar* [History of Ibn Khaldun: Book of Evidence, Record of Beginnings and Events from the Days of the Arabs, Persians and Berbers and Their Powerful Contemporaries]. 7 vols. Beirut: Muassasat al-Alami lil-Matbuat, 1971.

Khalidi, Rashid. *Resurrecting Empire: Western Footprints and America's Perilous Path in the Middle East.* Boston: Beacon Press, 2004.

Khazeni, Arash. "Helmand." *Encyclopaedia Iranica* 12/2 (2003): 173–76.

Ibn Khordâdhbeh. *Kitâb al-masâlik wa'l-mamâlik* [The Book of the Routes of the Kingdoms], ed. M. J. De Goeje. Leiden: E. J. Brill, 1967.

Khvandamir, Ghiyath al-Din. *Tarikh-i Habib al-Siyar* [The History of Habib al-Siyar], vol. 4, ed. Muhammad Dabir Siyaqi. Tehran: Intisharat-i Khayyam, 1380/2001.

Kinglake, Alexander. *Eothen; or, Traces of Travel Brought Home from the East.* Oxford: OxfordUniversity Press, 1906.

Kirk, George. *The Middle East in the War, 1939–1946.* London: Oxford University Press, 1952.

———. *The Middle East, 1945–1950.* London: Oxford University Press, 1954.

Konchin, M. "La Question de l'Oxus." *Annales de Géographie* (1895–96): 496–504.

Koppes, Clayton R. "Captain Mahan, General Gordon and the Origins of the Term 'Middle East.'" *Middle East Studies* 12 (1976): 95–98.

Krasner, Stephen D. *Structural Conflict: The Third World Against Global Liberalism.* Berkeley: University of California Press, 1985.

Krieger, Joel. *Reagan, Thatcher, and the Politics of Decline.* Cambridge: Polity Press, 1986.

Kull, Christian A. *Isle of Fire: The Political Ecology of Landscape Burning in Madagascar.* Chicago: University of Chicago Press, 2004.

Laffitte, Pierre. *Les grands types de l'humanité: Appréciation systématique des principaux agents de l'évolution humaine.* Paris: E. Leroux, 1875.

Lamb, H. F., F. Damblon, and R. W. Maxted. "Human Impact on the Vegetation of the Middle Atlas, Morocco, During the Last 5000 Years." *Journal of Biogeography* 18, no. 5 (1991): 519–32.

Lamb, H. F., U. Eichner, and V. R. Switsur. "An 18,000-Year Record of Vegetation, Lake-Level and Climate Change from Tigalmamine, Middle Atlas, Morocco." *Journal of Biogeography* 1, no. 16 (1989): 65–74.

Lamport, W. J. "Légende Ateniénne." *La rivista Europea* 4 (1872): 402–4.

———. "Levantine Sects." *Theological Review* 10 (1873): 268–76.

Laroui, Abdallah. *L'histoire du Maghreb: Un essai de synthèse.* Paris: Maspero, 1970. Trans. into English as *The History of the Maghrib: An Interpretive Essay.* Princeton, NJ: Princeton University Press, 1977.

Lashkar, Mirza Qahraman Amin. *Ruznama-yi Safar-i Khurasan* [Travel Memoir of Khurasan], ed. Iraj Afshar and Muhammad Rasul Daryagasht. Tehran: Asatir, 1374/1995.

Lawson, Fred H. "Domestic Transformation and Foreign Steadfastness in Contemporary Syria." *Middle East Journal* 48 (Winter 1994): 47–64.

Leach, M., and R. Mearns, eds. *The Lie of the Land: Challenging Received Wisdom on the African Environment*. London: International African Institute, 1996.

Leimdorfer, François. *Discours académique et colonisation: Thèmes de recherche sur l'Algérie pendant la période coloniale (le corpus des thèses de droit et lettres, 1880–1962)*. Paris: Publisud, 1992.

Le Strange, G. *Lands of the Eastern Caliphate: Mesopotamia, Persia, and Central Asia from the Moslem Conquest to the Time of Timur*. Cambridge: Cambridge University Press, 1905.

Létolle, René. "Histoire de l'Ouzboi, cours fossile de l'Amou Darya." *Studia Iranica* 29, no. 2 (2000): 195–240.

Létolle, René, Philip Micklin, Nikolay Aladin, and Igor Plotnikov. "Uzboy and the Aral Regressions: A Hydrological Approach." *Quaternary International* 173–74 (2007): 125–36.

Levesque, Paul. "Mapping the Other: Lion Feuchtwanger's Topographies of the Orient." *German Quarterly* 71 (1998): 145–65.

Lewis, Bernard. "Rethinking the Middle East." *Foreign Affairs* 71 (1992): 99–119.

———. *What Went Wrong? The Clash Between Islam and Modernity in the Middle East*. New York: Harper Perennial, 2003.

Lewis, Martin W., and Karen E. Wigen. *The Myth of Continents: A Critique of Metageography*. Berkeley: University of California Press, 1997.

Livingston, Steven G. "The Politics of International Agenda-Setting: Reagan and North-South Relations." *International Studies Quarterly* 36 (1992): 313–30.

Lockman, Zachary. *Contending Visions of the Middle East: The History and Politics of Orientalism*. Cambridge: Cambridge University Press, 2004.

Lorcin, Patricia. *Imperial Identities: Stereotyping, Prejudice, and Race in Colonial Algeria*. London: I. B. Tauris, 1999.

Lowdermilk, Walter C. *Palestine: Land of Promise*. New York and London: Harper & Brothers, 1944.

Lowell, Percival. *Chosön: The Land of the Morning Calm: A Sketch of Korea*. Boston: Ticknor and Co., 1886.

Luce, Henry. "The American Century." In *The Ideas of Henry Luce*, ed. John K. Jessup. New York: Atheneum, 1969 [1941].

Luciani, Giacomo. "Economic Foundations of Democracy and Authoritarianism: The Arab World in Comparative Perspective." *Arab Studies Quarterly* 10, no. 4 (Fall 1988): 457–75.

Ludlow, James Meeker. *The Age of the Crusades.* New York: Christian Literature Co., 1896.

Mackinder, Halford J. "The Geopolitical Pivot of History." *Geographical Journal* 23, no. 4 (April 1904): 421–44.

"Mağrib." *İslam Ansiklopedisi,* vol. 7. Istanbul: Milli Eğitim Basımevi, 1950–58.

"Mağrib." *Türkiye Diyanet Vakfı İslam Ansiklopedisi,* vol. 27. Istanbul: Türkiye Diyanet Vakfı, 1988–.

Mahan, Alfred T. "The Persian Gulf and International Relations." *National Review,* September 1902. Reprinted in Alfred T. Mahan, *Retrospect and Prospect: Studies in International Relations, Naval and Political,* 209–51. Boston: Little, Brown and Co., 1903.

Malley, Robert. *The Call from Algeria: Third Worldism, Revolution, and the Turn to Islam.* Berkeley: University of California Press, 1996.

Al-Mamalik, 'Ali Naqi Khan Hakim. *Ruznama-yi Safar-i Khurasan* [Hakim al-Mamalik's Travel Memoir of Khurasan]. Tehran: Intisharat-i Farhang-i Iran Zamin, 1356/1977.

Mandeville, Sir John. *The Travels of Sir John Mandeville.* Trans. C. W. R. D. Moseley. Middlesex: Penguin Books, 1983.

Map Link. *Middle East.* 1:4,500,000. Santa Barbara, 1998.

Maraval, Pierre. *Lieux saints et pèlegrinages d'Orient: Histoire et géographie des origines à l'conquete arabe.* Paris: CERF, 1985.

Marriott, John Arthur R. *The Eastern Question: An Historical Study in European Diplomacy.* Oxford: Calderon Press, 1940.

Marston, Sallie A., Paul L. Knox, and Diana M. Liverman. *World Regions in Global Context: Peoples, Places, and Environments.* Upper Saddle River, NJ: Prentice Hall, 2002.

Marvin, Charles. *Merv, the Queen of the World; and the Scourge of the Man-Stealing Turkomans.* London: W. H. Allen and Co., 1881.

Marx, Karl. *The Eastern Question: A Reprint of Letters Written 1853–1856 Dealing with the Events of the Crimean War,* ed. Eleanor Marx Aveling and Edward Aveling. London: S. Sonnenschein & Co., 1897.

Matthews, Charles D. "Palestine, Holy Land of Islam." *Journal of Biblical Literature* 51, no. 2 (1932): 171–78.

McAlister, Melani. *Epic Encounters: Culture, Media, and U.S. Interests in the Middle East, 1945–2000.* Berkeley: University of California Press, 2001.

McCann, James. *Green Land, Brown Land, Black Land: An Environmental History of Africa.* Portsmouth, NH: Heinemann, 1999.

McCarthy, Justin. *The Story of Gladstone's Life.* New York: Macmillan, 1898.

McChesney, Robert. "'Barrier of Heterodoxy'? Rethinking the Ties Between Iran and Central Asia in the Seventeenth Century." In *Safavid Persia: The History and Politics of an Islamic Society,* ed. Charles Melville, 231–67. London: I. B. Tauris, 1996.

McDougall, James. *History and the Culture of Nationalism in Algeria*. Cambridge: University of Cambridge Press, 2006.

McNeill, J. R. "Observations on the Nature and Culture of Environmental History." *History and Theory* 42 (2003): 5–43.

Meadows, John. "The Younger Dryas Episode and the Radiocarbon Chronologies of the Lake Huleh and Ghab Valley Pollen Diagrams, Israel and Syria." *The Holocene* 15, no. 4 (2005): 631–36.

Meadows, Thomas Taylor. *The Chinese and Their Rebellions*. London: Smith, Elder & Co., 1856.

———. "Communications with the Far East." *Fraser's Magazine for Town and Country* 54 (November 1856): 574–81.

Mearsheimer, John J. *The Tragedy of Great Power Politics*. New York: W. W. Norton, 2003.

Melman, Billie. *Women's Orients: English Women and the Middle East, 1718–1918: Sexuality, Religion, and Work*. Ann Arbor: University of Michigan Press, 1992.

Merrill, Selah. "Within Thy Gates, O Jerusalem." *Biblical World* 12, no. 5 (1898): 293–302.

Messerli, Bruno, and M. Winiger. "Climate, Environmental Change, and Resources of the African Mountains from the Mediterranean to the Equator." *Mountain Research and Development* 12, no. 4 (1992): 315–36.

Al-Mes'udi. *Meadows of Gold and Mines of Gems*, vol. 1, trans. Aloys Sprenger. London: Oriental Translation Fund, 1841.

Michelet, Karl Ludwig. *Das System der Philosophie als exacter Wissenschaft enthaltend Logik, Naturphilosophie und Geistesphilosophie*, vol. 4. Berlin: Nicolaische Verlags-Buchhandlung, 1879.

Mikdashi, Zuhayr. "The OPEC Process." In *The Oil Crisis*, ed. Raymond Vernon, 203–16. New York: W. W. Norton, 1976.

Mikesell, Marvin. "The Deforestation of Mount Lebanon." *Geographical Review* 59, no. 1 (1969): 1–28.

Milchunas, Daniel G., and W. K. Lauenroth. "Quantitative Effects of Grazing on Vegetation and Soils over a Global Range of Environments." *Ecological Applications* 63, no. 4 (1993): 327–66.

Millard, Thomas F. *Our Eastern Question: America's Contact with the Orient and the Trend of Relations with China and Japan*. New York: Century Co., 1916.

Miller, James A. *Imlil: A Moroccan Mountain Community in Change*. Boulder, CO: Westview Press, 1984.

Miller, W. "Europe and the Ottoman Power Before the Nineteenth Century." *English Historical Review*, 16 July 1901: 452–72.

Mirkhvand. *Rawzat al-Safa* (Garden of Purity). British Library, India Office, Or. 5736, folio 368.

Mirniya, Sayyid ʿAli, ed. *Vaqaʿiʾ-yi Khavar-i Iran dar Dawra-yi Qajar* [Events in Eastern Iran During Qajar Era], vol. 1. Mashhad: Intisharat-i Ardashir, 1366/1987, 179–90.

Mitchell, Lucy Myers Wright. *A History of Ancient Sculpture.* New York: Dodd, Mead and Co., 1883.

Mojtahed-Zadeh, Pirouz. *Small Players of the Great Game: The Settlement of Iran's Eastern Borderlands and the Creation of Afghanistan.* London: Routledge, 2004.

Monroe, Elizabeth. *Britain's Moment in the Middle East.* Baltimore: Johns Hopkins University Press, 1963.

Monroe, Will Seymour. *Turkey and the Turks: An Account of the Lands, the Peoples, and the Institutions of the Ottoman Empire.* London: G. Bell, 1908.

Montagne, Robert. "France, England, and the Arab States." *International Affairs* 25, no. 3 (1949): 286–94.

Montalembert, Comte de. "Sardinia and Rome." *Brownson's Quarterly Review* 2 (July 1861): 403–16.

Morey, William Carey. *Outlines of Ancient History: For the Use of High Schools and Academies.* New York: American Book Co., 1906.

Moser, Henri. *A travers l'Asie centrale.* Paris: Librairie Plon, 1885.

Mouterde, Paul. *La végétation arborescente des pays du Levant.* Beyrouth: L'École Française d'Ingénieurs, 1947.

Murphey, Rhoads. "Bigots or Informed Observers? A Periodization of Pre-colonial English and European Writing on the Middle East." *Journal of the American Oriental Society* 110, no. 2 (1990): 291–303.

Murphy, Craig. *The Emergence of the NIEO Ideology.* Boulder, CO: Westview Press, 1984.

———. "What the Third World Wants: An Interpretation of the Development and Meaning of the New International Economic Order Ideology." *International Studies Quarterly* 27 (1983): 55–76.

Murphy, Craig, and Enrico Augelli. "International Institutions, Decolonization, and Development." *International Political Science Review* 14 (January 1993): 71–85.

Najmabadi, Afsaneh. *The Story of the Daughters of Quchan: Gender and National Memory in Iranian History.* Syracuse, NY: Syracuse University Press, 1998.

National Geographic Society. *Iraq and the Heart of the Middle East.* 1:1,983,000. Washington, DC, 2003.

———. *National Geographic Atlas of the Middle East.* Washington, DC: National Geographic Society, 2003. 2nd ed., 2008.

———. *National Geographic Atlas of the World.* 6th ed. Washington, DC: National Geographic Society, 1990. 8th ed., 2005.

National Liberal Federation. *Proceedings in Connection with the Twentieth Annual Meeting.* London: Liberal Publication Department, 1898.

Nau, Henry R. "Where Reaganomics Works." *Foreign Policy* 57 (Winter 1984–85): 14–37.

Neep, Daniel. "Dilemmas of Democratization in the Middle East." *Middle East Policy* 11, no. 3 (Fall 2004): 73–84.

Nesadurai, Helen E. S. "Bandung and the Political Economy of North-South Relations: Sowing the Seeds for Revisioning International Society." Working Paper 95. Nanyang, Singapore: Institute of Defence and Strategic Studies, 2005.

Neumann, Roderick P. *Imposing Wilderness: Struggles over Livelihood and Nature Preservation in Africa*. Berkeley: University of California Press, 1998.

"The New Essayists: Dr. Williams and Others." *The Ecclesiastic* 22 (1860): 240–60.

Newsom, David D. *The Imperial Mantle: The United States, Decolonization, and the Third World*. Bloomington: Indiana University Press, 2001.

Niamir-Fuller, Maryam. "The Resilience of Pastoral Herding in Sahelian Africa." In *Linking Social and Ecological Systems: Management Practices and Social Mechanisms*, ed. F. Berkes and C. Folke, 250–85. Cambridge: Cambridge University Press, 1998.

Obenzinger, Hilton. *American Palestine: Melville, Twain, and the Holy Land Mania*. Princeton, NJ: Princeton University Press, 1999.

O'Brien, Richard. *Global Financial Integration: The End of Geography*. London: Pinter, 1992.

O'Donovan, Edmund. *The Merv Oasis: Travels and Adventures East of the Caspian During the Years 1879–80–81*, vol. 2. New York: G. P. Putnam's Sons, 1883.

Olsvig-Whittaker, Linda, Eliezer Frankenberg, Avi Perevolotsky, and Eugene D. Ungar. "Grazing, Overgrazing and Conservation: Changing Concepts and Practices in the Negev Rangelands." *Sécheresse* 17, nos. 1 & 2 (2006): 195–99.

Ottavo, Anno. "L'Obolo per la fede." *La Civiltà cattolica* 6 (1857): 385–400. Rome: Coi Tipi della Civiltà cattolica.

Ó Tuathail, Gearóid. *Critical Geopolitics: The Politics of Writing Global Space*. Minneapolis: University of Minnesota Press, 1996.

Ouis, Pernilla. "'Greening the Emirates': The Modern Construction of Nature in the United Arab Emirates." *Cultural Geographies* 9, no. 3 (2002): 334–47.

Oye, Kenneth A. "International Systems Structure and American Foreign Policy." In *Eagle Defiant: United States Foreign Policy in the 1980s*, ed. Keneth Oye, Robert J. Lieber, and Donald Rothchild, 3–32. Boston: Little, Brown and Co., 1983.

Packenham, Robert A. *Liberal America and the Third World: Political Development Ideas in Foreign Aid and Social Science*. Princeton, NJ: Princeton University Press, 1973.

Paolillo, Charles. "Development Assistance: Where Next?" In *The U.S. and the Developing World: Agenda for Action 1974*, ed. James W. Howe, 107–23. New York: Praeger/Overseas Development Council, 1974.

Parker, Kenneth, ed. *Early Modern Tales of Orient: A Critical Anthology*. London: Routledge, 1999.

Pearcy, G. Etzel. *The Middle East—An Indefinable Region*. Department of State Publication 7684, Near and Middle East Series 72. Washington D.C.: Government Printing Office, June 1964.

Peloubet, Francis Nathan. *Select Notes on the International Sabbath School Lessons*. Boston: W. A. Wilde Co., 1879.

Pepin, Alphonse. *Deux ans de règne, 1830–1832*. Paris: A. Mesnier, 1833.

Perevolotsky, Avi, and Noam G. Seligman. "Role of Grazing in Mediterranean Rangeland Ecosystems." *BioScience* 48, no. 12 (1998): 1007–17.

Périer, Jean Andre Napoleon. *Exploration scientifique de l'Algérie, Sciences médicales: De l'hygiène en Algérie*. 2 vols. Paris: Imprimerie Royale, 1847.

Perris, George Herbert. *The Eastern Crisis of 1897 and British Policy in the Near East*. London: Chapman and Hall, 1897.

Phillips, Walter Alison. *Modern Europe, 1815–1899*. 4th ed. London: Rivingtons, 1905.

Polk, William R. *Understanding Iraq: The Whole Sweep of Iraqi History, from Genghis Khan's Mongols to the Ottoman Turks to the British Mandate to the American Occupation*. New York: Harper Collins, 2005.

Powell, Colin L. "The U.S.–Middle East Partnership Initiative: Building Hope for the Years Ahead." Speech at the Heritage Foundation, December 12, 2002. http://2001-2009.state.gov/secretary/former/powell/remarks/2002/15920.htm.

Price, David H. *Anthropological Intelligence: The Deployment and Neglect of American Anthropology in the Second World War*. Durham, NC: Duke University Press, 2008.

Pulsipher, Lydia Mihelic. *World Regional Geography*. New York: W. H. Freeman, 2000.

Pumpelly, Raphael. *Explorations in Turkestan*, vol. 2. Washington, DC: Carnegie Institution of Washington, 1908.

Pye, Lucian. "Military Development in the New Countries." Center for International Studies Working Paper no. C/62-1. Washington, DC: Smithsonian Institution, 1961.

Qaragazlu, 'Abdallah Khan. *Majmu'a-yi Asar* [Collection of Writings], ed. Inayatallah Majidi. Tehran: Mirasi Maktub, 1382/2003.

Quandt, William B. "New Policies for a New Middle East?" In *The Middle East and the United States: A Historical and Political Reassessment*, 4th ed., ed. David W. Lesch, 493–503. Boulder, CO: Westview Press, 2007.

Rajan, S. Ravi. *Modernizing Nature: Forestry and Imperial Eco-Development, 1800–1950*. Oxford: Clarendon Press, 2006.

Rand McNally and Co. *Goode's World Atlas*. 21st ed. Chicago: Rand McNally, 2005.

———. *Indexed Atlas of the World*, vol. 2: *Foreign Countries*. Chicago: Rand, McNally and Co., 1908.

———. *The New International Atlas*. Chicago: Rand McNally, 1989.

———. *Quick Reference World Atlas*. Chicago: Rand McNally, 2005.

Ranke, Leopold von. *Historisch-politische Zeitschrift*, vol. 2. Berlin: Duncker & Humblot, 1833–36.

Reclus, Elisee. *The Earth and Its Inhabitants: The Universal Geography*, vol. 1, *Asiatic Russia*. London: J. S. Virtue & Co, 1898.

Reifenberg, Adolf. *The Struggle Between the Desert and the Sown: Rise and Fall of Agriculture in the Levant*. Jerusalem: Jewish Agency, 1955.

Reinaud, M. "Mémoire sur les relations politiques et commerciales de l'Empire romain avec l'Asie orientale." *Journal asiatique* 6 (1863): 93–297.

Renton, James. "Changing Languages of Empire and the Orient: Britain and the Invention of the Middle East, 1917–1918." *Historical Journal* 50, no. 3 (2007): 645–67.

Résidence Générale de France à Tunis, S.D.A.I. (Standard Data Access Interface). *Historique de l'annexe des affaires indigènes de Ben-Gardane*. Bourg: Imprimerie Victor Berthod, 1931.

Richards, Alan. "Economic Reform in the Middle East: The Challenge to Governance." In *The Future Security Environment in the Middle East*, ed. Nora Bensahel and Daniel L. Byman, 57–128. Santa Monica, CA: Rand Corporation, 2004.

Richter, Thomas. "The Political Economy of Regime Maintenance in Egypt: Linking External Resources and Domestic Legitimation." In *Debating Arab Authoritarianism*, ed. Oliver Schlumberger, 177–94. Stanford: Stanford University Press, 2007.

Rist, Gilbert. *The History of Development: From Western Origins to Global Faith*. London: Zed Press, 2006.

Ritchie, James C. "Analyse pollinique de sédiments holocènes supérieurs des hauts plateaux du Maghreb oriental." *Pollen et spores* 26, no. 3–4 (1984): 489–96.

Roberts, Neil. *The Holocene: An Environmental History*. Oxford: Blackwell Publishers, 1998.

Roberts, Sue, Anna Secord, and Matthew Sparke. "Neoliberal Geopolitics." *Antipode* 35, no. 5 (2003): 886–97.

Roemer, H. R. "The Safavid Period." Chapter 5 in *The Cambridge History of Iran*, vol. 6: *The Timurid and Safavid Periods*, ed. Peter Jackson and Laurence Lockhart. Cambridge: Cambridge University Press, 1986.

———. "The Successors of Timur." In *The Cambridge History of Iran*, vol. 6, *The Timurid and Safavid Periods*, ed. Peter Jackson and Laurence Lockhart, 126–27. Cambridge: Cambridge University Press, 1986.

Rogers, Daniel. "Exceptionalism." In *Imagined Histories: American Historians Interpret the Past*, ed. Anthony Molho and Gordon S. Wood, 21–40. Princeton, NJ: Princeton University Press, 1998.

Rognon, P. "Late Quaternary Climatic Reconstruction for the Maghreb (North Africa)." *Palaeogeography, Palaeoclimatology, Palaeoecology* 58, no. 1–2 (1987): 11–34.

Röhricht Reinhold. *Bibliotheca Geographica Palaestinae*. Berlin: H. Reuther's, 1890.

Romm, James. *Herodotus*. New Haven, CT: Yale University Press, 1998.

Roosevelt, Kermit. "The Middle East and the Prospect for World Government." *Annals of the American Academy of Political and Social Science* 264 (July 1949): 52–57.

Rosen, Georg. *Mesnewi oder doppelverse des Scheich Mewlânâ Dschelâl-ed-dîn Rûmî* [Mesnevi or Double Verses of Sheikh Mowlana Jalal ad-Din Rumi]. Leipzig: F. C. W. Vogel, 1849.

Rosen, Steven A. "The Decline of Desert Agriculture: A View from the Classical Period Negev. In *The Archaeology of Drylands: Living at the Margin*," ed. Graeme Barker and David Gilbertson, 44–61. London: Routledge, 2000.

———. "Desertification and Pastoralism: A Historical Review of Pastoral Nomadism in the Negev Region." In UNESCO, *Encyclopedia of Life Support Systems*. Oxford: Eolss Publishers (http://www.eolss.net), 2006.

Ross, Michael L. "Does Oil Hinder Democracy?" *World Politics* 53, no. 3 (April 2001): 325–61.

Rubbi, Andrea. *Poesie ebraiche* [Hebrew Poetry]. Venice: A. Zatta e Figli, 1793.

Ruggie, John Gerard. "International Regimes, Transactions, and Change: Embedded Liberalism in the Postwar Economic Order." *International Organization* 36 (Spring 1982): 379–415.

Rumohr, Carl Friedrich von. *Italienische Forschungen*. Berlin and Stettin: Nicolaische Buchhandlung, 1827.

Russell, Michael. *Palestine; or, The Holy Land from the Earliest Period to the Present Time*. New York: J. and J. Harper, 1833.

Ryan, Curtis R. "Peace, Bread and Riots: Jordan and the International Monetary Fund." *Middle East Policy* 6, no. 2 (October 1998).

Rycaut, Paul. *The Present State of the Ottoman Empire*. London: J. Starkey & H. Brome, 1667.

Sadiki, Larbi. "Popular Uprisings and Arab Democratization." *International Journal of Middle East Studies* 32 (2000): 71–95.

Sahli, Mohamed. *Décoloniser l'histoire: Introduction à l'histoire du Maghreb*. Paris: François Maspero, 1965.

Said, Edward. *Orientalism*. New York: Vintage Books, 1979.

Sala, George Augustus. *Echoes of the Year Eighteen Hundred and Eighty-three*. London: Remington and Co., 1884.

Al-Saltana, 'Ali Quli Mirza I'tizad. *Tarikh-i Vaqa'i' va Savana-yi Afghanistan*, ed. Mir Hashim Muhaddas. Tehran: Amir Kabir, 1365/1986, 47.

Saposnik, Arieh Bruce. "Europe and Its Orients in Zionist Culture Before the First World War." *Historical Journal* 49 (2006): 1105–23.

Satia, Priya. "The Defense of Inhumanity: Air Control and the British Idea of Arabia." *American Historical Review* 111, no. 1 (2006): 16–52.

Satloff, Robert. "Jordan's Great Gamble: Economic Crisis and Political Reform." In *The Politics of Economic Reform in the Middle East*, ed. Henri J. Barkey, 129–52. New York: St. Martin's Press, 1992.

Sayigh, Yusif A. *The Economies of the Arab World: Development Since 1945*. London: Croom Helm, 1978.

Schacht, Joseph. *An Introduction to Islamic Law*. Oxford: Clarendon Press, 1964.

Scheffler, Thomas. "'Fertile Crescent,' 'Oriens,' 'Middle East': The Changing Mental Maps of Southwest Asia." *European Review of History* 10 (2003): 253–72.

Schueller, Malini Johar. *U.S. Orientalisms: Race, Nation and Gender in Literature, 1790–1890*. Ann Arbor: University of Michigan Press, 1998.

Seddon, David. "Dreams and Disappointments: Postcolonial Constructions of 'The Maghrib.'" In *Beyond Colonialism and Nationalism in the Maghrib: History, Culture, and Politics*, ed. Ali Abdullatif Ahmida, 197–232. New York: Palgrave, 2000.

Sewall, John, and John Mathieson. "The United States and the Third World: Ties That Bind." In *Rich Country Interests and Third World Development*, ed. Robert Cassen, Richard Jolly, John Sewell, and Robert Wood, 41–93. New York: St. Martin's Press, 1982.

Seymour, Charles. *The Diplomatic Background of the War, 1870–1914*. New Haven, CT: Yale University Press, 1916.

Sfakianakis, John. "The Whales of the Nile: Networks, Businessmen, and Bureaucrats During the Era of Privatization in Egypt." In *Networks of Privilege in the Middle East: The Politics of Economic Reform Revisited*, ed. Steven Heydemann, 77–100. New York: Palgrave Macmillan, 2004.

Sharp, Jeremy M. "The Middle East Partnership Initiative: An Overview." CRS Report for Congress #RS21457. Washington, DC: Congressional Information Service, Library of Congress, July 23, 2003.

Showers, Kate B. *Imperial Gullies: Soil Erosion and Conservation in Lesotho*. Athens: Ohio University Press, 2005.

Sick, Gary. "The United States in the Persian Gulf: From Twin Pillars to Dual Containment." In *The Middle East and the United States: A Historical and Political Reassessment*, 4th ed., ed. David Lesch, 315–31. Boulder, CO: Westview Press, 2007.

Sladen, Douglas Brooke Wheelton. *Queer Things About Persia*. London: Nash, 1907.

Smith, Charles D. *Palestine and the Arab-Israeli Conflict: A History with Documents*. 5th ed. Boston: Bedford / St. Martin's, 2004.

Smith, George A. *The Historical Geography of the Holy Land*.16th ed. New York and London: Hodder & Stoughton, 1896 [1894].

Solomon, Robert. *The International Monetary System, 1945–1976: An Insider's View*. New York: Harper & Row, 1977.

Sorel, Albert. *The Eastern Question in the Eighteenth Century*. New York: Howard Fertig, 1969.

Soucek, Svat. *A History of Inner Asia*. Cambridge: Cambridge University Press, 2000.

Sowards, Steven W. *Moderne Geschichte des Balkans: Der Balkan im Zeitalter des Nationalismus*. Seuzach: Books on Demand, 2004.

Sowers, Jeannie L. "Allocation and Accountability: State-Business Relations and Environmental Politics in Egypt." Dissertation, Department of Political Science, Princeton University, Princeton, New Jersey, 2003.

Spiro, David E. *The Hidden Hand of American Hegemony: Petrodollar Recycling and International Markets*. Ithaca, NY: Cornell University Press, 1999.

Stanley, Hiram M. "New Books of Travels." *The Dial* 23 (1897): 330–38.

St. Clair, S. G. G., and Charles A. Brophy. *Twelve Years' Study of the Eastern Question in Bulgaria*. London: Chapman and Hall, 1877.

Steed, Henry Wickham. "The Quintessence of Austria." *Edinburgh Review* (October 1915): 225–47.

Streeten, Paul. "Development Ideas in Historical Perspective." In *Toward a New Strategy for Development: A Rothko Chapel Colloquium*, ed. Rothko Chapel, 21–52. New York: Pergamon Press, 1979.

Strong, William Ellsworth. *The Story of the American Board: An Account of the First Hundred Years of the American Board of Commissioners for Foreign Missions*. Boston: Pilgrim Press, 1910.

Survival on Land and Sea. Prepared for the U.S. Navy by the Ethnographic Board and the Staff of the Smithsonian Institution. Publications Branch, Office of Naval Intelligence. United States Navy, 1943.

Suskind, Ron. "Without a Doubt: Faith, Certainty and the Presidency of George W. Bush." *New York Times Magazine*, October 19, 2004.

al-Suyuti, Jalal al-Din Abd al-Rahman. *The History of the Temple of Jerusalem*, trans. James Reynolds. London: A. J. Valpy, 1836.

Swift, Jeremy. "Desertification: Narratives, Winners and Losers." In *The Lie of the Land: Challenging Received Wisdom on the African Environment*, ed. Melissa Leach and Robin Mearns, 73–90. London: International African Institute, 1996.

———. "Dynamic Ecological Systems and the Administration of Pastoral Development." In *Living with Uncertainty: New Directions for Pastoral Development in Africa*, ed. Ian Scoones, 153–73. London: Intermediate Technology Publications, 1995.

Tannous, Afif I. "Land Reform: Key to the Development and Stability of the Arab World." *Middle East Journal* 5 (1951): 1–20.

Taylor, Bayard. *The Lands of the Saracen; or, Pictures of Palestine, Asia Minor, Sicily and Spain*. New York: G. P. Putnam, 1860.

Tenca, Carlo. "Della litteratura Slava." *La rivista Europea* 5 (1847): 53–67.

Thirgood, J.V. *Man and the Mediterranean Forest: A History of Resource Depletion*. New York: Academic Press, 1981.

Thompson, Elizabeth. "The Climax and Crisis of the Colonial Welfare State in Syria and Lebanon During World War II." In *War, Institutions, and Social Change in the Middle East*, ed. Steven Heydemann, 59–99. Berkeley: University of California Press, 2000.

———. *Colonial Citizens: Republican Rights, Paternal Privilege, and Gender in French Syria and Lebanon*. New York: Columbia University Press, 2000.

Thomson, William M. *The Land and the Book; or, Biblical Illustrations Drawn from theManners and Customs, the Scenes and Scenery of the Holy Land*. London: T. Nelson and Sons, 1901.

Tibawi, Abdul L. *American Interests in Syria, 1800–1901*. Oxford: Clarendon Press, 1966.

———. *British Interests in Palestine, 1800–1901: A Study of Religious and Educational Enterprise*. Oxford: Oxford University Press, 1961.

Tickner, J. Ann. "Reaganomics and the Third World: Lessons from the Founding Fathers." *Polity* 23 (Autumn, 1990): 53–76.

Tiffen, Mary, Michael Mortimore, and Francis Gichuki. *More People, Less Erosion: Environmental Recovery in Kenya*. Chichester: John Wiley & Sons, 1994.

Times Books. *The Times Atlas of the World*. London: Times Books, 1990.

Todorova, Maria. *Imagining the Balkans*. New York: Oxford University Press, 1997.

Touati, Houari. "Algerian Historiography in the Nineteenth and Early Twentieth Centuries: From Chronicle to History." In *The Maghrib in Question: Essays in History and Historiography*, ed. Michel Le Gall and Kenneth Perkins, 84–94. Austin: University of Texas Press, 1997.

Townshend, Frederick Trench. *A Cruise in Greek Waters with a Hunting Excursion in Tunis*. London: Hurst and Blackett, 1870.

Toynbee, Arnold J. *The Murderous Tyranny of the Turks*. London: Hodder & Stoughton, 1917.

———. *The Western Question in Greece and Turkey*. London: Constable and Co., 1923.

Turhan, Filiz. *The Other Empire: British Romantic Writings About the Ottoman Empire*. New York: Routledge, 2003.

Twain, Mark [Samuel Clemens]. *The Innocents Abroad; or, The New Pilgrims' Progress*. New York: Heritage Press, 1962; New York: Signet Classics, 1980 (original, 1869).

Tyler, Mason Whiting. *The European Powers and the Near East, 1875–1908*. Minneapolis: University of Minnesota, 1925.

Tyler, Warwick P. *State Lands and Rural Development in Mandatory Palestine, 1920–1948*. Brighton: Sussex Academic Press, 2001.

UNDP. *Arab Human Development Report 2002: Creating Opportunities for Future Generations*. New York: United Nations Development Programme, 2002.

———. *Arab Human Development Report 2003: Building a Knowledge Society*. New York: United Nations Development Programme, 2003.

Upham, Francis W. "Upham on the Star of the Nativity." *Methodist Quarterly Review* 57 (1875): 437–51.

Urquhart, David. "Islam and the Constitutional System." *Diplomatic Review* 24 (July 1876): 177–82.

———, ed. *The Portfolio: A Collection of State Papers*, vol. 5. London: J. Maynard., 1837.

——. "Turkey, Egypt, and the Affairs of the East." *Blackwood's Edinburgh Magazine* 46 (July 1839): 100–115.

Vámbéry, Arminius. *Travels in Central Asia: Being the Account of a Journey from Teheran Across the Turkoman Desert on the Eastern Shore of the Caspian to Khiva, Bokhara, and Samarcand Performed in the Year 1863.* London: John Murray, 1864.

——. *Western Culture in Eastern Lands: A Comparison of the Methods Adopted by England and Russia in the Middle East.* London: John Murray, 1906.

Vámbéry, Hermann [Arminius]. *Der Islam im neunzehnten Jahrhundert: Eine culturgeschichtliche Studie.* Leipzig: F. A. Brockhaus, 1875.

Van Lennep, Emile. "The Interdependence of Nations." *OECD Observer* 67 (December 1973): 16–18.

"Van Lennep's Bible Lands." *London Quarterly Review* 46 (1876): 502–4.

Varisco, Daniel Martin. "The Archaeologist's Spade and the Apologist's Stacked Deck: The Near East Through Conservative Christian Bibliolatry." In *The United States and the Middle East: Cultural Encounters*, ed. Abbas Amanat and Magnus T. Bernhardsson, 57–116. New Haven, CT: YCIAS Working Paper Series, 2002.

——. *Islam Obscured: The Rhetoric of Anthropological Representation.* New York: Palgrave, 2005.

——. *Reading Orientalism: Said and the Unsaid.* Seattle: University of Washington Press, 2007.

Vitalis, Robert. *America's Kingdom: Mythmaking on the Saudi Oil Frontier.* Stanford: Stanford University Press, 2007.

Vitalis, Robert, and Steven Heydemann. "War, Keynesianism, and Colonialism: Explaining State-Market Relations in the Postwar Middle East." In *War, Institutions, and Social Change in the Middle East*, ed. Steven Heydemann, 100–148. Berkeley: University of California Press, 2000.

Wagley, Charles. *Area Research and Training: A Conference on the Study of World Areas.* Pamphlet no. 6. New York: Social Science Research Council, June 1948.

Wagner, Johann Jakob. "Einige vorläufige Angaben und Bemerkungen." *Bildermagazin für allgemeine Weltkunde* (1834): 172–76.

——. *Jahrbücher der Literatur* [Annals of Literature]. Vienna: C. Gerold, 1833.

——. *Der Staat.* Würzburg: Im Verlage des Verfassers, 1815.

Waliszewski, Kazimierz. *Ivan le Terrible.* Paris: Plon-Nourrit, 1904.

Waltz, Kenneth. *Theory of International Politics.* Reading, MA: Addison-Wesley, 1979.

Wansbrough, John. "Decolonization of North African History." *Journal of African History* 9, no. 4 (1968): 643–50.

Ibn al-Wardi. *Ajaib al-buldan* [The Wonders of the Countries], ed. Anwar Mahmud Zanati. Cairo: Maktaba al-Thaqafa al-Diniyya, 2007.

Weber, Shirley H., ed. *Voyages and Travels in Greece, the Near East and Adjacent Regions Made Previous to the Year 1801.* Princeton, NJ: American School of Classical Studies at Athens, 1953.

Weethe, J. P. *The Eastern Question in Its Various Phases: Egyptian, British, Russian, Hebrew, American, and Messianic.* Columbus, OH: J. L. Trauger, 1887.

Weiner, Myron, ed. *Modernization: The Dynamics of Growth.* New York: Basic Books, 1966.

Weinryb, Bernard D. "Industrial Development of the Near East." *Quarterly Journal of Economics* 61, no. 3 (May 1947): 471–99.

Wendt, Alexander. *Social Theory of International Politics.* London: Cambridge University Press, 1999.

Wengler, Luc, and Jean-Louis Vernet. "Vegetation, Sedimentary Deposits and Climates During the Late Pleistocene and Holocene in Eastern Morocco." *Palaeogeography, Palaeoclimatology, Palaeoecology* 94, nos. 1–4 (1992): 141–67.

Westoby, Mark, Brian Walker, and Immanuel Noy-Meir. "Opportunistic Management of Rangelands Not at Equilibrium." *Journal of Range Management* 42, no. 4 (1989): 266–74.

Wheeler, Benjamin Ide. "Alexander's Invasion of India." *The Century* 57 (August 1899): 525–39.

———. "The Old World in the New." *Atlantic Monthly* 82 (1898): 145–53.

White House. Office of the Press Secretary. "President Bush Discusses Freedom in Iraq and Middle East." Remarks by the President at the 20th Anniversary of the National Endowment for Democracy, November 6, 2003. http://georgewbush -whitehouse.archives.gov/news/releases/2003/11/20031106-2.html.

———. "Press Briefing: Situation in the Middle East." Strelna, Russia, July 16, 2006. http:// georgewbush-whitehouse.archives.gov/news/releases/2006/07/20060716-2.html.

Wilken, Robert L. *The Land Called Holy: Palestine in Christian History and Thought.* New Haven, CT: Yale University Press, 1992.

Wilkinson, John, trans. *Egeria's Travels.* Warminster, UK: Aris & Philips, 1999.

Williams, Frederick Wells. "The Russian Advance in Asia." *Yale Law Journal* 8 (1899): 306–19.

Wilser, Ludwig. "Weltbetrachtung eines Ariers." *Politisch-Anthropologische Revue: Monatsschrift für das soziale und geistige Leben der Völker* 2 (1904): 409–29.

Wilson, Henry B. "Séances historiques de Genève: The National Church." In *Essays and Reviews: The 1860 Text and Its Reading,* ed. Victor Shea and William Whitla, 275–344. Charlottesville: University Press of Virginia, 2000.

Wilson, Jeremy. *Lawrence of Arabia: The Authorised Biography of T. E. Lawrence.* London: Heinemann, 1989.

Woods, Ngaire. *The Globalizers: The IMF, the World Bank, and Their Borrowers.* Ithaca, NY: Cornell University Press, 2006.

Wright, Arnold, and Thomas H. Reid. *The Malay Peninsula: A Record of British Progress in the Middle East.* London: T. F. Unwin, 1912.

———. "Near East: Our Interests in the Philippines." *Outlook* 59 (August 13, 1898): 904–7.

Yapp, Malcolm E. *The Making of the Modern Near East, 1792–1923*. London: Longman, 1987.

———. *The Near East Since the First World War: A History to 1995*. 2nd ed. London: Longman, 1996.

Yasuda, Yoshinori, Hiroyuki Kitagawa, and Takeshi Nakagawa. "The Earliest Record of Major Anthropogenic Deforestation in the Ghab Valley, Northwest Syria: A Palynological Study." *Quaternary International* 73/74 (2000): 127–36.

Yergen, Daniel. *The Prize: The Epic Quest for Oil, Money and Power*. London: Simon and Shuster, 1991.

Yoshihara, Mari. *Embracing the East: White Women and American Orientalism*. Oxford: Oxford University Press, 2003.

Young, Mary J. L., John D. Latham, and Robert B. Serjeant, eds. *Religion, Learning and Science in the 'Abbasid Period*. Cambridge: Cambridge University Press, 1990.

Yücesoy, Hayrettin. "Ancient Imperial Heritage and Islamic Universal Historiography: Al-Dīnawarī's Secular Perspective." *Journal of Global History* 2 (2007): 135–55.

INDEX

Page numbers in italic indicate tables and figures.

Islam: Christian missionaries and, 133; Christian travel literature and, 129, 131; defining the "Middle East" and, 233, 234–35, 238; the Holy Land and, 122, 123; Jerusalem and, 256n20; Middle East / Central Asia boundary and, 140; sacred geography and, 137, 138; settlement names and, 158

Islamicate civilization, 139

Islamicate Eurasia: defining the "Middle East" and, *156*, 239, 262n1; indigenous geographical usages, 152–54, 166–69; personal identity and, 162–66, *163–65*; places, 154–59, *157*; political power and, 159–62; tolerance, pragmatism and trust and, 265n48; Western Europeans and, 264n35

Islamic countries: defining the "Middle East" and, 37, 78, 98; geographical identity of, 14–16; geopolitical identity and, 2–4; Maghribi nationalism and, 110; North Africa / Southwest Asia Realm, 80, 82

Islamic extremism, 7

Isma'il I, Shah, 140, 146

Israel: Arab-Israeli conflict, 51–52, 102, 214; Cold War and, 49; environmental conditions and, 184–86; historical divisions and cultural context, 6; U.S. arms supplies and, 54

Italian terminology and usage, 18, 24

Italy, World War II and, 45

I'timad al-Saltana, Muhammad Hasan Khan Sani' al-Dawla, 145, 150–51, 262n44

Itinerarium Burdigalense, 128

James, Preston, 61

Japan, 29

Jerusalem: Ezekiel and, 127; Islam and, 256n20; religious faith and, 258n46; sacred geography and, 123, 124, 138, 244n17, 256n14

Judaism, 122, 123, 133, 137, 138

Kanne, Johann, 18

Keddie, Nikki, 98, 238

Keohane, Robert O., 217

Khurasan, 146, 149, 150–51

Khvandamir, Ghiyath al-Din, 146

Kinglake, Alexander, 17, 129

Kissinger, Henry, 201

Knox, Paul, 57–58, 79

Kramer, Martin, 252n52

Kuwait, 203

Labor activism, 206

Laffitte, Pierre, 24

Lakshadweep, 159, 263n22

Lamport, W. J., 20

The Land and the Book (Thomson), 125–26, 130–36, 138

Land reforms, postwar economic policies and, 195

Land tenure laws, 180

Land use laws, 179–80, 182, 183, 232

Revival of the Eastern Question, 33

Lashkar, Mirza Qahraman Amin, 261n43

Latin American Studies Association, 60

Lawrence, T. E., 173

Le Maghreb entre deux guerres (Berque), 104

Le Maroc et le monde Arabe (Filali), 255n27

L'Étoile Nord Africaine (North African Star), 110

Levant, the: defining the "Middle East" and, 24, 32, 37; environmental conditions, 174–75, 181–86

Lewis, Bernard, 127

Lewis, Martin, 58, 60–61, 94, 140

The Lexus and the Olive Tree (Friedman), 213

Libya, 86, 253n1

Linguistics: area studies and, 62; defining the "Middle East" and, 235; ethnolinguistic groups, 98; Indus Valley and, 16; Yemen and, 256n7

Littoral settlements, Islamicate Eurasia and, 155–59

Liverman, Diana, 57–58, 79

Lowdermilk, Walter, 184–85

Ludlow, James M., 24

Lyell, Charles, 173

Mackinder, Halford, 39–40

"Maghreb and Its Neighbors," 82

Maghrébins (Maghribi immigrants), 111–12, 255n29

Maghrib, the: colonial era, 101–5; defined, 253n1; environmental conditions, 175–80, 266n12; ethnolinguistic groups and, 111–13; independent nation-states and, 105–9; nationalism and, 109–11; self-identification and, 100–101, 113–16. *See also* North Africa